KABBALAH AND THE FOUNDING OF AMERICA

Kabbalah and the Founding of America

The Early Influence of Jewish Thought in the New World

Brian Ogren

NEW YORK UNIVERSITY PRESS
New York

NEW YORK UNIVERSITY PRESS
New York
www.nyupress.org

References to Internet websites (URLs) were accurate at the time of writing. Neither the author nor New York University Press is responsible for URLs that may have expired or changed since the manuscript was prepared.

Library of Congress Cataloging-in-Publication Data
Names: Ogren, Brian, author.
Title: Kabbalah and the founding of America : the early influence of Jewish thought in the New World / Brian Ogren.
Description: New York : NYU Press, 2021. | Includes bibliographical references and index.
Identifiers: LCCN 2020041598 (print) | LCCN 2020041599 (ebook) |
    ISBN 9781479807987 (hardback) | ISBN 9781479807994 (ebook) |
    ISBN 9781479808007 (ebook)
Subjects: LCSH: Cabala. | United States—Civilization—Jewish influences. |
    Protestantism—United States—History—17th century. | Protestantism—
    United States—History—18th century. | United States—Intellectual life.
Classification: LCC BM526 .O37 2021 (print) | LCC BM526 (ebook) |
    DDC 261.2/6097309032—dc23
LC record available at https://lccn.loc.gov/2020041598
LC ebook record available at https://lccn.loc.gov/2020041599

New York University Press books are printed on acid-free paper, and their binding materials are chosen for strength and durability. We strive to use environmentally responsible suppliers and materials to the greatest extent possible in publishing our books.

Manufactured in the United States of America

10 9 8 7 6 5 4 3 2 1

Also available as an ebook

To Mom and Dad,

who implanted in me both a curiosity concerning Jewish thought

and a deep interest in what it "means" to be an American.

CONTENTS

LIST OF FIGURES

NOTES ON LANGUAGE

All Hebrew and Aramaic translations throughout are mine unless otherwise noted. In some cases I have consulted prior translations, but I have looked back at the original texts in order to understand and to convey how it is that the language is being used and interpreted.

Where a Hebrew transliteration in this book is in a direct quotation, I have left the forms of words as they were in the original. Thus, George Keith may use "Cabala" while Ezra Stiles may use "Kabbala." In my own text, I use the conventional "Kabbalah" when it is not in a specific quotation, for the sake of consistency. The same holds true with "Adam Kadmon." There is no semantic distinction being made between "Kabbalah," "Kabbala," "Cabala," "Cabbala," etc., or between "Adam Cadmon" and "Adam Kadmon," or other such terms.

Seventeenth- and eighteenth-century English abbreviations from manuscripts have been spelled out in the main body of the book for greater flow and easier readability. Thus, "Y^e" has been spelled out as "the," "sd" has been rendered "said," "y^t" as "that," "w^{ch}" as "which," "wth" as "with," "y^m" as "them," "Garm^t" as "Garment," "Cabb." as "Cabbala," "Gd" as "God," and "combin^g" as "combining." In the appendices, such abbreviations and spelling have been left as they are in order to remain as true to the original text as possible.

The term Trinity (with an uppercase T) is used to denote the Christian Trinity, while the term "trinity" (with a lowercase t) is used to denote more general trinities, as in Plotinus's system, or triads within the sefirotic system. A glossary of key kabbalistic terms that appear throughout is included at the end of the book for those who are not specialists in kabbalistic literature.

Introduction

*Kabbalistic "Diamonds in a Dunghill": On Reductionism and
Inclusivity in Early American Explorations into Jewish Thought*

Toward a New Intellectual History

This book offers a new intellectual history of religious thought in colonial
America, illuminating the role that the Jewish esoteric lore known as Kabbalah played in intellectual exchanges and in American religious-identity
formation. It correspondingly utilizes the history of Kabbalah in America as a lens through which to critically examine subsequent American
notions of religious liberty, tolerance, plurality, and American exceptionalism. Jewish thought and its perceived role in the shaping of a cosmic and
historical ethics indeed occupied significant founders of the American
republic, including Thomas Jefferson and John Adams, as well as some of
their key colonial predecessors, including Increase and Cotton Mather. In
turn, engagement with Jewish thought by such figures, in some of its more
esoteric and mystical iterations known collectively as Kabbalah, helped to
shape some major elements of early American religious identity. These elements include the syncretism of multiple sources, an attempt to recapture
a more pristine apostolic form of Protestantism for the American public,
and biblical hermeneutics as enacted in space and unfolding in time. Such
components would unwittingly lay the foundations for eventual, albeit
historically anachronistic and conceptually guileless perceptions of religious plurality and diversity, a "Judeo-Christian" American culture, and a
divinely designed and eschatologically driven American exceptionalism.[1]
Needless to say, these notions have had great resonance regarding what it
"means" to be an American, to this very day.

This book examines some of the historical precedents of such ideas by
tracing early American uses of Jewish kabbalistic thought. In so doing,

it stands at the intersection between colonial American history and Jewish Studies. It provides context by offering a nuanced, text-based understanding and a recognition that a presentist reading of the notions mentioned above is historically fraught. As such, this book offers a new intellectual history regarding early colonial American interpretations of sacred "Truth" and religious doctrine, not anachronistically based on pluralism and exceptionality but centered on real-time competitions for textual and intellectual hegemony. In this regard, it recognizes and fleshes out an early American plurality of divergent interpretations and conceptual rivalries.

Indeed, there is no such monolith as "the" early American ethos, and any understanding of the foundations of religious sensibilities must consider a tapestry woven of divergent threads. To that effect, this volume spans from the mid-1680s to the mid-1780s, in order to provide a full prerevolutionary and immediate postrevolutionary picture. In order to engage divergent strands, it includes a prominent early Quaker thinker who helped to shape Quakerism in North America, two important Puritan divines who were at the forefront of American Congregationalism, an outstanding convert from Judaism who taught at Harvard, and a renowned revolutionary-era educator and intellectual who was both a Congregational minister and the president of Yale. We will become familiar with these figures throughout the book. Some of them migrated from Europe to the American continent; others were born in the colonies. What ties the threads of these individuals' thoughts together are the common themes of Jewish esotericism and mysticism as stemming from kabbalistic literature; what weaves the tapestry are historical and ideational intersections.

Jewish thinkers and scholars do show up in this story and at points play important and intriguing parts. Moreover, one case involves a former Jewish convert who was seen well into his Christian life as a Jew. Nevertheless, it is important to note that Jewish thinkers as representatives of the Jewish community do not play a central role in the narrative told here. This is not a book about Jews; it is a book about Protestant American colonial and revolutionary uses of Jewish texts and thought, and their resultant impact on views of Judaism and on the shaping of wider American religious sensibilities. In fact, the early influences of kabbalistic thought discussed throughout this book came despite the minuscule Jewish population in the colonies, which according to at least one estimate was less than one-twentieth of 1 percent of all of British North America.[2] What is more, the kabbalistic influences on the figures discussed were profound despite the fact that no major Jewish Torah scholars resided upon the North American continent, and no repositories readily provided such kabbalistic texts.

The paths that led non-Jewish early American thinkers to an interest in Kabbalah are as varied as their backgrounds and religious inclinations. For some, the interest stemmed from serendipitous studies with kabbalists that then flowered into fuller examinations. For others it came from an attention to current world events and messianic stirrings in Europe and the Near East. For still others, it derived from their participation in the Republic of Letters and the role that Kabbalah had come to play in Europe in biblical exegesis, in the writings of philosophers such as the seventeenth-century group of thinkers known as the Cambridge Platonists, and in the work of Protestant historians such as the French man of letters Jacques Basnage.

The influence of the Republic of Letters holds true for all of the thinkers discussed throughout this book. Extending beyond the colonial period, this camp also included individuals such as Thomas Jefferson and John Adams. These two, in fact, were perhaps the most prominent postrevolutionary thinkers to engage in kabbalistic discourse, precisely spurred by books of European philosophy. In order to frame our narrative and to gauge the importance of such discourse leading up to the establishment of the new republic, it is with these two American statesmen that we begin, though they were writing of such matters not toward the colonial beginning, but later into the already established nation.

Jefferson, Adams, and the Reductive Search for Truth

On October 12, 1813, then-septuagenarian Thomas Jefferson wrote to John Adams, his senior of seven years, concerning the question of universal morals as based on religious principles. As a member of the Republic of Letters, Jefferson had recently read the English abridgment of Johann Jakob Brucker's *Historia Critica Philosophiae*, published by the British Unitarian minister William Enfield in 1791; and he was interested in some of Enfield's claims. Among the assertions that Jefferson wanted to discuss with Adams were Enfield's statements that "ethics were so little studied among the Jews" from the time of the Talmud, and that there was also a "low state of moral philosophy among the Jews in the Middle age."[3] Jefferson framed his own initial critical inquiry, flowing out of his reading of Enfield, as such:

> To compare the morals of the old with those of the new testament, would require an attentive study of the former, a search thro' all it's books, for it's precepts, and through all it's history for it's practices, and the principles they prove. as [sic] commentaries too on these, the philosophy of the Hebrews must be enquired into, their Mishna, their Gemara, Cabbala, Jezirah, Sohar, Cosri and their Talmud must be examined and understood, in order to do them full justice.[4]

Jefferson goes on in his letter to Adams to claim that Jesus attempted to undertake a reformation of Hebraic morality. According to Jefferson, by further isolating Jesus's own words from elements such as Platonism, Plotinianism, Aristotelianism, and Gnosticism, which he seems to allege surreptitiously made their way into the Gospels, one could arrive at "the most sublime and benevolent code of morals which has ever been offered to man."[5] By doing away with the "Logos & Demi-urgos, Aeons & Daemons male & female, with a long train of Etc. Etc. Etc.," or what he blatantly termed "Nonsense," Jefferson thought that he could find what he poetically refers to as "diamonds in a dunghill."[6] This was the thinking, and the operation, behind the now famous Jefferson Bible.

Significant in the present context is the role that Jewish thought, and Jewish mysticism specifically, played in the shaping of Jefferson's thinking about religious morality.[7] In fact, at center stage, along with the Mishnah, the Gemara, the *Cosri* (*Kuzari*), and the Talmud, are the Kabbalah and some of its central texts, the *Yetzirah* and the *Zohar*. In the above, Jefferson shows some interest, though taken together with his assessment of the "Logos & Demi-urgos, Aeons & Daemons male & female," etc., which he blatantly calls "nonsense," it is somewhat negatively formulated. But unfortunately, there is no evidence that he heeded his own rejoinder, stated in the above quote from his letter to Adams, that these seminal texts and systems of Jewish thought "must be examined and understood, in order to do them full justice."[8] Rather, in Jefferson's quest for hidden diamonds, they seem to have been thrown upon the dunghill along with their Platonic, Plotinian, Aristotelian, and Gnostic counterparts.

Adams, for his part, was even less charitable than Jefferson. In his letter of response to Jefferson dated November 14, 1813, Adams writes, "To examine the Mishna, Gemara, Cabbala Jezirah, Sohar Cosri and Talmud of the Hebrews would require the life of Methuselah, and after all, his 969 years would be wasted to very little purpose."[9] This statement comes despite Adams's now oft-quoted statement of just four years earlier that "the Hebrews have done more to civilize Men than any other Nation."[10] Despite the notion brought forward there that Judaism had propagated "to all Mankind the Doctrine of a Supreme intelligent wise, almighty Sovereign of the Universe,"[11] Adams appears to have had markedly less patience than his friend Jefferson for what he clearly perceived to be "nonsense," as contained in the extrabiblical books of the Jews.

Jefferson and Adams were perhaps the most famous early Americans to offer an opinion on the matter of post–Second Temple Jewish thought in relation to morality and truth, and both held to what might be termed an eliminative reductionism. That is, to borrow from the imagery of the New Testament, they thought they could separate the wheat from the chaff.[12] Notwithstanding, Jefferson and Adams were by no means the most definitive voices on the matter, nor were they the most educated on the subject. What is more, they were certainly not the earliest to weigh in; a long line of precedent that more carefully considered the Jewish textual tradition stretches as far back as the 1680s. And some of Jefferson's and Adams's Protestant American predecessors had very different, more textually inclusive approaches to mining for diamonds within extrabiblical Jewish texts. Indeed, some very influential figures prior to the Revolution had followed Jefferson's initial notion, expressed above, that such texts "must be enquired into . . . examined and understood." Many of these figures focused attention on the Kabbalah, and this book tells their story. More precisely, this volume offers the story of a cluster of five prerevolutionary American thinkers and their own unique understandings of kabbalistic thought, which weave together as a tapestry that played a central role in American religious-identity formation.

The group on which this book focuses includes Jefferson's and Adams's older contemporary and occasional correspondent Ezra Stiles (1727–1795), who was an important Congregational minister and the seventh president of Yale College.[13] It also includes Jefferson's, Adams's, and Stiles's older contemporary Judah Monis (1683–1764), who was the first full-time Hebrew instructor at Harvard and ostensibly Adams's teacher during the latter's time at that institution. In addition to these are the sixth president of Harvard and Puritan minister Increase Mather (1639–1723), and Increase's famous Puritan son Cotton Mather (1663–1728). But perhaps the oldest American case of treating Jewish esoteric lore and mining it for diamonds of wisdom, which is discussed here, belongs to the Scottish Christian Quaker theologian George Keith (1638–1716), who took the position of surveyor-general of East Jersey in 1685 and who immediately preached a kabbalistically inflected brand of Quakerism throughout the colonies.

By focusing on this intellectual cluster of thinkers rather than a single individual, this book seeks to trace cross-generational and interreligious influences, thereby illuminating wider trends in early American religious thought. It is a story of quests for knowledge, and of the shaping of American religious sensibilities leading up to but also well before the likes of Jefferson and Adams. It is a story of interreligious polemic, but also of interfaith dialogue. It is a story not of a Jeffersonian stripping away in order to isolate the truth, or a narrow Adamsian focus on the Hebrew God, but the very opposite: it is the story of more comprehensive examinations of Jewish thought that were inclusive of wider texts and traditions, carried out in order to sometimes inadvertently mold and create a new American truth.

In fact, this entire book hinges on notions of "the Truth," on its revelation, and on its formation; and I thus use the term quite deliberately—although, as will become clear as the volume unfolds, it is not only my usage. Judah Monis, for example, entitled his seminal treatise, written and published upon his baptism, *The Truth, the Whole Truth, and Nothing but the Truth*. The last part of this (*Nothing but the Truth*) is filled with his kabbalistic reflections. What is more, kabbalists are often referred to as "masters of the Wisdom of Truth," as was known to the thinkers discussed here and referenced by them.[14] Their endeavors are also searches for, and often creations of variant truths. Sometimes this involves novel textual hermeneutics. Sometimes it involves messianic understandings of an eschatological history running through America. At other times it involves real-time dialogue, between Quakers and Congregationalists and between Protestants and Jews. At the core of all of this, as will be seen throughout this book, are what were perceived to be the ancient Jewish traditions of the Kabbalah, or *received* Truth.

Kabbalah as Received Oral Torah

In order to do our protagonists justice, it is imperative to understand what is meant by the term Kabbalah and how it is that the protagonists are employing it. The Hebrew term literally means "reception," or "that which is received," and in its most austere religious sense it denotes the reception of a tradition handed down either metaphysically from a higher source or temporally from prior generations.[15] In its earliest rabbinic usage it represents an uninterrupted chain of transmission going back to the theophany at Mount Sinai. Hence the famous dictum from the Mishnaic tractate *Avot*: "Moses *received* the Torah from Sinai and transmitted it to Joshua; and Joshua to the elders; and the elders to the prophets; and the prophets transmitted it to the men of the Great Assembly."[16] Here Kabbalah, or "that which is *received*," is in its active verbal form in direct relation to Moses. It carries unequivocal divine sanction in that it traces back to Torah at Sinai, but it is ultimately an operational prophetic action carried out by Moses. This then leads to its flip side in the *transmission* of that which has been received.

Yet since in the biblical story, when the Hebrews were offered the Torah "*all* the people answered together and said 'all that the Lord has spoken we will do,'"[17] and "*all* the people saw the voices,"[18] the rabbinic pronouncement from *Avot* specifying leaders, prophets, and elders has been traditionally understood as a more elite history of reception and transmission. It has been understood to go beyond the reception of the Pentateuch, or the "Written Torah," and to include full bodies of commentary, law, and ethics, parallel to Jefferson's sample register in the quote above, and collectively known as "Oral Torah." The traditional rabbinic idea is that the five books of Moses, given to *all* the people, could not be properly understood, and could not be brought to life, without the Oral Torah, which Moses simultaneously received with the Written Torah and then transmitted to the elites as a veritable instruction manual for operating the latter.[19] This is certainly in direct contradistinction to Jefferson's dunghill idea. Not only is truth superadded, but in this formulation even later antique and medieval superadditions, called the "philosophy of the Hebrews" by Jefferson, are understood to go back to Sinai and thus take on a truly proleptic, divinely revealed character. They are active and living elements of divine Mosaic prophecy.

Some of the protagonists of this book indeed understood Kabbalah as anciently revealed wisdom of biblical proportions, in the same sense as it is understood by tractate *Avot*. Nevertheless, they cast doubt on the specific *Jewish* line of transmission since the men of the Great Assembly and up until their own present. A case in point is George Keith, who states of the Jewish rabbis that "their present Cabbala is not the same altogether with that antient Cabbala, that Moses & the Prophets had."[20] He later favorably, albeit hesitatingly states, "I doe not approve of every thing in the said Cabbala so I cannot but say, I have found some very excellent things in the same, which I greatly approve & savour well, not only agreeing with the Holy Scriptures of the O.T. [Old Testament] but especially with the N.T. [New Testament]."[21]

Ezra Stiles similarly makes the case that Kabbalah is "the most antient Learning," and he then explicitly lists as kabbalists ancient rabbinic sages who lived roughly from 170 BCE to 30 CE, known as *zugot* or "pairs." These are, as listed by Stiles, Jose ben Joezer and Jose ben Jochanan, Joshua ben Perachya and Nittai of Arbela, and Judah ben Tabbai and Simeon ben Shetach.[22] Yet remarkably similar to Keith, Stiles then goes on to discuss "the blindness, errors, delusions and false interpretations of the succeeding Doctors of the Law," averring that "the great and learned Hillel laid the foundation of this delusory system."[23] For both Keith and Stiles, Kabbalah is indeed pristine and potentially enlightening; but both hold that something got drastically lost in the specifically *Jewish* line of transmission. It is now partly their goal to recover the truth that they believe was lost by the Jews and to apply it to their own Christian systems.

Increase Mather remains neutral, in that his reading is not fundamentally textual but is of Judaism in relation to mystical current events of his own times. His son Cotton Mather and his protégé Judah Monis, however, both take a somewhat different approach. Like the older Jewish notion that all of Oral Torah is "Kabbalah," or *received tradition*, Cotton Mather has no problem juxtaposing the *Zohar*, which is the seminal thirteenth-century kabbalistic compendium out of Spain that came to be attributed to the second-century Judean rabbi Shimon bar Yochai, with the first-century Jewish philosopher and exegete Philo of Alexandria and with medieval Hebrew biblical commentary.[24] He is thereby blurring boundaries and lumping different systems and literatures together as varied parts of the Jewish received tradition. Yet in the same instance he claims "that the Jewish Rabbis let their Fancies please themselves,"[25] indicating a sense of delusionality. While all may be Oral Torah that may in some way shed light on Judaism and its inner workings, Mather has no room for a sweeping rabbinic, divinely revealed prolepsis reflecting the inner workings of God.

Monis, for his part, writes regarding the Jews and the Jewish textual tradition of Oral Torah: "I shall take another Method with them, to let them see the Brightness of our Doctrine if I can, namely, by quoting to them some of their own Authors, by which Means, I hope to bring them by Degrees out of Darkness, to see the Brightness of the *Sun of Righteousness*."[26] Monis seems to believe, or at least to entertain the idea, that the Jewish oral tradition is revealed Torah. Yet for him, in its truest form, what it reveals is the truth of Christianity.

Despite these foundations in which Oral Torah as a chain of transmission gets conflated with Kabbalah as that which is received, the term Kabbalah indeed comes to mean more than just "received Oral Torah" in its entirety. In fact, already starting in the Middle Ages, Kabbalah had come to denote a sacrosanct esoteric tradition as based on elements of mysticism and hermeneutics, and as fundamentally tied to Jewish praxis. To be sure, for traditional kabbalists, Kabbalah is the heart of the Oral Torah received by Moses and transmitted to the elites, but in itself it has a very specific theosophical character. It is the core esoteric element of received Oral Torah, but it is not for everyone and it is not inclusive of all revealed strands. Rather, it is the strand of revelation that somewhat paradoxically remains concealed. This concealed element plays well into the narratives of the protagonists of this book, who argue that it is not a case of ontological apophatism, but that the concealed truth has been esoterically elite in nature, and can and should be revealed as pointing the way toward an old-new apostolic Protestantism.

Esoteric Kabbalah

At the very center of the concealed strand as traditionally understood, whether by Jews or by Christians, lies a model of ten divine hypostases known as *sefirot*, and a view of the Hebrew language as a manifestation of the divine. These ideas initially derive from an assertion in an ancient text known as *Sefer Yetzirah* that God formed the world with thirty-two paths of Wisdom, namely, the ten *sefirot* and the twenty-two Hebrew letters. When examined, the *sefirot* and the Hebrew language can thus teach about the enigmas of creation, and they can also act as a bridge between finite creatures and the infinite Creator. Traditionally attributed to the patriarch Abraham and considered by traditionalists to have been written down in its final form by the second-century Rabbi Akiva, *Sefer Yetzirah* is a foundational text not only for Kabbalah as understood from the medieval period onward, but also for many of the early American thinkers examined in this book. Another foundational text for both Kabbalah in general and for the American thinkers expounded on here is the thirteenth-century *Sefer ha-Zohar*, pseudepigraphically attributed to Rabbi Akiva's student Shimon bar Yochai and highly developed in its expositions concerning both the Hebrew language and the *sefirot*.

For most of the thinkers discussed in this book, the kabbalistic textual tradition takes center stage. George Keith was in direct contact with and learned from the chief architects of the 1684 Sulzbach edition of the *Zohar*, and as we will see, this engagement profoundly affected his own kabbalistic thinking. Cotton Mather was a meticulous copyist who faithfully transcribed kabbalistic texts as he encountered them; though as we will see, this was sometimes muddled as it came through secondary materials. Increase Mather was not text based, but his protégé Judah Monis relied on his European yeshiva training in drawing on texts such as *Sefer Yetzirah* and the *Zohar*, and he even had a full compendium of important sixteenth-century Hebrew kabbalistic works that includes commentaries on the *sefirot* and the *Zohar*. Ezra Stiles was perhaps the most text-savvy of all of the thinkers analyzed here, as he not only drew upon the likes of Monis and the Sulzbach kabbalists but also had his own copies of texts such as *Sefer Yetzirah* and the *Zohar*, which he studied with Jewish adepts in their original languages.

It is important to note that for all of these thinkers, Kabbalah was stripped of its Jewish practical element, known as *ta'amei ha-mitzvot* or "reasons for the commandments." This is an interpretive stratagem that gives cosmic significance to even the most mundane aspects of Jewish law, transforming an observant Jew into an embodied vector for divine revelation. An example of this, as we will see, is the obligatory recital of the prayer known as the *Shema'*, which in its liturgy speaks of the oneness of God and in its kabbalistic exegesis is transformed into a theurgic practice of personal and divine unification. The Protestant thinkers discussed here naturally had little regard for the obligatory commandments of Jewish law and thus naturally discarded such theurgic and explanatory elements. For them Kabbalah was primarily a system of textual hermeneutics by which to uncover their own respective truths.

It is further worthwhile to note in this regard that as Protestants, the thinkers within this book had little regard for Christian Kabbalah as coming out of the late medieval and early modern Catholic world. This includes thinkers such as the late fifteenth-century Italian humanist Giovanni Pico della Mirandola and the early sixteenth-century Venetian Franciscan Francesco Giorgi, as well as the German-born Catholic humanist Johann Reuchlin.[27] While such sources perhaps presented a viable precedent in finding Christian "truths" within kabbalistic lore, the eighteenth-century Protestant disdain for Catholicism seems to have made them problematic.

When relying on Christian kabbalistic precedents, Keith and Stiles lean heavily on the Protestant Sulzbach kabbalists, who framed the 1684 edition of the *Zohar* and the famous Latin text known as *Kabbala Denudata*. Cotton Mather filters everything through Protestants such as Robert Fleming, Johannes Buxtorf, and Jacques Basnage, even when he is quoting Catholic kabbalists like the late fifteenth- and early sixteenth-century Italian friar Minor Petrus Galatinus. Monis at one point cites Agrippa von Nettesheim, who was only nominally Catholic and was Lutheran-leaning, and this is only in an obscure manuscript entry that was not certainly penned by Monis himself. In addition, Keith, as will be shown, was also tapped into a full Protestant kabbalistic school at Ragley Hall in England, which he helped to convert to Quakerism. Moreover, beyond these trends, Monis and Stiles returned to specifically *Jewish* kabbalistic texts, in their original Hebrew and Aramaic languages. All of these factors worked together to set the stage for new, specifically American Protestant trends in Christian Kabbalah, which will be displayed and examined throughout this book.

Structure of the Book

The book follows a relatively chronological order, though it is composed of five distinct but highly interrelated historical chapters. It then concludes with a detailed evaluation of current historiography in light of the findings. The first chapter traces the earliest known beginnings of Kabbalah in North America to George Keith and his brand of Christian Quakerism. Keith was born in Aberdeenshire, Scotland, to a Presbyterian family, and in his early twenties he joined the Society of Friends. He soon became an intimate of George Fox, William Penn, and Robert Barclay, and after the latter became the nonresident governor of the part of present-day New Jersey then known as East Jersey, Keith was sent there in 1685 to take the post of surveyor-general.

The first chapter traces Keith's exposure to kabbalistic thought during his missionary travels in England, and his transmittal of that thought to the American shores. In the 1670s in England, Keith had come into contact with a kabbalistic circle centering on the eminent philosopher Anne Conway, which extended to the famed Christian kabbalists behind the *Kabbala Denudata* and the 1684 publication of the *Zohar*. Not only did Keith successfully convert significant people from this circle to Quakerism, including Conway herself, but he was reciprocally converted into a kabbalist. He eventually took this kabbalistic learning with him to America and integrated it into his own form of Quakerism known as "Christian Quakerism." This chapter uncovers and examines a previously unidentified kabbalistic manuscript by Keith that was written in 1688 during his time in North America and that is now housed at the American Antiquarian Society in Worcester, Massachusetts. In light of both the manuscript and several of Keith's printed works, the chapter argues that many of the ideas of Christian Quakerism, which were developed upon American soil, were taken from an originally Jewish kabbalistic system of thought.

In the early 1690s, Keith's manuscript and some of his other writings made their way into the hands of the then twenty-seven- or twenty-eight-year-old New England Puritan minister Cotton Mather. This sparked debate centering on kabbalistic topics, which is the subject of chapter 2. Unlike Keith, Mather was born upon the American continent, in Boston, and he was from a long family line of prominent Puritan ministers. The same year that Keith had arrived upon the North American continent, Mather had assumed full responsibilities as pastor of Boston's Second Congregational Church. This was a prominent position, and Mather was on his way to becoming one of the most important and prolific colonial voices.

In 1691 Mather published a treatise against Quakerism, focusing largely on the thought of George Keith. Part of the criticism was directed at Keith's kabbalistic musings, including those found in his previously unidentified kabbalistic manuscript. This chapter explores the intellectual exchanges between these two great early American luminaries, also bringing into play other kabbalistic speculative writings from both. The chapter highlights the flow of ideas in the formation of early American religious identity between disparate Protestant sects, and it brings into focus some of the contrasts but also some of the commonalities between Jewish Kabbalah, Keithian Christian Quakerism, and the Puritan Congregationalism represented by Cotton Mather. Of particular interest are the Protestant textual bases for Mather's knowledge of and statements concerning Kabbalah, which fit with his authorial role as a compiler but also seem to shape his worldview in terms of both Quakerism and Jewish thought.

While Cotton Mather was heavily text based in his approach, and in fact busied himself with textual polemics and the Puritanization of Kabbalah, his famed father Increase was occupied with a more enacted form of mystical hermeneutics, meaning that he saw events playing out not in the text but in real time. Increase's reading of Scriptures and of history saw America as transformed into the *New Earth*, or "New World" as he called it, predicted in the twenty-first chapter of the Book of Revelation. He was the first member of his family to be born in the Massachusetts Bay Colony after the participation of his nonconformist parents in the Great Migration from England, and he seems to have subscribed to the reading spelled out by his son Cotton, in which John Winthrop aboard the *Arbella* was a new Moses leading his people to redemption through the sea.[28] In one of the earliest marks of the notion of American exceptionalism, Increase saw the messianic end of times as running through the "New World" of America. The third chapter of this book traces the trajectory and impact of Increase's messianic thought.

Increase was spurred in his thinking not only by the parallels between Winthrop and Moses and between the Atlantic and the Red Sea but also by false mystical messianic stirrings in the Jewish world during his own lifetime. Specifically, an Ottoman Jew by the name of Shabbetai Tzevi, who was a student of Kabbalah, had created a mass fervor throughout the Jewish world during 1665 and 1666. As a part of Increase's own messianic thinking, he had become obsessed with the conversion of the Jews. The historical events of the false Jewish Messiah during his own lifetime gave him further impetus to convert the Jews to a belief in the "true" Messiah, Jesus of Nazareth. This chapter traces Mather's thought, which culminated in the actual conversion of a Jew in the Boston area some fifty-six years after the false advent of Shabbetai Tzevi. The converted individual was none other than Judah Monis, who was the first Jew to receive an advanced degree in North America and who would go on to become the first full-time Hebrew instructor at Harvard. In addition to tracing the messianic thought and activities of Increase Mather, this chapter uncovers Monis's heretofore unknown kabbalistic background, and it shows how Monis as a figure was used and understood by Increase and others in the casting of their own, distinctly American mystical eschatology.

Upon Monis's conversion to Congregational Christianity in 1722 under the aegis of Increase Mather, Monis gave a very public discourse at Harvard's College Hall, which was attended by then president of Harvard John Leverett, prominent ministers Nathaniel Appleton and Benjamin Colman, and others from the community and from Harvard Corporation. This was a significant event, not only in the lives of the elder Mather and of Monis but also in the life of Harvard College. It was also important for New England perceptions of Judaism and of Congregationalism henceforward.

Shortly after the baptismal event with the public discourse, Monis published three resulting tracts together with introductions by Increase Mather and Benjamin Colman, which reached popular circulation. Monis entitled these three tracts *The Truth, the Whole Truth, and Nothing but the Truth*, respectively. The third of these, *Nothing but the*

Truth, is heavily infused with kabbalistic thought and citation; in fact, it appears to be the first kabbalistic text wholly produced and published in North America. Chapter 4 provides a deep textual analysis of this treatise, paying close attention to the Jewish sources that Monis had at his disposal.

The chapter examines not only Monis's textual sources but also the exegetical manner in which he transforms Jewish kabbalistic ideas to fit a Congregational Christian narrative. It argues that Monis was merely paying lip service to Judaism, and that by using Kabbalah he actually sought to convince his Christian interlocutors, including Mather, Colman, and Appelton, of the truth of his new convictions. Interestingly, during his excursions he does not venture beyond the Jewish text for sources of kabbalistic authority. Monis sought to exhibit the compatibility of Jewish thought and Kabbalah, as specifically *Jewishly* conceived, with American Protestant Christianity. Correlatively, he sought to do so *as a Jew* who was converting to Christianity. Through his published discourses, this project would prove to have implications beyond Monis's own time and community.

In fact, one figure who was markedly influenced by Monis's Jewish-Christian kabbalistic treatise was Ezra Stiles, the influential pastor of the Second Congregational Church in Newport, Rhode Island, who would go on to become the seventh president of Yale College. Stiles had read Monis's baptismal discourses about forty-seven years after the latter's momentous conversion, an activity that would set him on a kabbalistic journey for the remainder of his life. Similar to Monis and influenced by him, Stiles saw Kabbalah as a system that was not only compatible with Christianity but that, stripped of archaic ritual and law, could act as the ultimate foundation for what he saw as a true old-new Judeo-Christian divine Covenant. The final chapter of this book examines Stiles's project and its fascinating history, which seems to have begun with a reading of Monis but then branched out into deep textual forays into Jewish mystical books such as the *Zohar* and *Sefer Yetzirah*.

Like Ezra the Scribe of old, who brought a purified Torah back to Jerusalem from the Babylonian academies and established one of the first postexilic "colleges" in the Holy Land, Ezra Stiles saw himself as bringing forth a new type of learning based on rabbinic and kabbalistic thought. He thought that this old-new learning should pervade what he perceived to be American "sacred" colleges in the mold of the Babylonian and Jerusalem academies, such as Yale. Stiles even directly stated so in great detail in his first public commencement address at Yale in 1781, which had first been drafted in Hebrew in 1778. The final chapter of this book traces the history of how Stiles arrived at such thinking. In an unusual twist, it shows how this involved interreligious friendships and learning with various rabbis, sophisticated kabbalistic hermeneutics on the part of Stiles, and his drafting of original documents in Hebrew. The chapter also uncovers some previously unexamined documents, including some accounts of the early interreligious intellectual exchanges and musings on Jewish texts, all centering on various understandings of Kabbalah.

The conclusion brings the historical narrative set forth in the rest of the book to bear upon the historiography of early American thought since World War II. In light of the textual evidence presented throughout the book, it questions notions of a lack of Jewish conceptual involvement in the development of American religious thought on the one hand, and it problematizes ideas of pluralistic thought and religious diversity on the other hand. Taking the historical record of kabbalistic speculation into consideration, it looks at the uses of the history of the early American involvement of Jewish thought by post–World War II Jewish leaders such as Lee Max Friedman, then president of the American Jewish Historical Society, in forging a new understanding of Judaism's place within American society. In this regard, it brings forth age-old historiographical questions of national-identity modeling that center on the melting pot vs. cultural pluralism, especially in relation to American Judaism and its self-perception of its role in American history, subsequent to the Nazi atrocities.

The conclusion further queries notions of American exceptionalism as propounded by the likes of the eminent post–World War II Americanist Perry Miller and as critically discussed until this very day by the likes of Abram Van Engen. It brings to bear religious attempts to recapture a pristine apostolic Jewish-Christianity through the use of kabbalistic thought, eschatological biblical hermeneutics as historically enacted, and the forging of an old-new Torah stemming from the American context. It takes into account conversion, not only in regard to Jews and Jewish thought but also in regard to American Protestantism as it is influenced by Jewish Kabbalah.

Concluding Remarks

In this final introductory analysis, we return to Thomas Jefferson with whom we began. It is reported that after signing the Declaration of Independence, Jefferson, along with John Adams and Benjamin Franklin, was commissioned by the Continental Congress to design the Great Seal of the United States. On July 4, 1776, the very first Independence Day of the new republic, Jefferson, for his part, proposed a scene from the Exodus of the Israelites. Specifically, he wanted to depict "the children of Israel in the wilderness, led by a cloud by day and a pillar of flame by night."[29] This ultimately lost out, but it was Jefferson's first bid.

The great scholar of American Studies Sacvan Bercovitch suggests that Jefferson's choice of a scene from the Hebrew Bible was no accident. Despite his rhetoric of eliminative reductionism in relation to "the philosophy of the Hebrews," more commonly known as Oral Torah, Jefferson had bought into what Bercovitch, borrowing from Erich Auerbach, calls the Puritan "figura." By this Bercovitch means a scriptural "type" that presupposes a historical framework that is external to the self. This "figura" or "type" is in contradistinction to the "symbol." Bercovitch explains, "The symbolist, that is, seeks meaning through a subjective interaction between experience and the imagination; the figuralist or typologist assumes a 'plot of God,' independent of the self."[30] This idea smacks of destiny, and for Jefferson, following in the footsteps of his predecessors, the American figura was of a redeemed people that became a redeemer nation, in line with the Israelites of old and perceptions of the role of the Jews in the future.

In the 2011 preface to his seminal *The Puritan Origins of the American Self*, informed in part by his own situatedness as a Jewish scholar of Americanism, Bercovitch notes that similar to Jefferson, at later stages, America

invited the "majestic past" as it were to participate as the American Way to the Future. The American newness was a rhetorical design in which a fresh start signaled a historical culmination. And the key to that design, here as before, was the colonizing hyphen in "Judeo-Christian"—which is to say, the cultural work of the Puritan *figura*. The creative power of the "Old Testament" was nowhere more evident than in its appropriation by the "New," and it was precisely that enveloping embrace which allowed Christianity so fully to appropriate it.[31]

While perhaps controversial in its notion of "American newness," which improperly understood could be taken to refer to the American experiment itself, this seems to be an astute reading of postcolonial American cultural rhetoric. As Bercovitch states, it certainly characterizes much of the current language of multiculturalism, and much of the idea of exceptionalism through historical culmination. Yet the idea is not only characteristic of Jefferson, or of later stages in American thought, in drawing on the Puritan *figura*. It is also not relegated to ideas of the Old Testament as subsumed in the New. Rather, as will be shown in this book, it is a way of thinking that has roots in mystical and messianic as well as exegetical thought. It extends beyond Puritans to include Quakers and (at least instrumentally) Jews, and it includes extrabiblical literature. Here in this book, it is exemplified by "Judeo-Christian" forms of Kabbalah. The earliest known of these upon the North American continent was in fact not propounded by a Bercovitchian "Puritan figura" but by the very Quaker kabbalist George Keith. It is to him that we now turn.

1

American Christian Quakerism and Jewish Mysticism

Jacob Boehme in America and the Lost Kabbalistic
Manuscript of George Keith

Kabbalistic Epistle to Daniel Leeds

In the archives of the American Antiquarian Society in Worcester, Massachusetts, there exists an extraordinary kabbalistic manuscript in beautiful cursive English script, which extends to twenty-five pages and dates to the late seventeenth century. The manuscript was entirely concealed until 1935, when Robert W. G. Vail, then librarian at the American Antiquarian Society, spotted it among Quaker tracts formerly owned by Increase Mather; Vail then cataloged it as a "seventeenth century manuscript on the Jewish Cabala."[1] Since 1935 the manuscript has remained completely unstudied.[2] Nevertheless, a perusal of it reveals some astonishing information concerning early colonial American attitudes toward and uses of Jewish mysticism.

A close examination of the Antiquarian Society manuscript seems to reveal the identity of the author to be none other than George Keith, the famed Scottish Quaker thinker who was active on the North American continent and who later became an anti-Quaker Anglican missionary. If it is indeed the case that Keith authored this text, then here we have a very significant, previously unidentified kabbalistic manuscript from one of the most important early Quaker thinkers, who was also formerly a significant part of the esteemed intellectual circle centering on the philosopher Anne Conway at Ragley Hall in Warwickshire, England. Such a conclusion would add an entirely new element to our understanding of the impact of kabbalistic thought coming out of the Conway circle. The evidence for Keith's authorship, which I will show here, seems sound; yet even if it is not the case that

Keith wrote this manuscript, it was clearly written by someone from the Keithian milieu who had great familiarity with the Kabbalah of the Ragley circle and who was now in North America. As such, regardless of who wrote it, the Antiquarian Society manuscript sheds great light on seventeenth-century New World philosophical connections to the European continent, as well as on early developments in Quaker thought in relation to Kabbalah.

The manuscript is in epistolary form, and it begins as follows:

> So: Friend, having seen what Thou hast lately published in print, as a Compendium of Jacob Behmen's Works, which thou callest the Temple of Wisdom, it came to my Remembrance, of what I have sometimes formerly thought of J. Behmen's Works, to wit, that he has had some Converse with some Rabbies of the Jews, which abound in Germany, & has learned from them some imperfect notions of their Cabbala or Mystick Theology, which he not well understanding, has strangely disguised & mingled with some very imperfect & unsound notions of his own.[3]

This opening salvo is already quite revealing. Not only do we learn that the author seeks to set the record straight in the epistle concerning the "Cabbala or Mystick Theology" of the Jews, we also learn that he or she is directly addressing the author of a compendium of the works of the German mystical thinker Jacob Boehme, entitled *The Temple of Wisdom for the Little World*. Such association, and the use of the opening epithet "Friend" help us better gauge both the importance and the predilections of the unnamed author of the epistle.

The Temple of Wisdom, to which the Antiquarian Society manuscript is responding, is a remarkable book that appeared in 1688 in Philadelphia out of the press of the Quaker printer William Bradford. It was among the first books printed south of New England, and its author was the surveyor-general of West Jersey and former member of the local assembly, Daniel Leeds. Leeds, who was born in England, had been a Quaker since 1672 and an American colonist since around 1677. According to one recent scholarly biography, had he "lived a generation later, we might speak of him as one of the Founding Fathers."[4] Indeed, his service in the assembly helped to establish laws, and his work as surveyor helped to establish boundaries; but he was a pioneer not only in terms of government and terrestrial positioning. He was also a trail-blazer in terms of publishing and the transmission of ideas.

As surveyor, many of these ideas stemmed from ruminations on the environment and seasons, which resulted in an astrologically infused almanac that was published, also by William Bradford, one year before the publication of *The Temple of Wisdom*, in 1687. Leeds's almanac indeed made waves, but perhaps not in the manner that either Leeds or Bradford had hoped for. It was immediately suppressed by the Philadelphia Quarterly Meeting, which was a regional forum that met at least once a quarter to make decisions about issues of concern to the local Quaker population. The Meeting ordered Bradford to cease sales and to hand over his unsold stock to a leading Friend.[5] The astrological content consisting of signs of the zodiac, which is highly common in almanacs, was apparently far too heterodox, even for the early American Quakers. Nevertheless, such censure did not put a full stop to either Leeds or Bradford. Instead, it would set both men on a path that would eventually see them abandoning Quakerism completely.

Yet before that point, Leeds and Bradford would try again to disseminate their purportedly nonconformist ideas. In 1688, with the censure of the almanac still fresh in mind, Bradford brought to press Leeds's *Temple of Wisdom*. This work has as its first part a compilation of texts, in English translation, of the late sixteenth- and early seventeenth-century German Pietist Jacob Boehme. According to Leeds himself, it is a "treating of The Being of all Beengs, And whence every thing hath its original, as Heaven, Hell, Angels, Men and Devils, Earth, Stars and Elements. And particularly of all Mysteries concerning the *Soul*; and of *Adam* before and after the Fall."[6] Astrology reappears, but here is accompanied by controversial mystical musings on God, creation, and the human soul.

Within the published text, Leeds expressly guarantees that Boehme's works are in his "own words and sentences, in his own phrase and sense."[7] Much of Boehme's corpus had already been translated into English and published in London from 1645 to 1662.[8] Leeds's project was now an attempt to collate and to distill the essence of Boehme's thought from these texts. This includes ideas unorthodox to Christianity, such as the *coincidentia oppositorum* of Light and Darkness in God, and the androgynous nature of the virginal Adam before the Fall, by which

Boehme held that before rupture, Adam in the Garden was both male and female. No matter how radical, Leeds clearly saw value in Boehme's words and ideas, and he did not want to alter or interpret them. He merely wanted to transmit them to the American Quaker public.

The relationship between early Quakerism and Jacob Boehme's thought is quite complex; some Quaker thinkers, like Leeds, embraced it and were influenced by it while others outright repudiated it.[9] In the case of Leeds, his effort led to censure by the Philadelphia Meeting of Quakers.[10] *The Temple of Wisdom* was condemned. Here, for the second time after his zodiacally suffused almanac, both Leeds and his publisher Bradford were being publicly and officially scorned for ideas that were perceived to be unorthodox to proper Quaker theology.

However, the condemnation of such ideas based on astrology and a Boehmian mystical piety did not reign in the two men; rather, it only served to estrange them even further. Such estrangement, in turn, seems to have eventually led to the early alignment of both men with the Christian Quaker schismatic faction. This faction held that in addition to the classical Quaker idea of an internal Light that is inherent in each individual human, the notion of an external Christ as read through ideas such as the kabbalistic *Adam Kadmon* was also essential to salvation and to an understanding of the cosmos.[11] *Adam Kadmon*, literally translated as "Primordial Man," is a mystical idea based in part on Ezekiel 1:26, which refers to "a likeness as the appearance of man," and Genesis 1:26, which states "Let us make man in our image," indicating a divine man, or "Adam," reflected in creation. It represents various ideas of divine emanation, and already in kabbalistic literature of the thirteenth century it acts as the very first effluxion from the infinite and thus a key component of the intermediary bridge between God and creation. This is all very much in line with some of the notions championed by Boehme concerning the first Being emanated from the infinite aspect of God.

The Christian Quaker faction that espoused such ideas of both an inner and an outer Christ as connected to emanation began around 1691 and was instigated and led by none other than the aforementioned Scottish theologian who had arrived in the New World in 1685 to be a land surveyor like Leeds, George Keith.[12] Keith himself states concerning his faction's break from orthodox Quakerism, "[It was] ever since the Year,

1691. that the Dispute betwixt them and me began in *Pensilvania*, about Christ without, and Faith in him."[13] Somewhat ironically, about fourteen years prior, Keith had been one of the chief architects of the Quaker notion of an inner Christ, which is the idea that a Light emanates from the Source into every individual. That inner Light, which in a mixed metaphor is planted like a seed, will grow if properly cultivated and should act as a guiding principle for truth, goodness, and salvation. This came to be a signature feature of Quakerism, distinguishing it from other English Protestant denominations. In his *The Way Cast Up* of 1677, Keith writes:

> God through Christ is in us, and thus Christ doth declare himself to be the Mediator betwixt God and Man, as he is in them, *Thou in me and I in them*, here Christ is the middle-man or Mediator as being in the Saints, which confuts the *gross* and most *comfortless doctrine* of the *Presbyterians* and others, who affirme that Christ as Mediator is only without us, in heaven, and is not Mediator in us, whereas he himself in this place hath declared the contrary, *thou in me and I in them, that they may be made perfect in one.*[14]

While Keith's problem with "*Presbyterians* and others" was the belief that "Christ as Mediator is only without us," his problem now with the direction of Quakerism was the belief that Christ was *only* from within. Keith proposed that *both* the internal Light *and* the external Christ were necessary for salvation, and were actually one and the same. These are ideas that he garnered, in part, from his own kabbalistic learning back in England. They are also ideas that made their way, in a kabbalistic key, into the Antiquarian Society manuscript.

As we will see, the evidence shows that Keith's authorship of the Antiquarian Society manuscript, which is a commentary on Leeds's *Temple of Wisdom* and is related to the Jewish "Cabbala or Mystick Theology," is most probable. At the very least, he seems to have been behind many of its ideas. As will also be shown, the manuscript is significant in that it represents, perhaps unwittingly, the very first attempt at a full-length treatise on Jacob Boehme and the Kabbalah; and this is in the company of first-rate thinkers such as Georg Wilhelm Friedrich Hegel, Gershom Scholem, and more recently Elliot Wolfson, who have all speculated about the connection between Boehme and the Kabbalah.

Thus, what we have with *The Temple of Wisdom* is a Boehmian treatise deemed "unorthodox" for Quakerism, which ushered two important
figures toward an American Quaker schism led by a Christian Quaker
kabbalist. The friendly responding epistle now housed at the American
Antiquarian Society seems to be one of the very first written iterations
of that schismatic Christian Quaker theology, using the philosophy of
Jacob Boehme as a springboard for ideas heavily infused with Keithian
Kabbalah. It is a speculative piece on Boehme and the Kabbalah that at
once sheds light on the theology of George Keith and an early strand of
Quakerism, while giving us a better understanding of the transmission
of kabbalistic thought to the North American milieu.

George Keith's Quaker-Kabbalistic Soul

Before establishing Keith's authorship of the manuscript, it is important to review his kabbalistic background. Prior to his arrival in North
America in 1685, Keith had a markedly prominent theological career
upon the European continent that included extensive exposure to Kab-
balah.[15] He had been a close associate of Quaker leaders George Fox and
William Penn, and in 1675 he visited the philosopher and viscountess
Anne Conway at her residence of Ragley Hall as a stand-in for Penn.
Conway had apparently invited Penn, but he was unable to travel due
both to illness and to a Quaker emergency in Parliament. Thus he sent
Keith in his stead, and along with Keith a letter to Conway stating, "I
have been the more earnest with the Bearer, my innocent, learned,
Christian Friend, George Keith, to visitt thee, who comes in the Spirit
of Jesus."[16] This visit would lead to a long and fruitful relationship that
would have a profound effect not only on Conway, who would go on to
convert to Quakerism in 1677, but also on Keith, who would be deeply
affected by Conway's keen interest in Kabbalah.

About five years prior to Keith's visit, the famed Christian kabbalist
and renowned physician Francis Mercurius van Helmont had moved
into Ragley. Conway had been suffering from what appear to have been
acute migraines, and her friend, the Cambridge Platonist Henry More,
had convinced van Helmont to help. Yet his medical skills were to no
avail. Nevertheless, he apparently became enamored of Conway and the
activities at Ragley, and she must have found his presence pleasing too,

as he took up residence there until Conway's death in 1679. During that time he taught her Kabbalah, collaborated with her on several kabbalistic projects, and brought her into contact with the thought and manuscripts of the famed German Christian kabbalist who was the principal architect of the seminal *Kabbala Denudata* of 1677 and 1684, Christian Knorr von Rosenroth.[17] During that time Conway also wrote her *Principles of the Most Ancient and Modern Philosophy*, which is a remarkable work of early modern philosophy that is highly informed by kabbalistic notions.[18] It is into this intellectual milieu that Keith was entering upon his visit to Ragley in 1675. And he did not merely enter into this milieu; he dove head-first.

In fact, Keith's exposure to Kabbalah and his association of it with his own Quaker theology was immediate and profound. He had apparently discussed his ideas with both Conway and van Helmont, and all three found an instantaneous connection between his brand of Quaker theology and kabbalistic thought. As much as he was a skilled proselytizer for the Quaker cause, he was an enthusiastic proselyte of Christian Kabbalah. This led Keith to draft a letter, apparently while still at Ragley and still fresh off his conversations with Conway and van Helmont, to the most renowned Christian kabbalist of his day, Knorr von Rosenroth, also known by the pseudonym Peganius.

In a spirit of fervor for his newfound interest, Keith evidently shared this letter with Conway. In her own letter to Henry More of a few weeks later, Conway writes, "G.K. in his letter to Peganius seems to be of the Jewes opinion, that there may be many soules in man, and that our sensitive soul is really distinct from that endued with understanding, since his finding them to agree with him in his opinion, about the extension of the soul of Christ has been an occasion of his so readily adhering to them in this other opinion."[19] The idea of multipart souls in men is prevalent in Jewish thought, and Keith, through van Helmont and Conway, could have been drawing on any number of sources.[20] One pertinent example is a passage from the *Zohar* commenting on the story of the creation of man in the second chapter of Genesis. Specifically, verse 7 states, "Then the Lord God formed man of the dust of the ground, and breathed into his nostrils the breath of life (*nishmat hayyim*); and man became a living soul (*nefesh hayyah*)."[21] Remarking on this soul that was breathed into the first man, the *Zohar* writes:

This soul is made up of three levels, and thus, as an example of the supernal secret, there are three names for the soul: *Nefesh, Ruach, Neshamah.*
The *Nefesh* was established as the lowest of all. The *Ruach* is the entity that
rules over the *Nefesh* and is a level above it, so as to suitably stand over it
regarding everything. The *Neshamah* is the highest entity above all, and
it rules over all; it is at a holy level, supernal to all.[22]

Based on the Platonic notion of a tripartite soul, the *Zohar* goes on to
discuss the actualization of the different levels of the soul through service to God. Once a person has thus purified both his *Nefesh* and his
Ruach, which may relate to the appetitive and the spiritual parts respectively, then the holy *Neshamah*, which may relate to Plato's rational
faculty, rests upon and saturates him, "in order to crown him with the
level of supernal holiness."[23] For the author of the *Zohar*, this has salvific implications, as the actualization of the holy *Neshamah*, the Breath,
which was granted by God in love according to the *Zohar*, grants the
individual merit for the World-to-Come, i.e., the afterlife as broadly
conceived. One way to possibly understand this is that the *Neshamah*
represents the very first inner Breath of God as He prepares to exhale.
The *Ruach* is that breath passing through the divine lips and into the
nostrils of man, and the *Nefesh* is that breath as it embeds in man and
becomes his own deep breath.

Whether or not Keith was familiar with this specific Zoharic passage is not known, but he was certainly familiar with and captivated by
the ideas expressed therein. In fact, Keith's understanding of the connection between Quakerism and Kabbalah partly rests on such ideas
of the soul, which were seemingly first presented to him at Ragley
and which would stick with him well into his later developments in
thought. This is evinced in his *True Christ Owned* of 1679, where he
writes:

> *Adam* (beside that Divine *Nishma*, or Soul of Christ) had also, a Rational
> Soul, as we also have, and all men; but the Center of the Divine *Nishmah*,
> or Soul of Christ, was not breathed into *Adam*, nor into any man, besides
> Christ himself; nor doth it follow, that it should be the Center, which was
> breathed into him, because the *Nishma* is the excellency of his Soul above

ours: I say, this reason doth not hold, for not only the Center, but also that emanation or ray of the Divine Soul of Christ, that is in us, is exceedingly more excellent, than our Souls.[24]

Keith's use of the Hebrew term *Nishmah* (an alternative spelling for *Neshamah*) for the salvific soul of Christ that is within Adam does not seem to be mere coincidence. What is at play here is a notion of the extension of the soul or breath of Christ, which is breathed into Adam but only in Christ is inherent as the source of breath. Or in another kabbalistic metaphor employed here, it emanates like a ray of divine Light into the inner being of each individual human. It is not inherent, but is superadded to the human rational soul.

Like the passage from the *Zohar*, Keith's language here goes beyond Platonism and is markedly kabbalistic; and given the notion of divine breath, it is conceptually quite parallel to the Zohar passage quoted above. But in Keith's Quaker formulation, such a notion of the soul seeks to account for both an external Christ and the inner Light of salvation that is dependent on that external Christ.[25] Like the *Zohar* passage, Keith's comment is playing off Genesis 2:7, where God breathed into Adam's nostrils *nishmat hayyim*, i.e., "the breath of life." Keith's idea is that the external Christ breathes the *Neshamah*, which is a Hebrew term for "soul" that is linguistically related to breath, into the human. Yet in a platonically emanatory manner, it is not the Center or Source that is implanted but the effluence. This is like the rays from the sun or the smell from a flower; the essence is transmitted and even internalized, but the Source, or Center, remains outside. The only human to actually carry the Center, according to Keith, was Jesus, i.e., Christ made flesh. For all others, his incarnate soul within is an extension. In the language of Conway, by whom Keith may very well have been influenced, this is a distinction between the *Logos ousios*, or "the essential word," and the *Logos proforikos*, or "the word which is expressed and revealed."[26] While for Conway the former is wholly apophatic and concealed and the latter extends to all of the world, including the historical Christ, for Keith the former is made manifest only in the historical figure of Christ. Such ideas would continue to occupy Keith into the New World and through the Christian Quaker schism of the early 1690s.

The Soul of Christ in *Arikh Anpin* and *Ze'ir Anpin*

Concerning Keith's notion of "the extension of the soul of Christ," Conway writes in her letter to More about Keith that "his opinion, if true, would facilitate the understanding of many places in Scripture, as well as it would make better sense of the Cabbalists Soir-Aupin and Arich Aupin."[27] What Conway is referring to here is the kabbalistic notions of *Ze'ir Anpin*, literally "the Small Countenance," and *Arikh Anpin*, literally "the Long Countenance." These are two aspects of an otherwise singular divine emanation of the One God that show up in Zoharic thought and are fully systematized in sixteenth-century Lurianic Kabbalah. In relation to the ten classical kabbalistic emanations or hypostases known as *sefirot*, *Arikh Anpin* is usually associated with the uppermost *sefirah*, called *Keter* or "Crown," while *Ze'ir Anpin* is usually associated with the eight *sefirot* from *Hokhmah*, or "Wisdom," to *Yesod*, or "Foundation."[28] The attributive theology of these two countenances is rather intricate and complex within kabbalistic thought, but what is especially important for Keith, Conway, and van Helmont is the representation of inner and outer, or the macroscopic and the microscopic views of an entity that is ultimately one and the same.

In some kabbalistic texts, that entity, which is ontically one but present as two, ultimately brings the salvific Light of the infinite divine. In a text discussing the salvation of the Israelites in the desert from hunger via manna from heaven, for example, the *Zohar* states:

> At that time, holy dew dripped from the Concealed Ancient One, and filled the head of *Ze'ir Anpin*, a place that is called "Heavens." And from that dew of the supernal holy Light manna would flow and descend downward. And when it would descend, it would splinter into small icicles and would congeal below. As it is written, "thin as frost on the ground." (Exodus 16:14)[29]

Within this example from classical Kabbalah, *Arikh Anpin*, which is represented by "the Concealed Ancient One," infuses *Ze'ir Anpin* with supernal Light, which takes on a concrete material form by which Israel can be saved. This is certainly in line with, albeit not entirely identical to Conway's own notion that "Spirit is light, or an eye contemplating its own image, and body is the darkness that receives this image when spirit looks upon it."[30] While the metaphor of the eye does not cross over, in Conway the spirit and the body represent the two sides of Logos, which fulfill the same role as the Zoharic *Arikh Anpin* and *Ze'ir Anpin* in their extension of the Light into matter. In this regard, the *Zohar* passage is also in line with Conway's monistic assertion "that originally spirit and body were of one nature and substance and that a body is nothing other than a fixed and condensed spirit."[31] However, lest one understand the Zoharic passage in purely mechanistic terms, the *Zohar* reminds its readers, "We have learned, when Israel came to peace below, it was as an example of that which is on high."[32] As above, so below. This is in accord with Keith's notion of a more cosmic Christ and a more personal embodied inner Light, which for him are the two entities that are one and the same, rather than Conway's spirit and body.

In his letter to Knorr von Rosenroth referenced by Conway in her own letter to More,[33] Keith most certainly makes the connection between *Arikh Anpin* and the cosmic Christ, and to the embodied Christ and *Ze'ir Anpin*; but instead of the inner Light, he ties the latter to the historical Jesus. Apparently van Helmont had shown Keith a kabbalistic manuscript from Knorr, and by means of his letter to Knorr, Keith was seeking further clarification and confirmation. Referring to Christ as divine emanation, Keith writes:

> This is the first man, concerning whom the Jewish Cabbalists have spoken so much, both the Macroprosopos whom they name Arich Anpin, and the Microprosopos, whom they call Dseir Anpin. For Christ is the Great man and the small; he is Great, for it is by him that all things visible and invisible are made, and he is small, that he was able to lie for nine months in the womb of the Virgin Mary when he assumed the flesh.[34]

The "first man" referred to here is not the historical Adam but the cosmic *Adam Kadmon* of the Kabbalah. As Michael Birkel has noted, Keith uses 1 Corinthians 15:45, which states that "the first man Adam became a living being, the last Adam a life-giving spirit," to Christologically tie the kabbalistic idea to the soul of the Messiah extended across the universe.[35] He is also using it to tie the first cosmic man to the savior in

Christ. This relates directly to the notions written about here, of "the Great man and the small." The soul of Christ is both at once.

In this regard, Sarah Hutton surmises that "Keith's proposed interpretation of the *partsufim* [countenances] Arikh Anpin and Dseir Anpin appears to recapitulate Philo's theory of the dual-faceted *logos*."[36] While in Philo it is both eternal archetype and first created being, in Keith it is both cosmic epitome and historical apex. Keith's notion is thus indeed Philonian in tone, yet at the same time it is more. For Keith, this dual Logos is also the incarnate soul of Christ within each individual. Later in the same letter, Keith explains, "But the soul of this great man, whose center resides in the small man born of Mary, according to the flesh, is extended through all the saints, and in a certain sense through the whole human race, nay rather through the entire Creation."[37] In a follow-up letter to Knorr of about a year later, he terms this extended soul the "Neschama Christi."[38] Unsurprisingly, both the terminology and the ideas expressed parallel those discussed above from his *True Christ Owned* of a few years later, which displays echoes of Zoharic thought on the multipart soul.

Kabbalistic ideas of the soul and of the cosmic *Adam Kadmon* in *Arikh Anpin* and *Ze'ir Anpin* are among the themes that would stick with Keith for the rest of his life. They would continue to inform his notions of an inner Light and an outer Christ, as related to both cosmic time and soteriological history. They would shape concepts that would eventually lead to his Christian Quaker schism in the New World in the early 1690s, and they would filter into the epistle of 1688 found among the Mather family papers in Worcester, which offers a kabbalistic commentary on Jacob Boehme to Daniel Leeds of West Jersey.

Lodowick on Keith: Who Wrote the Epistle?

Given Keith's kabbalistic background, it seems reasonable to posit that he may have been the author of the Antiquarian Society's "seventeenth century manuscript on the Jewish Cabala." After all, no other known figure in late seventeenth-century North America would have been as familiar with the kabbalistic thought and language that appears in the epistle as was Keith. Moreover, during the Keithian controversy that led to schism, Leeds was one of Keith's main supporters, and even became the standard-bearer of the Christian Quaker faction in North America after Keith's departure for England in 1694.[39] The two controversial Quaker surveyors and thinkers most probably personally knew each other, and it is not unreasonable to assume that upon the publication of Leeds's mystical compilation of Boehme, Keith would want to offer his friend his own kabbalistic musings.

Yet at first glance, the evidence is fraught with difficulties. For instance, even though the Antiquarian Society manuscript is in epistolary form, the final page is torn and its lower half is missing. Thus, it bears no signature. There are no other identifying markings and the original provenance has been lost to history. Hence the authorship of the epistle cannot be established by way of direct evidence. Moreover, a comparison with two other manuscripts signed by Keith, one from his 1686 account ledger and another from a letter of 1677 to Anne Conway, shows a different script from that of the kabbalistic epistle to Leeds.[40] What is more, at one point the manuscript states "See Jesa. 43.7,"[41] which is the shorthand for the Germanic version of the name Isaiah, i.e., Jesaja. There is absolutely no reason that a Scotsman like Keith would write this in an English-language document, and it rather points to a Germanic hand. All of this seems to completely rule out the direct scribing of the Antiquarian Society manuscript by Keith, and to cast doubt on Keith as the author.

Notwithstanding the dismissal of Keith as scribe, the evidence against his original authorship is easily dispelled; and in fact there is strong evidence that he composed the epistle. In a letter dated 1691 to Cotton Mather from a certain Christian Lodowick of Rhode Island, formerly of Eilenburg near Leipzig, Germany,[42] Lodowick writes that he is sending Mather "Three, Books penned by G. *Keith*, with a Manuscript of His, Written by Him about Three years ago."[43] "Three years ago" would be 1688, the precise date of the commentary on *The Temple of Wisdom*. What is more, the manuscript of the commentary was found within the Mather family papers at the American Antiquarian Society among other Quaker tracts, several of which were authored by George Keith.[44] This would all make perfect sense if Lodowick had sent a copy of the commentary on *The Temple of Wisdom* to Mather in 1691.

"By the Manuscript," Lodowick writes rather sardonically to Mather, "You may further understand the Dotages of this Notional Man, which some obscure Passages in his late Books have reference unto."[45] Such "Dotages" involve kabbalistic notions, such as "the *Ænsoph's* having clothed himself with the Manhood, called *Adam Cadmon*."[46] *Ænsoph* (or *Ein Sof*) is the kabbalistic name for the infinite aspect of God, while *Adam Cadmon* (or *Kadmon*) is the first emanated being from out of infinitude, as related to Keith's discussion of the first man in *Arikh Anpin* and *Ze'ir Anpin*. In the Antiquarian Society manuscript, it is explicitly stated that "God in himself, called the Ænsoph, hath no Similitude or Form that created understanding can conceive, & that he did expressly forbid to make any Similitude of him, yet Adam Cadmon or the Son of God as is generated or emanated from the Father, hath a Similitude."[47] This is precisely one of the "Absurdities" that, for Lodowick, "follow from *G. Keith's* assertion, that the *Word was made Flesh* in the beginning, and that this Flesh is the Rabbies *Adam Cadmon*."[48] The ideas being expressed in the Antiquarian Society manuscript are the precise ideas being criticized by Lodowick. Beyond the ideas, it is worth mentioning that the fairly atypical spelling *Adam Cadmon*, which more commonly shows up as *Adam Kadmon* in sources such as the *Kabbala Denudata*, is identical in both Lodowick's letter and the Antiquarian Society manuscript.

In another critique of Keith, Lodowick writes:

> And because G. *Keith*, as he told me last Summer, favours the Twelve Revolutions or Transmigrations of our Souls, whereof R. *Jischack*,[49] a whimsical Jew in the Eastern Countries, (who pretended to Revelations,) hath written most largely, (which notion he perhaps learned of some of the *Turks* in some of those parts, who greatly favour the Pythagorean *Metempsychosis*) therefore he is of late very fickle concerning the *Resurrection-body*.[50]

What is being discussed here is a notion from a work on reincarnation by Francis Mercurius van Helmont, which states that there are "twelve distinct intervals of life, which every man receives upon this earth."[51] Keith was long suspected of collaborating on van Helmont's reincarnation project, along with Anne Conway, and the main idea behind it seems to have been one of universal salvation through multiple chances for rectification and purification.[52] What is important for our purposes is to note that the Antiquarian Society manuscript states:

> For there is no visible Creature but it comes into man by parts & degrees, either immediately or mediately, by that called the Gilgal, in Hebrew, i.e. the Wheel or Revolution, for as man eateth and drinketh many things, as Herbs, Corn, flesh or Beasts, birds & fishes, so he also by this means partaketh of the minerals & metals, & also of the Sun & Moon & Stars, & all the elements, & the earth itself springeth up into Herbs & Fruit & Flesh of beasts, & man eating these things, receiveth part of the earth daily into him, which if he be an Holy man, is perfected in him, & through much of what man eateth, turneth to Excrements, yet a part is purified & perfected in him, so that it dos neither turn to Excrements nor Dust, but is preserved to be his Resurrection-body.[53]

What is being espoused here is an idea of metensomatosis, which is notably different from the notion of twelve migrations for a single soul as recounted verbally to Lodowick by Keith and as written in van Helmont's treatise. Nevertheless, it is explicitly regarded here as "Gilgal," or the "Wheel or Revolution," as connected to purification and universal salvation.[54] Moreover, it explicitly mentions in this regard the "Resurrection-body," the precise element that Lodowick accuses Keith of being very fickle about, in the precise idiosyncratic manner of expression.

Judging from Lodowick's account, Keith indeed seems to be the author of the Antiquarian Society manuscript. But what are we to make of the handwriting that is clearly not Keith's, as confirmed by two documents that were signed by him that do have matching handwriting to each other, but not to the Antiquarian Society manuscript? The answer to this lies back with Lodowick. The manuscript of a letter directly signed by Lodowick in 1694 reveals a beautiful script that is remarkably similar to that used for the Antiquarian Society manuscript.[55] The Antiquarian Society manuscript thus seems to have been penned by Christian Lodowick.

Could Lodowick have been the author? This would be possible, especially given his German origins and the fact that he states that he had tutored the children of "a Learned Noble Man in *Germany*"[56] who had

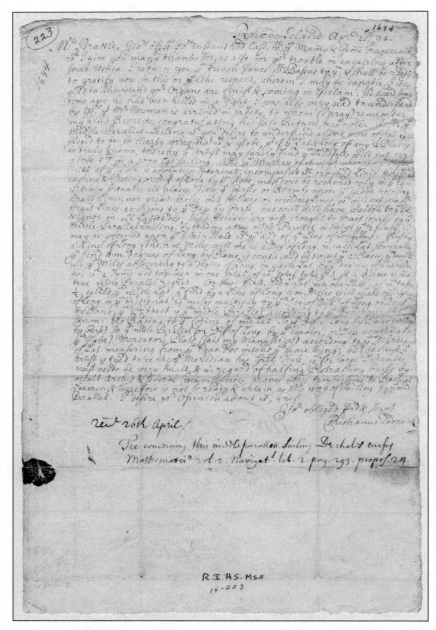

Figure 1.1. Letter from Christian Lodowick to Thomas Brattle, 1694, mss. 9003, vol. 14. Courtesy of the Rhode Island Historical Society.

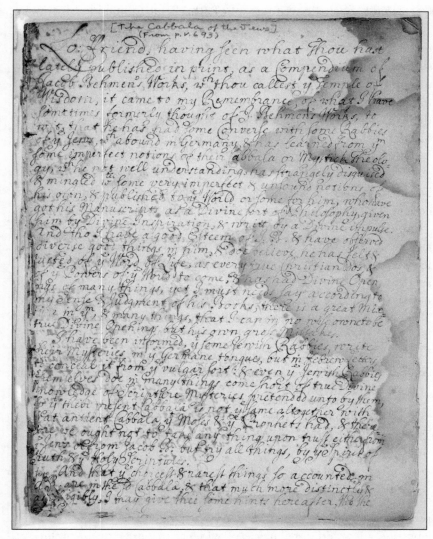

Figure 1.2. George Keith, *The Cabbala of the Jews*, mss. Miscellaneous boxes B, commentary on Jacob Behmen and The Temple of Wisdom, p. 1. Courtesy of the American Antiquarian Society, Worcester, MA.

translated kabbalistic writings into Latin. Prior to making his way to America, Lodowick seems to have been the tutor for Knorr von Rosenroth's children;[57] thus Lodowick quite possibly would have imbibed some kabbalistic learning from his employer. Nevertheless, his great disdain for Kabbalah as displayed by his letter to Mather, and the critiques in that same letter of specific elements that positively appear in the Antiquarian Society manuscript, seem to rule out the possibility of his authorship. Lodowick's background may have aided him in understanding; but unlike Keith, it did not lead him to Kabbalah.

Nevertheless, Keith and Lodowick did meet and discuss such kabbalistic concepts, as is evident from Lodowick's statements to Mather concerning Keith on the transmigration of souls, "as he told me last summer."[58] Keith was certainly in Rhode Island in the summer of 1691, and the records show that while there he debated Lodowick on the merits of Quakerism at the house of a certain Walter Clark.[59] Thus, what seems to be the most likely scenario for the kabbalistic manuscript now housed at the American Antiquarian Society is that on his visit to Newport, Keith gave Lodowick a copy of his own letter to Leeds, and Lodowick then copied it out in his own handwriting and presented it to Mather. This then ended up in the Mather family papers, and thus the copy that we have at the Antiquarian Society is Keith's letter to Leeds in Lodowick's handwriting.

The Great High Priest and Bridegroom and Husband of the Church

Beyond Christian Lodowick's testimony, which was both direct in terms of mentioning a Keithian manuscript in his letter to Mather and indirect in terms of issues such as handwriting and the corroboration of language, a few additional pieces of evidence that are internal to the text of the Antiquarian Society manuscript point to Keith as the author. One of these is a discussion of the ten *sefirot* in relation to the notion of *Adam Kadmon*. The manuscript states:

> And these 10 Divine Lights or Emanations are understood to be placed in such an order as the Members of a Man's body, to which the Members of the body of man bear an Analogy, & they make up that Aziluthick System

called Adam Cadmon, i.e. the first or great Adam, otherwise called by ~~the~~ name, the heavenly Adam, the great High priest & Bridegroom & Husband of the Church; And generally they give him all those names given to Christ in the Scripture, & therefore Christ is that Adam Cadmon or heavenly man.[60]

This idea of ten divine Lights "placed in such an order as the Members of a Man's body" would possibly have great significance for the Christian Quaker notion of the outer and inner Christ, which are One. Here the idea is by way of analogy, and the emanated "great Adam" as Christ has clear reverberations with the idea of Christ as the "Great man" in Keith's letter to Knorr, which he penned at Ragley.

Perhaps more significant, however, for a connection to Ragley than such reverberations between the "great Adam" and the "Great man" is the fact that the passage carries the distinctive epithets of the "heavenly Adam," the "great High priest," and the "Bridegroom & Husband of the Church," which all have a clear and direct resonance with Anne Conway. In her *Principles of the Most Ancient and Modern Philosophy*, posthumously published in 1690 but probably written around the time that Keith was at Ragley in the 1670s, Conway writes that:

> The ancient Kabbalists have written many things, namely, about the Son of God, how he was created, and about his existence in the natural order before all creatures; and moreover, that all receive a blessing and sanctification in him and through him, whom they call in their Writings "the celestial Adam," "Adam Kadmon," or "the first human," "the great Priest," and "the Husband, or Betrothed, of the Church."[61]

Not only are the epithets similar, the ideas expressed are alike as well. Indeed, the Antiquarian Society manuscript later states that "every Creature, be it Mineral, Vegetable or Animal, &c. hath 10 forms or Properties in it."[62] It goes on to state that this is parallel to the divine Lights, for the purpose of "imitating them as the shadow dos the body, & deriving a continual influence from them, without which all is dead, bare & empty."[63] While Conway does not mention the *sefirot*, her idea that by way of the Son of God who precedes creation "all receive a blessing and sanctification in him and through him" is quite analogous. The parallels between the Conway passage and the one from the Antiquarian Society manuscript are far too remarkable to be coincidental.

But what is perhaps even more remarkable for a direct connection between the Antiquarian Society manuscript and Keith than the Conway text is a passage from Keith's *True Christ Owned* of 1679. There he writes:

> I did understand some Hebrew Doctors, or Teachers, who call this Heavenly Man *Aziluth*, which is to say, in English, Emanation; as also they do call him, the Heavenly *Adam*, the great High-priest, the Bridegroom and Husband of the Church: and they say plainly, if this man were not, the world could not consist: and who is this but Christ Jesus, although they do not express these names.[64]

Here there is direct mention of *Aziluth*, like the "Aziluthick System" mentioned in the Antiquarian manuscript, in reference to the World of Emanation, which is also directly mentioned in both texts.[65] Moreover, the terms "Heavenly *Adam*, the great High-priest, the Bridegroom and Husband of the Church" to describe this first emanated entity that is associated with Christ are not only identical here and in the manuscript, they are listed in the very same order. Similar to the Conway text, this one does not mention the ten divine Lights or Emanations. Similar to both the other texts but perhaps more forceful and concise, this text states that "if this man were not, the world could not consist." Here again there is a strong correspondence of both terminology and concepts; and here there is a direct, undeniable connection to George Keith.

Given the dates of the three different pieces, one explanation for the parallels is that both Conway and the author of the Antiquarian Society manuscript were copying from Keith's *True Christ Owned*. Yet it is important to keep in mind that Conway introduced Keith to the Kabbalah, and as Sarah Hutton has noted, Keith's overall more confused treatment of kabbalistic doctrine than that of Conway "would suggest that he owed more to her than the other way around."[66] Another possibility is that they were borrowing from the same source; yet a perusal of the kabbalistic literature that would have been familiar to both (or all three, if we grant a different author to the manuscript) yields no direct parallels, in contradistinction to the parallels that we have within the above three texts.

Yet another possibility is that Conway influenced Keith and then a separate author of the manuscript was influenced by Keith's *True Christ Owned*. Given the dates, this is certainly possible. However, in the *True Christ Owned*, Keith does not explicitly mention *Adam Kadmon*. The Antiquarian Society manuscript does mention it, as does Conway in her treatise. This links the Conway piece to the manuscript without the intermediary of Keith's *True Christ Owned*, which is a scenario that would make sense only if Keith were the author of the manuscript. Given these overlaps, and given the evidence from Lodowick discussed above, the most reasonable and sensible scenario for the "Husband of the Church" passage that appears in all three sources is that Conway influenced Keith, who authored both the *True Christ Owned* and the manuscript held within the Antiquarian Society. Not only does this further establish Keith as the author of the manuscript, it shows that Conway, through Keith, had a direct influence on American Christian Kabbalah and American Christian Quaker theology.

The Spiritual Body

Similar to Conway's "Husband of the Church" passage, another textual bit of evidence for Keith's authorship of the Antiquarian Society manuscript also relates to *Adam Kadmon*. This one, however, is based more on conceptual and terminological correspondences between the text and known pieces by Keith, and less on direct citation. It is also based on a critique in Lodowick's letter to Mather of Keith's notion of a "*Heavenly Body* or Divine Intermediate Substance."[67] Lodowick clarifies that there is a small sect of more learned Quakers including Keith and Robert Barclay, whom he calls "semi-foxians," which allows for something substantial beyond the mere internal Light of the pure Foxians, who were followers of the English dissenter George Fox (1624–1691). That something "'tis a create or rather *Emanated* Being," he writes, "Emanated from God in the beginning before all things, *VIZ*. A measure of the *Essence* of the *Heavenly Man*, which they generally call the *Light* and *Spirit* of Jesus Christ."[68] Lodowick goes on to state that for Robert Barclay, "it is a *Measure of the Heavenly Body of Christ*."[69] In contradistinction to Keith, who, as Lodowick notes, "will have it to be the *Neshamah* of the *Heavenly Man extended into us*,"[70] here the emanated being is cast in terms of flesh and blood.

As a follow-up to this notion, in Keith's *Fifth Narrative* of 1701 he writes:

> Those Rabbins by the notion of *Adam Cadmon*, do not mean, *Adam* the Protoplast that sinned, but another *Adam* that never sinned nor could sin, that pre-existed before him from the beginning of the Creation, but not from Eternity, and so was not the Godhead but *Vehiculum Dei*, and was wholly Spiritual and Invisible. This I show, that the *Quakers* may not have to Glory, as in some new discovery given them by immediate Revelation, of this Heavenly and Spiritual Flesh and Blood of the heavenly Man; being an old Cabbalistical notion.[71]

In this treatise written during his post-Quaker phase, Keith is commenting on his erstwhile friend Barclay, who had received attention from Lodowick concerning the same topic. In this latter text, Keith claims that Barclay got the notion of the *vehiculum Dei* from him, and explains here that it is an intermediary Spiritual Body, which at once sustains the world and brings forth infinitude into finitude. As with the heavenly Adam who is the "Husband of the Church," here the "Spiritual Flesh and Blood" are related to *Adam Kadmon*.[72] Similarly, as with the heavenly Adam, Keith writes in his *Fifth Narrative* that the Spiritual Body is "the first Man, who is the great *Atlas* who supports the World, and were it not for him the World could not consist one Moment."[73] That "Spiritual Flesh and Blood of the heavenly Man" is preexistent from the beginning, and without it nothing could have duration; but significantly, Keith here states that it is not from eternity. Also significantly, it is not *Neshamah*, but is Body.

Lest one think that Keith had a change of heart here from the notion of an eternal essence of Sublime Soul, it is important to note what he asserted in his *True Christ Owned* of 1679. There he states:

> A Spiritual Body, can well enough penetrate another that is, either, not spiritual; or if Spiritual, yet not in that degree, as the other. Now, when I say, according unto the Scripture, that Christ had Spiritual Flesh and Blood from the beginning, wherewith he fed the Saints; by that Flesh and Blood, I mean a Spiritual Body, in the highest degree.[74]

This seeming discrepancy between *Neshamah* and Spiritual Body can be explained by way of Conway's notion mentioned above, which would have been imbibed by Keith, that "spirit and body are of one nature and substance, and thus convertible into one another."[75] In terms of Christ, she writes that "just as he participates in both mutability and immutability, and in eternity and time, he thus can be said to participate in being both spirit and body and, consequently, in both place and extension."[76] Given the relationship between Conway and Keith, it is plausible to surmise that he was influenced by such monistic ideas and that for him, the *Neshamah* of Christ and his Spiritual Body are two close degrees of the same substance.

Keith's thought on this matter can also be explained in terms of a vessel. As Michael Birkel has suggested, the term *vehiculum* translates into the Hebrew word *merkavah*, or chariot, which is the entity that carries the ineffable God in the book of Ezekiel, and which denotes an esoteric realm throughout Jewish literature.[77] It is also a vessel that bridges between the heavenly and the earthly realms, as with the transport of Elijah out of this world. In this context, *Adam Kadmon* as the Spiritual Body, which is the first, preexistent point of creation, is an emanated intermediary that carries forth the infinite Light into finite creation. It is not itself the eternal, but it is from the substance of eternity and is the beginning of time that liminally acts as the bridge between eternity and time. It contains within itself the eternal Light in an incarnate manner, and while it is emanated from the Light, it is not itself that Light in its absolute, infinite essence.

This would thus be closer to Lodowick's understanding of the pure Foxians as claiming "that the Visible Body Born of *Mary*, was but a *Garment* of the *true Christ* tabernacling in it."[78] It is also a reading that would be substantiated by the Antiquarian Society manuscript's statement that the

> Ænsoph & Supream Being doth cloth himself with these 10 Lights, as with so many Garments, as the Scripture saith, he is Clothed with Light as with a Garment, & with honour & majesty ψ 104.12 by which he may be apprehended known & enjoyed by his creatures, the which Lights are not created Lights, but pure Divine Emanations.[79]

It is important in this context to note that in another place, the manuscript equates "Vehicle" and "Garment," thereby conceptually bridging between this passage and that quoted above from the *Fifth Narrative*.[80] Lest one claim that here the manuscript is being used to show the intent of Keith's printed passages and a possible misunderstanding in Lodowick's discourse, rather than Keith's known works and Lodowick's arguments showing Keith's authorship of the manuscript, it is important to recall the final caveat of the above quote from Keith's *Fifth Narrative*. There he explicitly states that the "Heavenly and Spiritual Flesh and Blood of the heavenly Man" is "an old Cabbalistical notion." The claim here is, then, far from circular reasoning. Rather, it shows a harmonic reverberation, and taken together with the elements of proof above, Keith's kabbalistic text from the Antiquarian Society can begin here to provide further context for his overall thought.

Keith immediately goes on in his *Fifth Narrative* to state concerning this idea of the Spiritual Flesh and Blood of *Adam Kadmon*, "*Jacob Behmen*, and other German Enthusiasts and Familists, Originally had [such ideas] from those Jewish Authors, as I could largely show, by comparing them with the Rabbinical Authors I have by me."[81] Significantly, the Antiquarian Society manuscript similarly states, "I shall now proceed to give thee some hints which I promised of some of those things that are accounted choice & rare in J.B. [i.e., Jacob Behmen] his Writings, [*sic*] that I have found more distinctly & intelligibly in the Cabbala, which gives me occasion to suppose at least that he hath borrowed many of these things from some Rabbies among the Jews that abound in Germany."[82] The claim for kabbalistic influence on Boehme is the very same, with a similar tenor. One of these influences as outlined in the manuscript is as follows:

> J.B. agreeth with the Cabbala in saying, this gross, material & visible World, did come from a Spiritual & invisible, [*sic*] & that all created Nature was at first as a Garden or Paradise; But the Cabbala saith, it was but the inferiour Paradise, for the superiour Garden or Paradise, was the Aziluth or Aziluthick Systeme, that is above created Nature; & that every thing in this whole visible World to the lowest grain of Sand or Dust, did preexist in another invisible World, where all were Spiritual, but that the Fall has made things so gross & material by occasion of their Deprivation of Life in great part.[83]

Similar to the passage from Keith's *Fifth Narrative*, here is mentioned a world that preexisted created Nature, which is wholly "Spiritual & invisible." Here this is the "Aziluthick Systeme" or World of Emanation, which, as we have seen in Keith's thought, is synonymous with *Adam Kadmon*. The Antiquarian Society manuscript further elaborates in a more explicit manner that it "is that glorious & Divine body, so to speak, wherein God hath made himself spiritually seen & injoyed by Holy Angels & Souls of men, which is Christ Jesus the Image of the invisible God, in whom the Fulness of the Godhead dwells bodily."[84] This is directly parallel to the "Spiritual Flesh and Blood" of the *vehiculum Dei* written about in the *Fifth Narrative*, which is not in itself the Godhead in its infinite aspect, but which carries the fullness of the Godhead into the world.

As with the Conway text on the celestial Adam and the parallel texts from Keith's *True Christ Owned* and from the Antiquarian Society manuscript, the textual and conceptual parallels here are striking. So are the dual references to Jacob Boehme and the rabbis, which come in very similar contexts related to the Spiritual and Invisible Body of the heavenly Man, and which make very similar claims of influence and authenticity. Such parallels seem to point to a common authorship, thereby further establishing George Keith as the author of the Antiquarian Society manuscript while simultaneously allowing that kabbalistic manuscript to fill in gaps and to shed light on Keith's overall thought.

Neshamah

Both in his printed works and in his manuscript, then, Keith accounts for the Spiritual Body of the heavenly Christ; but what about the soul, or as Keith refers to it in its Hebrew locution, the *Neshamah*? After all, as we have seen from Anne Conway's letter to Henry More in 1675, the various parts of the human soul and the extension of the soul of Christ were some of the very first issues of enduring importance discussed in a Quaker-kabbalistic key by Keith, Conway, and van Helmont. Moreover, as we have seen, whether properly conflated with Barclay's "Heavenly Body of Christ" or not, Lodowick notes that Keith holds the essence of the heavenly Man "to be the *Neshamah* of the *Heavenly man extended into us*."[85] What Lodowick is commenting on here seems to be the following passage from Keith's *The Way Cast Up* of 1677:

But when I say, *the Soul* or *Spirit* of *Christ* as Man *is extended into us*, I do
not understand the *Nephesch* of his *Soul*, but the *Neschamah* or *Nischmah*,
even that *Divine Spirit of Life*, that God *breathed into Adam*, and is that
which *Solomon* calls *the Candle of the Lord searching all the inward parts
of the belly*;[86] and *James* the *Ingrafted Word*,[87] and *John* the *Word made
flesh*, or Incarnate Word, that *dwelleth in us*.[88] By the *Nephesch* I understand that of the *Soul* of Christ common to him with the Souls of other
men, as namely, the Root and Life of the Animal Senses, and discursive
parts. By the *Neschamah* or *Nischmath* I understand, that *Substantial dignity* and *excellency* of the *Soul of Christ*, that it hath in its nature (being a
Divine Nature, so to speake) above and beyond the Souls of all other men,
and Spirits of the most excellent and holy Angels.[89]

Two parts of the soul are being spoken of here, the *Nefesh*, which is the
common life force related to Plato's appetitive part of the soul, and the
Neshamah, which is divine.[90] For Keith, this latter is both deeply internal and immanent within humans and utterly transcendent and beyond.
It is both the efflux and the font, and without being a tertium quid in
its own right, it divinely connects each individual to the One. As Keith
states in his *True Christ Owned*, "the Heavenly Man-hood or *Nishmah*
of the Soul of Christ, is distinct in essence or substance from the Godhead, although by a most excellent and wonderful union united with the
same for ever, and yet is not any third essence."[91] This is a critical notion
for Keith's overall Christian Quaker theology, related to the Light within
and the Christ without.

Given the gravitas of this notion of the soul for Keith's overall theology, and its direct connection both by him and through Conway to
Jewish thought, one would expect it to show up in the Antiquarian Society manuscript. This is especially the case since it is a richly kabbalistic manuscript related to emanation. And indeed, the idea does appear
there, within a discussion of the four kabbalistic worlds of existence,
which Keith describes in detail in his *True Christ Owned*:

Besides this visible and corruptible world, of Heaven and earth, which
they call *Asiah*, or faction; they understand that there is another more
excellent world, or creation, invisible unto our outward eyes; and this
they call *Jezirah*, as to say in English, formation; and besides this, yet a

more excellent, which they call *Briah*, in English, creation; namely that which is strictly and properly so called, (the other two, although commonly named, Creations, yet not so properly or strictly) for which distinction of three Worlds, they alledge *Isaiah*, 43.7. where all these three *Hebrew* words are used; and besides all these, yet one most excellent of all, and which doth in the Nature thereof, approach nearest unto God himself, and this highest and most Noble production, above all things Created, visible, or Invisible, they call *Aziluth*, which is to say in English, Emanation.[92]

The idea here is one of effluvial clotting, similar to Conway's monistic degrees of materiality. Emanation from the infinite Source ontically precedes and provides the building blocks for creation, which ontically precedes and provides the building blocks for formation, which finally precedes and provides the building blocks for fabrication, or what Keith here calls the "faction" of our visible and corruptible world. In relation to the creation of man and his soul, the Antiquarian Society manuscript states:

> When God made man in the beginning, he made him an Epitome or Abridgement of all these 4 Worlds, & gave him a Degree out of each of them, to wit, the Nephesh or lowest Degree properly called Soul, out of Asia, the Ruchoth i.e. Spirits out of Jezirah; & Nishmah i.e. Mind out of Briah, & out of the Divine Systeme called Aziluth, he gave him that Nishmah Lenishmah, i.e. Mind of the mind, otherwise called Chajah, i.e. Life, which hath also its various Degrees too long here to enumerate.[93]

Man is a microcosm whose soul is made up of the classical three parts: *Nefesh* from the world of *Asiah*, or Fabrication; *Ruach* from the world of *Yetzirah*, or Formation; and *Neshamah* from the world of *Briah*, or Creation. Yet there is a fourth part superimposed on these and infused into man, which is the *Neshamah l'Neshamah*, or what Keith here calls the "Mind of the mind" from the world of *Aziluth*, which is a world that, as we have seen, is none other than *Adam Kadmon*. For Keith, this *Neshamah l'Neshamah* would be the *Neshamah* of the cosmic Christ of *Adam Kadmon*, emanated into him from the infinite Light and breathed from him into each individual to form the inner Light.

Keith could have been drawing from any number of sources, though one highly viable possibility is the late sixteenth-century kabbalist Abraham Cohen de Herrera's *Gate of Heaven*, which made its way, in Latin translation, into Knorr von Rosenroth's *Kabbalah Denudata*. There Herrera adds the ultimate aspect of God's boundless Light and states that there are five worlds: "1. the world of the infinite, 2. the world of emanation, 3. the world of creation, 4. the world of formation, and 5. the world of the foundation or making."[94] These, he writes, are the correlative sources of "1. yeḥidah or perfect and superior unity of soul, 2. ḥayyah or nešamah of the nešamah, that is, the actual deified mind joined in intercourse with the higher deity, 3. nešamah or the fixed understanding, consistent and whole in itself, 4. ruaḥ or reason and discourse, which, inclined toward the body, shapes and rules it, and 5. nefeš or guiding and corporeal life infused into the ordered natural substance of the body by the higher ones."[95]

Herrera goes on to write that the "nefeš resides in the liver, ruaḥ in the heart, and nešamah in the brain, while the nešamah of the nešamah or ḥayyah is located externally and outside but with the roots of the three lower [ones] which it not only contains in itself but projects out of itself and assigns to the body."[96] This "nešamah of the nešamah or ḥayyah" here is highly reflective of the *Neshamah l'Neshamah*, or "Mind of the mind, otherwise called Chajah, i.e. Life," written about in the manuscript. And the fact that it "projects out of itself and assigns to the body" is in line with Keith's "Neschama Christi," which is an external life force that becomes internalized.

Another possible source may have been Keith's friend van Helmont, who, in his *Seder Olam*, writes of the "*Neshama* of the World of Creation, *Ruach* of the World of Formation, and *Nephesh*, of the World of Fabrication; moreover," he writes, "*Nephesh* is the Cloathing or Vehicle of the τõ *Ruach*, and the *Ruach* is the Vehicle of the τõ *Neshama*."[97] He goes on to explain that "the *Hebrews* call the World of Creation *Briah*, the World of Formation *Jezirah*, and the World of Fabrication *Asiah*."[98] There is another world called *Aziluth*, "which signifies the nearest to the most high and supreme God himself, and this cannot agree to any other than Christ, the Saviour and Mediator between God and Men."[99] This last statement is remarkably similar to what is written in the Antiquarian Society manuscript, that *Aziluth* "signifies neer or next, as being most near or next to the Ænsoph or Supream Being, & are the Son of God come forth or emanated from God as his outspoken word."[100] The only problem is that *Seder Olam* was published in Latin in 1693 and in English in 1694, so it could not possibly have been the source for the Antiquarian Society manuscript. Regardless, if the manuscript was indeed written by Keith, then such ideas could very well have been transmitted orally or privately before publication, through Keith's friendship with van Helmont.

Whatever the case may be for sources and influences, there is no mistaking the correlation. In regard to the four worlds and the four levels of the soul, the Antiquarian Society manuscript was clearly being influenced by the type of Lurianic Kabbalah presented by both Herrera and van Helmont. If Keith was the author, then this would certainly accord with Lodowick's accusation that Keith was drawing from the theories of "*R. Jischack*, a whimsical Jew in the Eastern Countries,"[101] i.e., Rabbi Yitzhak Luria. Lurianic Kabbalah as filtered through the likes of Herrera would also precisely be the type of Kabbalah that Keith imbibed indirectly from his contact with Conway, who did not see the *Kabbalah Denudata* but who may very well have learned of ideas within it, and more directly from van Helmont and Knorr von Rosenroth. And through the latter's *Kabbalah Denudata*, Keith may have even had direct access to Herrera's text. The correlations further corroborate Keith's authorship of the manuscript, and simultaneously further shed light on his overall theology regarding the parts of the human soul and the relationship of the *Neshamah* to both the human and the divine.

Jacob Boehme and the Kabbalah

Now that the probability of Keith's authorship of the manuscript has been established, and the kabbalistic ideas within the manuscript can be shown to shed light on Keith's overall Christian Quaker theology, it is worth addressing the connection established by the manuscript between Jacob Boehme and the Kabbalah. After all, this has been an important theme in analyses of the flow of mystical ideas, and in the span of intellectual history, Keith's Antiquarian Society manuscript does not stand alone in this connection that it makes. As historical theologian Cyril O'Regan has noted, there is a longstanding interpretive tradition of claims to a clear kabbalistic influence on Boehme, going back to 1699 and the publication of the Lutheran theologian Gottfried Arnold's *Unparteiische Kirchen—und Ketzerhistorie*.[102] Other thinkers making the claim include the eighteenth-century Lutheran mystic Friedrich Christoph Oetinger and the early nineteenth-century German Idealist philosopher Georg Wilhelm Friedrich Hegel.[103] In more recent historiography, Gershom Scholem made an important phenomenological parallel in his seminal *Major Trends in Jewish Mysticism*, and even more currently, Elliot Wolfson, who is also a scholar of Jewish mysticism, has taken up the mantle.[104] Within this long line of history, the Antiquarian Society manuscript seems to have been one of the very early readings of Boehme through the lens of Kabbalah, and given the seriousness and stature of scholars who have read Boehme as such, it occupies a significant pride of place as the very first to be scribed as a full-length treatise.

O'Regan has noted that much of the focus from Oetinger onward "has been on the extraordinary overlaps between Boehme and the Kabbalah with respect to the depiction of the initial move from the depths of divine mystery to manifestation and the constitutive matrix of divine manifestation."[105] This notion is indeed picked up on in the Antiquarian Society manuscript, which states in regard to manifestation that "J.B. agrees with the Cabala In affirming that the Properties of Nature became divided, & were severed asunder in great part by the Lapse or Fall of certain created Spirits."[106] Nevertheless, it seems to grossly misinterpret Boehme here as seeing the divided state of nature as representing two principles within the depths of divine mystery. The manuscript states that Boehme "understands 2 Principles to be in God, viz Light & Darkness, Love & Anger, Good & Evil."[107] This, it asserts, "is contrary to Scripture, that sais God is Light, & in him is no Darkness at all, & in God there is perfect Unity."[108] In this last regard, the Antiquarian Society manuscript sees the kabbalistic notion of infinite Light as offering a better framework than that of Boehme.

What the manuscript is commenting on here seems to be the following passage from *The Temple of Wisdom*:

> The Beeing of all Beeings, is but one only Beeing, but in its generation it
> severs it self into two Principles, *viz*. into Light and Darkness, into Joy

and Sorrow, into Evil and Good, into Love and Anger, into Fire and Light; and out of these two eternal Beginnings [or Principles] into a third beginning, *viz.* into the Creation to its own Love play and Melody, according to the Property of both eternal Desires.[109]

Contrary to the Antiquarian Society manuscript's characterization, God as Being in-itself, as displayed here, is clearly One; only through two "eternal Desires" is it able to generate, by necessarily severing itself into two principles, or eternal beginnings.[110] The language here seems to be deliberately paradoxical, and it is thus no surprise that it confounded Keith. After all, how can something be both eternal and a beginning? How can the Being of all Beings be one only, but at the same time have two eternal desires?

As Elliot Wolfson astutely remarks on similar passages from Boehme, this "is astoundingly close to the idea of jouissance that kabbalists impute to the initial act of the infinite to emanate and to establish itself as the ground."[111] What Wolfson has in mind is the kabbalistic concept of *Shaʾashuʾa*, the eternal autoerotic desire of *Ein Sof*, the infinite God prior to distinction, for that which is indistinctly distinct. In theosophical terms, the one desire eternally gives rise to "two eternal Desires" that stem from the two opposite principles, or beginnings, out of the one eternal Being. The two desire each other: Light desires Darkness and Darkness desires Light; Joy desires Sorrow and Sorrow desires Joy; Evil desires Good and Good desires Evil; Love desires Anger and Anger desires Love; and finally Fire desires Light and Light desires Fire. As Wolfson poetically frames the mystical paradox, "Light and dark, love and anguish, are differentiated in virtue of their identity in the will of the primordial nothing that is prior to all opposition, since it evinces the twofoldness of an irreducible duality, the quality, above all else, that justifies the characterization of the nonground as the absolute indifference beyond the dyad of being and nonbeing."[112] What is at stake here is how the nondifferentiated One can give rise to difference in plurality as related to creation, while still maintaining its status as the all-encompassing Source.

One answer, whose commonality to both Kabbalah and Boehme has been picked up on by commentators, including the Antiquarian Society manuscript, relates to seven spirits emanating out of the infinite realm.

Boehme, filtered through *The Temple of Wisdom*, calls these *"the* Seven Forms *or* Properties *of the* Eternal Nature."[113] According to Scholem, if Boehme was not directly taking such ideas from Kabbalah, then he "discovered the world of the Sefiroth all over again."[114] Similarly, according to the Antiquarian Society manuscript:

> As to the forms of nature which J.B. sometimes calls 7 & sometimes 10, this doth agree to the Cabbala, which saith, there are 10 Divine Lights, that have emanated or flowed forth from the most high & Supream Being, called the Ænsoph i.e. Infinite, which no Creaturely Understanding can reach unto, by any Positive Concentration, & that the Said Ænsoph & Supream Being doth cloth himself with these 10 Lights, as with so many Garments.[115]

Just how the author arrives at ten from Boehme's seven is left unexplained. But Wolfson, for his part, who assumes that Boehme actively borrowed from Kabbalah, notes that kabbalists frequently divide the theosophical realm into the upper three emanations and the lower seven. He suggests that Boehme "obfuscated this distinction and viewed divinity as being constituted by seven qualities that are also manifest in creation."[116] And indeed, the characterization of some of these qualities by Boehme and the Kabbalah is strikingly similar. For example, *The Temple of Wisdom* states:

> The seventh Property is rightly and truly called the ground or place of Nature, wherein the other Properties stand in one only ground, the Contents of the other six, in which they work as the Life doth in the Flesh, also it is a Food of the Fire, where the Fire draweth Essence for its sustenance, wherin it burneth, and the seventh is the Kingdom of the divine Glory.[117]

Concerning this type of statement from Boehme and its possible relation to Kabbalah, Wolfson quotes the Danish clergyman Hans Martensen, who in his 1882 study of Boehme writes, "Böhme agrees with the Kabbala, which asserts in God seven Natural Properties, the last of which is the Kingdom (*Malkuth*)."[118] While the Antiquarian Society manuscript does not make such a direct connection, it does state that

Holy Influence "comes from the Ænsoph into Kether & descendeth from Kether through all the Divine Sephiras into Malchuth, which is the last Divine Measure or Vessel."[119] Other than the name, the connection between *Malkuth* (literally "Kingdom") and Boehme's seventh property as "the Kingdom of divine Glory" is not explicitly stated here; but given the previous quote of "7 & sometimes 10" forms of nature, pursuant to Boehme and by which the *Ænsoph*, the infinite aspect of God, emanates Light, this may very well be implied.

In extension of the idea of the emanated *sefirot* as parallel to Boehme's Seven Forms is the idea of *Adam Kadmon*, "Primordial Man," which, as we have seen extensively employed by Keith, is God's self-expression out of nonself and nonexpression. For both Boehme and the Kabbalah, this Primordial Man is an androgynous figure that contains within itself the ultimate in *coincidentia oppositorum*, both masculine and feminine characteristics that are often very physically described. This commonality has been picked up on by interpreters, such as the late seventeenth-century Gottfried Arnold, who "pointed to both the androgynous nature of Adam and the presence of the prelapsarian Adam of Sophia in Boehme's texts as indicating an especially close link between Boehmian and Kabbalistic discourse."[120] More recently, Elliot Wolfson has mentioned that it is interesting to consider the kabbalistic symbol of the androgynous *Adam Kadmon* in conjunction with Boehme's notion of the original Adamic figure as both androgynous and genderless.[121]

The Antiquarian Society manuscript, which was prior to both Wolfson and Arnold, states that "J.B. agreeth with the Cabbala that saith, Adam & Eva were made both in one body or person, the woman in the man."[122] It continues to comment on Boehme's idea, drawn from the Aristophanic notion portrayed in Plato's *Symposium*, that the soul is in the form of a round globe that divides itself into two parts standing back to back. According to the manuscript, this is explained by the Kabbalah as Adam and Eve, who were "made but one intire man & their Soul was one, & their body one, as an entire Globe."[123] The notion of the divine androgyne and how it is reinterpreted by the Antiquarian Society manuscript is too complex to enter into here in detail, and it deserves a separate study.[124] For the time being, and for the purposes of this present study, it is worth noting that this method of understanding two from one and two contained within both one and each other was picked up on by the manuscript as relating to both Boehme and the kabbalistic idea of *Adam Kadmon.*

In addition to a duality of gender for the one that is genderless, the entire notion of *Adam Kadmon* as an objectivation of the Objectless and as a graspable intermediary for the ungraspable is another kabbalistic idea that interpreters have compared to the thought of Boehme. In his notes of 1821, for example, Hegel writes:

> To grasp the relation of human and divine nature in a philosophically speculative way, however, in pure thoughts, is to be mentioned that namely the *first man*, that is man per se, was grasped by them [the philosophers, partly heretics, partly Christians] as inborn, Son of God, as the moment of God's objectivation in the divine Idea—Adam Kadmon, J. Böhme, Logos, Urmensch.[125]

Cecilia Muratori notes that while Hegel does not refer to any particular concept in Boehme's thought, his conjoining of Boehme with the idea of Logos and with *Adam Kadmon* represents a certain sense of divine objectivation.[126] It bears mention that this is not only an objectivation from the nonobject, which is God, but that also in reverse, for Hegel, it was an objectification of this "*first man*" that "was grasped" by the philosophers, some heretics and some Christians.

The Antiquarian Society manuscript understands the *first man* in the same way. In fact, the manuscript states that it is not in *Ænsoph* that the kabbalists come to an understanding of the qualities of God, "but in Adam Cadmon which they hold to be a middle Being or mediator between God & the Creatures."[127] This, as we have seen, is a driving theme throughout the treatise, based on Boehme's thought but expanded in a more perfect way into the kabbalistic thought of the Jews, which the manuscript claims acted as the entire metaphysical basis for Boehme's thought in the first place. Such a claim is precisely in line with George Keith's statement, cited earlier, that "the heavenly Man, being an old Cabbalistical notion," is precisely that "which *Jacob Behmen*, and other German Enthusiasts and Familists, Originally had from those Jewish Authors."[128] Given the high probability that Keith wrote the Antiquarian Society manuscript, the resonance here seems to be far from merely coincidental.

Concluding Remarks

In September 1692, the Philadelphia Yearly Meeting of Quakers, the major gathering to decide regional affairs, disowned George Keith and his Christian Quaker followers; yet his continued agitation led to his arrest, trial, and finally conviction on charges of sedition by the Philadelphia Court of Quarter Sessions.[129] Along with him were apprehended a few of his associates, including William Bradford, the very printer who had published *The Temple of Wisdom* four years prior.[130] In February 1693, Keith returned to England to argue in vain for vindication from the London Yearly Meeting, which ultimately disowned him for his attacks.[131] George Keith's kabbalistically infused influence on Quakerism had come to an end; but in Pennsylvania his Christian Quaker movement still continued for a short period, with Daniel Leeds as one of its key representatives.

An early account of the trial in Philadelphia relates that a major impetus for the divide, and perceived agitation that ultimately led to Keith's ouster, was an accusation against Keith

> of Preaching Two Christs, because he held forth (as necessary to our Salvation) the Faith of Christ as he died for our Sins, rose again for our Justification, and ascended into Heaven, and is in Heaven in the true and intire gloiried Nature of Man, and Mediator with the Father; and also, that Christ was spiritually present by his Light and Life, in all his Children.[132]

This idea of a dual Christ was directly related to the kabbalistic notions of *Arikh Anpin* and *Ze'ir Anpin*, which Keith had learned about many years before during his time at Ragley Hall. Correlatively, it is related to ideas of the *Neshamah l'Neshamah* and the *Neshamah* as an emanatory extension of the soul of Christ to all of creation, both cosmically and historically in the personage of Jesus of Nazareth.

Later in the same treatise of 1693, it is recounted that Keith publicly admonished as an "Impudent Rascal" an individual who unfortunately, though unknowingly to Keith, happened to be a magistrate. Due to the person's position, this was taken to be an act of sedition, leading to Keith's ultimate downfall. But the treatise explains:

> But this Person whom they mention went about to deceive his Neighbours by false and weak Arguments, *viz. That he did not expect to be saved by that which died at* Jerusalem; *And that God was not present in all his Creatures;* which Unchristian and Atheistical Principles G. K. being about to refute in a Monthly Meeting, and holding forth, *That God was present in all his Creatures,* this Person stood up, and with much opposition questioning, as *Paul's* Fool did about the Resurrection, said in a rude and boysterous manner, *What,* George, *doth the Spirit of God speak in Trees?* Whereupon G. K. said (being greatly provoked by his interrupting of him, and Unchristian Behaviour and Discourse) *Thou Impudent Rascal, who saith the Spirit of God speaks in Trees, as it doth in Men?*[133]

What Keith was quite possibly insinuating here was the kabbalistic notion of soul revolutions, or "Gilgal" as he terms it, as espoused within the Antiquarian Society manuscript.[134] Here the idea is that God is present in all of his creatures but that only through the soul of a believing Christian can anything be saved; in the manuscript everything from herbs to corn to the elements and the earth can be redeemed by being imbibed by a holy man and being perfected in him to be his resurrection body.

While ultimately controversial and sometimes seemingly cryptic or contentious, Keith's ideas were well considered and the kabbalistic thought within becomes apparent when his works are read intertextually. This is especially so in light of the kabbalistic manuscript housed at the American Antiquarian Society, which is a well-written piece in line with Keith's thought that, by all indications, seems to have been composed by Keith himself. As the famed Quaker scholar of mysticism Rufus Jones wrote over a hundred years ago, Keith was intellectually a great man and his writings are marked by an excellence of style and a clearness of thought. "Had he died in 1690," Jones continues, "they would have ranked high as Quaker classics."[135] In light of the Antiquarian Society manuscript and the analyses undertaken throughout this chapter, it should be added to Jones's remark that had American Quakerism been ripe for Kabbalah, and had Keith been able to explain himself publicly in the kabbalistic terms from which he was ultimately drawing, the end picture may have been quite different.

Perhaps due to its unorthodox and non-Christian character, such an explicit appeal to Kabbalah would have garnered the same backlash for Keith as that experienced by Leeds and Bradford for their appeal to both astrology and the mystical thought of Jacob Boehme. Whatever the reason for Keith's reticence to publicly espouse a Quaker form of Kabbalah, there was the private espousal to Christian Lodowick in Rhode Island, and to Daniel Leeds through his kabbalistic commentary on *The Temple of Wisdom*. Keith seems to have shared this latter piece with Lodowick, who then sent it on to Cotton Mather. Not only did it then become preserved in the Mather family papers at the American Antiquarian Society, but as we will see, it seems to have had an effect on the thought of Cotton Mather himself. Though intended as a critique, Lodowick's transfer of Keith's ideas to Mather seems to have had the opposite effect, and from Quakerism to Congregationalism, Jewish kabbalistic ideas were now becoming an integral part of the fabric of early American Protestantism.

2

From Christian Quakerism to American Puritanism

George Keith, Cotton Mather, and Kabbalistic Polemics

Puritanism, Quakerism, and Kabbalistic Dialogue

On September 1, 1691, a twenty-seven-year-old Cotton Mather, who was from a dynastic line of Puritan clergymen and was one of the most renowned New England Congregational ministers of his generation, published a 110-page tract in Boston entitled *Little Flocks Guarded against Grievous Wolves: An Address Unto those Parts of New-England which are most Exposed unto Assaults, from the Modern Teachers of the misled Quakers.*[1] Within this tract, Mather states that George Keith "has in his Writings, tho less *Truth*, yet more *Hebrew* and *Greek*, than ever *Pilate* had upon the *Cross*."[2] He goes on to state that Keith is "upon all occasions drawing back into many Languages; and indeed *he draws into confusion* too."[3] Mather also states, seemingly targeting Keith, that it would be more tedious than useful to transcribe "horrible passages, which continually fall from the Pens of the greatest *Rabbi's* among the *Quakers*."[4] In what is perhaps a deliberately mixed metaphor that places Pilate among the rabbis, Mather at once shows both respect and great disdain for Keith's Hebrew and rabbinic learning.

Included within this critique are ideas of Jewish Kabbalah as cloaked by Keith in a Christian Quaker garb. In an interesting twist, the crossover of Kabbalah into Puritan Congregationalism becomes a point of both contention and extended dialogue. As will be shown in this chapter, the lens of exchange sheds light on Mather's overall employment of kabbalistic ideas and sources throughout his corpus. In addition, this lens of exchange highlights the flow of ideas and the formation of early American religious identity. It brings into focus some of the contrasts but also some of the commonalities between Jewish Kabbalah, Keithian Christian Quakerism, and the Puritan Congregationalism represented by Cotton Mather.

On the Revolution of Souls

Within his *Little Flocks Guarded*, Mather twice mentions Christian Lodowick, the same figure who had copied out George Keith's kabbalistic commentary on *The Temple of Wisdom* specifically for Mather. In one of those mentions, Mather writes that "Mr. *Lodowick*, a Gentleman of *Rhode-Island* lately Recovered out of *Quakerism*, in a Challenge to the Quakers, tells them, If this your foundation stand sure, it would follow, That all honest Pagans, Jews, and Mahometans, are in Christ as well as you."[5] Lodowick's contemptuous letter against Quakerism, which he had sent to Mather seven months earlier along with Keith's kabbalistic commentary and two other Keithian treatises, was part of a larger discussion and had not gone unnoticed or been disregarded.

In the above quote regarding "Pagans, Jews, and Mahometans," Mather seems to be referring to the Quaker notion of the manifestation of Light within, also characterized by a different metaphor as the Seed of Grace. This is the idea that within every single human, regardless of belief, upbringing, or national origin, there is implanted a divine seed. By this, according to Lodowick, the Quakers claim that "some have been and may yet be saved, to whom the Gospel is not outwardly Preached, nor the History of Christ outwardly known."[6] In his letter to Mather, Lodowick goes on to implicate Keith directly. Lodowick recognizes Keith's ultimately schismatic support for *both* the inward Light, or divine seed, *and* the external historical Christ in regard to salvation. In this context, Lodowick writes, "I suppose also that he believes, that honest *Pagans*, at some of their Revolutions receive the knowledge of Jesus of *Nazareth*, (& according to his late absurd Notion) are then perfectly Justified and Saved."[7] Lodowick's allusion here is to the notion that Keith, and Lodowick in his wake, terms in Hebrew "GALGAL" and then translates as "*Revolution* of Soul,"[8] referring to the kabbalistic concept of reincarnation.

According to Lodowick, it is not only by way of a belief in the inner Light that Keith is mistaken but also by way of his support for this kabbalistic concept of soul revolutions. What is being referenced here is a point of speculation among anti-Keithian Quakers such as Caleb Pusey, the erstwhile business partner of William Penn and a Pennsylvania pamphleteer, that Keith taught a doctrine of twelve reincarnations for each individual soul in order to allow for an eventual exposure to and acceptance of the Gospels.[9] For Keith, such an idea would allow for both a universality of salvation and the particularity of the Christian doctrine; though in Keith's actual case, instead of permitting him to have his cake and eat it too, it opened him up to scrutiny from all sides.

From the side of Puritan Congregationalism, Keith's kabbalistically tinged Christian Quaker ideas of the Light within and of external reincarnation were certainly not lost on Mather. In his attack on Quakerism, Mather writes, reflecting Lodowick's original claim:

> So then the *Quaker* holds, that the *Indians* and *Negroes*, and the *Pagans* beyond *China*, have *Sufficiency of Grace and means of Salvation*. He therefore holds according to what *Keith* adds upon it, *That the Light that is in every man, is sufficient to enable him to do any work acceptable to God*.[10]

To be sure, what is being attacked here is the standard Quaker idea of the manifestation of the Light within, and it is not the Keithian notion of *both* internality *and* externality as essential requisites for redemption. Keith's external notion of the acceptance of the narrative and lessons of the historical Christ as a necessary condition for salvation would theoretically have been amenable to Puritan Congregationalism. Perhaps for that reason, it is not stated here as a problem for Mather. Nevertheless, Mather warns, "*George Keith* is not the *Man* which he is taken to be, but a most absurd and wicked *Seducer*, and one from whom all good men should with Detestation *Turn away*."[11] This sets Mather up for a slightly, though perhaps deliberately, understated kabbalistic critique.

In a subtle quip whose sharp rhetoric is indeed better understood against the backdrop of the kabbalistic accusations against Keith both from within the Quaker camp and from Lodowick, Mather writes:

> Were the *Transmigration of Souls* a Truth, you might, when you see *Keith*, imagine that you see *Alexander the Coppersmith*, alive among us, *doing*

much harm to the Religion of which he once made, like *Alexander*, a no mean profession, with a no less *brazen* Impudence, than *knocking* Diligence, *hammering* of mischief against the true Ministers of God.[12]

Here Mather is associating Keith with a figure from 2 Timothy 4:14, who the Bible tells us did harm to Paul's ministry. Not much is known about this figure, but many Christian commentators assume that he was the same Alexander mentioned in Acts 19:33 and 1 Timothy 1:20, who was at one point pushed forward as a spokesman for the Jews of Ephesus in the face of idolatry, and who was later delivered by Paul unto Satan. Perhaps Mather is tacitly accusing Keith of Judaizing here, which would fit with Keith's promotion of kabbalistic concepts; but Mather more explicitly seems to be advancing the narrative that like Alexander the coppersmith, Keith was at one point open to the Christian Gospel but then later turned against the Church.[13] In fact, he writes that Keith "has been enlightened, and had formerly much of his education and conversation among the people of God; nevertheless he is a most Infamous *Apostate* from the Truths and Ways of God, professed among them."[14] According to Mather, Keith may be erudite and well-spoken, but this makes him all the more so a dangerous heretic who can seduce others.

Perhaps more important than the actual association of Keith with Alexander the coppersmith for our purpose of understanding the role of Kabbalah within this discourse is the fact that Mather is shrewdly associating Keith here with the transmigration of souls. He is then incisively associating the entire structure, and also the entire personage of Keith, with heresy. Mather's hermeneutic circle rests back on the kabbalistic notion that was brought to his attention by Lodowick. Not only is Keith given over to Satan like Alexander the coppersmith, he is also being delegitimized through the very kabbalistic exegetical methods that he intends to foster. It does not matter that Mather's use of transmigration here is clearly allegorical. It has the same effect of dialectical nullification, while simultaneously still showing a restrained acquiescence to the very kabbalistically tinged idea that it seeks to nullify. Here the idea of transmigration is ever so inconspicuously being used as a subtle cudgel in the hands of Cotton Mather. Elsewhere kabbalistic ideas inadvertently lead to theological discourse and the honing of ideas.

"Rabbinic Fopperies" and Divine Names

Another area of theological discourse into which Mather ambles in his exchanges with George Keith hinges on the divine name in relation to the Quaker idea of divine Light. Writing of Keith's theology, Mather at one point states, "Can any thing be so *Ridiculous* as the Rabbinical Fopperies, which he sometimes makes ostentation of?"[15] As an example of such "Fopperies," Mather later wisecracks in his typical manner of banter, "Is not the man *Light-headed*, when he says, *Light* being used as a Name of God, *is no Figurative or Tropical Expression?*"[16] Not only does Mather attempt to undermine the gravitas of Keith's entire theological argument, he pejoratively links Keith's ideas of Light as related to the divine name, or essence of God, to rabbinical thought. In doing so he is cleverly delegitimizing the idea by extracting it from the realm of orthodox Protestant theology.

In a tract of 1692 directly addressing Mather, Keith responds that his own ideas are "well warranted in holy Scripture, and well approved by Christian Writers of great esteem for Piety and Learning."[17] Mather's ideas, on the other hand, lack true Christian knowledge in Keith's assessment. Keith goes on, in a fairly awkward grammatical style, to openly declare regarding Mather's statements,

> that he and his Brethren call *Rabbinical Fopperies*, in that they show their great Ignorance in good Learning; for it is generally acknowledged by *Christians*, as well as *Jews*, yea, and by *Protestants* of good Note, *That the* Hebrew *Names of God, mentioned in Scripture, being various, some of them are greater than others*; and the greater Names do answer to the greater Measures of the divine Light.[18]

If Keith is "Light-headed" in the eyes of Mather, then Mather is ignorant in the eyes of Keith. The concept that the various Hebrew names of God represent differing degrees of divine Light is certainly Jewish, but for Keith it is *also* Christian, and even more prodigiously, it is supported by respected Protestants.

Keith recognizes the importance that Mather attaches to Protestant *auctoritates*, texts deemed worthy because they were perceived to give clear witness to Protestant truth. To this end he plays Mather's own game by mentioning the famed Swiss Christian Hebraist Johannes Buxtorf the Elder, who in his *Lexicon Hebraicum et Chaldaicum* of 1607 discusses the four-letter divine name, commonly pronounced *Jehovah* by many in Keith's and Mather's respective cohorts.[19] Through Buxtorf, Keith attributes this pronunciation to the early sixteenth-century Italian Christian kabbalist Petrus Galatinus, though he claims that until Galatinus the name was actually ineffable, "consisting of quiescent Letters, and having no proper Vowels of its own."[20] It is thus one of the greatest names of God, reflecting and revealing one of the highest points of divine Light.

Galatinus, for his part, relies on the anti-Jewish Christian kabbalistic works by the fifteenth-century Spanish convert Paulus de Heredia to make the case that the ineffability of the divine name lies not in pronunciation but in the mystery of the Trinity latent within.[21] To this effect he first quotes Heredia's *Iggeret ha-Sodot*, pseudepigraphically attributed to the tannaitic rabbi Nehunia ben Ha-Kanah, in order to establish the apophatic nature of God in relation to human understanding:

> God does not have a name that we can fully comprehend, because His essence is His name, and His name is His essence. And even though we cannot attain knowledge from His essence, all of His names provide instruction. Accordingly, the four-letter name is more essential according to His actions, and it teaches a more complete knowledge that is more essential, according to that which we are able to receive. From this are joined all of His names. Accordingly, this name is called the "Explicit Name," not because it is His essential name, but we say this because this is all that our faculties can understand, and we cannot rise higher than this.[22]

Once God's essence is established to be both beyond His name and taught about through His various names, Galatinus goes on, in typical Christian kabbalistic fashion, to show that the highest, "Explicit Name" contains within its deepest recesses the notion of the Trinity. For this he turns to Heredia's *Galei Razaya*, falsely attributed to the second-century *tanna* Judah ha-Nasi. "From this Explicit Name is derived the twelve-letter name," he quotes, "for it is *Av-Ben-v'Ruach-ha-Kodesh* (Father, Son, and the Holy Spirit), which in our Hebrew language is a twelve-letter name, written as such."[23] That is to say, when spelled out in Hebrew, the words for "Father," i.e., *Av* (*alef-bet*), "Son," i.e., *Ben* (*bet-nun*), "and Holy Spirit," i.e., *v'Ruach-ha-Kodesh* (*vav-resh-vav-het-heh-kuf-dalet-shin*) comprise a total of twelve letters.

What Galatinus is tacitly interpreting in the above two quotes is a passage from the Talmud that discusses the ineffable name of God:

> The Holy One, Blessed is He, said, "I am not called as I am written; I am written with *yod-heh* and I am called by *alef-dalet*." The Rabbis taught that at first they would transmit the twelve-letter name to every man. When those who were corrupt increased, they would transmit it only to humble members of the priesthood.[24]

Yod-heh in this passage seems to be shorthand for the Tetragrammaton, i.e., YHWH (*yod-heh-vav-heh*), while *alef-dalet* seems to be shorthand for *Adonai* (*alef-dalet-nun-yod*). In the context of Galatinus's discourse, it is important to note that the traditional Jewish pronunciation of the Tetragrammaton is euphemistically, and purposefully circuitously *Adonai*, i.e., "my Lord."[25] What the "twelve-letter name" refers to in the Talmudic passage is not entirely clear, but it does seem to be related to the Tetragrammaton, and the ambiguity lends it to interpretation, such as that of Heredia via Galatinus.

In line with Galatinus's overall discourse on the name, George Keith states that the Tetragrammaton "is generally acknowledged to be one of the greatest Names of God" and that only Moses among the prophets "knew the inward force and efficacy signified by that Name."[26] Carrying this discourse and its rabbinic undertones into his argument with Mather, Keith states, "And though I do no wise approve *Rabbinical Fopperies*, or *Jewish Fictions* or *Fables*, yet what I find either in *Jewish* or *Gentile Writers*, that doth well accord with the divine Oracles of the holy Scripture, I do well receive it and relish it."[27] Like Galatinus, and Buxtorf in his wake, Keith sees fit to use "Jewish" wisdom inasmuch as it carries forth his Christian message. In order to make rhetorical inroads, this is an idea that Keith particularly and explicitly seems to be emphasizing in his argument with Mather.

Mather and Christian Hebraism

Keith's rhetoric of using Christian Hebraism as a common ground of discourse seems to be fairly sound. Indeed, Mather, for his part, was no stranger to the thought of Petrus Galatinus and his usage of kabbalistic linguistics to prove the Trinity, or to the linguistics of the Buxtorf family concerning the Tetragrammaton. Among his mentions of the former, for example, Mather quotes the Anglican bishop Richard Kidder and states that "*Galatinus* appeals to R. *Simeon Ben Johai*" in expounding on the triple mention of the word "Holy" in Isaiah 6:3: "*Holy,* זה אב *This is the Father: Holy* זה בן *This is the Son: Holy* זה רוח הקדוש *This is the Holy Ghost.*"[28] He goes on to state concerning Galatinus, "Indeed, for what he saies of R. *Simeon*, I must confess . . . I can affirm nothing upon my own Knowledge."[29] This confession does not seem to be disingenuous, and his lack of knowledge in this specific instance does not necessarily stem from a lack of familiarity with Zoharic thought.

Rather, Mather cannot affirm Galatinus's citation because it does not seem to appear anywhere in extant Zoharic literature. To be sure, the *Zohar* does attach trinitarian significance to this verse, but it is in an entirely different manner and for a different purpose. In a passage from the *Idra Rabba*, for example, the triple utterance of "Holy" refers to the Torah scroll, "whose case is holy, and for whom the ark, or Temple is holy, and which itself is holy."[30] Within none of the trinitarian iterations is there mention of a divine Father, Son, and Holy Ghost. Galatinus's appeal thus seems to be a forgery. Regardless, its full citation by Mather exhibits a keen awareness by Mather of Galatinus's work and thought. Moreover, regardless of a lack of Mather's own voice here, there is a reason why he introduced the above quote, and it is certainly reasonable to surmise that he would have been supportive of such a Trinitarian reading as stemming from this purportedly Zoharic interpretation of Scriptures. This places him on par, rather than at odds, with Keith.

Mather also seems to be more on par with Keith in terms of kabbalistic readings of the Tetragrammaton. While Keith refers to Johannes Buxtorf the Elder, at one point Mather references Johannes Buxtorf the Younger, filtered through the French theologian Philippus Riboudealdus Cabilonensis, as quoting the *Zohar* in relation to Exodus 28:30. There the Bible states, "You shall put in the Breastplate of Judgment the *Urim* and

Thummim; and they shall be upon Aaron's heart when he comes in before YHWH." According to Mather's citation, the *Zohar* holds "That the *Urim* and *Thummim*, were the *Four-Lettered Name* יהוה putt within the Folds of the *Breast-Plate*, thro' the Influences whereof, the *High-Priest* had Secret and Future Matters Revealed unto him."[31] The name itself was thus a type of amulet, acting in a similar manner to Keith's notion of the Tetragrammaton as the highest possible divine-human medium.

Mather explains that according to this theory, the Tetragrammaton put within the breastplate was inscribed by God Himself; it was thus of heavenly origin, not only in its signification as a name but also in its formation. As such, it could act as a medium for the high priest between material manifestation and the invisible world of the divine. He continues on to state, referencing his ancestor Samuel Mather, that "the Loss of the *Urim* and *Thummim* under the *Second Temple* . . . was to praepare the People of God, for the Coming of the Lord Jesus Christ."[32] With the advent of Christ, a new, more direct medium between the people and God's essence in the Tetragrammaton was introduced that negated the need for both the high priest and the *Urim* and *Thummim*.

As with the Galatinus passage on the Trinity, here too attribution to the *Zohar* is mistaken. Riboudealdus, whom Mather is quoting, does not quote the *Zohar*. He does mention the *Zohar* in relation to the *Urim* and *Thummim*, but he also names Jonathan ben Uzziel, Rashi, Gersonides, and Nachmanides, and he also mentions that Buxtorf more fully and explicitly brings forth all of these.[33] Buxtorf, for his part, quotes the following passage from the *Zohar*:

> Indeed, this has been interpreted: *the Urim* [i.e., "lights"] which enlighten. This is the secret of the enlightening looking glass,[34] and this is the engraving of the Holy Name according to the secret of forty-two, from which worlds were created; and they were embedded in it. And the *Thummim*, this is the secret of those letters that are contained within the looking glass that does not enlighten, which functions according to the seventy-two engraved letters, which are the secret of the Holy Name; and all of them are called *Urim and Thummim*.[35]

The complexities of this multifaceted passage, which engages classical tropes of priestly divinization with linguistic hermeneutics, are far too intricate to enter into here and would take us too far afield.[36] What is important to note for our purposes is that while this passage does mention the Holy Name, it is not understanding it in the same way that Mather is employing it.

Another classical Jewish text, however, which is quoted by Buxtorf, does approximate Mather's usage. This is the commentary of the late eleventh- and early twelfth-century French exegete Rabbi Shlomo Yitzhaki, known by the acronym Rashi, which states about the *Urim* and the *Thummim*, "This was an inscription of the Explicit Name, which was placed within the folds of the Breastplate; and by means of it he would enlighten and fulfill its statements."[37] Rashi is engaged in deliberate wordplay here; "enlighten," i.e., *me'ir*, is of the same root as *Urim*, while the word "fulfill," i.e., *metamem*, is of the same root as *Thummim*. In terms of the "Explicit Name," Buxtorf translates this as "Nominis Tetragrammati,"[38] directly reflecting Riboudealdus as read through the *Four-Lettered Name* of Mather.

What we have here with Mather is the case of Rashi inadvertently being turned into a Zoharic kabbalist. Such is the result of third-hand textual knowledge and the failure to consult the *Zohar*, Rashi, or even Johannes Buxtorf the Younger. Perhaps this was due to a lack of access to these sources. Whatever the case may be, as is the situation with Galatinus's Zoharic Trinity as appropriated by Mather, text-historical accuracy ultimately takes a back seat to Christology.[39] Part of the reason for this stems from Mather's Christian Hebraic exposure to such kabbalistic ideas. In effect, this places Mather in the same boat as George Keith, who was ultimately imbibing kabbalistic wisdom from the likes of Anne Conway and Francis Mercurius van Helmont. Perhaps the difference lies in the fact that Keith rarely cites the *Zohar* or other specific Jewish sources, even as filtered through a Christian Hebraist cadre. He also rarely cites the Christian Hebraists from whom he is learning, whether through text or personal contact. Rather, unlike Mather, who often plays the role of a meticulous compiler, Keith takes the kabbalistic concepts to be part and parcel of his own Christian Quaker theology.

Kabbalistic Wisdom and Christ

In at least one instance, Mather does seem to break with his own norm by tacitly addressing a kabbalistic topic, with the indistinct caveat that

"The Jewes observe," without directly citing or referencing either a Jewish or a Christian Hebraic source. This is a topic that extends the discussion of divine names beyond the Tetragrammaton and shows further accord, rather than discord, with Keith. Specifically, in his *Biblia Americana* on Genesis, Mather writes:

> The Jewes observe, That in the First of *Genesis*, throughout the whole Chapter, unto the Finishing of the six days Work, the Creator is called, אלהים, *Elohim*, which is a Name that signifies, *Power*; and this, no less than Thirty Two Times over. An Intimation, That the *Power* of God, is eminently display'd in the *Creation* of the World.[40]

What is being alluded to here is a notion that shows up in kabbalistic literature, which equates the thirty-two times that the specific Hebrew divine name *Elohim* is mentioned within the story of creation with the thirty-two paths of Wisdom mentioned at the very outset of the Hebrew speculative mystical tract known as *Sefer Yetzirah*. Through these thirty-two paths, according to that work, the world was formed.[41] Other than acknowledging that *Elohim* "is a Name that signifies, *Power*," which brings into question Keith's argument that Mather was ignorant of the idea "*That the* Hebrew *Names of God, mentioned in Scripture*" are variant, and that "*some of them are greater than others*,"[42] key here is the tacit equation of the divine name with the "Wisdom" accounted for in *Sefer Yetzirah*.

In an important follow-up hinging on the notion of Wisdom as a divine epithet, which does invoke both Jewish thinkers and Christian Hebraists, and which indirectly sheds light on the entire kabbalistic argument with Keith, Mather writes concerning the first word of the Pentateuch:

> No less Persons than *Origen*, and *Basil*, and *Jerom*, and *Austin*, and *Bede*, and *Junilius*, look upon the Word ראשית here, which wee will translate, *The Beginning*, to bee a Name of the *Messiah*. Yea, the *Chaldee* Paraphrast had some such thing in his Eye, when hee renders it, בחוכמא *By Wisdome*, God created. *Galatinus* well argues, That this must bee the *Messiah*, because *Wisdome* is called in Prov. 8.22. by the Name of ראשית *The Beginning*. And thus, our Lord Jesus Christ being asked, in Joh. 8.25. *Who art thou?* Answered, *The Beginning*.[43]

Here Galatinus clearly comes back into play among other Christian authorities, as do kabbalistic notions of the divine name. In this context, however, those notions masterfully link God as Creator with God as the Messiah through Wisdom personified in Jesus. ראשית (*Reshit*) is "Beginning," as in the very first verse of Genesis, "In the beginning;" בחוכמא (*b'Hokhmah*) is "By Wisdom," and the ancient authoritative Aramaic translation of the Bible known as *Targum Jonathan* translates the first verse of Genesis as *b'Hokhmah bara 'alma*, i.e., "By Wisdom God created the world." In kabbalistic literature the two terms are often bridged by reference to Psalm 111:10, which begins *Reshit Hokhmah*, i.e., "The Beginning is Wisdom." The idea in kabbalistic literature is that the second *sefirah*, which is *Hokhmah*, is the beginning by which the world was created. Here in the quote from Mather the parallel is clear, though in line with orthodox Christology, the second hypostasis is the Messiah, who is Jesus Christ as *The Beginning*, i.e., *Wisdom*. The influence of Galatinus's Christian Kabbalah is unmistakable.

In another instance, Mather quotes a lengthy passage from the late seventeenth- and early eighteenth-century Scottish Presbyterian minister Robert Fleming the Younger, which itself is translating and quoting the mysterious seventeenth-century German Christian Hebraist Johann Stephan Rittangel, who is referring to the Jewish kabbalistic text known as *Tikkunim* or *Tikkunei ha-Zohar*. Not much is known about Rittangel, but he was rumored to have been born a Jew, to have become a Catholic, and then later to have converted to Lutheranism. He reportedly dressed like an eastern European rabbi but also lived in Turkey and had insight into the Karaites.[44] According to Fleming through Mather, commenting on the passage that he brings forth, "This *Rittangelius* had been a Jew, and was once a *Rabbi* among the Jewes; tho' when he wrote this Book, he was become a *Christian*."[45] Once again by way of an argument from authority, Mather is keen on clearly Christianizing his use of kabbalistic texts. This is through the figure of Rittangel and also that of Fleming.

Commenting on the personification of Wisdom in Proverbs 8, the passage at hand states that it is an aspect of God, and "That He is supreme WISDOME, proceeding from His *Father*, (whom they call, *the supreme Crown*, or *Majesty*,) by Eternal and Ineffable Generation."[46] Rittangel's original Latin text has an additional statement not copied by Fleming, or Mather in his wake, that the supreme Wisdom is "the second Intellectual Numeration in the archetypal world, that is, the Living Word of God," and that the supreme Crown is the first of the Intellectual Numerations within the archetypal world, from out of eternity.[47] What is being referred to here in Rittangel's original is the idea of the ten *sefirot*, neoplatonically cast as archetypes within the eternal mind and emanated from eternity itself. Whether or not the omission by Fleming, and subsequently Mather, was purposeful, it certainly changes the nature of the idea being discussed. Jesus as Wisdom proceeding from his Father, without consideration either for the eight other Numerations or for the abyss of eternity, more easily stands within a clean Protestant Trinitarian framework.

In order to buttress this argument, the passage brought forth by Mather, from Rittangel through Fleming, goes on to directly quote from *Tikkunei ha-Zohar*:

> There is a *Man*,—who is not simply called, a *Man*, but the *First Man*, and the *Highest* of all Men, and the *supreme Crown*; the Hidden and Occult; the Cause of Causes; the Beginning of Beginnings. Of this *Man*, it is said Prov. 8.30. Then *was I by Him, as one brought up with Him.* And to this *Man* it was said [namely, by God the Father,] *lett us make Man.* So that this Man is the *Wisdome*.[48]

Similar to George Keith, who was shown in the last chapter to have expounded heavily on the kabbalistic notion of *Adam Kadmon*, Mather, along with the two sources sequentially informing him, seems to take this "*First Man*" who is *Wisdome* as a reference to Jesus Christ. The Aramaic passage from *Tikkunei ha-Zohar*, however, continues on to discuss the first man in relation to the supernal Mother, and in relation to the Man of the World of Creation, the Man of the World of Formation, and the Man of the World of Fabrication. These ideas, which we have seen in a different framework extensively adopted and adapted by Keith, throw the Christological idea into relief in this specific instance. If the first man as supernal Father is related to a supernal Mother, and if there is a supernal Man in four different Worlds of Existence, then the entire hypostatic structure is altered.

This is an additional example in Mather's corpus of a thrice-removed citation that simultaneously holds authority and is radically transformed. Whether Mather was cognizant of this, or whether it is a classic case of inevitable mistransmission in the game of "telephone" is not entirely clear. Whatever the case may be, this kabbalistic text works for Mather precisely because it is removed from its context; at the same time, however, it maintains an air of authority as a specific "ancient" citation. It also works for Mather because it is filtered through both Rittangel and Fleming. If the former removed it from Judaism and perhaps dragged it through Catholicism on his way to Lutheranism, the latter was an uncontested Scottish Presbyterian who thus baptized the kabbalistic text for orthodox Protestant use.

Wisdom Personified in *Adam Kadmon*

George Keith takes a completely different approach to hypostatic Wisdom as informed by Kabbalah. In one of the tracts that sparked his dispute with Mather, entitled *The Presbyterian and Independent Visible Churches in New England and else-where, Brought to the Test*, which was originally published by William Bradford in 1689, Keith writes in regard to the personification of Wisdom in the book of Proverbs:

> Wisdom is a degree above Understanding, and Understanding a degree above Knowledge, all which divine Measures are set in order, as the parts of a Tree, with Root, Branches and Tops, or as the Members of a Mans Body, by way of Allegory and Analogy, *Cochmah, Binah* and *Daath* belonging to the Head, *Gedulah, Geburah* to the right and left Hand and Arm, *Tipheret* to the Body, *Nesah, Hod* and *Jesod* to the Thighs and Legs, &c. and *Mulcuth* lowest of all; all which make up, by way only of allegory and analogy the Parts and Members of the *Son of Man*, or heavenly *Adam*, as both *Ezekiel* and *John* saw him upon his Throne. The English Names of these Hebrew words, all which are found in Scripture, in their true order, are these following, *Cochmah*, i.e. Wisdom, *Binah*, i.e. Understanding or Prudence, *Daath*, i.e. Knowledge, (see I *Chron.* 29. 11) *Gedulah*, i.e. Magnificence, *Geburah*, i.e. Power, *Tipheret*, i.e. Beauty, *Nesah* and *Hod*, i.e. Victory & Glory, *Jesod*, i.e. Foundation, and *Mulcuth*, i.e. the Kingdom.[49]

Keith does not mention *Keter* here, thereby placing Wisdom, or *Hokhmah*, at the very top of the emanatory, sefirotic structure of ten.

Here it is the first point of extension from the infinite aspect of God. And as might be expected from Keith's overall theology, he links it here, "by way only of allegory and analogy," to the heavenly Adam.[50] For Keith, the idea is less about Trinity and more about the all-encompassing cosmic Tree of Christ as *Adam Kadmon*.

Quite unlike Mather, and as is typical of Keith's overall theology, the above passage by Keith does not quote any kabbalistic source, whether Jewish or Christian. Also dissimilar to Mather, and characteristic of Keith, this passage seeks to fully integrate the kabbalistic concepts being discussed, and it attempts to make them into an organic part of his overall thought. For Mather, Wisdom at the beginning of God's ways is Christ, and any kabbalistic ascription only seems to hold weight insofar as it is filtered through Protestant sources of authority. For Keith, Wisdom is part of a larger structure that comprises *Adam Kadmon*, and its Christlike character holds weight only by way of general analogy between the human and the divine.

To be fair, Mather does bring forth a very lengthy passage from Fleming, which is translated from the *Kabbala Denudata* of Keith's friend, Christian Knorr von Rosenroth; it is a series of translations from the *Zohar*, which discuss *Adam Kadmon* at length. Mather's citation from Fleming, which is alternately paraphrastic and direct, focuses on the *Idra Rabba* and the *Idra Zuta* sections of the *Zohar*. The passage discusses "a mystical Repraesentation of God the *Father*, and the *Logos*,"[51] and it states:

> The first is called *The Ancient*, and *The Ancient of Dayes*; and, *Adam Kadman*, or *The most Ancient Adam*, as likewise, *The most Holy one*, or, *The Holiest of all*. But the most usual Name of this glorious Person in the *Zohar*, is *Arich Anpin*, which is, as the *Zohar* explains it, one whose *Face* is infinitely extended. The Latin Translator calls Him therefore, *Macroprosopus*.
>
> The second is, the *Logos*; who in the *Zohar* is constantly called, *Seir Anpin*, one whose *Face* is lesser, & shorter, or *confined*; as it were one Way, in His looking towards Men; which the Latin Translation renders by the Greek Word, *Microprosopus*.[52]

This has clear resonance with Keith, who, as we have seen in the previous chapter, corresponded directly with "The Latin Translator" of this text, Knorr von Rosenroth, precisely concerning the notions of *Macroprosopus* and *Microprosopus*. It is not known whether Mather was aware of Keith's direct connection to Knorr, or of Keith's correspondence with Knorr regarding *Arikh Anpin* and *Ze'ir Anpin*. What is known from this passage is that Mather was clearly aware of both the concepts and some of the sources on which Keith was basing much of his Christian Quaker kabbalistic theology.

It is important to note that within this passage brought by Mather via Fleming, *Logos* stands for divine Wisdom. Further along, the passage states:

> When the *most Ancient Holy one*, who is altogether *Hidden* from us, was desirous to render himself conspicuous, he found out a Way to represent Himself in the Form of *Man*. For this End, the *Wisdome*, which comprehends all things, and which is *Begotten* by and shines from the *most Ancient Holy one*, chose to be represented by *Man*, Male and Female. As *Wisdome*, He is the *Father*; and as *Intelligence, Information*, and *Prudence*, He is the *Mother*. And so it is said, [Prov. 8.12.] *I Wisdome dwell with Prudence. Wisdome* and *Prudence* are in the same Scale, united as *Man* and *Woman*.[53]

Within this passage, a complexity comes into play that is much greater than the reductionist notion of Christ as the kabbalistic personification of Wisdom. Specifically, the androgynous nature of the hypostatic realm is allowed for here, which is an idea that we have seen addressed by Keith in his commentary on Jacob Boehme. Moreover, Wisdom is not the Son; He is the *Father*, and in an interesting turn of gender fluidity, He is also the *Mother*. Thus, although Wisdom is "*Begotten*," and "shines from the *most Ancient Holy one*," it cannot be understood here in the traditional Christian sense of Jesus as Logos.

There is a clear disparity here between this usage of Zoharic quotation, which brings the androgyny of *Adam Kadmon* into the picture, and the previous citation taken from Rittangel, which casts Wisdom as the hypostatic Son of the divine Father. One small glimmer of insight into Mather's mind may shed some light on the disparity. Paraphrasing Fleming, Mather writes of all of the above Zoharic quotations, "If we suppose R. *Simeon* to have been a satanical Imposter, the Quotations from his Book, will therefore have the more of Cogency in them."[54] Fleming's original sentiment was that there are arguments in the *Zohar* that confirm Christianity, but that Shimon bar Yochai was "raised up by the Devil to ape Christ, in order to keep them [i.e., the Jews] from falling in with him as the true Messias."[55] Mather later states, in what appears to be his own voice, "These are wonderful Passages, to come from a *Jew*, an Infidel *Jew*. And they will help to Illustrate many of the scriptural Oracles. A contemplative Mind, may make a good and great Use of them."[56] The idea being expressed by Mather seems to be along the lines of Fleming, that as an infidel Jew and satanic impostor, Rabbi Shimon's purported writings in the *Zohar* hold many false thoughts that may seduce the reader into error. These may include ideas such as the androgynous heavenly Adam. Notwithstanding, according to Mather in divergence from Fleming, a keen contemplative mind that has been exposed to the true Way of Christianity can separate the wheat from the chaff and can utilize such passages for better understanding. Whether someone the likes of George Keith has, in the eyes of Mather, such a keen contemplative mind is an entirely different question.

The Divine Feminine

A similar passage to Keith's explanation of Wisdom as the first sefirotic emanation of ten within his discourse against Congregationalists and Presbyterians in New England, including Mather who is explicitly named, appears in the Antiquarian Society manuscript discussed in the previous chapter. As should be recalled, that manuscript, which was copied from a text written in 1688, just a year prior to the publication of Keith's *The Presbyterian and Independent Visible Churches in New England*, seems to have been composed by Keith, transcribed by Lodowick, and delivered to Mather. The similar language of "analogy" between the body of *Adam Kadmon* and the *sefirot*, and the similar means of transliteration and translation thus not only further substantiate the claim of Keith's authorship of the manuscript; the transmission of the manuscript from Lodowick to Mather also provides a further point of contact in the fray between Keithian Kabbalah and the Congregationalism of Cotton Mather.

Similar to the quote from *The Presbyterian and Independent Visible Churches*, in which the ten hypostases are in the shape of a "Mans Body, by way of Allegory and Analogy," Keith writes within the Antiquarian Society manuscript, regarding the *sefirot*:

> These 10 Divine Lights or Emanations are understood to be placed in such an order as the members of a man's body, to which the members of the body of man bear an analogy, & they make up that Aziluthick System called Adam Cadmon, i.e., the first or great Adam, otherwise called by the name, the heavenly Adam. . . . Now the names of these 10 are in Hebrew & English thus: 1. Kether i.e. the Crown. 2. Cochma i.e. Wisdom. 3. Binah i.e. Prudence and Understanding. 4. Daath i.e. Knowledge. And these 4 belong to the Head of this great man. . . . 5. Gedulah otherwise called Chesed i.e. Munificence, Bounty or Mercy & Clemency, the right shoulder arm & hand. 6. Geburah i.e. Fortitude, vigour & Severity, the left shoulder, arm & hand. 7. Tiphereth i.e. beauty & body of this great man. 8. Nezah i.e. Victory, the right thigh, Leg & foot. 9. Hod i.e. Glory, the left thigh, leg & foot. 10. Jesod i.e. the Foundation answering to the member of generation in the male. And to this Adam they assign his Wife which is called Malchuth i.e. the Kingdom having also the feminine members by way of analogy.[57]

Unlike the previous passage, which begins with *Hokhmah*, here *Keter* is given pride of place as the first emanation. In order to maintain the structure of ten, *Malkhut* is divorced from the unified structure of *Adam Kadmon* and is set as his female counterpart. Keith goes on to call this divine feminine "Mount Zion, & the heavenly Jerusalem . . . the Supernatural Chavah i.e. Life who is in the truest sense the Mother of all living."[58] *Chavah*, which means "life" and is the Hebrew name of the biblical Eve, is, on the supernal level, not merely the embodiment of God in the Church; she is truly the divine feminine, the female complement of *Adam Kadmon*.

Due to the integrative nature of the text and the lack of attribution, it is not clear from where Keith is deriving his ideas concerning the divine feminine. One possible source is the *Idra Zuta*, which he would have access to filtered through Knorr von Rosenroth. The *Idra* comments on the male as called *Tiferet*, and analogizes him to bodily parts made up of the *sefirot*. While *Netzah* and *Hod* make up the testicles, the final of these is the "Phallus of the Male—consummation of the whole body, called *Yesod*."[59] The text continues on to state that "all the desire of the Male toward the Female inheres in this *Yesod*—entering the Female, to the place called Zion and Jerusalem, which is the place of covering of the Female, like a woman's vagina."[60] While the notion of body parts, and the epithets of "Zion" and "Jerusalem" are the same, the Zoharic source is much more sexualized than Keith's text. Moreover, it does not contain Keith's notion of "feminine members by way of analogy." In Keith's somewhat astonishing formulation, the female counterpart has all of the bodily members paralleled in the supernal Adam, and thus can also be imaged as a structure of ten. What we have in his text, then, is a veritable *Chavah Kadmonit*, i.e., a Primordial Eve, who stands in relation to *Adam Kadmon*, Primordial Adam.

Mather is not entirely in disagreement with this seemingly radical notion, and he gives a version of it voice in his commentary on the Song of Songs. But yet again, unlike Keith, he more explicitly filters it through Christian Hebraism in a manner that more forcefully connects it back to the Christian canon and to the Church of Christ on earth. In another instance of triple filtering, Mather directly quotes the Anglican bishop and theologian Simon Patrick, who is paraphrasing the famed Cambridge Platonist and Christian kabbalist Ralph Cudworth. Cudworth, for his part, quotes from the early seventeenth-century *Shefa Tal* by the Jewish kabbalist from Prague Shabbetai Sheftal Horowitz, the sixteenth-century Italian Franciscan Archangelus de Burgonovo, the fifteenth-century Italian Platonist and veritable father of Christian Kabbalah, Giovanni Pico della Mirandola, and the thirteenth-century Spanish Jewish exegete Moses ben Nachman.[61] The passage ultimately brought forth by Mather states:

> The profoundest of the Hebrew Divines, had such a Notion as this among them; *That sensible things are but an Imitation of things above.* And, that for Instance; There was an original Pattern of that Love and Union, which is between a Man and his Wife, here in this World. This they expressed by the Kindness of *Tipheret* unto *Malcuth*; which are the Names they give unto the Invisible *Bridegroom* and *Bride* in the upper World. This *Tipheret* [or, Beauty,] they call also by the Name of, the *Adam on high*, and the *great Adam*; in Opposition to the earthly & little *Adam* here below. This *Malcuth* [or, Kingdome,] they also call by the

Name of *Cheneseth Israel*, or, *The Congregation of Israel*; who is united, they say, unto the *Coelestial Adam*, as *Eve* was to the *Terrestrial*.[62]

While there is mention here of the "*Bridegroom* and *Bride* in the upper World," and while the former relates to the *great Adam*, the emphasis in terms of the latter is on *The Congregation of Israel*, i.e., the community of believers. As the passage goes on to state regarding these "Hebrew Divines," "In sum, They seem to say the same, with our Apostle *Paul*, Eph. V.32."[63] Within that verse, Paul states, "This is a great mystery: but I speak concerning Christ and the church." The emphasis is thus entirely drawn away from any notion of a supernal feminine, even though that idea remains latent within the text.

In the text brought from the *Idra Zuta* as translated by Knorr von Rosenroth and quoted from Fleming, Mather reiterates in his commentary on Proverbs, "When this *Matron* is married unto the *King*," [that is, when *Zion*, or the Church, is married unto the *Logos*,] "these *Two* become *One*."[64] The quote continues:

> This *Matron* being married unto the *King*, the whole World receives a Blessing by it, & the Universe rejoiceth. Now as the *King* [i.e. God essentially considered] consisteth of a *Trinity*, so all things bear the *Resemblance* of this. And His Wife does not Receive the *Blessing* otherwise than from the whole *Trinity*; which *Three Degrees* are called, The *Supereminency*, the *Glory*, and the *Foundation*.[65]

Supereminency, *Glory*, and *Foundation* are *Netzah*, *Hod*, and *Yesod*, respectively, and as we have seen in the above passage from the *Idra Zuta*, in the original context they are sexualized and represent the testicles and the phallus of *Adam Kadmon*. Here, by contrast, they are cast in a Trinitarian light. Moreover, the Matron is cast as the Church.

It is worth recalling that Keith had a direct line of contact with Knorr, and it bears mention that Ralph Cudworth, who was the ultimate source for Mather in the above quote from Simon Patrick, was in deep connection with members of the Ragley circle; this is the precise milieu out of which the Kabbalah of George Keith was formed. Thus, at the core of ideas of the divine feminine propounded by these two thinkers stands a commonality of sources and a commonality of ideas. In the case of Mather, it seems that he was privy to Keith's direct conceptualizations through the latter's Antiquarian Society manuscript. In both cases, perhaps due to the filters of Cudworth and Knorr von Rosenroth, the sexualization of the divine couple has largely been neutralized, thereby lending it a more "puritanical" air. Notwithstanding, Mather takes the notion in a different direction than Keith by refraining from any opinion different from the sources that he quotes, and thereby sticking to a more conservative notion of the Church as the Bride of Christ.

The Light Within

In moving from the realm of the divine couple to the question of the relationship between Christ and the individual Christian, Mather's critique of Keith and his ilk becomes more forceful. In fact, in his direct argument with Keith and the Quakers, Mather takes up the issue of divine Light and offers an oblique criticism of Keith's kabbalistic understanding of the concept. Following up on the trope that Keith is "*Light-headed*," Mather states that this must be the case when he says that "*Light is immediate, though it comes through a Medium.*"[66] Within the same treatise, he writes of the Quakers:

> Grant them, that we have a Light which is a Ray *from the Sun of Righteousness*, as being the work and gift of our Lord, who was the Creator of Man, and has put a *Conscience* into him. It is this *Conscience*, which is *The Candle of the Lord*. Yet let them know, that you can distinguish between *Causes* and *Effects*. You can distinguish between a *Light* given by Christ, and *Christ* Himself, who gives the Light . . . the *Light* in all men which Rebukes them when they do amiss, is not, *The Man Christ Jesus*.[67]

The phrase *The Candle of the Lord* is a direct quote from the book of Proverbs, which states, "The Candle of the Lord is the soul of man (*nishmat Adam*), which searches all of the inward parts."[68] Taken in this light, Mather's statement here is a clear attack on Keith's kabbalistic notion of the *Neshamah* as the soul of Christ, as discussed in the previous chapter.

Human conscience, for Mather, is a Ray of Light given off by Christ, but it is not emanated in a purely essentialist manner. Rather, it follows the physical example of cause and effect, by which effect points to and informs of the cause but is not in essence one and the same with the cause. In a later treatise Mather affirms:

> I would not speak of my SOUL as a *Part* of GOD; so on the other side, I take my SOUL to be such an *Emanation* from Him, that I may look on Him as more immediately the *Father of my Spirit*, than of my *Flesh*. HE 'tis who *forms the Spirit of Man within him*; and it proceeds from HIM so *Immediately*, that there is no Chain of *Intermediate Causes* between HIM and *That*.[69]

In Aristotelian terms, for Mather, a statement like "Light of Christ" would denote Christ as efficient cause, and while Christ himself may be the final cause, he is neither the material nor the formal cause of the soul. Keith's kabbalistic idea of the Light as the *Neshamah* thus does not accord.

Whether out of willful disdain or a failure to notice Mather's subtle critique of the kabbalistic *Neshamah* of Christ, Keith does not enter into that discussion, and he takes the argument about the simultaneous immanence and transcendence of Light in a different, albeit still definitively kabbalistic direction. In a rather stunning move, he ties the Quaker notion of inner Light to kabbalistic prophecy. Astutely careful to link his discussion with his fellow Protestants back to the New Testament, he notes, referencing James 1:17, that "we read in Scripture, that *God is the Father of Lights*." Of these Lights, he writes, "some are higher, and some lower, which some mystick Writers, both among *Jews* and *Christians*, have taken notice of, out of the Scripture it self."[70] From there he goes on to detail what these mystic writers think about biblical prophecy:

> Hence they say, *Moses* drank at the Fountain, *Samuel*, *David*, *Solomon*, and some others, drank at the Streams; and others of an inferior degree, at the Pond or Cistern. And they further say, *Moses* had his Revelations from *Binah*, *Abraham* from *Gedulah*, a step lower; *Isaac* from *Geburah*, yet lower; *Jacob* from *Tipheret*, yet lower, but partaking of both, signified by his dwelling in Tents, betwixt the Tents of *Abraham* and *Isaac*; *David* sometimes from *Tipheret*, and sometimes from *Nezah* and *Hod*; hence we read some of the Inscriptions of his *Psalms* to *Nezah*; and sometimes from *Malcuth*; and they say that the ordinary Prophets had their Revela-

tions from these two divine Measures, *Nezah* and *Hod*, called, *Exod.* 38.8. *The Looking-Glasses of the Lords Hosts that Assemble at the door of the Tabernacle*, (see the *Heb.* text) But *Moses* had liberty to go into the heavenly Tabernacle it self, and so had some others. And that God did make himself more known to *Moses*, than to *Abraham*, *Isaac*, and *Jacob*, is clear from these words of his to *Moses* at the Bush, *I appeared to* Abraham, Isaac *and* Jacob *by the Name of God Almighty, but by my Name Jehovah, was I not known to them*, Exod. 6.3.[71]

In this extraordinary passage, Keith returns to the sefirotic structure to once again explain his notion of emanated divine Light. Here it is specifically related to prophecy, and taken in conjunction with some of his former ideas, it can be conjectured that he is linking the Quaker notion of the inner Light with the divine authority of the biblical patriarchs. This has a somewhat radical, twofold purpose. First of all, if that inner Light is Christ, then it effectively retroactively christens the Old Testament prophets. Second, if the inner Light is something that is still latent within all humans, then mystical prophecy in the guise of Quaker illumination is still available to everyone, on various levels. With both of these purposes Keith is setting himself apart from the likes of Mather, though he is perspicaciously doing so through the kabbalistic use of biblical citation. By invoking both the Old and New Testaments, he is seeking to set himself on equal Protestant footing.

And indeed, at a different point within his corpus, through the medium of Simon Patrick, Mather does invoke the very same verse from the New Testament in order to discuss the *sefirot*. Directly quoting Patrick, Mather writes that the kabbalists

make the *Three First* of them, to be more than the other *Seven*, and they call them, the *Primordial*. The First, they call, *The Wonderful Intelligence*, and, *The first Intellectual Light*, (as the Apostle *James* calls God, *The Father of Lights*,) and, *The First Glory*. The Second, they call (among other Names,) *The Illuminating Intelligence*; (as the Evangelist *John* saies, The Eternal WORD *enlightens every one that cometh into the World*,) and, *The Second Glory*. The Third, they call, *The Sanctified Intelligence*; probably they mean, *The Holy Intelligence*; which is the very same with, *The Holy Spirit*. All this we find in the Book *Jetzira*, which they fancy was

made by *Abraham*. From whence we learn, that they had an obscure Notion of the *Trinity*; and that the Apostles used such Language about it, as
was usual among the Jewes.[72]

While this passage clearly cites James 1:17 like Keith, as well as John 1:9, there
is absolutely no reference to the Old Testament or to notions of prophecy.
The emphasis is also on the first three *sefirot*, and the goal is unmistakably
Trinitarian. Mather, utilizing Patrick, is interested in the *sefirot* only inasmuch as they can promote a Trinitarian understanding of the Godhead. In
this case "the Book *Jetzira*," attributed to Abraham, is employed to buttress
the language of the Apostles within the New Testament,[73] in direct contradistinction to Keith who uses the New Testament verse as a point of entry
into kabbalistic exegesis on Old Testament prophets.

Unlike Mather who quotes Patrick whole cloth, Keith does not cite
sources and he seems both to paraphrase and to mix and match concepts. This is frustratingly common for Keith, and in this instance it
makes it difficult to definitively assess from where it is that he is getting
his ideas on prophecy. One possible candidate is the thirteenth-century
Spanish kabbalist Joseph Gikatilla, whose book *Sha'arei Orah* (*Gates of
Light)* influenced Knorr von Rosenroth.[74] Gikatilla associates the patriarchs with various *sefirot* throughout that work, with Abraham always
being coupled with *Gedulah*, Isaac with *Gevurah*, and Jacob with *Tiferet*.
For example, in the fifth Gate, or chapter, Gikatilla writes that "Abraham
is set against *Hesed*, Isaac is set against *Din*, and Jacob mediates between
them as *a complete man dwelling in tents*."[75] *Hesed* is a common syn-
onym for *Gedulah* and *Din* is common for *Gevurah*. *Tiferet* is commonly
placed as a mediator between the two, or as an entity "partaking of both"
in the language of Keith. In complete accord with Gikatilla, he notes that
Jacob is "signified by his dwelling in Tents." The case for influence here
thus seems plausible at the very least.

In another place, Gikatilla specifically mentions "*The Looking-Glasses
of the Lords Hosts that Assemble at the door of the Tabernacle*" of Exodus
38:8, which in the above quote Keith has beseeched his readers to look
up in Hebrew. Gikatilla states:

Moses our Teacher, may peace be upon him, enters the Tabernacle and
speaks with YHWH, which is the clear looking glass, face to face. The rest

of the prophets speak with YHWH by way of Adonai, which is the looking glass that is not clear. And this is the secret of the verse *"I appeared to Abraham, Isaac and Jacob as El Shaddai, but I did not make myself known to them by my Name YHWH."* (Exodus 6:3)[76]

This is virtually identical to the concluding portion of the passage from Keith. It also interestingly ties back to the *Zohar* passage on the *Urim* and *Thummim* discussed above, which was quoted by Buxtorf and confused by Mather with Rashi. In both cases the divine name is connected to prophecy; though here in Keith, who was probably drawing on Gikatilla, this prophecy is reflected through the Light shining through the lenses of the *sefirot*.

The Inner Light, Resurrection, and "Plastical Dew"

The argument concerning the inner Light centers not only on the soul and prophecy; it also involves the complex notion of resurrection and the body. In a telling comment to Mather regarding Keith, Lodowick writes:

> He told me last Summer, that this *our Flesh* which goes into the grave shall not rise again, but there is an Invisible *Bone* dispersed thro' the Body, called by the Cabbalists *Luz*, which is the *Seed Sown*, unto which God shall give a *Spiritual Body*: and he said, that he asked some of the Jews in these parts, what *Luz* signified, and they [because they understood nothing of that *Cabbala*, and perhaps knowing that the word, *Luz* in the *Portugal* and *Spanish* Tongue signifieth *Light*] told him it means *Light* and so G. *Keith* is hugely pleased with the fancy of it, and thinks it fitteth bravely with their *Light* and *Seed*. And when I told him, that the Cabbalists said, that this *Invisible Bone* is only a Small Bone in the back, he answered, that *Wise men would not tell all at once*.[77]

From this remarkable passage we learn that Keith was in contact with some of the members of the Jewish community of Rhode Island, which indeed was Sephardic and thus Portuguese and Spanish speaking, and which was established as early as 1658. We also learn that Lodowick seemingly had contact with the seventeenth-century New England Jews as well, and, probably accurately, had little esteem for their kabbalistic learning. Keith, on the other hand, lends them an air of esotericism as wise men. Perhaps this is due to the fact that while philologically not sound, homiletically the equation of *Luz* with Light jibes well with his overall theology. Whatever the case may be, here we have the extraordinary instance of three religious groupings, Quaker, Congregational, and Jewish, meeting in real time to discuss differing interpretations of common concepts.

Mather, for his part, addresses the kabbalistic concept of *Luz* in his commentary on the book of Isaiah. Copying almost verbatim from the seventeenth-century English religious thinker John Gregory, Mather writes:

> The Jewes in the Book *Zohar*, tell us, That at the last Day, a Kind of *Plastical Dew* shall fall down upon the *Dead*, and ingender with *Luz*, the praeserved *Bone*, out of which the whole Man shall again spring forth. Jewish Fancies I indulge not; but I am sure, wee shall bee at last quickened by the Influences of Him, *whose Head is filled with the Dew, & whose Locks with the Drops of the Night.*[78]

While the *Zohar* does at various points discuss a preserved bone of the spine from which the resurrected will be reconstituted at the end of days, it does not use the term *Luz*.[79] Rather, this specific term, which relates to the shape of a small nut and which Keith later associates with Light, comes from the rabbinic tracts *Ecclesiastes Rabbah* and *Leviticus Rabbah*.[80] The idea of a dew descending upon and reviving the dead, by contrast, does appear in the *Idra Rabba* and acts as a metaphor for divine emanation of the life-giving force from above.[81] The mistake of the *Luz* bone may derive from the fact that in the Zoharic imagery, the dew trickles from the skull of *Arikh Anpin*, and thus its dripping on a bone of the spine would entirely make sense.

Whatever the reason may be for the error, the nitpicking details are no matter for Mather, who is copying from Gregory in any case, or for Gregory, who at any rate expressly does not indulge in "Jewish Fancies." What is important here is not the matter of the *Luz*, whether Light or Bone. Nor does the authority of the *Zohar* seem particularly compelling to either Gregory or Mather. This is despite that fact that they seem to be drawing from the *Idra Rabba*, possibly as filtered through the *Kabbala Denudata*.[82] What does seem to be important for Gregory, and by extension for Mather, is the notion of resurrection by means of divine influence.

Notwithstanding, the question deserves to be asked as to why it is that the *Zohar* is mentioned in the first place. It also deserves to be mentioned that Mather mostly repeats this formula in his commentary on 1 Samuel, which is something that he presumably would not have done had he found it unimportant. There he writes:

> The Jewes, in the Book *Zohar*, tell us, That at the Last Day, a *plastical Dew, shall fall down upon the Dead*, and Revive them. Wee won't ask, *who shall beget these Drops of Dew?* Tis Hee, *whose Head is fill'd with the Dew*. In the great Morning of the World, the *Dew* shall fall first upon the *Dead of Christ*, as the *Dew* fell upon the Fleece of *Gideon*.[83]

Here the *Luz* bone is curiously absent, as is the follow-up regarding "Jewish Fancies." This may well indicate what it was that was distasteful to Mather in the previous quote. It does not seem to have been the *Zohar* per se, nor was it the notion of the "plastical Dew."

In fact, several current scholars of Mather's thought note that he was fascinated by the concept of a plastic spirit or substance, and that from it developed his own idea of the vital spirit.[84] This is an intermediary between the spiritual and the physical that Mather significantly refers to in several of his treatises by the Hebrew name the *Nishmath-Chajim*, i.e., the breath or soul of life, which is a locution taken from Genesis 2:7.[85] It has also been observed that the doctrine of a plastic nature that binds the universe and acts as a link between the material and immaterial realms was widely discussed in the seventeenth century and beyond.[86] What seems to be of concern to Mather, thus, is not this idea but the doctrine of the *Luz* as an eternal structure inhering within the human, be it in the form of a physical bone, or as seems to be the case for Keith, in the form of Light. For Mather, a plastical dew as coming from Christ and falling upon the dead is sound in principle and perhaps even theoretically intriguing. This is the case even if it is coming from a source such as the *Zohar*. The idea of a deep-seeded immortal element within the human, by contrast, is problematic and perhaps even idolatrous. And this can especially be dismissed precisely because it is coming from Jewish kabbalistic and not good Protestant sources. The doctrinal argument between Mather and Keith, again hinging on kabbalistic interpretation, thus seems to return to the question of the inner and the outer Christ.

Spiritual Bodily Garments

For Mather, the question of resurrection hinges not on an inner, inherent essence but on an outer, external garment. This is perhaps unsurprisingly parallel to his understandings of Christ's place in the cosmos and history, and is thus of great consequence to his overall soteriology of grace. In order to emphasize the point, Mather brings forth 1 Corinthians 15:54, which, discussing the resurrection of the body, states in the King James version that "when this corruptible shall have put on incorruption, and this mortal shall have put on immortality, then shall be brought to pass the saying that is written, Death is swallowed up in victory." Here Paul is discussing the idea that some mortals will become immortal, and that at the time of resurrection their perishable bodies of flesh will be transformed by clothing themselves with the imperishable.

Mather emphatically exhorts concerning this, "Behold, a Matter that calls for great Attention!" He then goes on to universalize the significance of the issue, stating that not only the Scriptures but "all the Ancients, do speak of a *Cloathing*, which will be *putt on* the *Raised Bodies*."[87] As prooftext he quotes the controversial Anglican priest Daniel Whitby, who states in his *Paraphrase and Commentary on the New Testament* of 1703 that

> the Conjecture of the Jewes, is this; That it shall be a *Cloathing of Light*, or of a *Pure Flame*. So the old Book *Zohar* saies, *The Bodies of the Just, shall be cloathed with the Light of Glory*. Tis a Saying of R. *Phineas*, The Blessed God will give to the Bodies of the Just, יפיות *An Ornament*; According to that, Isa. 58.11. *He shall satisfy thy Soul* בצחצחית *with white, or splendid Things*. Tis a Saying of R. *Levi*, That the *Soul, in the State of its Glory, sustains itself by the superiour Light*; and when it returns to the Body, it shall *come with this Light, & then the Body shall shine, as with the Brightness of the Heavens*. This agrees well enough, with the Transfiguration of our Lords Body, and His Appearance to *Paul* and *John*; and the Descriptions

made in the Old Testament, of the Just Rising from their Graves, and then *shining, as the Brightness of the Firmament, & the Stars forever*; and in the New, that they shall *shine as the Sun in the Kingdome of the Father*.[88]

Emphasizing the importance of this passage, Mather adds, "Every Line of this Illustration is, to me, worth an Ingott of Gold!"[89] The transfiguration of Christ's body, coupled with individual postmortem salvation, becomes key, not only to Mather's argument with Keith but to his entire soteriological sensibility.

Whitby for his part is drawing here on Joseph de Voisin of Bourdeaux's commentary on Raimond Martini's *Pugio Fidei*, which in its turn is drawing on the *Zohar*.[90] The only substantial difference from the original Hebrew text of the *Zohar* is that there Rabbi Phineas says that "in the future the Holy One, blessed is He, will beautify the bodies of the righteous, like the beauty of the first man when he entered the Garden of Eden."[91] This sentence does show up in the Voisin text, and it is a trope that, as we will see, later becomes important to Mather. The reason for its omission in the Whitby text quoted by Mather is not apparent. Regardless, the pattern here certainly is evident. What we have here, again, is a polemical melding that leads to an ultimately Protestant baptism of Zoharic thought. Jewish text makes its way through Catholic anti-Jewish polemics and into Protestant Christian Hebraism in a way that is slightly altered but once again palatable for Mather. In this case, however, the alteration does not contribute to the palatability, as is seen by the fact that the message of the omitted sentence later reappears for Mather, in a different context.

In fact, in his eschatological *Triparadisus* of 1727, Mather repeats this passage almost word for word. This further indicates that the topic was more than just of passing interest to him, especially since his *Triparadisus* contains much more than just copying and exhibits some of his more mature ideas. In this regard, it is important to note that in contradistinction to the quotation within the commentary on 1 Corinthians, in his *Triparadisus* Mather pointedly adds:

We have shrowd [sic] Reasons to think, That our *First Parents* while they continued in their Sinless Integrity, had something of this *Luminous Garment* upon them, and had, in it, both their *Shelter* and their *Beauty*. Tis called, *Vestis Onychina* in the Jewish Tradition of it; from its Resemblance to an *Onyx* in the Colour of it; and unto the *Nails* on our Fingers, in some other Circumstances. Tis thought, that on the Sin of our First Parents, this *Luminous Garment* vanished from them; and this was the *Nakedness*, wherein they were *Asham'd* and *Afraid* of appearing before the Glorious GOD.[92]

Here the sentiment of the Zoharic sentence omitted from the Whitby quote, concerning "the beauty of the first man when he entered the Garden of Eden," makes a bold reappearance in Mather's thought. Yet here it is even more pronounced, either than in the *Zohar* text or in the explications of that text by Voisin. What seems to be at play is a different passage from the *Zohar*, which metaphysically discusses the idea of "plaited garments," called *bigdei s'rad* in Hebrew. These are garments that God commands the people of Israel to make in Exodus 31:10 and 39:1 for service in the Tabernacle. Concerning such garments the *Zohar* states that "the soul cannot ascend to be seen before the Holy King until it merits being clothed with supernal garments, by which it can be seen there."[93] It goes on to clarify:

The first man, when he was in the Garden of Eden, was clothed in the garments of the supernal realm, and these are garments of the supernal Light. Since he was exiled from the Garden of Eden and was in need of the hues of this world, what is written? *And the Lord God made garments of skin for the man and his wife, and he clothed them* [Genesis 3:21]. At first they had garments of Light, which was the same supernal Light that was utilized in the Garden of Eden. . . . And if he had not first been clothed in that Light, he would not have been able to enter into there. . . . Likewise here they made plaited garments in order to serve in holiness and to enter the Holy.[94]

This bears striking resemblance to Mather's passage from the *Triparadisus* quoted above, and it may very well be the source for his notion there of the *Luminous Garment* of our *First Parents*, which vanished from them when they sinned. It is also possible that the *Vestis Onychina*, which Mather claims is from the Jewish tradition, is a reference to the "plaited garments" mentioned here. Whatever the case may be for Mather's source, the main idea remains for him, and is buttressed by these texts: Light of salvation ultimately comes from without, and it acts as a garment that clothes the individual and brings him or her into the realm of the Holy. It is not inherent and it can be stripped at any time.

Perhaps unsurprisingly, the notion of the garment makes its way into Mather's argument with Keith. Yet there it is conceptually the inverse, and it somewhat surprisingly carries no explicit kabbalistic overtones. In order to attack Keith, Mather goes after Keith's older contemporary, the famed English Quaker Isaac Pennington, who writes that we "can never call the bodily garment Christ, but that which appeared and dwelt in the body."[95] Similar to the Zoharic notion of garments of skin for the exiled first couple, when God comes into this world he must take on corruptible bodily form. Mather continues on to critically state of the Quakers that "all this is no more than they professed also of *Themselves*."[96] In a reversal of that which is proposed above concerning the luminous garment, Mather sees the Quakers as proposing a bodily garment that clothes a luminous divine essence. And this is not only for the historical Christ; it is for every individual human being.

It is from this context that Mather brings his argument to Keith. He writes:

> It seems, that unto such a sense as *this*, you must accommodate all *Keith's* Confessions about the Man *Christ Jesus*. You must imagine, 'twas this more *Spiritual Body*, which was *Crucify'd* in that more gross *Bodily Garment* which was deriv'd from the Virgin *Mary*, and you must imagine that *Body* to be in *every* Body as in a *Garment, Crucify'd* over again; thus the whole Story of the Gospel is acted over again every day, as Literally as ever it was at *Jerusalem* of old; it is all transacted by unaccountable Dispensations within our selves; and *Christ* is in every *Quaker*, as properly as he was in that Garment of man, which was hang'd upon the *Tree*.[97]

The heresy here for Mather is twofold. The first point of sacrilege is the clear, dualistic separation being made between the divine and the human elements in Christ. The body of Christ was not a mere garment, and the passion play was much more tangible and potent for him than what would be allowed by Keith's inner Spiritual Body. The second point of blasphemy here is that *every* body is a mere garment enclothing a luminous essence. If this is the case, then "the Quakers are so compleat Christs, as ever the Son of *Mary* was; for they also have the Divine Nature of Christ, dwelling in a Body of Spiritual Flesh and Blood, and those their Bodies which we see, are but the outward Tabernacles of the God, and the Man Christ Jesus."[98] On account of radical apotheosis, there is no difference between the individual and the historical Jesus Christ.

Keith answers the first critique thus: "If we consider Christ, as he was before the World was, by whom all things were created, and in respect of his Godhead, the Body was not that, but the Garment of it, when he assumed it."[99] Though he does not explicitly state so, what Keith is hearkening back to here is the cosmic notion of Christ as *Adam Kadmon*.[100] For him Christ preexisted his historical assumption of the body in an array of emanated Light. In regard to the second critique, he writes, "As the Body of the head is of far more dignity than the Body of the inferiour Members, and hath the Soul, or Spirit and Life of man otherwise dwelling in it than the inferiour Members, so much more the soul and Body of Christ hath the eternal Word living and dwelling in the same, than any other."[101] While individuals are Christlike, the historical Jesus remains forever unique in degree as the epicenter in time and space of the incarnation of the eternal Word. While he does not explicitly mention it here, what Keith is referring to is his kabbalistic notion of the *Neshamah* of Christ, which was embodied in Jesus and which otherwise emanates into every human being.

Concluding Remarks

The polemical nature of the discourse between Cotton Mather and George Keith interestingly relies heavily on kabbalistic thought throughout. The originally Jewish metaphysical system thus acts as a pertinent lens through which to examine some of the key differences between American Congregational Christianity and Christian Quakerism, as propounded by two of the early leading thinkers of each respective group.

Differences lie not only in variant interpretations that are shaped to fit their particular molds but also in their methodologies of utilization. Mather, for his part, is an adamant, assiduous copyist. Very rarely does his own voice break through in regard to kabbalistic matters, and as we have seen, it often takes speculative work and textual archaeology in order to try to hear his underlying point. Repetitions of passages seem to be indications of importance, for example, and the context of citations sometimes points to the opinion being conveyed.

As a compiler, however, Mather does not seem to be very systematic, and the texts that he brings forth sometimes give differing interpretations. For example, as we have seen, there is a disparity between his Genesis commentary extolling Wisdom as a Logos-like Christ and a later lengthy, more mythological excursus taken from the *Idra* sections of the *Zohar* as filtered through Fleming. Given that the *Biblia Americana* remained in manuscript during Mather's lifetime, it is possible that he never had a chance to edit it. It is also possible, given the expanse of time and the immense breadth of Mather's writing, that he had changes of heart. Due to the paucity of Mather's own voice in relation to many of the texts and ideas that he brings forth, it is virtually impossible to tell. One point, however, stands out very clearly, and that is Mather's consistent citation from Protestant Hebraic sources. Rarely does he cite Catholic sources, and when he does they are usually filtered through Protestant authors such as Fleming and Buxtorf. Never does he cite original Hebrew or Aramaic kabbalistic sources. Perhaps paradoxically for a Protestant, the reason for this seems to be a notion of proper authority and the prior "baptism," so to speak, of originally Jewish ideas.

Keith, for his part, is much less meticulous with his citation and it is often difficult to distinguish from where it is that he is garnering his kabbalistic ideas. The main exception seems to be in his direct argument with Mather, within which he cites Galatinus and "*Protestants* of good Note" such as Buxtorf. In doing so, he seems to deliberately be playing into Mather's game in order to be able to argue with him on even ground. Otherwise, kabbalistic thought is appropriated and more integrated into his work, such as the manuscript that was copied by Lodowick and sent to Mather, discussed in the previous chapter. Notwithstanding, other than Lodowick's account of Keith's discussion of the *Luz* bone with the Jews of Rhode Island, there is no evidence that Keith consulted with Jews or Jewish Hebrew and Aramaic texts; instead, he seems to have been heavily dependent on Protestant sources. These came by way of direct contact with the individuals who penned the texts standing at the heart of Mather's materials, and also possibly by way of textual transmission.

In regard to this last detail concerning the lack of dependence on Jewish sources on the part of both Keith and Mather, one final point deserves mention. In their respective usages of Kabbalah, neither Keith nor Mather necessarily exhibited any great esteem for Judaism or Jewish thought per se. In Keith's Antiquarian Society manuscript, for example, he writes at the outset that "the Jewish Rabbies themselves doe in many things come short of true Divine knowledge of Scripture mysteries pretended unto by them, so that their present Cabbala is not the same altogether with that antient Cabbala, that Moses & the Prophets had, & therefore we ought not to take any thing upon truth"[102] that is recounted by them. Rather, it should be filtered in order to get back to the ancient truth of Moses and the prophets, and in the case of Keith through the early 1690s, that filter should be Christian Quakerism.

Mather, as we have seen, had no problem quoting and parroting John Gregory when he wrote, "Jewish Fancies I indulge not."[103] Michael Hoberman surmises that Mather's primary motivation for learning about the Jewish Kabbalah was to anchor the words of the Bible in their ancient context, and that along the way his kabbalistic studies taught him about the spirit world.[104] Yet it is important to reiterate Mather's consistent usage of Protestant texts and contexts, from which Mather's kabbalistic learning ultimately comes about. He is not drawn to Judaism for Judaism's sake, nor is he particularly interested in reviving the "antient Cabala" of Moses and the prophets as is Keith.[105] Rather, he is quite explicit about his Puritan sensibilities, and if Kabbalah fits, then perhaps it can be of interest as a means of reinforcement. If not, then he has no problem discarding it or even historicizing it.

An example of historicization comes in his "Appendix to the Book of Acts" in his *Biblia Americana*. There he appropriates a passage from the French Protestant historian Jacques Basnage, which states concerning the Jewish kabbalists:

They had [A.C. 1290] another Imposture. The Rabbin *Moses* was a learned man, but poor, & called unto the Government of a Synagogue, the salary whereof was not enough, to maintain his numerous Family. The Doctors had in their hands, diverse loose sheets of the *Zohar*, a work ascribed unto *Simeon Jochaides*, which *Moses* observing to be distributed by pieces & infinitely esteemed, imitated the style, finished what was wanting, and sold the work as compleat. He sold such a number of copies, as relieved the necessities of his Family. But after the Discovery, the Disgrace confounded him.[106]

The intricate history of this claim is somewhat complex and would take us too far afield to enter into here.[107] What is important for our context is to note that Mather's approach to Kabbalah was multifaceted. Where its metaphysics helped to reinforce Protestant claims, it could be useful. Where a more detached historical view could cast Judaism and Jewish thought in a certain light, that could be useful too. What is important, as might be expected, is that even the historicist view on display here comes through the filter of a Protestant theologian.

Mather's variegated metaphysical and historicist approach as filtered through the Protestant textual tradition comes to a head in his commentary on Deuteronomy, where he takes the notion of Kabbalah as the handmaiden to Christianity even a step further. There he recounts the contents of an epistle by a certain Ludovicus Carretus of Genova, who converted from Judaism to Christianity largely based on kabbalistic reflection.[108] This includes reflection on the Trinity and on the godliness of the Messiah. Mather's point in bringing this story forth is clear; if used and understood properly, Jewish thought could do more than just support Christian truth claims; it could lead to the conversion of the Jews. And such stories as that of Carretus did not have to remain in faraway Italy. In fact, an Italian Jew, with whom Mather would become acquainted, would later make an appearance in the Boston area and would become somewhat of a pet project for Mather's famed father Increase. Indeed, the elder Mather set himself to the sentiment of conversion through mystical and eschatological Judaism even more vigorously than his son.[109] It is to this idea, as moored within an American sense of apocalypticism, that we now turn.

3

Sabbateanism and Mystical Conversion in the New World

From Increase Mather to Judah Monis

The Father, the Son, and Unholy Sabbateanism

In an appendix to the book of Acts within the *Biblia Americana*, Cotton Mather tells of "the famous Impostor, *Zabathai Tzevi*, in the last century."[1] Mather goes on, in a lengthy account that is entirely cribbed from the 1708 English translation of *The History of the Jews* by the French Protestant historian Jacques Basnage, to recount that this impostor Tzevi had set himself to persuade the Jewish people that he was the Redeemer of Israel. It is important for the present Protestant context to note that according to the narrative of Basnage brought by Mather, this was in light of "the *Kacams* of the Jewish Nation, who declared that they expected a *Messiah*, & could not worship the *Christ*, whom their Fathers had crucified."[2] The Jews were not only Christ-killers; now their *Kacams* (*hachamim*), "wise men," were rejecting the truth of Christ's messianism for the false Messiah Tzevi.

Tzevi was an Ottoman Jew born in Smyrna in 1626 who had learned Kabbalah, and at a certain point, according to Basnage's account, he met with a kabbalist, "a *Jew* of Reputation at *Gaza*, called *Nathan Levi*, to whom he communicated his Design."[3] Nathan would go on to set himself up as the new Messiah's new Elijah and to disseminate the message, based on kabbalistic calculation, of the advent of the final eschaton. Such ideas of messianism and the end of days had great resonance with Mather, and as we have seen in the previous chapter in regard to his own kabbalistic forays, the Protestant casting of Basnage, emphasizing the truth of Christ in opposition to the impertinence of the Jewish wise men, had implications for a larger agenda of conversion. As seen previously, in other contexts this related to the likes of Ludovicus Carretus, who saw the Light of Christ precisely through kabbalistic narrative. Here, by contrast, the Jews as a nation were being deceived by an impostor and his kabbalistic prophet, and they were being led down a false path.

This narrative would lead Cotton Mather's famed father Increase to campaign for a new soteriology, placing the "true" conversion of the Jews to Christianity at the center of redemption. In 1666 he would give a series of sermons that would eventually be turned into his publication *The Mystery of Israel's Salvation*, and about forty years later, just one year after the English publication of Basnage's work, he would publish *A Dissertation Concerning the Future Conversion of the Jewish Nation*. Increase saw the conversion of the Jewish nation to Christianity as imperative, and this eventually led to an enacted hermeneutics based on the idea of America as salvifically beyond time and space. In the American wilderness, the false path of Shabbetai Tzevi could be cosmologically redirected toward the "truth." Increase's salvific enactment of "truth" involved the eventual, very public conversion of a kabbalistically driven Jew in the Boston area named Judah Monis, who himself had an anti-Sabbatean background, albeit from a rabbinic perspective.

Increase's ruminations centering on Shabbetai Tzevi were known to his son Cotton, as was Monis, who would go on to become the first full-time Hebrew instructor at Harvard. It is thus a bit perplexing that Cotton Mather cites at length from Basnage in his *Biblia Americana* concerning the Sabbbatean affair, but he never mentions his father's understanding of this affair; nor does he discuss Monis, or his father Increase's religious uses of Sabbateanism in the latter's conversion. One possible explanation for this lack is that the selections in the younger Mather's appendix to Acts were simply textual reproductions for him, as a veritable part of his library, and were not meant to put forth his own theses. Or perhaps they were copied before Cotton was able to fully formulate his ideas about his father, Shabbetai Tzevi, and Jewish conversion. Whatever the case may be, by remaining faithful to Basnage's text, Cotton seems to be one of the first, if not *the* very first North American to explicitly mention Shabbetai Tzevi and to directly recount the Sabbatean story. This is in the context of his Bible commentary, which he had hoped to publish and disseminate, and it is from out of the framework of a specifically Protestant history concerning the Jews.

However, Cotton's relation to that story is rather distant and inscrutable. Yet again we have the case of a faithful copyist and diligent compiler. In fact, there is nothing particularly extraordinary about Basnage's account as brought forth by Mather in relation to Mather's thought, since, as Mather is wont to do, he copies the text entirely from Basnage without adding any commentary of his own. Yet again, this makes it very difficult, if not impossible, to parse out any original ideas or intention. Increase, by contrast, curiously never mentions Shabbetai Tzevi by name, and he does not quote him or his story out of any specifically known text or history. Nevertheless, the messianic fervor sparked by Tzevi extends beyond the text for Increase and consumes him in a more enacted manner of redemptive history. While the son sticks to the text, the father textualizes current events. This approach then goes on to shape certain American views of both Jewish and Protestant messianism, and even to bring forth an American Protestant kabbalistic text, as we will see within this chapter and into the next.

The End of Times and the New World

Basnage's account as recounted by Cotton is fairly accurate. According to contemporary historiography, during 1665 and 1666 the astonishing messianic campaign of the mystical Messiah Shabbetai Tzevi of Smyrna indeed swept over the Jewish world. And indeed, with the help of his prophet, the visionary kabbalist Nathan of Gaza, Tzevi proclaimed himself Deliverer and spread news of the coming of the end of history.[4] By all accounts, Tzevi had suffered from what today might be diagnosed as bipolar disorder, and he had gone to Nathan to seek his help as a renowned healer of souls. Nathan was a kabbalist in the tradition of the sixteenth-century Tzfat notable Isaac Luria, who was both a spiritual healer and a cosmic theorist. Nathan had picked up both the healing and the eschatological aspects of Lurianic Kabbalah, and when Tzevi arrived with his woes, instead of healing him, Nathan saw in his bipolar episodes kabbalistic evidence of messianism. As the eminent historian of Sabbateanism Gershom Scholem has described and documented in great detail, in Nathan's theological treatises, he describes Tzevi's psychical experiences of melancholia as a "fall" into the nether regions. There, according to Nathan's soteriology, Tzevi was to extract divine sparks from the broken shards of an unredeemed creation, which he was then to raise up during his times of illumination.[5] According to this narrative, it is only natural that the Messiah would experience such acute mental states. Tzevi could redeem both individual divine sparks and the cosmos as a whole precisely by wavering between depressive and manic episodes.

For Nathan of Gaza, redemption appeared to be at hand; and people the world over were ready for it. This was the case not only for elite kabbalists like Nathan of Gaza himself but also, and primarily, for the masses. Indeed, as Moshe Idel and Ze'ev Gries have convincingly argued, it is not that Lurianic Kabbalah led to the spread of Sabbateanism. Rather, it was quite the opposite: Sabbateanism helped to spread Lurianic Kabbalah throughout the Jewish world.[6] Whatever the historical case may be for the dissemination of Kabbalah, the fervor of Sabbatean messianism most certainly caught like wildfire, and Jews from Gaza to Aleppo to Alexandria, to Salonika to Amsterdam to London, as well as many places in between, gathered together behind their new mystical Messiah. Jews all over the world began to sell their property, to leave their lives behind, and to move to Palestine in order to await the final eschaton.

This narrative, erected by careful twentieth-century historians, accords well with the story told by our early eighteenth-century Protestant protagonists. Nevertheless, Cotton Mather, and Basnage on whom he was drawing, do not tell the entire story. In fact, as we have seen above, their narrative paints a bleak picture of a gravely mistaken Judaism. But in truth, neither the news nor the fervor was confined to the Jewish world. Indeed, as Michael McKeon has shown regarding Shabbetai Tzevi, early on in England, "observers of apparently diverse ideologies and connections—royalists, republicans, amateur scientists, professional astrologers, Puritan prophets—were ready to entertain news of him with some enthusiasm."[7] Paul Rycaut, who was a British diplomat in Smyrna at the time and was one of the main Western authors to first recount the story of Shabbetai Tzevi, reports a tale that a ship with sails of silk inscribed with the motto "The twelve tribes of Israel," and with a Hebrew-speaking crew, arrived in the northern part of Scotland in that very same period.[8] It seems that just as in the Jewish world, in the British Isles people were ready for the messianic advent. In this vein, Richard Popkin describes no less than three non-Jewish popular early English accounts of Shabbetai Tzevi;[9] and on the elite stage, Christian millenarians such as the secretary of the Royal Society of England, Henry Oldenburg, and Oldenburg's son-in-law, the theologian John Dury, were trying to make sense of the Sabbatean craze and to fit it into Christian notions of the end of days.

It is from this Sabbatean background that Increase Mather's new soteriology placing the conversion of the Jews at the center of redemption sprang forth, eventually leading to an enacted hermeneutics based on the idea of America as salvifically beyond time and space. Shabbetai Tzevi may have started the end of history, but his end was ultimately *within* history. The true end had to break through from beyond the end that it sought to bring about. In order for this to happen, it had to leave the European continent, upon which it seized Christian attention, and enter into the liminal New World wilderness of America.

In his *A Dissertation Concerning the Future Conversion of the Jewish Nation* of 1709, which incidentally coincides with the English publication of Basnage's *History of the Jews* just one year earlier, Increase Mather writes of the end of times.[10] He comments, "The *New Heaven* and *the New Earth* which God has promised, i.e. *the New World* which shall begin with the Resurrection, will be another kind of World than what this which we see is, and has been ever since the Fall of *Adam*."[11] Increase goes on to state, a little bit later in the same treatise:

> As for the *New World*, which is now well known and called by the Name of *America* . . . in Honour to the first *European* Discoverer; it was not known in the Days in which the Penmen of the Holy Scriptures lived. Those Parts of the Earth which do not include *America* are in Scripture Dialect *all the World*.[12] . . . It is certain that the *American Hemisphere* was unknown to the Ancients a long Time after the Apostles Days.[13]

Here the use of the term New World as that which "shall begin with the Resurrection" and also as that which is "called by the Name of *America*" is striking. It is certainly possible that the use of this term here is equivocal; Mather may be referring to the New World promised in Revelation 21 in a completely different, less mundane manner than his reference to America as the New World. Nevertheless, the fact that he explicitly transforms the phrase New Earth into New World in the first, eschatological mention is telling. So is his explanation that it "will be another kind of World than what this which we see is, and has been ever since the Fall of *Adam*," along with his caveat in the second quote that America as the New World "was not known in the Days in which the Penmen of the Holy Scriptures lived," and that it was not known to the ancients.[14] America, in essence, can be seen as "another kind of World" that is beyond history.

The idea exemplified here, which comes into play in Mather's uniquely American employment of Sabbateanism, is perspicaciously outlined, albeit in exaggerated form, by the Canadian Jewish Americanist Sacvan Bercovitch, who writes of the Puritans:

> They took possession by designating America as text and then interpreting the text as themselves. This was their legacy: a New World whose newness is moral or spiritual and therefore beyond mere geographical definition; a community defined by its sacred origin and telos and therefore impervious to cultural relativism; a corporate symbol, "America," whose meaning transcends territorial limits.[15]

While Christian supersessionism of God's ancient Israel was by no means unique to the American context, and while Bercovitch may indeed be prone here to a form of extreme generalization that promotes a myth of American exceptionalism, the idea of text being propounded here seems to hold in the specific case of Increase Mather. America as text outside of the biblical text calls for a new hermeneutics, which allows for a transformation beyond the Bible and beyond history. What unfolds from the American context thus takes on a lived prophetic and ultimately messianic character. Shabbetai Tzevi may have acted as a catalyst; and a "New Jerusalem" as written about in Revelation 21:2 is integral to the eschaton. But the real messianic force for Mather, which is prompted by Sabbateanism and which involves the conversion of the Jews, begins in Revelation 21:1 with the "New World" of America.

Shabbetai Tzevi in America

The messianic interest in and excitement around Shabbetai Tzevi indeed spilled over from England into British North America, into the sermons and expositions of Increase Mather. It is not clear from where Mather received the news, though his biographer Michael G. Hall surmises that he first heard about Shabbetai Tzevi in early 1666. This is based on Mather's diary entry of February 12, 1666, which states, "A.M. Transcribed preface &c, and news about Jews."[16] Mather does not state what the "preface &c" was, nor does he explain the "news about Jews." Nevertheless, the timing certainly matches up with the Sabbatean craze, and Hall's surmise is supported by an account of Increase's son Cotton. In Cotton's memoir of his father from 1724, the younger Mather writes:

> About the Year, 1665. the World was Allarmed with Rumors of Motions among the *Jews* in several Parts of the World, that made some who were *waiting for the Consolation of Israel,* to hope, that the *Lord* was going *to set His Hand again the second time, to recover the Remnant of His People, and assemble the Outcasts of Israel, and gather together the Dispersed of Judah.* Mr. *Mather* [i.e., Increase] Preached a *Monthly Lecture.* . . . And he took this Occasion, to give his Auditory some Elaborate & Judicious Lectures on that *Mystery*; Rom. XI.26.[17]

Here too specific names are omitted, which is somewhat peculiar given Cotton's unambiguous, lengthy account of Shabbetai Tzevi and Sabbateanism as drawn from Basnage. Notwithstanding, the reference here in this piece from 1724 seems to be clear. Given both the date and the narrative, this can be an allusion to none other than Shabbetai Tzevi and Sabbateanism. News of the Jewish mystical Messiah had stirred something in Cotton's father, the famed American Puritan minister, which led him to a campaign of preaching and teaching regarding the salvation of the Jews.

The Sabbatean background to Increase Mather's conversionary impulse is further attested to by an epistle of 1667, written by the famed English Puritan minister who helped to found the colony of New Haven, John Davenport. Regarding Mather's activities, Davenport wrote in what would eventually become a preface to Mather's sermons reworked as *The Mystery of Israel's Salvation*:

> These Sermons [were] being preached in a time when constant reports from sundry places and hands gave out to the world, that the *Israelites*

were upon their journey towards *Jerusalem*, from sundry Foreign parts in great multitudes, and that they were carryed on with great signs and wonders by a high and mighty hand of extraordinary providence, to the admiration and astonishment of all that heard it, and that they had written to others of their Nation, in *Europe and America*, to encourage and invite them to hasten to them.[18]

As with Cotton Mather's 1724 account, and as with Increase's own diary entry, no explicit reference is made here to Shabbetai Tzevi. Nevertheless, given the fact that these sermons were delivered in the summer of 1666, the "journey towards *Jerusalem* . . . in great multitudes" and the "great signs and wonders" mentioned by Davenport seem to be a clear indication of Sabbateanism.

Curiously, throughout the early American dealings with Sabbateanism, no writer, other than Cotton Mather patently and meticulously copying Basnage, ever mentions either Shabbetai Tzevi or Sabbateanism by name. Perhaps this was deliberate, so as not to lend Shabbetai Tzevi any historical weight. Or perhaps it is a stark reflection of what Moshe Idel, Richard Popkin, and other historians in the wake of Gershom Scholem have called "Sabbateanism as a widespread movement."[19] That is to say, the influence on Increase Mather and his cohort was not Shabbetai Tzevi as a particular figure but the historically messianic effect of Shabbetai Tzevi on the entire Jewish world. It was not the specific figures within the narrative that were of importance but the messianic stirrings of the Jews as an entire body. Yet if this is the case, then this type of attenuation seems to have been posthumous to Shabbetai Tzevi's conversion to Islam in September 1666.

Prior to the conversion, Increase seems to have been stirred to messianic action by the news of Shabbetai Tzevi himself. As Cotton had mentioned, his father's sermons of 1666 had focused on Romans 11:26. That verse, in the King James rendition, states, "And so all Israel shall be saved: as it is written, there shall come out of Sion the Deliverer, and shall turn away ungodliness from Jacob." Despite Cotton's later, postconversion caveat regarding Sabbateanism, that Increase "verily Believed the Motions then talked of *would come to nothing*,"[20] Increase's sense in the summer of 1666, as based on this verse, seems to point in a different direction: as the verse from Romans states, "there shall come out of Sion the Deliverer." In this case it *does* seem that Shabbetai Tzevi himself was important to the narrative; he had come to deliver the people of Israel away from ungodliness and eventually into the hands of Christianity, where they could meet their true Deliverer in Christ.

Yet how was this to occur when Shabbetai Tzevi was Jewish and had set himself to the task of taking on the sultan? The answer to this seems to lie in Mather's two-stage notion of historical soteriology. The first stage would see the overthrow of the Ottoman and the Roman Catholic kingdoms by the Israelite and the Protestant armies, respectively. As English Puritan minister William Hooke wrote regarding the conversion of the Jews in his own preface to Mather's *The Mystery of Israel's Salvation*:

> God now removeth this hindrance out of the way of the *Kings of the East*, who at present have two great impediments obstructing their conversion. 1. The Idolatry of *Rome*. 2. The power and prosperity of the Turk, the potent and professed enemy of Christianity. And though the first of these shall be removed in the ruine of *Rome* by the pouring out of the fifth vial upon the seat of the Beast, yet the second impediment lyeth still in the way, till by the sixth vial the waters of the great River are made fordable; and dreined so low, that the *Jews* may be able to wade thorow them to joyn with the *Gentiles*, to the utter overthrow both of the Turk and Pope.[21]

Hooke's reading is based on the book of Revelation, which speaks of "the seat of the beast" and "the great river Euphrates," which was "dried up, that the way of the kings of the east might be prepared."[22] In Hooke's interpretation, the epithet " *Kings of the East*" refers to the Jews, the "seat of the Beast" refers to the Pope, and the "waters of the great River" Euphrates refers to Ottoman borderlands. Reflecting on Mather's treatise through the lens of the book of Revelation, Hooke agrees that prior to the conversion of the Jews, both the Pope and the sultan would have to go.

Mather's second eschatological stage, after the defeat of the Pope by Protestantism and the overthrow of the sultan by Shabbetai Tzevi, would see the ingathering of the exiles of Israel and their complete conversion to Christianity.[23] In this scenario, Shabbetai Tzevi was at the very least to be the bulwark against the Ottomans and the impetus for a return of the Jews to the Holy Land. At the very best, the false Messiah would usher in the true messianic age. Such, in the summer of 1666, seems to have been Mather's sense of sacred history and a beginning of the end of times.

Sabbatean Heresy in the American Narrative

Regardless of Mather's detailed sense of sacred history, secular history had different plans. In September 1666, upon word that Shabbetai Tzevi was fomenting sedition, he was taken prisoner by the Turkish authorities in Gallipoli.[24] The sultan called upon Tzevi to account for his behavior, and he was immediately given a choice: face death or convert to Islam. Shabbetai Tzevi chose the latter, thereby uprooting the messianic narrative and turning it on its head. It was not Shabbetai Tzevi who came to conquer the Ottomans; instead, it was the sultan himself who ultimately quashed any hopes for messianic salvation through the figure of Shabbetai Tzevi.

Faced with the new reality, the world had to adjust. Some within the Jewish kabbalistic theological camp claimed that this was an unfolding of the final stages of redemption. As Nathan of Gaza had argued, Tzevi's melancholic states were in order for him to fall into the realm of the broken shards of our unredeemed world and eventually lift up divine sparks therein during his more manic states. His idea was that the same was now happening on the cosmic level of history. The Messiah had to become profane through conversion in order to redeem the world.[25] Others faced a crisis of faith, and some eventually became radically anti-Sabbatean.

Increase Mather, for his part, seems to have been forced to revise his own narrative.[26] In May 1667 he began to work tirelessly on redrafting his hypotheses, and by June he had managed to transform his sermon notes into a book-length manuscript.[27] The eventual product was *The Mystery of Israel's Salvation*, which was published in London in 1669. Within that work, Mather explains:

> The Jews have heretofore many a time and often made fruitless and miserable attempts to deliver themselves out of their present *tribulation*. Such hath been the dreadful, direful wrath of God against that stubborn and

stiff necked people, that he hath left them often to be deluded with vain hopes and attempts of salvation . . . the *Jews* have vainly sought to deliver themselves . . . by hearkening unto false Christs that have risen up amongst them. Thus the true *Messias* told the *Jews* that it would be, *John* 5:43. *I am come in my father's name, and ye receive me not, if another shall come in his own name, him you will receive.*[28]

This statement comes in the context of a discussion of a long line of Jewish false Messiahs, including Bar Kokhba (whom Mather bitingly notes was subsequently referred to by the Jews as "Bar Koziba," i.e., "the Son of lying"),[29] Moses of Crete, and David Alroy.

Mather assures his readers that there are many others who "hath risen amongst the *Jews*, who, by signs and lying wonders, hath seduced many."[30] The most recent, of course, was Shabbetai Tzevi. And for Mather, lest one think that he is being unfair to both the Jews as God's Chosen People and their God who chose them, he later writes that he does not intend "to cast a darkness upon the providence of God in the present stirrings which we hear are amongst the *Israelites*."[31] Rather, he now sees the false messianic fervor up until and through Shabbetai Tzevi as an opportune occasion for true salvation. As he explicitly states in his *Dissertation Concerning the Future Conversion of the Jewish Nation*, "the *Jews*, after they had refused the true *Messiah*, were plagued with many false ones; for which Cause it is said, *there are many Antichrists*."[32] The answer to the debacle caused by the false messianism of the likes of Shabbetai Tzevi is clear: acceptance of the "true" messianism of Jesus.

The specific mention in the above passage from *The Mystery of Israel's Salvation* of the "present *tribulation*," along with "present stirrings which we hear are amongst the *Israelites*" again leave no doubt that Mather is referencing Sabbateanism. Here, in the wake of Shabbetai Tzevi's conversion, Mather is masterfully turning the narrative on its head. In his revised opinion, the contemporary Sabbatean messianism of which he was receiving reports was all in vain for the Jews, as it was a completely false messianism. Nevertheless, if employed correctly it could play into a Protestant soteriology of prophetic witness and turn the Jews toward the "true" messianism of Jesus. This would eventually happen on the national level, though incrementally.

As Mather writes in the *Dissertation Concerning the Future Conversion of the Jewish Nation*, he is inclined "to think that it will be effected as *Paul's* was, by a miraculous Appearance of Christ to some of them, and be carried on by the Preaching of the Gospel, with a most glorious down pouring of the Holy Spirit therewith."[33] In other words, a select few will convert and then will bring the message forth to their brethren, as Paul had done subsequent to his Christophany on the road to Damascus. Mather would witness the beginning of what he perceived as this new Pauline process, this time not running through Damascus but through Cambridge, Massachusetts. Only he would have to wait thirteen years from the drafting of his final treatise on Jewish conversion to do so.

Judah Monis's Conversion

The beginning of the end of times came for Mather on March 27, 1722, about a year prior to the end of his own life. On that date his Jewish disciple Judah Monis entered into Harvard's College Hall in Cambridge, Massachusetts, as a Jew, in order to voluntarily, and very publicly, be baptized into the Congregational Christian faith. The baptism was presided over by Harvard president John Leverett and was performed by the Reverend Nathaniel Appleton of the First Congregational Church of Cambridge. The conversion was sponsored by the eminent Reverend Benjamin Colman of the famed Brattle Street Church, who was also a member of the Harvard College Corporation. Finally, though he was not present due to the failing health of old age, the octogenarian Increase Mather, now erstwhile president of Harvard, stood behind the entire process.

All of these figures, including Mather, were highly influential within colonial American intellectual life, pointing to the fact that this conversion was indeed no mere curiosity of history. Rather, it played directly into the sacred history that had already been outlined in detail by Mather, which involved Jewish conversion. In the preface to the published discourses stemming from the public baptism, Mather writes, reiterating his earlier thoughts, "There will a time come when there shall be a General Conversion of the *Jewish Nation*."[34] He goes on to state, "The Blessed Day is coming when all *Israel* shall be Saved, as I have Evinced in a Discourse on that Subject, written in the Year 1667."[35]

Here he is hearkening back to *The Mystery of Israel's Salvation*, and he is explicitly tying the thoughts therein to the events surrounding Monis's conversion.

For the eighty-three-year-old Mather, Monis's baptism some fifty-five years after the Sabbatean debacle was the beginning of a natural culmination of those patently false messianic events. Yet now, in Mather's estimation, those events were properly and concretely being redirected from falsehood to truth, or what Monis himself, perhaps at the urging of Mather, ultimately deems *The Truth, The Whole Truth, and Nothing but the Truth*.[36] For Mather, and for Monis perhaps unwittingly in Mather's wake, the calamitous history of Jewish false messianism was now beginning to come to its conclusion with the beginning of the willful conversion of a Jew, who would bring the message of the "true" messianism of Jesus forth to his brethren.

Judah Monis was a fine person for this task, as he was a moderately significant figure in his own right. Just two years prior to his baptism, he had earned an MA for his erudition in Hebrew linguistics, thereby making him the first Jew on American soil to be granted an academic degree. One month after his baptism, he would go on to become the first full-time instructor of Hebrew at Harvard. And finally, thirteen years later, in 1735, Harvard Corporation would publish his *Dickdook Leshon Gnebreet*, the very first Hebrew grammar written in the New World.[37] Thus, without a doubt, Monis was an important personage on the scene of Hebrew linguistics in colonial America, and he was at least perceived by his Christian contemporaries as a truly Jewish Hebrew authority.

Indeed, Monis's position as a purported expert in biblical Hebrew is no small matter, considering the strong connection of Puritanism to the Hebrew Bible and the corresponding self-identification of New England Puritan culture with a New Israel. According to this narrative, the early colonialists saw their own passing through the waters of the Atlantic in light of the story of the Israelites passing through the Red Sea.[38] The narrative especially solidified around the Great Migration of 1630 as prodded by the anti-Puritan stance of King Charles I, which led to the famous sermon of John Winthrop aboard the *Arbella* upon the Atlantic Ocean. Within that sermon, Winthrop writes of a new Covenant. "The Lord hath given us leave to drawe our own articles," he asserts, going on to state, "Now if the Lord shall please to hear us, and bring us in peace to the place we desire, then hath hee ratified this covenant and sealed our Commission."[39] Whether the first generation of the Great Migration saw itself in such a divine light, and both the historicity and impact of Winthrop's speech, are all matters of great debate.[40] It is important to remember that the generation of the 1630s to the 1650s in America was much different from the generation of the 1700s to the 1720s. Nevertheless, regardless of the sensibilities of the first generation, by that later generation a certain soteriological narrative had begun to solidify. Indeed, it was such a statement by Winthrop culled by Cotton Mather that led the latter, in 1702, to write of Winthrop, "*This* Eminent Person was, by the Consent of all, *Chosen* for the *Moses*, who must be the Leader of so great an Undertaking."[41] And if Winthrop was Moses, then his flocks were the people of Israel. But the narrative extends beyond mere metaphor. As Sacvan Bercovitch has taught, for early American thinkers like Cotton Mather, "the Puritan Great Migration stands revealed as the latest in a series of 'dispensations,' progressing from one 'elect people' to another, from Old Israel to New."[42] The divine Covenant was now in the hands of the American heirs of the early Puritan migrants.

But the biblical framing of this Puritan narrative of chosenness did not remain so neat. As Increase Mather states, "The *Jews* were the people of God before the *Gentiles*."[43] Basing himself on Paul's Epistle to the Romans 11:17, which describes Israel as original branches broken from the root and the Gentiles as wild branches grafted onto the root, Mather goes on to state that "the *Gentile*-Church which now is, is *Surrogate Israel*."[44] It will remain so, for Mather, until the final conversion of the Jews. In a similar manner, Benjamin Colman writes to the Scottish minister and historian Robert Wodrow, concerning Monis, of daily prayer "for the Conversion of that once beloved People."[45] In his public address at Monis's baptism, he further states, "WE *look* for the happy day of the Conversion of the *Jews* and of *Israel's* Salvation; we daily and earnestly *pray* for it with great desire; we *wait* for it with a holy Impatience; It will be *life from the dead* to the Christian World."[46] For Colman, as for Mather, the conversion of the entire Jewish nation will return the Jews to their rightful place as the beloved of God and will consequently usher in the final salvation. Here the existence of the Jews introduces a radical new element to the classical Puritan narrative of chosenness.

Within this latter mode of thought as expressed by Mather and Colman, Monis's baptism was more than just a symbolic move through water from the old to the new that paralleled the Israelite passing through the Red Sea as reflected in the Puritan migration over the Atlantic. Rather, it was seen as a further messianic fulfillment of prophecy that further legitimated the biblical hermeneutic of Puritan American history in the making. This was lent even more of a prophetic edge by Monis's identity, not only as a Jew, but as a Hebrew scholar who had apparently copied out an entire Torah scroll for a synagogue in Holland years earlier.[47] Monis was as close to an embodiment of the Old Testament within the New World as one could possibly get. "His knowledge is great in the Holy Scriptures, both of the Old and New Testament, and also in the Writings of the Rabbies," wrote Colman, optimistically adding, "he seems to be much set on doing something Considerable for the Conversion of his Nation, by the will of God."[48] In the same vein, Mather sanguinely wrote of Monis, "God Grant that he (who is the first Jew that ever I knew Converted in New-England) may prove a Blessing unto many, and especially to some of his own Nation."[49] The new Puritan hope as expressed by Mather and Colman was for mass conversion of the Jews, beginning within and spreading forth from the New Zion of New England; the thought was that Monis's conversion would be the perfect impetus.

Anti-Sabbateanism and Anti-Catholicism

Subsequent to his baptism, and in conjunction with both Mather and Colman, Monis published a treatise that was partly addressed to his "Brethren according to the Flesh."[50] The purpose of this treatise, at least seemingly, was to carry forth Mather's soteriology by bringing witness to bear on Monis's fellow Jews. Like Paul, Monis could preach the Gospel to the Jews and effect "a most glorious down pouring of the Holy Spirit therewith."[51] Thirteen years after the publication of Mather's *Dissertation Concerning the Future Conversion of the Jewish Nation*, the Puritan minister's vision was coming true through the personage of Judah Monis.

For that purpose, Monis employs several Jewish texts and cites several Jewish sources in arguing for the value and appeal of Christ. Yet he mentions only one who had been his contemporary, who had died only twenty-four years prior to his conversion. This was the most anti-Sabbatean Jewish authority of his day, one who, Monis writes, "was called by the Consent of all the Jewish Nation, even in his Life-time, *The perfect wise Man, The Pious or Godly, The Theologer. Glory of the wise Men, The Holy, Our Teacher, My Teacher, R. Jacob Sasportas.*"[52] Jacob Sasportas was one of the most important rabbinic figures of his day, and in 1665 while in Northern Europe between London and Hamburg, he began to investigate the rumors and the zeal surrounding Shabbetai Tzevi. In 1669, the very same year that Mather published his *Mystery of Israel's Salvation*, Sasportas edited his notes and letters into a book called *Zizath Novel Tzvi* (The Withering Flower of Tzevi).[53] Like Mather, Sasportas ultimately came down on the side of calling out Sabbateanism as false messianism. Unlike Mather, who saw in Sabbateanism an opportunity for the conversion of the Jews, Sasportas saw it as a crisis. His goal was to protect rabbinic Judaism from Sabbateanism's dire effects.

In terms of Christianity, Sasportas evinced very little interest. As Yaacob Dweck has recently shown in great detail, "Sasportas does not seem to have been particularly concerned with Christianity as an idea."[54] Rather, he used it intellectually as a comparative model for the nascent advent of Sabbateanism. Prior to his writings on Sabbateanism, however, Sasportas wrote a responsum in which he referred to Christianity as idolatry. Citing the twelfth-century rabbinic authority Abraham ben David of Posquières, Sasportas writes, "One who believes in that man from Edom is called a heretic."[55] This is fairly standard rabbinic rhetoric equating Edom with Rome, and hence with Catholicism; thus the "man from Edom" is probably a euphemism for Jesus.

Nevertheless, due to the relation of Edom with Roman Catholicism, such sentiments could be taken more papally and could thus actually accord with the sentiments of figures like Increase Mather. In fact, in his *Dissertation Concerning the Future Conversion of the Jewish Nation*, Mather writes:

> No Man that has any Acquaintance with the Writings of the *Jewish Rabbies* can be ignorant that when *Edom* is mentioned in the Scriptures, they still apply it to *Rome*, supposing that Vengeance must come on the City before the Redemption of *Israel*. There is undoubtedly a *Vial* to be poured

out on the *Seat of the Beast*, before the *Jews* return. The *Beast* has his Seat (which he will needs have it called *Sedes Apostolica*) in *Italy*.

As an anti-Catholic Puritan, Mather actually adopts the Jewish reading of Edom as espoused by the likes of Sasportas and applies it to his eschatological reading of Revelation 16:10. There is no evidence that Mather was reading Sasportas or that he was aware of him before his encounter with Monis, but the convergence is still significant. For Mather, Sasportas's "man from Edom" would perhaps signify the Pope who occupies the "Seat of the Beast" recounted in the book of Revelation. Mather would be in full accord that the Christianity of Edom is a form of heresy. For him, it is not idolatrous Catholicism but true Protestantism that the Jew should embrace. "As for the *Jews converted* to the *Popish Religion*, their Conversion was more to *Antichrist* than to *Christ*," he writes, continuing, "they were *perverted* to the old Idolatry of their Fathers in *Babylon*." Catholicism, as such, is worse than Judaism. In another place he writes, "*Few Jews have ever embraced the* Protestant, *which is the only true Christian Religion*."[56] Everything else is falsehood at best.

The skewed resonance between Mather and Sasportas on Edom may very well have had an effect on Monis, who was ultimately pulled into Protestant Christianity. Both the anti-Sabbateanism and the anti-Catholicism could very well have transferred from the Jewish teacher of his youth to the Puritan teacher of his later years. And indeed, Monis's statement in his baptismal treatise that Sasportas was his teacher does not seem to be mere hyperbole; in fact, it seems to be a real possibility.[57] If true, this would provide a glimpse into Monis's educational background and would show that he was perhaps exposed to both anti-Sabbateanism and anti-Catholicism already as an adolescent in Europe. The types of anti-Sabbateanism and anti-Catholicism of his earlier teacher, however, would be much different than that espoused by his later teacher, Mather.

In fact, if it is true that Sasportas was Monis's rabbinic teacher, then this would be a fairly ironic and unusual twist. This is not merely because Sasportas was the most anti-Sabbatean Jewish authority of his day. Rather, the irony comes from the fact that, as Isaiah Tishby and Rivka Shatz-Uffenheimer, and more recently Matt Goldish, Pavel Maciejko, and Yaacob Dweck have thoroughly shown, Sasportas was anti-

Sabbatean for the key purpose of defending Jewish religious law and Talmudic rabbinic authority.[58] This was in the face of a Sephardic converso population the likes of the Monis family, which might otherwise be tempted into antinomianism due to its own religiously ambiguous background. In this regard, the irony of history is as follows: Shabbetai Tzevi, perceived as a "false" Messiah, influenced Mather to convert the Jews to Christianity, while the most halakhically conservative rabbinic defendant of Judaism against Shabbetai Tzevi, who also perceived him as a false Messiah and was worried for the fate of Judaism in the face of ex-converso Jews, influenced the very Jew whom Mather would go on to aid in converting away from Judaism to an anti-Catholic, Protestant form of Christianity. Messianism, conversion, and identity all seem to have run in oppositely intended directions.

Jacob Sasportas as Judah Monis's Teacher

Regardless of the irony of history and identity in this specific episode, there are clear indications that Monis was actually Sasportas's student in Europe, and that Monis was not merely invoking him for an anti-Sabbatean stance that would square well with that of his later teacher Increase Mather.[59] Nor was Monis simply calling Sasportas "My Teacher" out of mere respect or metaphor, as with a common Jewish epithet like *Moshe Rabbenu*, "Moses our Teacher." One indication that Monis's claim to be a student of Sasportas was not mere hyperbole is the report in the local newspaper, the *New England Courant*, the day after Monis's fateful conversion. The paper states that he "commenced *Mashkil Venavon*, in the Jewish Academies of Leghorn and Amsterdam."[60] As some historians have explained, *Maskil* was an appellation used in Italy for one considered inferior to those who held the title of *Hacham*, and it was a designation for one who held a secondary rabbinical position.[61] Monis may very well have supplied this information to the newspaper himself, but there is nevertheless no reason to doubt that he did engage in some level of learning within the communities of Livorno and Amsterdam. After all, if he were lying, then why would he not give himself the more exalted title of *Hacham*? Moreover, his acknowledgment within his Hebrew grammar of indebtedness to Rabbi Shmuel Archivolti and to Judah Leon Templo, as well as his use of sources such as Menasseh ben Israel and Sasportas himself, reflect the curricula of Livorno and Amsterdam.[62] We know that Sasportas was the head of the yeshiva in Livorno and then became the head of the famous Etz Hayyim Yeshiva in Amsterdam in 1680. He was active there until his death in 1698, at which point Monis would have been fifteen years old. It is therefore not unreasonable to assume some direct contact.

Another possible piece of evidence strengthens this assumption. As the American Jewish scholar George Alexander Kohut observed already over 123 years ago, Monis is an extremely rare name among Jews.[63] Kohut goes on to discuss two epitaphs from Venice that he found with the name, from 1642 and 1644, respectively.[64] He surmises that, given the rarity of the name, these may very well have been relatives of Judah. Kohut's was an attempt to uncover some of Judah Monis's past, and while he may certainly have been correct, a document housed at the Mishkan Museum of Art in Ein Harod in Israel seems to be of even greater relevance. This is the *Ketubah*, the marriage contract, of David ben Avraham Monis, the groom, and Rachel bat Shlomo Monis, the bride.[65]

The *Ketubah* dates to 1679, which was four years before the birth of Judah Monis; and the place of consecration is none other than Livorno, Italy. What is perhaps even more interesting for our discussion is the fact that one of the official witnesses signed on to the union of David and Rachel Monis is none other than Jacob Sasportas, who at the time was indeed the head of the yeshiva at Livorno.

Were David and Rachel Monis Judah's parents? Considering the time and place of their wedding in relation to Judah's birth, it is certainly possible. Were they at the very least his relatives? Considering the rarity of the surname and the overlapping connection to Livorno, it seems most probable. Accordingly, we seem to have members of the Monis family in close connection with Jacob Sasportas in Livorno the year before Sasportas became the head of the Etz Hayyim Yeshiva in Amsterdam. It is quite conceivable under these circumstances that the family would eventually send their son Judah to study under the great rabbi, and it is entirely plausible that even though he was young, Judah would imbibe some of the anti-Sabbatean ethos espoused by his Jewish teacher.[66]

Figure 3.1. *Ketubah* of David and Rachel Monis, 1679. Courtesy of the Mishkan Museum of Art, Ein Harod, Israel, JUD 107.

Lurianism and Christian Kabbalah

In addition to anti-Sabbateanism, Monis would have imbibed a specific brand of Lurianic Kabbalah from both Sasportas and his European yeshiva environments, the same type of Lurianic Kabbalah disseminated by the likes of Nathan of Gaza about one hundred years prior. To this end, one final piece of evidence regarding Monis's European education, long before he fell into the company of Mather and his ilk, deserves some attention. This is a wonderful compendium of primarily Lurianic kabbalistic texts that was donated to Harvard College Library in 1764 by Monis's brother-in-law, the Reverend John Martyn of Westboro, Massachusetts. Many of the works copied are ostensibly in the handwriting of Monis himself, including *Emet l'Ya'akov*, a commentary on the *Idra* sections of the *Zohar* written by Sasportas's elder North African contemporary Jacob Marrache of Tetouan.[67] This is important not only because of its North African Lurianic character, which is in line with the thought of Sasportas, but also because of the fact that the *Idra* sections of the *Zohar* present what is perhaps the most anthropomorphic portrayal of God as *Adam Kadmon* within all of kabbalistic literature.

At the very end of the manuscript are three alphabetic ciphers that are based on the twenty-two letters of the Hebrew alphabet: *Scriptura coelestis* (Celestial Script), *Scriptura Malachim* (Angelic Script), and *Scriptura transitus fluuij* (Transfluvial Script). There is another cipher, based on Latin letters, entitled *De characteribus et sigillis spirituum* (On characters and signs of the spirit).[68] These are not from any Jewish Lurianic source but are in fact identical to those within Agrippa von Nettesheim's widely popular *De occulta philosophia*.[69] It is thus reasonable to surmise that they are taken from that source.

From the *De characteribus et sigillis spirituum* script is written out "Judah Monis Book," and on the prior page, in the *Scriptura transitus fluuij* is coded וצ״יץ מוניש יהודה, "Judah Monis YZ"O" (a righteous and upright one of the people of Israel).[70] Chances are that Monis would not have written such an honorific about himself. What is more, this is apparently not in his handwriting, which as mentioned, ostensibly marks the first forty-four pages of the manuscript and then another forty pages from the middle. Rather, these ciphers are in the hand of an anonymous copyist who wrote out the last eighty pages of this manuscript. These eighty pages include three treatises in Hebrew. The first is entitled "The matter of the connection of my rabbi with the companions and the companions with each other," which is about Isaac Luria, his disciple Hayyim Vital, and their companions in the Galilean town of Tzfat. The second is entitled "The matter of reincarnation and the matter of the calf." The third, immediately preceding the piece from Agrippa, is entitled "A commentary on the exposé concerning the footsteps of our forefather Abraham."[71] By virtue of such copying itself, the person who wrote all of this out had a clear familiarity with Jewish Lurianic kabbalistic sources. By virtue of writing out the passages from Agrippa, that person also had a clear knowledge of the Christian occult as employing Hebrew learning. What we have here, then, is the case of another mingled identity meeting on the pages of Judah Monis's kabbalistic compendium.

Just who this person was is impossible to tell. One guess would be John Martyn, Judah Monis's brother-in-law. After all, he did end up with the manuscript and he is the one who ultimately donated it to Harvard. Perhaps he had learned Kabbalah with Monis and then had added his own copies to the compilation. However, given the copyist's thorough knowledge of Hebrew, the skilled use of Hebrew script, and the distinctly Jewish use of the honorific epithet YZ"O, this is highly unlikely. There were also no known kabbalistic texts in the Westboro area from which Martyn could have copied. Moreover, Martyn donated this manuscript to Harvard upon Monis's death, along with other books including the kabbalistic *Kitsur Shnei Luhot ha-Brit* by Michael Jechiel Epstein.[72] Had he been even remotely interested in Kabbalah, he most probably would not have donated such rare works. Another possibility is that it was a different student of Monis from within the New World, perhaps from his days in New York before he arrived in the Boston area. Yet for many of the same reasons mentioned in regard to Martyn, this seems highly unlikely. Again, and most especially, there were no known kabbalistic texts in the New World from which anybody could have copied.

Still another possibility, which seems much more likely, is that this was all copied out in Europe, before Monis's arrival in the New World, by a fellow Jew who was either a peer or a student of Monis. The only conundrum here involves the cipher that reads out in English "Judah Monis Book." Why would someone in Sasportas's circle in Livorno or Amsterdam be writing in English? Perhaps this was written out during a stint in England, or perhaps it was added later, in the New World. There is simply not enough evidence to clearly know, and unfortunately no dates appear in the manuscript.

Yet if it was another Jew who wrote this, it would reveal a couple of important factors. One is that Monis was indeed tapped into a kabbalistic network moored in textual learning before arriving in North America, and that whoever copied the second half of this manuscript held some sense of esteem for him. Thus, Monis was not a total novice, and he was respected, at least in the eyes of one of his European Jewish peers. Another important factor is that the addition of the section from Agrippa reveals the entrance of non-Jewish occult Kabbalah into Monis's circle already when he was still in Europe and when he was still fully a Jew. Whatever the case may be for who this was, we have here a hybridity of thought that predates Monis's official conversion and that either involves at least one other Jewish kabbalistic copyist or one Christian kabbalist who was deeply familiar with Jewish kabbalistic texts.

Concluding Remarks

The events surrounding the figure of Shabbetai Tzevi led Increase Mather to a greater theoretical interest in the collective conversion of the Jews, which ultimately led to the actual conversion of Judah Monis. Monis, for his part, was a Jew in America who by all indications had been a student of Jacob Sasportas, the most anti-Sabbatean rabbinic figure in Europe. He had also been tapped into Lurianic Kabbalah, the same type disseminated by Shabbetai Tzevi's prophet Nathan of Gaza, and he also quite possibly subscribed to Christian occult philosophy as playing upon kabbalistic tropes. In a strange theological twist, the widespread messianism contained in Sabbateanism, perceived as a "falsehood" by both Increase Mather and Jacob Sasportas, converged in the figure of Judah Monis, a "real" Jew from the Old World with kabbalistic training who embraced Protestantism out of the New World Christian covenantal context. Within that context, Monis's distinctly *Jewish* identity indeed played a vital role.

But how much of a truly "Jewish" character did Monis maintain? In regard to the historical developments of Protestant messianism and of Monis's baptism, his own words of religious identity concerning the Messiah are perhaps quite telling: "THAT *we* believe that *He* is already come, is questionless, because whosoever among us should deny it, is no more a Christian, as whosoever believes among the Jews that he is already come, is no more a Jew."[73] Through the notion of belief, Monis affirms his Christianity here but at the same time seems to explicitly acknowledge that according to *Judaism* he is no longer a Jew.

Nevertheless, throughout his treatise Monis refers to the Jewish people as his "Brethren according to the Flesh."[74] Identity as such goes beyond belief. He also makes the following statement concerning the Jews:

> I hope they will be gathered from all parts where-ever they are, even since the Captivity of the Ten Tribes, into their Country, in a National Body as they were in former Ages, and be Settled, and Build Churches, as many and as pompous, as their hearts shall wish; and serve and worship the True and Living God through Christ; and be established for ever.[75]

Here he seems to be adopting a national sense of identity with a more complicated relationship to belief. This is directly in line with Increase Mather, who emphatically states that the Jews "shall never cease to be a Nation as long as the Sun and Moon endureth, as long as heaven and earth remain undissolved, as long as the frame of nature is kept from ruine."[76] The soteriological idea here is that it is incumbent on the "National Body" of the Jews, *as Jews*, to accept Christ. And precisely *as a Jew* it is Monis's mission to help make that happen. In fact, he explicitly declares, "I shall . . . turn my Face towards the *Jews*, who are my Brethren according to the Flesh, and for whom my Heart is ready to burst, when I Seriously think on them, to see them still in their Spiritual Darkness."[77] As a Jewish-Christian, Monis sees his role in salvific, veritably messianic terms.

Whether this role as presented by Monis and his Christian mentors was purely performative remains an elusive point of debate. As Milton Klein has noted, the famed Scottish minister Robert Wodrow had suggested that Monis's baptism would have more gravitas within the Christian community if it would indeed bring about the mass conversion of the Jews. To this end Wodrow advised that Monis could strengthen his position by both remaining faithful to Christianity and working toward the conversion of his fellow Jews.[78] In his very own day, then, Monis's convictions were being scrutinized, and his own salvific sense of identity and his outreach to his "Brethren according to the Flesh" may very well have actually been an outreach and response to his Christian critics.

Yet there is a need to be wary. As Michael Hoberman warns, "The question of whether Monis was a Jew or a Christian at heart . . . , besides being an impossible one to answer, represents an epistemological dead end." Hoberman continues, "What matters is why and how Monis's conversion, regardless of what his innermost spiritual leanings may have been was important to third-generation Puritans."[79] Indeed, through his public conversion Monis became a public figure, and his Jewish-Christian story became an American narrative. And while "true" convictions may indeed remain ever elusive, I would argue that personal thoughts as displayed through text, whether genuine or merely performative, play a key role in unlocking the importance that Monis's conversion had to both third-generation Puritans and subsequent generations.

In fact, within this entire hermeneutical narrative lies the rather complex and conflicted notion of identity formation: as a (former) Jew, Monis recognizes that by accepting Christ, he is no longer a Jew. But as a new Christian, the sacred history of the future salvation fundamentally depends on his acceptance of Christ *as a Jew*, and his subsequent turn to his "Brethren" *as a Christian*. His "Brethren," however, paradoxically no longer accept him as a brother, precisely *because* he is a Christian. The process, as such, seems to invalidate itself, and we have a classic case of what Sacvan Bercovitch, basing himself on the seventeenth-century poet George Goodwin, calls Puritan "Auto-Machia."[80] By this Bercovitch means a sense of self that is constantly at war with itself in that it both asserts and negates individual autonomy. In this sense, Monis as a Puritan Jew, who both is and is not Jewish (and whose Christianity is constantly questioned, for that matter),[81] perfectly embodies this complex developing American notion of the self. "At the deepest level, and as a powerful example of cultural liminality," writes Hoberman, "Monis was neither a Jew nor a Christian, neither a father nor a son, neither a teacher nor a student."[82] To this sense of liminality should be added a complex sense of mutuality; Monis was not only neither, he was also simultaneously both: both a Jew and a Christian, both a father and a son (at least metaphorically), both a teacher and a student.

Precisely because of Monis's complex personal identity, it is my contention that in his specific case, the Sabbatean events leading up to his baptism, in their very transgressive nature, did more than just provide a hopeful glimpse of salvation. Similar to America, which for Mather stood as the "New World" of the eschaton written of in the book of Revelation, which is beyond time and space and thus could bring about the beginning of the end of time and space, Monis as a liminally mutual figure, who was neither Jewish nor Christian and at the same time both, was key to the new messianic narrative. Moreover, in this American case, Monis's baptism and the events leading up to it were seen as a part of the discursive texts that they produced, that shortly thereafter were published for popular consumption, and that engage with scriptural reasoning and the hermeneutics of truth. Not only were these events part of the texts, they were perceived as providing prophetic witness in and of themselves. Jewish history, leading through America and as fundamentally attached to the politics of personal identity, provided a new hermeneutics that profoundly informed Puritan soteriology in various ways.

One final caveat remains in order. I have mentioned that the messianism of Shabbetai Tzevi stemmed partly from Kabbalah and then helped to disseminate that Kabbalah throughout the Jewish world. We have seen that Monis picked up on that same type of Kabbalah, perhaps through Sasportas. It is certainly reflected in his kabbalistic compendium, now in the Harvard archives. We see through that compendium that he was also tapped into a form of Christian occult Kabbalah, and that he may have been part of a larger group of people who employed such syncretic materials in fashioning their own theology.

In extension to this background, previous scholars have noted a possible affinity between Kabbalah and Monis's conversion to Christianity. As Milton Klein asserted, "It is quite possible that Monis's studies of the Cabala, a mystical interpretation of the Jewish Scriptures which viewed the Deity in terms of triads and emphasized the coming of the Messiah, led him to an intellectual acceptance of Christian theology."[83] Along the same lines, Shalom Goldman has noted that earlier researchers asserted that either Monis clung to some sense of Jewish religious identity or he embraced Christian doctrine and practice, whether out of convenience, pragmatism, belief, or some combination of these. Goldman has posited a greater "need to be nuanced" and wrote, "Kabbalism, of both the Christian and Jewish varieties, may be one key to Monis's interior life, and it might help to explain his assertion that his affirming view of Christianity's messianic claims was based on Jewish mystical writings."[84] Yet despite these bold claims to intellectual persuasion through Kabbalah on the one hand, and the need to be nuanced on the other hand, no deep analysis of Monis's kabbalistic musings has ever been undertaken. It is to such an analysis that we now turn.

4

Nothing but the Truth

The First Kabbalistic Text Published in North America

Truth, Text, and Practice

The new hermeneutics as set up by Increase Mather, of an American messianism beyond time and space and of a liminal figure both beyond and within both Judaism and Christianity, was not contained by the mere act of Judah Monis's conversion to Congregational Christianity. In fact, the hermeneutics of "truth" as engaged with scriptural reasoning was carried forward in a very textual manner. Shortly after the occasion of Monis's baptism in March 1722, a certain S. Kneeland printed what were officially rendered "Three Discourses Written by Mr. *Monis* himself"; though as historians have previously noted, Monis seems to have received a considerable amount of help from someone the likes of Increase Mather.[1] These were entitled *The Truth*, *The Whole Truth*, and *Nothing but the Truth*, respectively, and this trilogy, along with the preface by Increase Mather and the discourse of Benjamin Colman given at the baptism, entitled *Moses a Witness to our Lord and Saviour Jesus Christ*, was sold for popular consumption at the shop of Daniel Henchman, who was one of Boston's foremost printers.

In addition to an attestation to the truth of the messiahship of Jesus over false Messiahs like Shabbetai Tzevi, the title of the tripartite discourse, *The Truth, the Whole Truth, and Nothing but the Truth*, seems to hold other significance as well. As anyone even marginally familiar with Anglo courtroom drama can confirm, this is clearly playing off the notion of sworn testimony. Such is significant for Monis, as it seems to be a clear missive against anyone who might doubt the real motives of his conversion. And given the timing of his conversion in relation to his employment at Harvard shortly thereafter, in conjunction with the general Puritan notion of salvation through grace, as well as Catholic converso precedent, there were several individuals who doubted Monis's motives from the very outset.[2] Through the very title of his discourse, then, Monis seems to be swearing by the inner truth of his conversion to all Christians who might doubt him.

Notwithstanding his rhetoric of sworn testimony to the skeptical Christian world, the title seems to be placing the work within the Jewish world as well. In *Nothing but the Truth*, Monis explicitly mentions the Jews' "own authentick Authors, i.e., those that have the true understanding of the Law and of the Prophets . . . called by them, *Baugnaula hohmath hauameth*,"[3] literally "the masters of the Wisdom of Truth." By this Monis means the Jewish kabbalists, and thereby the very title of his discourse takes on a whole new dimension; *The Truth, the Whole Truth, and Nothing but the Truth* becomes a truly kabbalistic text. For Monis and his ilk, Kabbalah may not support the false messianism of those such as Shabbetai Tzevi, but it does support the "true" messianism of Jesus. Especially in the third and last section, Monis sets out to show *Nothing but the Truth* concerning the Christian Trinity by utilizing the works and tools of the Jewish masters of the Wisdom of Truth, that is, the kabbalists. What is more, he does so by focusing much of his kabbalistic attention on the *Shema'*, a part of the daily Jewish prayer service found in Deuteronomy 6:4 that many see as summing up the entire monotheistic truth claim of Judaism itself.

Within *Nothing but the Truth*, we have what seems to be the very first kabbalistic text published in the American colonies. As explained on its frontispiece, it is "A Short ESSAY, WHEREIN the Author proves the Doctrine of the Ever Blessed and Adorable TRINITY, Both out of the Old Testament, And with the Authority of the Cabalistical Rabbies, Ancient and Modern." The frontispiece goes on to note "that said Doctrine is not a *NOVELTY*, as his Country-Men do think, but as *ancient* as the *BIBLE* it self."[4] Interestingly, "Country-Men" here seems to refer to Monis's fellow Jews, since there is no reference anywhere to European origins, but in other places he refers directly to Jews, as we have seen, as his "Brethren according to the Flesh." Thus, what we have here is the very first American Christian kabbalistic polemical work, purportedly addressed to the Jews by one of their own.

Within the treatise, Monis uses Kabbalah to further Mather's Pauline agenda of filial witness. Kabbalah, as such, becomes a valuable Jewish source of Christian hermeneutics, or what Moshe Idel, in relation to Christian Kabbalah in general, has called "the keys, sacrosanct even in the eyes of the Jew, that could unlock the gates of the mysteries of the Scriptures and ultimately demonstrate Christian truths, using Jewish rules."[5] Nevertheless, given the paucity of Jews in the Boston area, and given the fact that Monis's discourses were ultimately circulated in English, it seems that his hermeneutics of truth within *Nothing but the Truth* were directed at his real Christian audience, at least as much as at his imaginary Jewish readership.[6] By using kabbalistic tradition, Monis sought to convince his interlocutors, including Increase Mather and Benjamin Colman, of the truth of his new convictions. By focusing on the extremely important liturgical text of the *Shema'*, he sought to exhibit the compatibility of Jewish thought with Christianity, as well as his true intent to offer witness to his Jewish brethren through their very own faith practices.

Foundations of Faith in the *Shema'*

Monis's kabbalistic exposition begins with the notion of faith, which he claims "is the Foundation which the whole Structure of Christianity depends upon."[7] He jumps straight to faith in the mystery of the Trinity, and brings it into dialogue with the professed monotheistic faith of Judaism. In order to do this, he turns to what he calls "that Great Tower, that Strong Bulwark, that Impregnable Fortification, which the modern *Jews*, learned and unlearned have and hold, against all those who do oppose the *unity* of the *Godhead*, either in Words or in Thoughts."[8] Here he is referring to the *Shema'*, the text of Deuteronomy 6:4, which states, "Hear, O Israel, the Lord is our God, the Lord is One." In Monis's juxtaposition, Christian faith in Trinitarianism meets a Jewish assertion of Oneness, or unity.

For Monis, words and thoughts coalesce in the recital of the *Shema'* in order to create a perception of unity within the Godhead. In his estimation, as based on the notion of faith as belief, this affects Jewish identity as fundamentally monotheistic in nature. Monis further notes that Jews teach "these Words (or this Text) in a more special Manner to all their

Children from their Infancy, with a Design they should be ingrafted into them as a second Nature, and they are oblig'd to repeat it three Times a Day at least, *viz.*, twice in Publick in their Synagogues, and once before they go to Sleep."⁹ Thus, in his assertion, it is truly one of the most important pillars of anything that might be called Jewish faith.

Monis is not entirely wrong. While Judaism does not, per modus operandi, dictate creed, the unity and uniqueness of God is indeed asserted as the second of what the great twelfth-century Jewish scholar Moses Maimonides terms the "thirteen foundations" of the principles of Jewish faith. This assertion is based directly on the *Shema'*. In his commentary on the Mishnah, Maimonides writes:

> THE SECOND FOUNDATION: The unity of the Lord, may He be blessed; that is to say, we should believe that He is the Cause of All. He is One but is not like one of a pair, nor like one of a species. Nor is He like one man, who is composite and is divided into multiple singular parts. He is not one like a simple body, which is numerically one but is subject to infinite partition and division. Rather, He, may He be exalted, is One in a unique sense of oneness that has absolutely no oneness like it. This second foundation is that which is taught about by that which is said [in the Bible]: "Hear, O Israel, the Lord is our God, the Lord is One."¹⁰

Speaking of the Jews, Monis calls the passage just quoted "the second Article of their Creed."¹¹ He goes on to cite, in his own translation, "*He is One, and not One like his Unity,*"¹² continuing to ask, "How can it be, for God to be one, and not one like unto him? This is against all Reason, for to be one and not one, and yet one."¹³ Here Monis is mistranslating the phrase that God's oneness "has absolutely no oneness like it" and is clearly missing the equivocal nature of Maimonides's entire discourse.

This mistranslation allows Monis to make a parallel: "So we Christians say, *That God is One and Three, and not Three, but One.* And I think there is more Regularity of Speech to say as we do, than to say as they say."¹⁴ Monis here targets Judaism on creed, and audaciously goes after Maimonides on a false sense of contradictory logic based on univocity in relation to the sense of the word "One." Wittingly or not, his sense of Maimonides's exegesis is wrong in that it does not take account of Maimonidean equivocation. But he is right that if anything might be considered akin to a "creed" in Judaism that might pose a problem for Trinitarian faith, it would be such a statement of oneness as framed by the likes of Maimonides. Not only did Maimonides comment on it in regard to the Mishnah, but the idea was printed, along with the other thirteen foundations, in an Ashkenazi prayer book already in 1558 in an unmistakably creedal form beginning "I believe with perfect faith." The fact that Monis was deeply familiar with this creedal formulation is readily apparent from his own translation of the Apostles' Creed into Hebrew, which appears at the very end of his *Dickdook Leshon Gnebreet* of 1735. There he begins with the exact formulation from the Jewish prayer book, "*Ani ma'amin b'emunah shlemah*," i.e., "I believe with perfect faith."[15] As Rachel Wamsley has noted, Monis adds the caveat *b'emunah shlemah*, i.e., "with perfect faith," which appears in none of the standard versions of the Apostles' Creed.[16] Beyond Monis, the idea also became a part of standard liturgy in the form of a hymn known as "Yigdal." It is thus an idea that reached beyond the elites and filtered deeply into Jewish life.

While Maimonides may have helped to cast the idea of oneness philosophically and to make it into a widely accepted "foundation of faith," it is important to remember that it does hearken back to Deuteronomy 6:4. And the biblical verse on which the idea is based has stood at the center of Jewish contemplative prayer since at least the second century of the Common Era. Observant Jews have been obligated to recite it each morning and evening, and it is customary to recite it once privately before bedtime. It is thus the last utterance before sleep, and for many martyrs it was the last utterance before death. Indeed, the Talmud relates that Rabbi Akiva, one of the greatest sages, was brutally tortured to death by the Romans for teaching Torah in public; before dying, he pronounced this verse, prolonging the word "One." At that point, the Talmud relates, a voice came forth from heaven, proclaiming, "Happy are you, Rabbi Akiva, that you are destined for life in the world-to-come."[17] Already in this Talmudic parable, an awareness of oneness, even in the face of suffering and death, leads to eternal life.

The word in the verse translated as "the Lord" is YHWH, the proper name for the God of Israel, which is linguistically related to the Hebrew word for "Being," HWYH. God, as a proper noun, is actually a temporally conflated verb of all that was, is, and will be. The Bible, and by extension the prayer, continues on to talk about love: "You shall love your God YHWH [or: existential Being] with all of your heart and with all of your soul and with all of your will."[18] Taken hyperliterally, the notion being propounded here is that God as Being is a unified whole, and it is proper to completely and totally love that unified Being through the wholeness of self.

In an early rabbinic comment that atypically concerns intentionality, the Mishnah tractate *Berakhot*, which is dedicated to "Blessings," remarks that the *Shema'* should be recited without distraction and with full concentration on the meaning of the words. "One who has said it with intention," proclaims the Mishnah, "has fulfilled the commandment [to recite it]. One who has not, has not fulfilled the commandment."[19] Louis Jacobs further elaborates on intentionality, returning to the first verse: "It is customary to place the right hand over the eyes while reciting the first verse as an aid to concentration, and, for the same reason, the first verse should be recited in a loud voice." He continues, "One should not wink or gesticulate while reading the *Shema* but should recite it in fear and trembling."[20] From the grave significance of intentionality regarding the *Shema'* and its fundamental messages of unity and love, it should be no surprise that it became a central vehicle for Jewish practices of contemplation concerning both the divine and the self, well into Monis's own day.

Indeed, an anonymous kabbalistic commentary on prayer copied out by Monis and now housed in the Harvard Archives adds to Jacobs's ritualistic description: "To uphold the positive command to say the *Shema'* and to love the Lord, may He be blessed, as it is written, *You shall love the Lord your God with all of your heart*, [one has] to close his eyes with his right hand during the [recital of the] first verse, according to the secret of the beautiful maiden who does not have eyes."[21] The secret being referred to here is a well-studied riddle from a section of the *Zohar* entitled *Sabba d'Mishpatim*, which states, "Who is a beautiful maiden who does not have eyes, whose body is concealed and revealed, who comes out in the morning and is covered during the day, adorning herself with adornments that are not?"[22] As Tzahi Weiss has noted, the phrase "beautiful maiden who does not have eyes" has no parallel in kabbalistic literature of the period of the *Zohar*, and its meaning is widely disputed.[23]

Nevertheless, in the case of the Lurianic Kabbalah as appearing in the text copied by Monis, Elliot Wolfson's notion that it signifies both Torah and *Shekhinah* seems to be instructive. He states that the maiden who does not have eyes indicates that "the text in and of itself is 'blind,' without sense," and that "whatever meaning the text has is imparted to it by the open eye . . . of the reader in the same manner that the Shekhinah assumes the forms that she receives from the *sefirah* of *Yesod*, the *membrum virile* in the divine organism."[24] In this sense, the interpreter opens and enters into the text and impregnates it with meaning, as the *Yesod* does to the *Shekhinah*. This certainly applies to the *Shema'*, which is not only a biblical text but is also, as we will see, an entire ecstatic contemplative system of unification on par with mystical intercourse. In Monis's case, however, the meaning with which the text becomes impregnated diverges radically from the traditional Jewish Kabbalah.

Monotheism and the Three Lights That Are One

Not only within his kabbalistic compendium but also within his *Nothing but the Truth*, Monis cleverly picks up a distinctively kabbalistic notion of intentionality in regard to the *Shema'*. "THE *kaubaunau Intention*, which their best *Cabalistical* Authors do oblige them to have," he writes, "when they read said Verse, is to unite the Godhead in these three *Numerations* or *Lights*."[25] Monis sees kabbalistic intention of thought, seemingly directed toward the "One" of the *Shema'*, as simultaneously directed toward what the kabbalists call the three *Numerations* or *Lights*. For him, this is synonymous with the Christian notion of divine personae, and the distinction is only a matter of linguistics. Further along in his treatise, he writes that "this is to quarrel about Words; and the Word *Persons* being only a Word that we use to convey our Ideas to the Hearers, and make them understand in some Measure what we mean by this Doctrine."[26] In a subtle twist, Monis seems to be stating that Christianity has adapted the primordial idea to a different language more suitable to Christian hearers as based on the more ancient concept espoused by Kabbalah. Nevertheless, he exhorts his fellow Christians regarding the Jewish kabbalists, "Let them use what Terms they will, either *Numerations*, *Lights*, or what they please; and in case they understand and believe the same as we do, I am contented."[27] In the end, for Monis, this is a matter of mere semantics.

In order to ground his notion of the purportedly ancient nature of the Trinity of *Numerations* or *Lights* within the One, and the corresponding intentionality to such within the *Shema'*, Monis bases himself textually:

> In that famous and most ancient of all the Books the Jewish Nation pretend to have, called *Sapher hauyatzeerau*, (a Book which some of them would have to be as ancient as our Father *Abraham*, and of his Composing also, as they say,) 'tis plain by what is said concerning the *Godhead*, that *God* is *Three* and *One*, as we Christians believe, tho' not with the same Expressions as we use, the *Father*, the *Son*, and the *Holy Ghost*; but he calls him *Numerations*, and *Lights*. . . . The Words are as follow. (*N.B.* I quote not the Page, because I forgot it; but the Sentences are to be found in it, as may be made to appear at any Time when the Book shall be produced.). "*They are three Lights, an* ANCIENT LIGHT, *a* PURE LIGHT, *and a* MOST PURE LIGHT, *nevertheless all these are only* ONE GOD."[28]

Here Monis seems to be allowing for the ancient nature of *Sefer Yetzirah*, but his jibe that it is a book that the "Jewish Nation pretend to have," along with the Trinitarian reading proposed, seems to cast hegemonic doubt. With the traditional attribution of *Sefer Yetzirah* to Abraham,[29] who Monis most certainly realized was considered by many to be the first monotheist, the Trinitarianism within would most certainly add an entirely new dimension to the ancient theology.

In fact, the mention of Abraham in relation to the One and the Trinity seems to carry with it a subtle allusion to the monotheistic notion of the eradication of idols. Monis was most probably aware of rabbinic midrashim such as *Bereshit Rabbah* 38:13, which discusses the worship of idols by Abraham's father Terah and Abraham's smashing of those idols.[30] This subtext would have indeed been significant for Monis in this context, since, as he states in his treatise, the "Blasphemous Doctrine of denying the Coequality of the three Persons, hath been a great Stumbling-Block to the *Jewish Nation*'s Conversion, as well as the worshipping of Images by the Papists, there being no other Difference between these two Opinions only this, *viz.* One worships Idols *in actu*, namely the *Papists*, and the other *in potentia* . . . and of the Two, I think, (if I may pass my Judgment,) the last is the worst."[31] By employing *Sefer Yetzirah* as an ancient prooftext, Monis is attempting to follow the path of Abraham in smashing the idols of the religion of his father and forefathers so as to allow for the conversion of the Jews.

The only problem with this subtle polemic engineered by Monis is that the quote from *Sefer Yetzirah* concerning the three Lights is not at all from *Sefer Yetzirah*. Rather, it is from an anonymous thirteenth-century Provençal text falsely attributed to the tenth- and early eleventh-century Talmudic scholar Hai Gaon.[32] The iteration paraphrased in the early fourteenth-century commentary of Bahya ben Asher to Exodus seems to be a probable candidate for Monis's source of this citation. This is due to the stark similarity of language, coupled with the fact that in another place, Monis explicitly mentions "Rabbanoo Bahauya."[33] The text of Bahya reads: "The tradition of the Gaon concerning their names is that they are a primordial Light, a purified Light, and a pure Light; and these three names are all one matter and one essence, attached with a firm attachment to the Root of all Roots."[34] Although it is pseudo-Hai Gaon and not the pseudo-Abraham of *Sefer Yetzirah* who states this, there is a clear trinitarian reading of three that are one.

In the text of pseudo-Hai as reported by Bahya, this relates to three divine Lights that are above the *sefirot*. By adding these three Lights to the ten *sefirot*, the author is attempting to square the thirteen divine attributes of mercy, as derived by the rabbinic tradition from Exodus 34:6–7, with the numerical pleroma of God. Bahya writes, "Even though we have encountered thirteen attributes and we have not encountered thirteen *sefirot*, the secret of the matter is that the three supernal Lights, which are above the ten *sefirot*, do not have a beginning because they are the essence of the Root of Roots."[35] The message is clearly trinitarian; there are three coequal, coeternal divine Lights that stand at the root of everything, including the *sefirot* that proceed from them. Yet Scholem's admonition is extremely important here: "What remains is a supreme intelligible triad more reminiscent of triads to be found in the spiritual universe of Proclus than in Christian dogmatics."[36] Here indeed uncreated Lights without a beginning illuminate each other, thereby bringing forth a beginning through the process of emanation. A correlation of trinities does not imply identity. Notwithstanding, the correlation does provide a convenient template that is readily accessible for Christian polemical use.

It is worth pointing out that Monis's Christological employment of the pseudo-Hai text on the three Lights was not entirely novel. In fact, it was already heavily used in this regard in 1667 by the Roman Catholic bishop Giuseppe Maria Ciantes in his *De sanctissima trinitate ex antiquoroum Hebraeorum testimonijs euidenter comprobata*. Within that work, Ciantes mentions what he believes is Hai Gaon's text several times, as filtered through Moshe Cordovero's *Pardes Rimonim*. For example, he quotes:

> Now I will show you, (it says), three sublime Lights that are above the ten *Sefirot*, (or Spirit)—We received the names from our holy forefathers; an intrinsic ancient Light, a clarified Light, a clear Light—These three Lights are Infinite in God.[37]

Ciantes goes on for the better part of his treatise to discuss this kabbalistic Trinity of Lights. But this Christian application of pseudo-Hai is not the only commonality with Monis. Ciantes also sought "to convert the Jews with their own principles,"[38] and like Monis, he preferred the usage of Jewish over Christian kabbalistic authorities.[39] Whether Monis was familiar with Ciantes is not at all clear, but given Ciantes's direct appointment by Pope Urban VIII as missionary to the Jews already in 1640,[40] and the fact that Monis ostensibly grew up on the Italian peninsula, it is certainly possible.

Another possibility is that Monis was aware of Jewish anti-Christian polemics, such as Profiat Duran's *Kelimat ha-Goyim* of 1397, which states, "The doctrine of the trinity, which they erroneously attributed to the deity, arose among them as a result of their missteps in this science [the Kabbalah] which established the primordial light, the radiant light and the transparent light."[41] This is clearly a reference to the three Lights of pseudo-Hai, framed in an unusually Jewish polemical manner within a Christian Trinitarian context. Whether Monis was aware of Duran's work is also not clear. What is clear is that Monis, like some of those before him, picked up on the trinity of divine Lights and superimposed it onto the Christian Trinity. The correlation was certainly enough for him to identify the two with each other, to identify himself as both a Jewish kabbalist and a Christian, and to bring the One of the *Shema'* into the purview of the three uncreated Lights within the hidden Root.

The Trinity of the *Shema'* in the *Zohar*

Perhaps more substantial to Monis for kabbalistic Trinitarianism than pseudo-Hai, which he thinks is *Sefer Yetzirah* on the three supernal Lights, is what he calls "that famous Book, more ancient than the *Talmud* itself, compos'd by one of the Sages of the *Mishnau*, by Name *Rabbi Simeon Ben Johauy* called *Zohar*, i.e., *a Light*."[42] Monis significantly goes on to explain that the title is because of "the great Light and Truths therein contained," and that it is "a Book of as great Value and Authority among them all (even those that know nothing about it) as the very Five Books of *Moses*."[43] In continuing with his metaphor of light, Monis clearly holds the *Zohar* in high esteem. But what is perhaps even more significant for his purported outreach to his "Brethren of the flesh" than his own esteem for this work is his note of its place of canonical authority among the Jews at the very level of the Torah itself. Whether his usage of the *Zohar* in this respect had an effect on his supposed missionary aims is unclear, as there is no record of any Jew reading Monis's tract let alone commenting on it. Notwithstanding, his high exaltation of it alone did undoubtedly bring it to a significant place of awareness in certain American Protestant circles, where it subsequently had an important influence on thinkers such as Ezra Stiles, as we will see in the next chapter.

In the context of the *Shema'*, Monis cites multiple passages from the *Zohar* that focus on the triune statement "YHWH, Eloheinu, YHWH," i.e., "The Lord, our God, the Lord." Within those passages, the three mentions of God indeed attach to hypostatic speculation, and as Isaiah Tishby has explained, such trinitarian formulations throughout the *Zohar* indeed provided ammunition for Christian kabbalists, who, in Tishby's words, "endeavored to show that the *Zohar* displayed Christian tendencies."[44] In terms of an ancient and central prayer like the *Shema'*, if the *Zohar* could be held as such, then so could the truly inner Jewish meaning of liturgy as derived from the Bible itself.

Furthering Tishby's work, Yehuda Liebes has shown that Christian theology, which includes the Trinity, had a distinct influence on certain Zoharic formulations of divine mystery.[45] This should come as no great surprise, since historically the *Zohar* made its first appearance in thirteenth-century Catholic Spain and could very easily have been influenced by the dominant religious culture. Regardless, Liebes offers a caveat that is highly important, especially in the context of Monis. He writes, "It should be noted that, although the author of the *Zohar* allowed himself to be influenced by Christianity, this does not mean that he felt any affinity for the 'Gentile Nations,' and particularly for those who converted to their faith."[46] In Liebes's estimation the *Zohar* indeed borrowed Christian formulations, but it fundamentally transformed them and made them into an essential part of a particularly *Jewish* Kabbalah. Such formulations became part of a much larger theosophical structure and pattern.

However, for one such as Judah Monis, reading the *Zohar* as a text penned in second-century Palestine by Rabbi Shimon bar Yochai, trinitarian intimations took on an entirely different sense. Whether through secondary sources such as Abner of Burgos and Paul of Heredia[47] or through fiat of his own understanding, Monis picked up on the Christian undertones within certain Zoharic passages and managed to reverse the process described by Liebes. Under Monis's pen, the *Zohar* became a Christian kabbalistic text.

The Trinity, the Voice, and the Holy Ghost

Monis's first citation from the *Zohar* regarding the *Shema'* in this Trinitarian regard is from a substratum of the *Zohar* known as *Raya Mehemna*, on the pericope *Bo*.[48] It should be noted that this precise passage is cited at length by Liebes in his seminal article.[49] Monis's translation is as follows:

> THE LORD, the first (*or antient*), and OUR GOD, THE LORD, these are all one, and therefore is read ONE. These are three Names, how are they one? Altho' we read One, this One (*or Unity*) by the Vision of the HOLY GHOST is known, and is as plain as the Eye-sight, that THESE THREE ARE ONE: And this is the Mystery like the Thunder; the Voice which is heard is One, and yet are included in it Three Colours (*or Things*), viz. Fire, Wind and Water; and all are One in the Secret of the Thunder, and none but One. So here also, THE LORD, OUR GOD, THE LORD, are One, Three Colours (*or Things*), they make all One; and this is that Union which every Day is manifested by the Secret of the HOLY GHOST.[50]

Monis offers no side commentary here. He lets the text stand on its own, and aside from some slight modifications like "as plain as the Eye-sight" for *b'heizu d'eyna stima* instead of the more cryptic though more accurate "with the sight of a sealed eye," or his naturalistic recasting of "the Voice" as "Thunder," the translation as it stands is fairly accurate. There is also the minor insertion of "the first (*or antient*)," which does not appear in the Aramaic and seems to be signaling the Ancient of Days or the Ancient Holy One.[51] But none of these changes Christologically alters the text.

There is, however, a slight omission that is of greater significance. It is of the following sentence that appears in the Aramaic, regarding the voice that, for Monis, is like thunder: "This is the voice that man makes in unifying, setting his will to the unification of the All, from *Ein Sof* [i.e., "that which is *Without End*"] until the end of the All, with this voice that he makes in terms of these three that are One."[52] The human voice written about here seems to be the voice that recites the *Shema'*, and the overall reference seems to be to the theurgic act of unification from end to end, from the Infinite to the All, through prayer. The agency of the voice is thus purposefully left ambiguous; it at once originates in the divine, like an overpowering thunder from on high, and in the individual, who recites and thereby unifies. It is an emanatory circle that at once flows from God and theurgically returns to God in connection and unity. Understood as such, Monis's explicit transformation of the voice to unambiguous, naturalistic thunder necessitates an omission of reference to the voice on the human plane. In the Aramaic context, it is the voice, and not specifically thunder, that bridges the gap.

Given this theurgic explanation, it is somewhat significant, beyond mere naturalistic explanation, that Monis omitted this specific sentence. This is because the omission radically divorces the Zoharic passage from that element of *Jewish* Kabbalah known as *ta'amei ha-mitzvot*, i.e., "reasons for the commandments." It is not important to Monis to promote Jewish prayer; what is important to Monis here is to utilize Jewish prayer, based directly here on the Hebrew Bible, to promote the Trinity.[53] As such, through this seemingly small omission, Monis has managed to transform this classical passage from the *Zohar* into a quintessentially Christian kabbalistic text.

A further Christianization of this text, directly related to the notion of the voice, is Monis's translation of the Aramaic term *Ruach Kudsha* as "Holy Ghost." This term appears in its Hebrew form in the Hebrew Bible, where it designates God's life force among humanity and particularly among Israel; in rabbinic Judaism it stands for individual prophetic inspiration.[54] As Adam Afterman has recently shown, "It is within medieval and early modern Jewish literature, both philosophical and mystical, that the term 'holy spirit' is elevated to prominence, as it becomes key for denoting the intimate communion between humanity and God."[55] Within that literature, it comes to designate a divine overflow from the supernal realm, which flows down into the human realm. In medieval kabbalistic literature specifically, the idea is that through the Holy Spirit, "God not only transmits his word, message, or ideas but his being and holiness as well."[56] Like the voice, it acts as a bridge through which mystical fusion and human transformation take place.

The Aramaic *Zohar* passage translated and quoted by Monis seems to be referencing the notion of *Ruach Kudsha* in this precise mystical manner of unity through the voice by placing it within the context of the theurgic recital of the *Shema'*. Through recital, God's life force, or *Ruach Kudsha*, is among Israel, to whom the very prayer is beckoning in the first place. Conversely, through that life force, the individual reciting the *Shema'* can achieve prophetic inspiration, or *Ruach Kudsha*, to see the very unity or oneness of God. The voice reflecting the Holy Spirit unifies, but unlike for Christianity it is not in itself a part of the tripartite unity of three names in one God.

For Monis, by contrast, that voice as spirit is a part of the Whole from on high. Monis's sense is entirely different from that of the original context of the *Zohar* in that it is nontheurgic and essentially hypostatic. For Monis, *Ruach* is not "spirit" in the sense of divinely stimulated conscience or divinely directed disposition; nor is it a divine overflow as mystically infused and promoting transformation and reciprocal unity. Rather, it is a more essentially substantive Being on an entirely different plane, in the sense of divine manifestation of the Trinity specifically, explicitly as "Ghost." What is more, as Paraclete, it aids in an unmediated Trinitarian reading of the biblical text. What is being pushed to the front, then, is the early Anglican, and by extension Congregational, notion of *Prima scriptura*, whereby Scripture, reason, and tradition form a triple source of religious authority.[57] In Monis's case in this specific instance, the Scripture is the *Shema'* of Deuteronomy 6:4, reason comes by way of the three mentions of God, who is explicitly stated to be One, and tradition is Zoharic Kabbalah.

Unification by Mystical Intercourse

Monis continues his Trinitarian reading of the *Shema'* with two additional passages from the *Zohar*. The first, which he calls an "excellent Exposition," comes from the *Zohar* on the pericope *Balak* and is as follows:

> THE LORD, OUR GOD, THE LORD: *This is his very Secret, from the Top of the Rock is it,*[58] (i.e. from the very Beginning,) *and it is united at the* HEAD, STEMME, *and* ROOT. THE LORD: *This is the Head above, a Spirit ascended.* OUR GOD: *This is the Stemme, which is called the Stemme of Jesse.*[59] THE LORD: *This is the Root which is beneath; and upon this Secret the Unity is united as it should be,* &c.[60]

As with the first *Zohar* passage quoted by Monis, this one is neither justified nor explained. Rather, it is left to stand on its own, and except for the rendering of *shvil* as "root" rather than "path," the translation is fairly accurate. Nevertheless, in the context of Monis's treatise, it has clear Christian implications, with the "Head above" indicating the Father, the "Stemme of Jesse" signaling the messianic Son, and the "Root which is beneath" pointing to the Holy Ghost.[61] In the Zoharic context, however, none of this applies. As Tishby points out, this passage and others like it allude to "the unification of names as a joining together of head, trunk, and path (*shevil*)," indicating "the unification of *Hokhmah, Tiferet*, and *Malkhut*."[62] What is being addressed here is the notion of mystical intercourse. One who recites the *Shema'* with proper intention unites the brain, thought to be the originator of semen, with the male body, and the male body with the female receptacle. Here we have another case of altered trinities through altered contexts.

The final Zoharic passage on the *Shema'* quoted by Monis is from the *Zohar* on the pericope *Terumah*, and it reads:

THE LORD: *This is the Mark of the Letter Yode the high Head of the Holy Name.* OUR GOD: *This is the Secret which is marked by the Letter Ha, the second of the holy Name.* THE LORD: *This is the Proceeding which proceedeth from beneath, in the Secret which is marked by the Letter Uau; these two Letters are drawn to be in this Place, and they are all one,* (one Unity,) *all these three are one Unity; since that each one is made in one Unity of themselves.*[63]

In contrast to the previous two passages, here Monis does offer a clarification before presenting this Zoharic text, stating that it can help the reader "to discover more fully the Deity of the *Holy Ghost* in particular, as proceeding from the Father and Son."[64] What he means by this is not entirely clear, as there is no clear indication of either the Father, the Son, or the Holy Ghost here, even within Monis's translation.

As with the previous passage quoted by Monis, this one, as it appears in the *Zohar*, comes in a discussion of mystical intercourse and a focus on the unification of the male and female aspects of God. Recital of the *Shema*' is all about theurgically uniting what the *Zohar* calls the supernal Husband with that which it calls the Matrona. The passage in the *Zohar* immediately preceding the one quoted by Monis on the *yod heh* and *vav* states:

At the same time that the Husband and the Matrona conjoin as one, a proclamation comes forth from the south, which arouses the celestial armies and legions, which reveal love to their Master. Then a celestial supervisor whose name is Boel the Great Legionnaire awakens, and in his hands are four keys that are taken from the four sides of the earth. On one key is inscribed the mark of the letter *Yod*, and on another key is inscribed the mark of the letter *Heh*, and on another key is inscribed the mark of the letter *Vav*. And he places these under the Tree of Life. These three keys, which are inscribed with these three letters, become one. Since they become one, the other key ascends and stands and conjoins with that other that includes the three. And all of those same celestial armies and legions enter with those three keys into the Garden, and all of them perform a unification, as is done below.[65]

In this remarkable passage, angelic action parallels human intention in the recital of the *Shema*'. The three first letters of the Tetragrammaton, which is recited twice in the *Shema'*, are conjoined into a single entity that then conjoins with the final *heh* that arises from below. This is what unlocks the Garden for the sake of celestial unification. One of the extradordinary elements here is the sense of human agency. The theurgic unification of the Husband and the Matrona through the human recital of the *Shema'* seems to literally unlock an entire cosmic process of unification through mystical intercourse and love.

This all seems to be a far cry from "the Deity of the *Holy Ghost* . . . as proceeding from the Father and Son," as mentioned by Monis. The one commonality seems to be the hypostatization of the letters, or at the very least the demarcation of the letters as symbols pointing to hypostases. In Monis, however, the *yod* seems to demarcate the Father, the *heh* seems to demarcate the Son, and the *vav* seems to demarcate the Holy Ghost, as it is "the Proceeding which proceedeth from beneath." In the Zoharic context, it seems to be the final *heh* of the Tetragrammaton that would act in any way that might be construed as *Holy Ghost*: it is below among the populace and it rises up to conjoin with the other three letters in order to complete the key that unlocks the key to the Garden. Yet even then, it helps to unlock the Garden for the hosts of heaven to perform a theurgic unification that is parallel to the unification performed by the recital of the *Shema'* below. It does not open the gate for the adepts below. Here again, whether wittingly or not, a change of context creates a change of meaning. Through a Trinitarian reappropriation of a triad, not only is complex Zoharic mythology eschewed but the ideas therein are completely recast.

Heikhal Ha-Kodesh, Mistaken Identity, and the Father and Son

Monis moves from the classical canon of Kabbalah into modernity, and in a final kabbalistic rereading of the *Shema'*, he ties the prayer to his own rabbinic teacher, Jacob Sasportas. Specifically, he brings a text from a popular kabbalistic book explaining Jewish prayer entitled *Heikhal ha-Kodesh*, or what Monis calls in English *The Holy Temple*. This is in fact the only modern kabbalistic work that Monis cites within his treatise.[66] In his discussion of the *Shema'*, Monis states:

> R. Jacob Sasportas in his Book called *The Holy Temple*, printed in *Amsterdam* about Seventy Years since, *Page* 15. says the following

Words, "THE LORD: *This is the Father most high*. OUR GOD: *This is the Head, most Ancient, the Eternal One, the Soul of Souls*."[67]

In addition to being a prominent anti-Sabbatean, as outlined in the previous chapter, Sasportas was a renowned kabbalist. Thus, if it is true that Sasportas was Monis's personal teacher, as maintained in the last chapter, then this somewhat sophisticated move of including Sasportas would offer a degree of kabbalistic pedigree to Monis's Trinitarian readings of the *Shema'*. After all, under the traditional Jewish schema, Kabbalah denotes a chain of transmission and reception from teacher to student; and if Monis was now purporting to be a kabbalistic authority, then the establishment of this lineage and the direct citation would play a key role.

Monis goes on to clarify regarding this text that he claims is by Sasportas: "HERE this worthy Author makes a Distinction in the Meaning of the Names, *The Lord*, and *Our God*, by which Words he says the same in Substance as we Christians believe, even that the Name of *The Lord* first mention'd, is the *Father* most high, and the Name of *Our God* is the *Son*, which is that White Head mentioned in *Dan*. 7.9."[68] Yet again for Monis, the *Shema'* as understood by kabbalistic thought only confirms Christianity. The Father and the Son are One Substance, and "the Lord" and "our God" are two explicitly distinguished names in the *Shema'* that actually coalesce into One. For Monis, as a new convert but also as an ostensible disciple of Sasportas by whom he brings this reading of the *Shema'*, such a confirmation would be both poignant and weighty.

This is all well and good, except for two fundamental problems. The first is that the book that he calls *The Holy Temple*, known in Hebrew as *Heikhal ha-Kodesh*, was *not* written by Jacob Sasportas. Rather, it was written between 1575 and 1599 by a lesser-known Moroccan kabbalist named Moshe bar Maimon Elbaz.[69] Sasportas most certainly had a role in publishing the book in Amsterdam in 1653, as he brought it to press from a manuscript that he apparently had in his possession. At that point and with Sasportas's name attached to the book, it became somewhat of a best seller throughout the Jewish world; but the ideas in it were not originally his. Sasportas also wrote a preface to the work, but the portion quoted by Monis is not from that preface. The second problem, in addition to the mistaken identity of the author of *Heikhal ha-Kodesh*, is that Monis greatly confounds the meaning of the passage that he quotes from that text. Whether purposefully or not, his reading radically transforms the theology of the text that he thinks was written by the rabbi whom he admiringly refers to as "*The Pious or Godly, The Theologer*," and it strips it of its meditative nature.

In order to see Monis's extreme Christological divergence as he interprets *Heikhal ha-Kodesh* on the *Shema'*, it is worth quoting the passage from the original text in full:

> The intended meaning of "*Shema'*" is "*Shem ayin*." "*Shem*" is *Malkhut*, and it is its own word. Thus, the big *ayin* is intended to show that "*Shem*" is its own word, and it is the attribute of *Malkhut*, which is called "*Shem*." And when it emits the big *ayin* from its mouth, with the sounding out of the *ayin*, all of the seven *sefirot* are intended, which are the secret of the groom, from *Yesod* until *Hesed*. And when one says "*Shema'*," the intention is to unite "*Shem*" with "*ayin*" and to make them into one composite, just as Scriptures made them one word: "*Shema'*." And when it says "Israel," the intention is the mother of the children, which is above the seven and is called "Israel," because there they are the souls of Israel. "The Lord" is the supernal Father. "Our God" is the White Head, may He be blessed, the Ancient of all Ancients, the Primordial Singular, the Soul of Souls. And when the thought of a man rises to this place, the soul will be drawn to *Keter* when he says the *alef* of *echad*, which is set against the White Head.[70]

The mythology at play here is quite intricate, but even a first glance without an elaborate understanding of the details reveals the fact that the passage goes far beyond Monis's dyad of Father and Son. In fact, here the *Shema'* in its entirety is associated with the entirety of the sefirotic structure, and there is no way to mistake it for anything Christological. Rather, it is being set up by Elbaz as a veritable ladder of ascent for one who recites it with proper intention.

The lowest and most accessible rung on the ladder is the *sefirah* of *Malkhut*, represented by the first part of the first word, *Shem*, while the last letter of the first word, *a'* (*ayin*), which is orthographically bigger than the rest of the word as it appears in a standard Torah scroll, represents the next six *sefirot* up, from *Yesod* to *Hesed*. These six *sefirot* are the groom, and *Malkhut* is the bride; in marital union as one word *Shema'*, they make up the seven lower *sefirot*. The second word, *Israel*, is the supernal Mother, i.e., *Binah*, and the third word, *YHWH*, "the Lord," is the supernal Father, i.e., *Hokhmah*. That makes nine. Finally, "our God" is the White Head, i.e., *Keter*. It is not, as Monis maintains, the Son.

Monis is right that *Heikhal ha-Kodesh* makes a distinction in regard to the *Shema'* between "the Lord" and "our God." But the distinction is not between Father and Son; it is between the divine Father and the Primordial Singular, who is above and beyond the divine Father. Moreover, the distinction is part of a larger system involving not three hypostases but ten *sefirot*. Thus, Monis's overall mistake in regard to this passage goes well beyond his attribution of *Heikhal ha-Kodesh* to Sasportas. Read in its own context, the passage holds nothing even tacitly suggestive of Christology; if anything, it is not Christ who is the immanent point of access but the supernal Bride and her divine Groom in union, as represented by the word *Shema'*.[71]

The Primordial Singular, *Adam Kadmon*, and Coeternality

According to *Heikhal ha-Kodesh*, when one recites *alef*, the first letter of *echad*, "One," which itself is numerically equivalent to one and which paradoxically has no sound in and of itself, all is unified. Moreover, the soul of the adept who is praying is elevated to a cosmic level of pure unity, standing against the White Head, or *Keter*, the Primordial Singular that precedes emanation. Elbaz cautions, however, that "one should not lengthen the *alef* of *echad* because it is set against the mysterium, and it is an attribute among which one's thought should wander for [only] an instant."[72] As a mystical experience, existence at the apex can and should be fleeting. Anything more could lead to a dissolution of the self into the (non)entity that is *alef*.

After reaching the summit point of the Primordial Singular in *alef*, Elbaz offers a reversal for the adept. In order to understand how the concepts from Elbaz are being reinterpreted by Monis, it is worth citing Elbaz's return from the apex of the *alef* of *echad*, in full:

> From there the soul will be drawn after the *het*, which is the secret of the supernal Wisdom (*Hokhmah*), with all of the eight *sefirot*, which are the Male World as they add up to eight, until the Foundation (*Yesod*). And

one should lengthen the measure of the *het* so that his thought can wander among all of the attributes, from *Hokhmah* until *Yesod*, in order to
draw the soul to them. . . . And after one has unified the Male World, he
should make them all one with one soul, with love and fraternity, through
the word "one." He should intend to further draw his soul to the *Shekhinah*, which is the *dalet* (or door), and he should connect that letter
with *ach* (brother), and they should become one (*echad*). For their soul
is one, and they are one body. Just as the human body is divided up into
limbs and his soul is one, so it is in the supernal realm. And this is the
true unification, which is received and desired. And behold, the enlarged
dalet is also intended to divide the word and to make it "one," for the Male
World hints to brother (*ach*), as we have clarified. It is a brother to the
dalet, which is the *Shekhinah*, for they are siblings from the Father and
the Mother.[73]

The Hebrew letter *het* is not only the second letter of the word *echad*, it
is the first letter of the word *Hokhmah*, Wisdom. Numerologically it also
equals eight, and Elbaz connects it to the eight *sefirot* from *Hokhmah*
to *Yesod*. *Dalet* is not only the third and last letter of the word *echad*,
in Hebrew it also literally means "door"; for Elbaz it symbolizes the
Shekhinah, which itself literally means "indwelling." The lowest *sefirah*,
and the lowest rung on the ladder, is a veritable two-way door for the
soul of one who recites the *Shema'*. On the way up and in, Elbaz designates this door *Malkhut*, or "Monarchy," while on the way down and
out, he designates it *Shekhinah*, or "Indwelling." The feminine aspect
of God provides a royal point of entry into the Godhead, but it also
provides a point of exit from which God still dwells with the soul of the
adept. One could argue that for the adept, on the way up the process is
one of sexually ecstatic union, while on the way down it is a process of
rebirth.

Here Elbaz is playing with the classical philosophical problem of
immanence vs. transcendence and the possibility of achieving transcendence through immanence. Within that schema, *ha-Yehid ha-
Kadmon*, "the Primordial Singular," acts as a lynchpin. As Dan Manor
has noted, the interplay of immanence and transcendence is a common theme throughout *Heikhal ha-Kodesh*, in which God as the "Primordial Singular" expresses Himself through the ten *sefirot*, and in

which an emphasis is placed on ultimate Unity of the Emanator with the Emanated.[74] In this specific instance, Elbaz masterfully plays on the dialectic by giving a sefirotic reading of the *Shema'*, which in its most literal rendering asserts divine unity. But here he goes beyond mere intellectual speculation through the mystical idea that every Jew can go beyond understanding and can elevate his soul, through progressive concentration on the *sefirot*, to a level of unity. From that experience of unity, which casts the "One" of the *Shema'* in an entirely different light, the adept can return to the mundane plane with a noetic sense of unity still intact.

For Monis, as we have seen, the central figure to this scheme, "the White Head, may He be blessed, the Ancient of all Ancients, the Primordial Singular, the Soul of Souls," as represented by the term "our God" in the *Shema'*, is not the high point of *Keter* above the Father but is the Son. And though he translates "the Primordial Singular," *ha-Yehid ha-Kadmon*, as "the Eternal One," he may have understood this as referring to *Adam ha-Kadmon*, "the Primordial Man." This is a term that shows up in thirteenth-century kabbalistic texts but gains prominence in the sixteenth century with Lurianic Kabbalah. Within that later context, as with individuals like George Keith whom we have seen, it signifies the most sublime manifestation of God as the first emanation of divine Light, which is partially accessible to human meditation;[75] at the same time, it is paradoxically entirely concealed.

Monis was presumably reading *Heikhal ha-Kodesh* in Hebrew, and he would have noticed both the linguistic and conceptual affinities between *ha-Yehid ha-Kadmon* and *Adam ha-Kadmon*. Moreover, he was certainly aware of the Lurianic concept of *Adam ha-Kadmon*, as is apparent from a manuscript copy, ostensibly in his own handwriting, of the late seventeenth- or early eighteenth-century commentary on the *Idra* sections of the *Zohar* by Ya'acov Marrache of Tetouan, *Emet l'Ya'acov*. Commenting on the term from the *Idra Rabba* of the *Zohar*, *Attika d'Attikin*, "the Ancient of Ancients," the copy of *Emet l'Ya'akov* penned by Monis states:

> This is *Adam Kadmon* [i.e., Primordial Man], which is called *Attika d'Attikin* [i.e., the Ancient of Ancients], since it is above the Ancient of Days of *Atzilut*. And because of this it is called "the Ancient of Ancients." It is also called "the Concealed of Concealeds," as it is concealed.[76]

It is significant to note that the passage from *Heikhal ha-Kodesh* explic-itly quoted by Monis employs the term *Attika d'kol Attikin*, a direct variant of "the Ancient of Ancients," which Monis translates as "most Ancient." It is thus reasonable to surmise that the same entity is being discussed here and that it was known to Monis.

The reason this is significant is because the term *Adam Kadmon* came to be associated with Christ in the seventeenth century by promi-nent Protestant Christian kabbalists such as Francis Mercury van Helmont and Christian Knorr von Rosenroth, and as we have seen, was carried over into the American context by George Keith and Cotton Mather. As van Helmont's Christian philosopher says to his Jewish kab-balistic counterpart in his *Adumbratio Kabbalae Christianae*, "Precisely what you call *Adam Kadmon*, we call Christ."[77] In a similar vein, Keith's other friend and teacher, the seventeenth-century English Platonist Anne Conway writes, "The ancient Kabbalists have written many things about this, namely, how the son of God was created; how his existence in the order of nature preceded all creatures; how everything is blessed and receives holiness in him and through him, whom they call in their writings the celestial Adam, or the first man Adam Kadmon."[78] Monis seems to be making the same Christian turn toward *Adam Kadmon* as his Christian predecessors, including Keith and Mather, by explicitly linking what he translates as "the Head, most Ancient, the Eternal One, the Soul of Souls" to the Son rather than to *Keter* above the supernal Father.

But why the subtelty in this matter, and even the translation of Elbaz's *Yehid ha-Kadmon* as "the Eternal One" rather than as "the Primordial Singular"? I would suggest that this was perhaps deliberate on Monis's part. The idea of *Adam Kadmon* as an emanated entity creates problems for Trinitarian notions of coequality and coeternality; this is not to men-tion Conway's notion that "the son of God was created." The translation of *Yehid* as "One" and *Kadmon* as "Eternal" puts this all immediately to rest. Under this formulation, which is not an entirely wrong translation, this entity, which for Monis is the Son, is indeed both coequal as "One" and coeternal as, well, "Eternal." This is all perhaps as much a subtle Congrega-tional Trinitarian recasting of earlier Protestant notions of *Adam Kadmon* from the circle of Anne Conway as it was a recasting of the Jewish ideas of Elbaz.

Numerology of the Father, the Son, and the Holy Ghost

Toward the latter part of the treatise, Monis moves from liturgy to numerology, linking *Adam Kadmon* and notions of a coequal and coeternal Trinity to the Holy Name of God. In a rather explicit claim to innovation, he states, "That all the three Persons are included and comprehended in the Name *Jehovah*, I do not know any who have shewed it before me."[79] Through a series of complex hermeneutics, Monis wants to be the first. Yet despite the proposed originality, Monis does rely on strong interpretive precedent and on rabbinic Midrash.

Monis begins by explaining gematria, or Hebrew numerology, by way of which each letter of the Hebrew alphabet holds a numeric value, in ascending order. Thus, the first letter *alef* equals "one," the second letter *bet* equals "two," and so on. According to this reckoning, Monis notes, the name *Jehovah* (*yod*=10; *heh*=5; *vav*=6; *heh*=5), whose root signifies "Being," holds the numeric value of 26. Yet from this, he remarks, through a spelling out of each of the individual letters of the name, kabbalists have come up with variants, including 45 (*yod-vav-dalet*=20; *heh-aleph*=6; *vav-alef-vav*=13; *heh-alef*=6) and 52 (*yod-vav-dalet*=20; *heh-heh*=10; *vav-vav*=12; *heh-heh*=10).[80] In reversing the numeric expression back to the alphabetic, 45 is *Mah* (*mem-heh*), or "what," while 52 is *Ben* (*bet-nun*), or "son."

The idea of the names *Mah* and *Ben* for the proper names of God deriving from the Tetragrammaton is part of a larger kabbalistic theme that also includes the names *'Av* (72; *yod-vav-dalet*=20; *heh-yod*=15; *vav-yod-vav*=22; *heh-yod*=15) and *Sag* (63; *yod-vav-dalet*=20; *heh-yod*=15; *vav-alef-vav*=13; *heh-yod*=15), and Monis could have potentially been drawing this from any number of sources. One candidate would be Hayyim Vital's *Ozrot Hayyim*, which, though published in 1783, was widely in circulation in Europe well beforehand.[81] Another candidate might be *Puerta Del Cielo* of Abraham Cohen de Herrera, translated into Hebrew from the Spanish as *Sha'ar ha-Shamayim*, and then translated into Latin from the Hebrew and included in the *Kabbala Denudata* of 1684. Within that work, Herrera writes "that *Adam* includes *alef* (one), *dalet* (four), and *mem* (forty) to show that in this 'Adam Qadmon there is a name of the hawwayah or essence projected in ten letters as follows: *yod-vav-dalet, heh-yod, vav-alef-vav, heh-alef*, which is explained by these being the numbers 72, 63, 45, and 52."[82] This seems to be quite in line with Monis's thought. Regardless, whether he had access to either of these sources is unclear; but the idea does clearly show up in Monis's kabbalistic compendium, specifically in the *Emet l'Ya'acov* of Ya'acov Marrache of Tetouan. There, however, it is in a much different context.

Within Monis's compendium, the idea of the numeric names of God appears in relation to a complex kabbalistic mythology regarding the death of the kings of Edom as recounted in Genesis 36:31–39. While the Bible tells of "the kings that reigned in the land of Edom, before there reigned any king over the children of Israel,"[83] the *Idra Rabba* section of the *Zohar* interprets these as primordial worlds that were created before the creation of our world but that did not have the proper male-female balance and were thus diminished. God needed to emanate and enter into the form of *Adam Kadmon*, with a proper balance of both the male and female principles, in order to fully and properly sustain the world. With this, the Primordial Kings remained but were transformed. As the *Zohar* states, "Once *Adam* was arrayed, they were called by different names and became fragrantly firm through existing in Him, enduring in their places."[84] Commenting upon this Zoharic verse in rather stilted language, the *Emet l'Ya'akov*, as copied by Monis, states:

> Once the aspect of Adam, the new Name *Mah*, called *Adam*, which came forth arranged as male and female, was arrayed and came forth into the world, then—these Kings that were broken, which were previously called points of the Name *Sag*—then, when the Name *Mah* came forth—then, these points of *Sag* were called *Ben*, so that they could become fragrantly firm and arrayed with the Name *Mah*. For if they were still called by the Name *Sag*, they would not be able to be arrayed with the Name *Mah* . . . these points were called by different names, as first they were called *Sag* and afterward they were called *Ben*, and afterward they became fragrantly firm through the Name *Mah*, which is called *Adam*.[85]

Here the different numeric iterations of the divine name YHWH, related to Being, correlate with processes of creation as the emanation of Being. *Av* is not mentioned, but this may be deliberate as it is beyond all comprehension. *Sag* is the first stage, from which points of the divine emerged. These were not stable and broke, but were transformed through *Ben* and then finally became stabilized through *Mah*, which is numerically equivalent to *Adam* (*alef*=1; *dalet*=4; *mem*=40). *Mah* is thus an allusion to *Adam Kadmon*, the point of divine balance that allows the world to come into being.

While Monis curiously does not mention any of this in his *Nothing but the Truth*, he does directly relate the name *Mah* to the creation of the world, and to Adam. Regarding the Jews, he writes:

> THEY teach that God created the World with the Name of 45. and they prove it out of Prov. 3. 19. *The Lord by Wisdom hath founded the Earth.* The Word in the Original is *Bahohmah*, and they turn said Word, which is translated, *By Wisdom*, according to their way of explaining the most part of the Scriptures, thus, *Bahohmah Bacoauh Mau, By Wisdom, By the Strength of Mau i.e.* by the Strength of the Name 45, saying, *The Lord by the Strength of this Name founded the Earth.*[86]

In line with the discussion within *Emet l'Ya'akov*, here the idea being propounded is that the earth came forth and was stabilized through the divine name *Mah*. *Hokhmah* as the second *sefirah* from the top turns to *Koach Mah*, i.e., the strength of the divine name *Mah*. This idea of *Hokhmah* as *Koach Mah* appears in the *Raya Mehemna* stratum of the *Zohar* and also in the book *Novelot Hokhmah* of Yosef Shlomo Delmedigo, which may have been known to Monis.[87] It also appears in Knorr von Rosenroth's *Kabbala Denudata*, which states, "*Hokhmah* is equivalent to *Koach Mah* that is strength *Mah*, which is the numerical equivalent of *Adam*."[88] In this sense, it is through *Adam Kadmon* as an iteration of *Hokhmah*, or supernal Wisdom, that the earth was founded.

For Monis, this is none other than Christ. "The Lord *Jesus Christ* is called *Adam*," he writes, "as the Apostle Paul says to the Corinthians, I Cor. 15. 45. *The first Man Adam was made a living Soul, the last ADAM was made a quickening Spirit.*"[89] In order to fully establish the kabbalistic connection, he continues, "Now the Word *Adam* following the same rule amounts to 45."[90] Given both the context and the use of 45 to describe Jesus as God, it is not far-fetched to read the New Testament verse brought forth by Monis in a kabbalistic manner. *Adam Kadmon,* the "Primordial Man," brought the world to life; Christ, the "last Adam," has the power to give life. Yet the two are essentially one and the same. As Monis later states, the 45 as "the true *Adam*" and "from Eternity with *Jehovah the Lord*" is "to show that the *Son* and the *Father* are all one, of the self same Numeration, i.e., one and the self same Essence."[91] In regard to the *Son*, Monis states, "THE more immediate Word for Son in the Original is *Ben*, this amounts according to the third Rule of Reckoning to 52, which is the same Numeration of the Name *Jehovah*, as the second Way of Spelling of it."[92] *Ben*, as we have seen, is the numerical equivalent of *Jehovah*, or YHWH, spelled out as *yod-vav-dalet, heh-heh, vav-vav, heh-heh*. Father and Son are thus One in the essential Being of *Jehovah*.

But what about the Holy Ghost? Monis attempts to link this third person of the Trinity in a rather convoluted manner of numerological gymnastics. Through variant forms of numeration, he shows that the Hebrew epithet *Ruach ha-Kodesh*, which signifies the Holy Ghost, amounts to 101.[93] YHWH, representing the Father, amounts to 26, and *Adonai*, which he claims to be representative of Christ, amounts to 65. "Both together makes 91, and with the Addition of the eight Letters of both Names, and the two Names themselves," Monis writes, "come to be in the whole 101 also, to show that the *Holy Ghost* proceedeth from both, *i.e.* the *Father* and the *Son*."[94] In addition, *Ruach* equals 16, which is the same as the numerical value of *Havah*, or "Being," the root word for the name *Jehovah*. This is all to show that the Holy Ghost not only proceeds from the Father and Son, but that they are all from the same root and essence, and are thus all coequal and coeternal.

"I hope I have plainly and fully demonstrated," writes Monis, "that the God which we adore and hope to be saved by, is not *three Gods* . . . but only One living and only true God; One in Substance and Essence, but Three Persons, *Father, Son,* and *Holy Ghost,* all equal in Power and Glory from all Eternity."[95] Monis's rather labyrinthine gematria, which leads from traditional kabbalistic layers of Zoharic and Lurianic thought on the divine name to more tortuous albeit inventive musings on the Holy Ghost, seeks to buttress his initial claims in regard to the *Shema'*. Yet here, rather than creed through biblically derived prayer, the focus is on what he sees as the essence of "Being," or more precisely, the proper name of God.

Concluding Remarks

After a full textual analysis of Monis's kabbalistic discourse, a series of questions naturally arises. One concerns the lack of explicit reference to anything from Monis's own handwritten kabbalistic compendium, which extends to a full 187 folio pages and includes intricate texts of Lurianic Kabbalah. It is certainly reasonable to expect some type of citation from these works, yet there is none. Even when he alludes to some ideas present in *Emet l'Yaakov*, as we have seen, he neither mentions nor cites this work. None of the other copied texts are cited either. The reason is perhaps that within his discourse, Monis attempts to stick as closely as possible to the sources he sees as classical Kabbalah, including what he thinks is *Sefer Yetzirah*, and several passages from the *Zohar*. The only truly modern source comes from what he thinks is the work of his teacher, Jacob Sasportas. Monis thus seems to be attempting to ground his assertions in the classical kabbalistic canon, and when he deviates, it is to establish his own personal kabbalistic transition from teacher to student.

Another question that arises concerns the lack of engagement with Christian kabbalistic sources. After all, Monis ostensibly grew up in Italy where Christian Kabbalah had flourished, and the inclusion of a passage from Agrippa's *De occulta philosophia*, as discussed in the previous chapter, provides some evidence that he was familiar with Christian developments in this lore. Moreover, as has been shown, there are close affinities between Monis's thought and that of Ciantes on the three Lights, as well as that of Abner of Burgos and Paul of Heredia in relation to trinities in the *Zohar*. And while he may have been unfamiliar with this research, he certainly could have sought it out as a resource. One reason for the lacuna may be Monis's attempt to establish a distinctly *Jewish* background for his arguments. If even for only performative rather than functional reasons, Monis sought to present himself as a *Jew* who was reaching out to his "Brethren according to the Flesh," and an explicit introduction of figures such as Ciantes would only serve to subvert that.[96] Another reason may be Monis's anti-Catholic view, prodded by the likes of Mather, of "the idolatrous Worship of the *Romish* Church,"[97] which he sees at the heart of the failure of previous forced attempts to convert the Jews. Under this assumption, an appeal to Catholic kabbalistic polemics would indeed be antithetical.

A third question involves the reach of Monis's kabbalistic ideas, and whether he was teaching them in his lifetime beyond the discourses that he published with Daniel Henchman. Beyond the fact that his texts do not seem to have been read by Jews, there was no Jewish community in the Boston area of his day and he does not seem to have had any further contact with any Jewish people. His texts were subsequently read by Christians, such as the reverend Humphrey Moore of Milford, New Hampshire, who quotes Monis as "A modern Jew" in his *Treatise on the Divine Nature* of 1824.[98] There Moore examines the *Shema'*, and he brings forth, as an example from Monis, "one of the most ancient Jewish books, a book said to be as ancient as Abraham himself," which discusses "*an ancient light, a pure light, and a most pure light*."[99] This, of course, is the pseudo-Hai text, attributed by Monis, and then here again through Moore, to *Sefer Yetzirah*. Monis's texts were also republished in their entirety in 1821 in *The Jewish Expositor and Friend of Israel*, which was the monthly proceedings of the London Society for Promoting Christianity Amongst the Jews.[100] The texts thus presumably reached a much wider audience in the nineteenth century.

One final question involves the Jewish nature of the Kabbalah produced by Monis within his published piece. How much of that, if anything, remains "Jewish," whatever this multifaceted term of identity may mean? Or how much of it depends on Judaism, even in a complex manner? After all, as Monis himself states in regard to the Jewish kabbalists: "IN quoting their Sayings, I do purposely design not to Criticise upon the Words, least [*sic*] they may say, that I draw and make them say what I have a mind to, but only quote & Translate them Faithfully, and let them Judge afterwards."[101] Given what we have seen with his interpretations of texts from the *Zohar* and from *Heikhal ha-Kodesh*, this is far from true. Monis is clearly drawing from those texts in a cherry-picking manner and both through interpretation and selective translation, he is making them say what he has a mind for them to say. He does not simply "quote & Translate them Faithfully," if this is even a possibility. Rather, he translates them faithfully into a language of Protestant cultural faith, and in so doing he transforms both the texts and the theology contained within.

Nevertheless, Monis's readings do maintain a nomian character as related to the divinely commanded Jewish recital of the *Shema'* and as related to the fundamental affirmation of God's unity, which Monis claims is common to Judaism and Christianity. In this sense, Monis's complex American Puritan "Jewish" identity seems to inform his hermeneutical ploy of reaching out to his "Brethren" in order to bring about a conversion of the Jews that is to be of messianic proportions. The result, however, is not the conversion of the Jews. In fact, there is no evidence that either Monis's conversion or his subsequent treatise had an effect on the Jewish community, and there are absolutely no known Jewish responses to his writings.[102] There are, however, American Protestant responses to Monis from key figures, such as the seventh president of Yale, Ezra Stiles. Monis's conversion and the kabbalistic text that it produced may not have led to the conversion of the Jews, but both the event and the text did lead to the conversion of American Protestant sentiments toward Jewish thought, even if inadvertently and only partially. In this regard, it is to Ezra Stiles whom we now turn.

Universal Kabbalah in the Colleges of America

Ezra Stiles and the Jewish-Protestant Interface

Ezra's Torah and Kabbalah

Over forty-eight years after Judah Monis's conversion to Congregational Christianity, Congregational minister and future president of Yale College Ezra Stiles outlined a detailed record of over seventy important dates and figures in the history of Jewish thought, culminating in 1720 with the very conversion of Monis.[1] Stiles writes of that date, "Rabbi Judah Monis becomes Christian: made Hebrew Professor in Harvard College Cambridge. Him I have conversed with."[2] With this statement, not only does the Christianized "Rabbi Judah Monis" mark the culmination of the history of Jewish theology up until Stiles's time, he also serves as a direct line of transmission of metahistorical, kabbalistic thought for Stiles himself. If Stiles has "conversed with" Monis, then it seems that Stiles too is privy to the authentic oral tradition, outlined in part, as we saw in the last chapter, in Monis's published baptismal discourses.

While Stiles's catalog ends with Monis as having personally conversed with Stiles, it begins with Cyrus the Great in 536 "Before the Christian Era" and then significantly immediately lists Stiles's eponym, along with his eponym's institution. "Ezra and the Great Synagogue and cessation of Prophecy"[3] were, for Stiles, the very first point of a systematization of Kabbalah, or "received tradition" as he saw it. They were also the first point of transmission of that received tradition, in the form of a newly canonized Torah. Through appellative parallelism, Stiles seems to be setting himself up as a new "Ezra": he is both the proper recipient and the appropriate transmitter of received tradition, framed as an old-new Torah. If, for Congregational divines, Monis was an embodiment of the Old Testament in the New World, as partly argued above in chapter 3,

Stiles, like his biblical namesake, was an apposite reformulator of that Old Testament and a suitable eventual disseminator of it, as kabbalistically understood. This reading is supported by Stiles's later obsession with the role of the biblical Ezra in the national exposure of the Pentateuch,[4] which especially comes to light in Stiles's first public oration delivered at a Yale commencement in September 1781.

Stiles begins his commencement oration, originally written in Hebrew in 1778, by quoting the book of Ezra 7:10: "For Ezra had prepared his heart to teach the law of the Lord and to do it and to teach in Israel Statutes and Judgments." He goes on to state:

> This wise and holy man found favor in the eyes of the Lord and in the eyes of the King of Persia, and in the eyes of all Israel; he was great among the Jews, and accepted with the multitude of his Brethren. Instructed by the Masters of Wisdom and Understanding at the university of the Captivity in Babylon, he became a ready writer of the Law; and filled with all divine Literature, he was great and perfect on every point.[5]

The epithet "Masters of Wisdom and Understanding" for the teachers from whom Ezra learned implies Kabbalah. So does the continuation of the description, whch states of Ezra, "The benign influences of the light from above distilled upon him like the dew. So that he erred not from the Way of Truth."[6] Here Kabbalah is signified by the "influences of the light," distilled dew, and the "Way of Truth," appellations that we have seen employed by both Monis and Cotton Mather, as well as Keith. Stiles's description of Ezra continues:

> And therefore thro' [all] whole his life he was good and holy. There is no memorial of his sin or of an imperfection in him, nor in him was ever found a crime. He was one of the very few without a blemish. In Noah there was a blemish; Abraham Moses Job and David all had their imperfections; but in Ezra there was nothing but benevolence and holiness.[7]

Stiles's eponym Ezra was more perfect than Noah, Abraham, Moses, Job, and David. What is more, he had learned and disseminated Kabbalah.

While Stiles does not explicitly implicate himself here, one cannot help but wonder why he chose this specific verse from the Bible to expound upon in his very first public address at Yale. It is significant to note that later in the oration he states regarding Jewish literature, "With desire I have earnestly desired to see it illuminating the scholars of Yale College, and also the literati of different cities in these goings down of the sun these ends of the world."[8] As will be shown in this chapter, like Ezra the Scribe, Stiles had learned from "Masters of Wisdom and Understanding," beginning with Monis but extending to both credentialed Jewish rabbis of note and Jewish texts of great importance. And like Ezra as the head of the Great Synagogue who brought the Torah to a renovated Jerusalem, Stiles, as president of Yale, was now in a position to transfer that old-new Torah to a New World, American context.

This reading of a historically enacted hermeneutics is further buttressed by the fact that Stiles drafts the list with which we opened, beginning with Cyrus and ending with Monis, within the context of the following statement, adapted from *Pirkei Avot*: "The Kabbala is, next to the Scriptures, the most antient learning. It was *orally* communicated from Adam to Moses, and from Moses to the CXX of the Great Synagogue."[9] Ezra's Great Synagogue was the direct recipient of Mosaic Wisdom. From there, for Stiles, it led all the way down to kabbalistic diffusion into American Congregational Christianity. Monis was the last Jew and first Congregationalist in the line of authentic transmission, before such Kabbalah began to reach Stiles himself. The latter would seek to further the process begun by Monis and his ilk, such as Increase Mather and Benjamin Colman, of its transplantation into the colleges of America and consequentially, into American Christianity more generally.

Stiles and Monis

Despite the fact that Stiles explicitly states that he had conversed with Monis, there are unfortunately no extant accounts of their conversations. This is somewhat unusual given Stiles's meticulous record keeping, which includes detailed descriptions of intellectual exchanges. Moreover, nowhere does Stiles indicate what it is that they may have discussed. It may be that they met prior to the time at which Stiles began his comprehensive documentation, which would make sense since Monis died in 1764 and Stiles began his literary diaries only in 1769. In fact, as early as 1769, we know that Stiles had read what he refers to as "Rabbi Judah Monis's Discourses at his Baptism in 1722."[10] Thus, while the personal conversation is not known, some of the content of Monis's kabbalistic thought as made known to Stiles is.

Monis's discourses and the Kabbalah within them, as discussed in the previous chapter, would prove to have a profound effect on Stiles's overall theology and his relationship to Jewish thought. In fact, about a year after having logged his reading of Monis's discourses, Stiles makes extensive use of the kabbalistic thought contained within them in an important public forum. This is his *Discourse on Saving Knowledge*, a sermon that Stiles delivered in Newport, Rhode Island, on April 11, 1770, at the installment of the famed Congregational abolitionist theologian Samuel Hopkins as pastor of the First Congregational Church. The discourse was shortly afterward published and distributed in Newport by Solomon Southwick. Within the discourse, Stiles writes that the "pious Hebrews of all ages, and particularly in the period between the two temples, accustomed themselves to worship and think of the great JEHOVAH under the idea of trinity."[11] In order to support this claim, he writes:

> R. *Simeon ben Johauy*, one of the sages of the *mishna*, out of the ancient and most spiritual writings compiled the Zohar, a book of the highest reputation with the Jews to this day. Speaking of the grand Shema, Deut. vi. 4. It says, "these are three names, how are they one?—These *three are one:*" and illustrates this by three things in thunder, viz. fire, wind and water "all one in the secret of the thunder"—and much more to the same purpose respecting three in one as to God.[12]

Contained in this passage is a direct quotation from the *Zohar* on the unity of the three mentions of "God" in the *Shema'*, which is the *exact* English translation of *Zohar* 2:43b that appears in Monis's *Nothing but the Truth*. There is no need to enter into a detailed explication here, as that has already been done in the previous chapter, but it is worth mentioning that in addition to the passage directly quoted, Monis too refers to *Simeon Ben Johauy*, spelled in the same idiosyncratic way, as "one of the Sages of the *Mishnau*."[13] Moreover, the naturalistic rendering of the term *kol*, i.e., "voice," as "thunder," discussed in the preceding chapter as an interpretive translation that neutralizes the theurgic element, carries over into Stiles's discourse. It is significant to note that Stiles did not receive a copy of the *Zohar* until 1772; but as we have already mentioned, he was certainly reading Monis as early as 1769. It is thus reasonable to surmise that even though Stiles does not provide reference, Monis was his direct Zoharic source for his discourse of 1770.

Monis's influence on Stiles extends beyond Zoharic thought and includes other Trinitarian readings of Jewish mystical texts. In fact, Stiles continues on in his *Discourse on Saving Knowledge* to state:

> The *Sapher Hajatzirah*, is allowed by the rabbins to be one of their most ancient books, some say as ancient as Abraham and composed by him. It is doubtless of great antiquity. This speaks of the Godhead as three in one,—these three are called *Lights* in God:—"they are three LIGHTS, an ancient light, a pure light, and a most pure light, all which are however but *one God*."[14]

This is virtually identical to Monis's statement that in "*Sapher hauyatzee-rau*, (a Book which some of them would have to be as ancient as our Father *Abraham*, and of his Composing also, as they say,) 'tis plain by what is said concerning the *Godhead*, that *God is Three and One*," called "*Numerations*, and *Lights*."[15] As we saw in the last chapter, Monis goes on to quote from memory what he mistakenly thinks is from this book: "*They are three Lights, an* ANCIENT LIGHT, *a* PURE LIGHT, *and a* MOST PURE LIGHT, *nevertheless all these are only* ONE GOD."[16] We have already treated the actual provenance of this statement, and there is no need to repeat it here. What is important in the present context is to note that Stiles repeats the identical mistake in almost the exact same language. As with the *Zohar* passage, here too Stiles fails to refer to his source; but here too it is perfectly sensible to conclude that Stiles was drawing from Monis's discourse.

At a later point in his own *Discourse on Saving Knowledge*, within which Stiles echoes Monis's previously discussed understanding of the Jewish *Ruach ha-Kodesh* as synonymous with the Christian Holy Ghost, Stiles states, "Whoever consults *Selden, Croijus, Le Clerc, Basnage, Monis, Pool*, among the christians, may be satisfied that the Hebrew cabbala holds forth a trinity in the glorious JEHOVAH."[17] Here Stiles explicitly lists Monis among Christian authors on Jewish subjects. Yet his earlier epithets in his catalog of the history of Jewish thought and in his literary diary, invoking "Rabbi Judah Monis," do not seem to be mere embellishment. Rather, Stiles sees Monis as a truly authoritative "Rabbi" *and* as a true Christian author. For Stiles, Monis represents a new paradigm as a veritable bridge between the old and the new. In the terminology of his notebooks and oration, Monis is a representative of the Mosaic Wisdom in the academies of Babylon, delivering that knowledge to Ezra who can reformulate it and disseminate it in the institutions of a new Jerusalem.

Monis, however, was not the final word for Stiles. In fact, his influence seems to have piqued Stiles's interest in this ancient Wisdom; but as a diligent student, Stiles was interested in exploring in greater depth. Stiles wanted to study the texts that Monis had referred to, and to know for himself. Already in 1768, before referencing Monis, Stiles had written of his own interests in learning the Hebrew language for the purpose of reading the Bible. In addition, he writes, "There is also another species of Writing which I could wish to examin with learned attention, I mean, the *Cabbala*. The *Zohar* I imagine contains the scattered Ruins of noble Truths revealed to antient Ages; & may yet derive to us glorious Lights."[18] Whether Stiles was familiar with Monis's writings at that earlier point is unclear. What is clear is that Stiles had already been acquiring the tools, and that by 1769 he had been prompted by the likes of Monis to explore specific texts. Among these were the two foundational sources cited by Monis and copied from him by Stiles, namely, the *Zohar* and *Sefer Yetzirah*.

Benjamin Franklin and the Sulzbach *Zohar*

On December 27, 1769, about eight months after having recorded his reading of Monis's baptismal discourses, Stiles wrote a letter of request to Benjamin Franklin, who was then living in London as a colonial representative. Within that letter, Stiles asked Franklin to acquire for him a number of esoteric texts that were presumably not yet available in the New World. Perhaps unsurprisingly in light of his early show of interest, Stiles listed among these: "Zohar. With the Latin translation if it be had: else in Hebrew alone."[19] A follow-up letter of precisely nine months later, dated September 27, 1770, reveals that Stiles had seen mention of the *Zohar* and its discussion of God's governing Lights in a list of authors similar to that in his *Discourse on Saving Knowledge* mentioning Monis, such as Selden, More, Croijus, and Cudworth. Stiles was intrigued by the theosophy of the *Zohar* as presented by these authors, as well as its possible concordance with Christianity; now he wanted to study it in the original, unfiltered. The seeds were thus sewn for what was perhaps the earliest recorded serious interest in unmediated Zoharic theosophical study on the North American continent.

Within the same follow-up letter to Franklin, Stiles conjectured concerning the *Zohar*: "We in the Xtian [i.e., Christian] ages have more ample conceptions of the religion for man, than the antients—they had the veil drawn aside and looking into the invisible State—took a more glorious prospect of the Œconomy of, and dominion of Angels, &c. in, the Intellectual World, than we."[20] By "the antients" Stiles purportedly meant the wisdom of Kabbalah as found in the *Zohar*, and his intuition was that modern Christianity better focused on the human condition. By "Œconomy" he meant not only the resources of, but also the providence and government of "the Intellectual World," by which he meant the divine realm. Here, it seems his intuition was that Zoharic Kabbalah offered better theosophical insight than contemporary Christianity. He was now interested in getting down to the nuts and bolts and in studying Kabbalah directly from the *Zohar* in order to forge a synthesis. Stiles was interested in a text-based fusion between the "more ample" Christian concept of religion for man and the unobstructed view of Kabbalah into the Œconomy of the divine realm, which he hoped would carry over in a new fashion into the seminaries of the New World.

Yet unfortunately for Stiles, his desire for a sound synthesis as founded on text-based study ran into obstacles. Franklin was seemingly unable to immediately fulfill Stiles's wish for Zoharic procurement, and Stiles would not receive an original copy of the *Zohar* until years later. In the same follow-up letter from nine months after the initial request, in a rather frustrated, impudent tone, Stiles writes, "I am surprised that you should fail. The Amsterdam Jews have an edition of the Zohar in quarto."[21] In a letter to Franklin the following day, dated September 28, 1770, which is indexed as "copy two," Stiles writes in a completely different tone, "I am sorry to have given you so much trouble." He later signs off, "With the greatest Respect, I am Dear Sir Your most obliged Friend and very humble Servant."[22] From this it appears that Stiles may have slept on his original, somewhat impudent letter and may never have sent it. Whatever the case may be, one thing is clear: Franklin was unable to obtain a copy of the *Zohar* for Stiles, and Stiles would simply have to wait.

Regardless of Franklin's initial failure to procure the *Zohar* for Stiles, the latter's interest did not wane and he seems to have adamantly persisted. Two years later, he finally received his own copy of the *Zohar*. In his diary entry of October 29, 1772, Stiles reports that he "received from London the Zohar, a Hebrew folio volume of 800 or 770 pages, Sultzbac Edition 1684, and published at Nuremberg."[23] While sitting in Newport, Rhode Island, Stiles could now study kabbalistic lore, not filtered through the likes of Monis but straight from the source. Whether Franklin was the one to procure this Sulzbach edition of the *Zohar* for Stiles is unclear, but it does seem to be the first recorded copy to have reached the American shores.

The fact that Stiles ended up with a 1684 Sulzbach edition of the *Zohar* is somewhat significant because this, the fourth ever printed edition of the *Zohar*, was the first that involved a cooperative effort between Catholics, Jews, and Protestants. As Boaz Huss has noted, this edition of the *Zohar* was the product of a "unique collaboration between Christian Kabbalists from different denominations, Jewish Kabbalists, and Jewish and Christian printers who operated in the court of Prince Christian August in the late 17th century."[24] The patron named was a Catholic prince, and included on the Jewish side were printers Moshe Bloch, Menahem Man ben Yitzhak, Abraham bar Issachar Gershoni of Prague, and Rabbi Moshe ben Yoseph Hausen.

In terms of the present context, the Protestant theologians involved in the Sulzbach *Zohar* are perhaps the most significant. These were no ordinary theologians; instead, they were the very same cohort that directly informed the Kabbalah of George Keith. In fact, at the collaborative project's helm stood Keith's friend, Christian Knorr von Rosenroth. As we have seen, Knorr was also the compiler and editor of the famed *Kabbala Denudata*, the second volume of which was uncoincidentally printed in 1684, the very same year as the *Zohar*. Another key figure was Keith's direct teacher in kabbalistic matters, Francis Mercury van Helmont.[25] Thus, in a certain manner, by delving into the Sulzbach edition of the *Zohar*, Stiles was arriving at the same point of departure for his Christian Kabbalah as that of George Keith. And in many ways, the project of Keith's mentors that produced the edition of the *Zohar* that finally reached Stiles paralleled Stiles's own projects of collaboration and Christian refashioning. As with its Protestant instigators' influences on Keith, it may very well have influenced Stiles through its Protestant-Jewish hybrid tenor.

It is important to note that the Protestants at the helm of the project also had similar sensibilities to those of Stiles himself. In fact, in line with Stiles's notion of the theosophically more adept ancients of the *Zohar*, as quoted above from Stiles's letter to Benjamin Franklin, Knorr von Rosenroth writes, "It immediately occurred to me that I should hunt out that same ancient philosophy which flourished at the time of Christ and the Apostles and which appears to have flowed from the stream of the sacred oracles."[26] He goes on to explain, "As I was about to examine those ancient opinions about God and other spiritual and theological matters, I fell upon this most ancient book of the Jews, which is called the Sohar, or Book of Splendor."[27] It is this that purportedly led Knorr to a deep study of the *Zohar* and its eventual publication in Sulzbach in 1684.

As Alison Coudert has noted, the Sulzbach kabbalists had a unique tendency to combine "the Renaissance *prisca theologia* tradition with the radical Protestant appeal for a return to simplified apostolic Jewish-Christianity."[28] Stiles falls in that same line of Protestant-appropriated *prisca theologia*, as evidenced by his mention in the 1770 letter to Franklin that the "Sabians, Persians, Indians are three distinct ramifications from antique original lights."[29] Prisca theologia was a popular Renaissance and early modern notion that a singular "ancient theology" of a pristine revealed truth can be found, in various forms, in numerous antique systems of thought. Despite the variety of the prisca theologia tradition, for Stiles, as for the Sulzbach kabbalists, the *Zohar* seems to be the most clear in its discussion of what he calls "the lights respecting the Œconomy or distributive government and dominion of the world of eternal light, the grand monarchical representative of the Universe."[30] Thus, as for Knorr von Rosenroth and his cohort, for Stiles a good Protestant apostolic Jewish-Christianity requires a deep study of kabbalistic theosophy as filtered through the *Zohar*. Stiles now had his own copy of the *Zohar* in order to carry out such a study.

Stiles's Personal Edition of the *Zohar*

What we know about Stiles's specific copy of the Sulzbach edition of the *Zohar* comes first and foremost from his journal entry of October 29, 1772. Interestingly, some of the most important and informative parts have been left out of the 1901 published edition of his diary, compiled and published by his twentieth-century chronicler Franklin Bowditch Dexter. In the original manuscript, Stiles lists the detailed contents of the book. This includes a specified mention of *"Siphra de Zeniutha, Haidra rabba,* & *Haidra Suta."*[31] It also includes a mention of "mystic secret spiritual Traditions concerning *God—the persons in the Divinity—divine names—the four Worlds or Universe—the soul & its Ascents—good & evil Angels—the MESSIAH—Man—Paradise—Hell—various state [sic] of the soul after Death—Virtues."*[32]

While all of these indeed appear on the Latin title page of the Sulzbach edition along with other topics, the fact that they are first mentioned in that edition and then further singled out by Stiles is somewhat significant. This is because, as we have seen, they stand at the core of the discourses of the previous protagonists discussed. These include George Keith, Cotton Mather, and Judah Monis, who, as we have seen, emphasized notions such as God, divine persons, divine names, and the four Worlds, and who also brought to the fore the *Sifra di-Tzniuta* and the *Idrot* of the *Zohar*. Within Stiles's diary, it is perhaps worth pointing out that he especially emphasizes the idea of *"the MESSIAH,"* which, while mentioned on the printed Latin title page, is not capitalized there.

In addition to gleaning such descriptions from Stiles's diary entry, which point to a specific direction for Protestant Kabbalah as begun by the Sulzbach kabbalists and as leading through George Keith, Cotton Mather, Judah Monis, and finally Ezra Stiles, we also learn more about Stiles's specific copy of the *Zohar*. Stiles writes, "Dr. Jonathan Gill Baptist Minister in London owned the volume in 1724; in a Note in his Hand Writing he says—'another Book called *Tekunim*, out of which *much of the Zohar* was gathered.'"[33] John Gill was a famed Calvinist Baptist who preached in London from 1720 to 1771. His six-volume nonconformist *Exposition of the Old Testament*, published in London from 1748 to 1763, was indeed heavily influenced by the *Zohar*, and his Sulzbach copy, which eventually reached Stiles, may have been the primary source for his exposition. Moreover, Franklin, who was indeed often in London during that time and was there when Stiles wrote to him requesting a copy of the *Zohar*, may have been the one to eventually procure Gill's volume for Stiles. Whatever the case may be, the copy's English life, prior to reaching Stiles on the American shores, is not well documented.

In terms of the volume's American life, two other documents besides Stiles's literary diary prove informative. One of these is an entry in the March 1918 *Proceedings of the Massachusetts Historical Society* by the early twentieth-century Harvard scholar George Foot Moore, entitled "Ezra Stiles' Studies in the Cabbala."[34] Within that entry, Moore notes that he chanced upon Stiles's copy of the *Zohar* at Harvard Library and was able to determine that its provenance was the library of John Gill.[35] This, of course, accords with Stiles's full diary entry as it appears in its original; but it seems that Moore had read only Dexter's redaction of the diary and had not seen the manuscript.

The other informative document is an unpublished letter by the same Moore, written to Dexter and dated April 3, 1918.[36] In that letter Moore mentions his account to the Massachusetts Historical Society of a month earlier, but he interestingly adds, regarding Stiles, "His interest in the Cabala ... antedated by some years this period of study; he had been writing about it also to Tutor Whittlesey and others, and I have wondered whether he possessed at any time Knorr von Rosenroth, *Kabbala Denudata*, which was and is the most practicable approach for a Christian scholar to the subject."[37] Moore's reference to "Tutor Whittlesey and others" refers to Chauncey Whittelsey of New Haven, and perhaps also Francis Alison of Philadelphia, who were two esteemed American ministers to whom Stiles purportedly wrote letters in 1769 discussing "the Trinity of the *Zohar*."[38] Unfortunately, these two letters do not exist in the Stiles Papers at Yale and they have not, as of yet, turned up in other archives around the country. In terms of the *Kabbala Denudata* of Knorr von Rosenroth, no evidence exists that Stiles had access; but Moore's sensibilities seem to have been correct. As shown above, Stiles's Protestant kabbalistic thought was certainly in line with that of Knorr and the Sulzbach kabbalists, well before he received and studied his Sulzbach edition of the *Zohar*.

From Stiles's diary, and from Moore's comments, we thus know a little about the provenance of the physical book itself. As for Stiles's engagement with the text of the *Zohar* itself, Moore notes:

A cursory inspection of the volume shows that Stiles had really been over, if not through, its formidable bulk. In all parts of it he had underlined places which from some reason interested him, and there are many marginal notes in his handwriting, indicating the contents of the passages thus signalized. . . . Occasionally there are longer notes, and in one or two instances translations or summaries.[39]

Stiles also apparently penned an index to his own notes on one of the flyleaves of the volume, as well as a catalog of the names of rabbis found throughout. According to Moore's description, this volume is a veritable gold mine for understanding Zoharic studies as first promulgated by English Baptism and then carried into and further developed by the American Protestant context.

Yet unfortunately, the Gill-Stiles copy of the *Zohar* is nowhere to be found. I have visited Harvard's libraries and have gone through all of their editions of the *Zohar*, including their one Sulzbach edition. I have consulted extensively with their librarians and with their archivists. I have reached out to other libraries and librarians across the globe. I have corresponded extensively with the Stiles archivist at Yale. Notwithstanding, Stiles's personal copy of the *Zohar*, with all of his plentiful annotations, is as of yet nowhere to be found. Its traces seem to have been lost with George Foot Moore over a hundred years ago.

Comparative Mysticisms with Rabbi Moses bar David

Shortly after receiving his copy of the *Zohar*, Stiles began a daily regimen of *Zohar* reading that would last for years. On November 9, 1772, just eleven days after first cracking open his volume, he reports having studied Hebrew and *Zohar* in the morning, and then having visited a learned Jewish rabbi who was traveling through town, named Moses bar David, i.e., Moses the son of David, whom Stiles describes as "an Ashcanazin of little Poland, of the holy synagogue at Apta."[40] According to Stiles, this rabbi was fifty-two years old, was well traveled, was learned in both of the Talmuds and in the *Zohar*, and was "well acquainted with the Rabbins of the Middle Ages as Maimonides, Jarchi, the Kimchis, &c."[41] He was a self-professed *Gaon*, or wise scholar, and he came bearing a letter of testimony from the rabbi of the Portuguese Synagogue in

London. Beyond what is reported by Stiles, nothing is known about this seemingly erudite figure.

On that same November 9, Rabbi Moses called upon Stiles for an afternoon visit. At that time, Stiles reports:

> I showed him the Zohar, with which he was much delighted, speaking with Raptures of the sublimity & mysteries of its contents; he told me if I could comprehend that Book I should be a master of the Jewish Learning & of the greatest philosophy in the World. He explained several passages in it respecting the *holy name*, and the *ten Saphirots*.[42]

At this juncture, Stiles has finally brought his study of the *Zohar* from secondary sources the likes of Monis, to solitary study of the actual text, to deliberation on the text here with a Jewish rabbi. In an astonishing turn of events, kabbalistic study brings a prominent early American Congregational minister into direct educational discussion with an official, learned representative of the Jewish community. To be sure, Stiles had already met with a certain Rabbi Moses Malki of Tzfat in December 1759, but this was prior to his having learned Hebrew and well before he had acquired any kabbalistic books. There is also no reference to any kabbalistic textual discussion with Malki within any of Stiles's records.[43] Here, by contrast, the *Zohar* stands at the center of discussion. What is more, Rabbi Moses bar David offers Stiles full legitimization for his sentiment that the *Zohar* is a great repository of Jewish learning and sublime philosophy.

In an extraordinary passage that is peculiarly absent from Dexter's 1901 printed version of the literary diary, Stiles continues writing of his Zoharic discussion with Rabbi Moses bar David:

> Of the *Saphirots* he spake with eyes turned up heavenward & with Fervor. He said R. Moses Ben Maimon had written upon *nine* of the *Gilgalim* or circles, but not on the *tenth*, which he left as too deep and mysterious. He said the ten גלגלים were *circles* upon which I shewed him the circles of the celestial Hierarchy of Dionysius Areopagite . . . and asked him whether they were the same as the 9 circles upon which Maimonides wrote? These circles denoting angelic orders around the Throne, or created Intelligences, they might be written upon & fully described; but the glorious

יהוה enthroned in the central Light was mysterious & incomprehensible & rather to be silently contemplated with humble Reverence, than to be badly described by a mortal pen. Whether this was the reason that Maimonides was deterred from writing on the Tenth? He doubted Dionysius' Names of the orders—he supposed the denoted circles of Beings, & the Incomprehensibility of the Xth deterred R. Moses.[44]

In a novel move of comparative mysticisms, Stiles here uses the late fifth- or early sixth-century Christian Neoplatonist Dionysius the Areopagite in order to discourse with the rabbi concerning the holy *sephirot*. Here he is referring to a diagram of concentric circles that he had sketched, misdated to July 14, 1792, which hierarchically radiates outward, with the Tetragrammaton in the center, Seraphim, Cherubim, and Thrones progressively extending outward, a further hierarchical triad of Powers, Dominions, and Authorities, and a final triad at the bottom of the overall hierarchy, of First Ones, Archangels, and Angels.[45] This is indeed the hierarchical schema of nine orders of angels surrounding the ineffable God as outlined by Dionysius the Areopagite, which Stiles is explicitly using here to make sense of the kabbalistic system of the ten *sefirot*.

In his conversation with the rabbi, Stiles is using what Yossi Chajes, borrowing from Christoph Lüthy, calls an "epistemic image," by which Chajes means a depiction created specifically to replace or to accompany linguistic explanations.[46] Here a simple diagram allows Stiles to dialogue concerning abstract concepts. Relatedly, it allows him and the rabbi to perceive the imperceptible, turning the traditionally perceived notion of a favored verbal over visual revelation in Judaism on its head.[47] While silent contemplation is better than bad description "by a mortal pen," Dionysian-inflected apophatism could still be discussed, and be compared to its Maimonidean form, through the medium of the epistemic image.

Stiles had received a copy of the works of Dionysius from London in April 1772, and in a rather unusual turn for a Protestant divine, Dionysius would eventually become one of his favorite authors.[48] In fact, in a letter of 1775 to the famed English astronomer Thomas Wright, Stiles would state, in the context of Trinitarianism as found within the *Zohar*, "I am inclined to think the works of Dionysius the Areop' far more genuine than seems to be allowed by the Protestant learned."[49] Stiles seems

to be responding to Martin Luther's famed denunciation of "that Dionysius whoever he was," who "Platonizes more than he Christianizes," as
well as John Calvin's condemnation of Dionysius's "monkish trifles" and
"wicked speculations."[50] Stiles has a rather opposite approach, involving
a more perennialist type of appreciation that crosses otherwise strict
religious boundaries. This leads him to state, on November 23, 1772:
"R. Moses spent the rest of the afternoon in my study, explaining the
Zohar to me," directly continuing: "This foremorn I spent reading Dionysius Areopagite whom I find to have the same sublime mysteries as
the Zohar." The thought of Dionysius the Areopagite gives Stiles a point
of entry to deeper discussions with the rabbi, and it allows him to put
Christian Trinitarianism into dialogue with Jewish mysticism.

What is perhaps most stunning about Stiles's account of his Dionysian Zoharic discussion with Rabbi Moses bar David, however, is the
Maimonidean inflection of the rabbi's kabbalistic explanation. In invoking "Moses Ben Maimon . . . upon *nine* of the *Gilgalim* or circles, but not
on the *tenth*," he is referring both to Maimonides's *Hilkhot Yesodei ha-
Torah* and to his *Guide of the Perplexed*. The former work states that "the
spheres are called heavens, firmament, celestial abode, and the celestial
plains, and there are nine spheres."[51] It then proceeds to name these nine
according to the designation of their heavenly bodies. The *Guide*, by
contrast, discusses these nine celestial spheres in light of the Aristotelian
idea of separate intellects. There Maimonides states:

> With regard to the opinion of the later philosophers that there are ten
> separate intellects, it may be explained by the fact that they counted the
> globes in which there are stars as well as the all-encompassing sphere,
> although in some of these globes there are several spheres. The globes
> are nine according to their reckoning; namely, the one that encompasses
> the universe, the sphere of the fixed stars, and the spheres of the seven
> planets. The tenth intellect is the Active Intellect, whose existence is indi-
> cated by the facts that our intellects pass from potentiality to actuality and
> that the forms of the existents that are subject to generation and corrup-
> tion are actualized after they have been in their matter only in potentia.[52]

The later philosophers mentioned here are al-Farabi and Avicenna,
and the idea here is of a series of ten emanating separate intellects,

nine of which are linked to their own celestial spheres, which they move. The tenth of these is the Active Intellect, which emanates directly from the Unmoved Mover, or God, and which does not have its own separate sphere but brings into actuality all of existence.

While there is nothing particularly kabbalistic about the Maimonidean discourse on the spheres, Rabbi Moses bar David follows a fairly long line of tradition in converting Maimonides into a kabbalist.[53] For him there are ten spheres in Maimonidean thought, which parallel the ten *sefirot* of the *Zohar* and other kabbalistic sources. Maimonides discusses only nine because the tenth is entirely unknowable, in the realm of the Unmoved Mover. Farabian and Avicennan Platonism ultimately lend Maimonides's intellectualized spheres to a sefirotic reading, and Maimonidean apophatism in relation to the Unmoved Mover ultimately lends Maimonides himself over to a Dionysian reading. This rather ecumenical picture comes full circle, so to speak, in the dialogue between the rabbi from Apta and the colonial Congregational minister, which was perhaps the earliest dialogue of its kind upon the North American continent.

Sefer Yetzirah and Maimonidean *Hevruta*

Rabbi Moses bar David of Apta was not only a noteworthy study partner for Stiles but also an important conduit for other significant kabbalistic texts, beyond the *Zohar*. On November 10 Rabbi Moses had given Stiles a copy of Joseph Gikatilla's *Sha'arei Orah* in order to help him better understand the *Zohar* and the names of the *sefirot*, and the day before, Stiles had asked the rabbi if the author of the *Zohar* had obtained such sublime matters from his master, Rabbi Akiba. Moses bar David answered in the affirmative. As a follow-up, a week later Stiles reports:

Rabbi Moses lent me a small volume called ספר שערי ציון which contained ספר יצירה supposed to have been written by the Patriarch Abraham; the present copy was composed by R. Akiba, i.e. as I suppose R. Akiba gave an Extract or summary of the Book of Abraham. It is contained in ten pages. I read it thro' immediately. It is in good Hebrew. The subject is, the Mysteries of the Godhead & the Ten Saphirots, & the several ways in which Deity acts himself forth in the Creation of the Universe: & some things of an *astronomical* & *Philosophic* kind respecting the Elements & Stellary Spheres—with mystic numbers & Letters of the Alphabet—& the Names of God. I spent the Evening with the Rabbi. I asked him whether the order of the Alphabet was the same in Abrahams as Akibas Day? He said yes. I asked, but he did not give any clear Illustration of the sublimities of the Saphirot &c.[54]

In this account of their November 16 meeting, which is just as remarkable as the account of the week before, we get a clear reporting of Stiles's first exposure to the primary text of *Sefer Yetzirah*, which had piqued his interest at least three years earlier with his reading of Monis. Yet here, in contradistinction to his exposure to the text of the *Zohar*, it is by way of a living Jewish rabbi who presents him with the book, who presumably is present during Stiles's reading of it, and who immediately acts as a live interlocutor regarding its contents. In the tradition of *hevruta*, or classical rabbinic partner study, Jewish textual learning had reached North America.

On December 14, 1772, Rabbi Moses set sail for the West Indies, thereby putting a permanent end to his learning sessions with Stiles.[55] Four weeks later, on January 11, 1773, Stiles revisited *Sefer Yetzirah* and provided what seems to be his own interpretation, perhaps informed or augmented by his erstwhile conversations with Rabbi Moses. There he comments on the first verse of *Sefer Yetzirah*, which according to the vowel ascription of his source *Sha'arei Tzion*, states that God created the world by three related things: a "book" (*b'sefer*), a "scribe" (*b'sofer*), and what Stiles calls a "thing written" (*b'sipur*). Stiles writes:

This seems at first view unintelligible. It is difficult to rend the primitive meaning of ספר. It is number, numeration, narration, &c. A scribe was not only a writer but Interpreter. The Book of Life is ספר חיים. The Ten Descriptions of God are called The Ten Saphirots. Numeration seems to make a part of the primary meaning. The Cabbalistic science is founded in certain mysterious Arrangements & Numerations of the 22 Letters, correspondent to the inferior Arrangments of the celestial Hierarchies. In Omniscience the whole is laid out. The omniscient mind is ספר, the great designer of all Things or God himself distinguished under this Character is סופר, and the plan or Thing designed & markt out is סיפור.[56]

Many of these ideas, including a connection of the term *sefer* with "number, numeration, narration," with "The Ten Saphirots," and with "mysterious Arrangements & Numerations of the 22 Letters," are commonplace within commentaries on *Sefer Yetzirah*, and it is virtually impossible to ascertain from where it is that Stiles may have been drawing these concepts. This is especially so given the oral nature of his exchanges with Moses bar David.

Nevertheless, the final sentence of the above quote, coupled with a brief note on the seal of a letter received by Stiles on May 1, 1772, from Monis's successor, Hebrew professor Stephen Sewell of Harvard, may give an indication as to the provenance of his ideas. There, on the edge of the envelope, is scribbled, "*Sefer Yetzirah* with the commentary of R. Moshe Botarel and the Ravad and the Rosh."[57] It seems that in addition to the version of *Sefer Yetzirah* in *Sha'arei Tzion*, Stiles may have had access to another copy with commentary. Or he may have discussed these commentaries with someone such as Moses bar David, who either jotted them down for him or dictated to him while he made note of them on the envelope, which was perhaps the closest piece of paper at hand. If this is so, then the statement of the late fourteenth- and early fifteenth-century Botarel, seemingly spuriously attributed to a certain "Rav Zakeni," may shed light: "*Sefer, sofer,* and *sipur* are 'the intellect,' 'the intellectually cognizing subject,' and 'the intellectually cognized object.'"[58] This seems to correspond to Stiles's "omniscient mind," "great designer of all things," and "Thing designed."

Such a reading of the three related things, or Books, also accords with Rabbi Moses bar David's propensity for a kabbalistic reading of Maimonides, though here the order is reversed: *Sefer Yetzirah*, seen as a kabbalistic text, is being read here through a Maimonidean lens. Chapter 68 of the first part of the *Guide* states regarding God "that He is the intellect as well as the intellectually cognizing subject and the intellectually cognized object, and that those three notions form in Him, may He be exalted, one single notion in which there is no multiplicity."[59] As the only perfect existent, God alone is a contained, active triad of subject, object, and verb, in that He intellectualizes Himself and is also the entire process of intellectualization.[60] By transferring this to the realm of *Sefer Yetzirah*, the idea invoked by Stiles, of the *sefer* as the "Book of Life," takes on a whole new philosophical meaning as related to the divine.

On *Sefer Yetzirah* as a Cypher of Formation

In continuation of the diary entry from January 11, 1773, Stiles offers an alternative interpretation of the notion of the "Book" as based on the homonymous character of the terms *sefer* and *cypher*. Particularly in regard to the third and final *sipur*, or "thing written" from *Sefer Yetzirah*, he seeks to introduce cryptography through conflation, writing:

> Agreeably the writing in a Book or character or cypher there is called
> סיפור *Siphur* from whence I suppose *Cypher*. These cyphers originally re-
> spected chiefly numerations: and when the Arabians bro't their literature
> into Europe, & their Arithmetic particularly, their numeral letters, like
> antient Cyphers, contained many hidden mysteries in numbers, so in Al-
> gebra & abra cadabra: now the antient characters denoting numerations,
> being unknown passed by the name of Cyphers—& the Art of combining
> them was *cyphering*—and sometimes o or nothing is a Cypher because
> what is unknown is nothing. Cyphers are retained on Rings &c. Thus the
> Word סיופר or cypher has sustained many metaphorical changes. But
> the nearer we run it back to the Original, we shall find it carrying the idea
> of Numeration.[61]

Up until here, Stiles follows a fairly accurate etymological tracing as based on the Arabic term *al-Ṣifr*, which, according to Arabist and science historian Juan Vernet, means "zero" or more precisely "void."[62] Interesting in this regard is Stiles's juxtaposition of "Algebra," the well-known study of mathematical symbols and equations, with "abra cadabra," the more arcane designation, which, into Stiles's time and beyond, was used for amulets and incantations.[63] Especially telling is the separation of the now popular magic formula by Stiles into two words, consistent with the conjecture that the term derives from the Aramaic formulation *evra k'davra*, i.e., "I will create like the word." This is also consistent with the context of *Sefer Yetzirah* as a book of formation out of the Hebrew letters, understood by some to actually be a grimoire. Whatever the case may be, by bringing algebra together with incantational magic, Stiles is bringing number systems together with letter systems. What connects the two is the art of combination through the method of cyphering.

Stiles is correct that from the Arabic *al-Ṣifr* as related to combinatorial equations hearkening back to zero, the term made its way into Medieval Latin as *cifra* and eventually came to mean any digit. As Juan Vernet has noted regarding the Arabic root, "Its doublet *s-f-r* signifies the opposite," leading to "the conceptual opposition between the two roots 'empty place' as against 'written place.'"[64] Vernet continues, "In the latter sense, the Hebrew *sefer* and Persian *sifr*, etc. 'book,' are encountered."[65] Thus, Stiles's reading is strikingly accurate. By understanding *sipur* as a "thing written" in relation to *sefer*, and as the source of *cypher* as numeration out of zero, Stiles is actually offering a genuine philological spin on *Sefer Yetzirah*.

From a sound philological base that is fitting for the future president of Yale, Stiles continues with his exposition concerning *sipur* as *cypher*:

> And it was antiently the usage to describe things by Numbers—sometimes by giving the number of the initial letter of a sentence or number of words descriptive of a matter; thus God is described by the number 45 &c. The Arrangment & ordinance of the universe is such, that in a Description of it on paper or in a Book the several orders of Being spiritual & bodily may be denoted by Letters or Numbers, as in a Plan of a city the public Building may be noted by Letters or figures referring to Descriptions in the margins. Thus the plan of the invisible & visible universe was delineated to the Patriarchs (who certainly knew the Pythagorian or Newtonian Systems for Instance) and by this they were enabled to form an idea of the creation, which they beheld in the סיפור cypher or written book.[66]

Not only does Stiles invoke Pythagoras and Newton here, he also calls forth the number 45, or *Mah* (*mem-heh*) according to gematria, in reference to God. As we have seen, this was discussed at length by Monis as calculated from one of the spelled-out versions of the Tetragrammaton, and in relation to Man, or *Adam*, as a designation for God.[67] Stiles, as noted, had certainly read Monis and may very well have been imbibing from him.

But the name of 45 is also discussed in a scribbled note on the very same envelope of the letter sent to Stiles from Stephen Sewell examined above, which mentions the commentary on *Sefer Yetzirah* of Moshe Botarel. In a passage purportedly translated from the *Zohar*, the note says, "The letters of the holy name יוד הא ואו הא [i.e., *yod heh vav heh* as spelled out] = 45 is called אדם [i.e., *Adam*] = 45. And אתפשט [i.e., *etpashet*, "I will spread out"]—his light to much Light—and this is the reckon for אדם [i.e., *Adam*] 45 = מה [i.e., *Mah*] = 45."[68] In this note, the Tetragrammaton is numerologically equated with the word "man" through the designation of *Mah*, or the name of 45. What is more, that note begins with a code for numerologically deciphering the otherwise alphabetical *cypher* of the Hebrew letters, spelling out the entire Hebrew alphabet.[69] Perhaps this was another carryover from Stiles's discussions with Moses bar David. Or perhaps it is one more piece of a common theme that piqued his interest. Whatever the case may be, there seems to be a connection related to *cyphering*, which led to a diligent yet novel reading of *Sefer Yetzirah* by one of colonial America's leading intellectuals.

Homoeroticism, from Hajim Isaac Karigal to Jesus

Moses bar David was perhaps the most important living rabbi for Stiles's kabbalistic development. He was the very first person with whom Stiles studied the *Zohar* after receiving his own personal copy. He was the one to bring Stiles important kabbalistic texts such as *Sha'arei Orah* and *Sha'arei Tzion*. Finally, it was he who studied *Sefer Yetzirah* with Stiles in a form of classical *hevruta*, from the actual textual version within *Sha'arei Tzion*, thereby bringing Stiles's understanding of the text to a whole new level. His reverberations seem to have been felt even after his departure, and the case could certainly be made that without Stiles's encounters with Moses bar David, Stiles's involvement with Jewish learning, and especially with Kabbalah, would not have reached the depths that it did.

Nevertheless, Rabbi Moses bar David was not Stiles's favorite or even most esteemed rabbinical interlocutor. That position was reserved for the next Jewish scholar in Stiles's life, whom he first encountered in March 1773, Rabbi Hajim Isaac Karigal of Hebron.[70] Writing of him in relation to six other rabbis whom Stiles had met, he remarks, "As Light expelleth Darkness, so far doth R. Karigal surpass and excel all the rest, particularly in the learning of the Talmud and on all points and questions of the Law of the Jews, on all which he discourses with singular ingenuity, a most amiable candor and profound erudition."[71] In another context, Stiles writes that Karigal "daily and without ceasing lifteth up his Eyes unto things on high, and is enlightened with the Dew of Lights from Jehovah, and has been initiated into the Secrets of Understanding & (sublime) Knowledge and perfected in the hidden mystery of the סוד [i.e., *sod*, "secret"] at the mouth of the masters of the Law and by the Tradition of the wise men of all ages."[72] While the first reference could be seen as emphasizing Karigal's expertise in the Talmud and Jewish law, the second categorically rests on kabbalistic notions of mystery, "Secrets of Understanding," and "sublime Knowledge." The Hebrew word employed by Stiles, סוד (*sod*), in fact means "secret" and is a specific epithet denoting Kabbalah. Stiles indeed had the greatest esteem for Karigal, extending beyond rabbinic learning and into the mystical realm.

Part of the mystical allure for Stiles seems to have rested on an exotic, mysterious, blatantly homoerotic appeal, initially prompted by a letter from Karigal.[73] Within that letter, the esteemed rabbi had written to Stiles, "Thy love is engraved in the inmost Thots of my heart that Volumes of Book would not suffice to write a thousandth part of the eternal Love with which I love you."[74] In his diary, Stiles significantly notes that he was surprised by so strong an expression of friendship, and that he had asked Karigal about it when they next met in person. He reports that Karigal remarkably replied that he "wished well to others besides his own Nation, he loved all Mankind,"[75] and that he quoted Leviticus 19:18: "Thou shalt love thy neighbor as thyself." Perhaps Karigal was reaching for a certain type of ecumenicism as based on love. Regardless, Stiles seems to have responded by quickly turning this universal language of love into an erotic exchange.

In fact, in an eventual letter directly reflecting the biblical relationship between David and Jonathan, Stiles would write to Karigal, "And thou my honorable Friend, who hast *been very pleasant unto me, whose Love to me is wonderful passing the Love of Women*, may you come forth at the Time and Stand in thy Lot."[76] In another letter, partially echoing the Psalms, he would write, "I remember with great pleasure thy society and conversation which was more sweet to my taste than Honey, and much more pleasant than the spicy incense and perfume of the High Priest."[77] Perhaps Stiles is responding to Karigal's initial love language in kind, though here the erotic tenor is unmistakable. Given this latter fact, what we have here seems to be a mystical sense of love in union, which blurs the boundaries between religious distinctions, between *eros* and *philia*, and between self and other.

Laura Leibman has written off the homoeroticism expressed here as an extremely hyperbolic expression of conventional letter writing of the 1770s.[78] And it is certainly true that conventions of written salutation have changed, and that such erotic expressions to convey deep friendship were not unusual for the time. Nevertheless, while it may be part of a larger pattern stemming from elite homosociality, the erotic tenor is unmistakable. This is especially the case here, where the precise biblical passages chosen by Stiles speak to a very specific type of love and desire. Moreover, in Stiles's oration of 1781, he lists off the six rabbis with whom he has studied, and only of Karigal does he state that he was "like Joseph of a comely aspect and a beautiful countenance."[79] Others, by contrast, are not portrayed physically but are described as eloquent, great kabbalists and philosophers, and profoundly versed in celestial Wisdom. What is more, throughout the literary diary Stiles incessantly describes Karigal's dress and appearance with a sense of awe.[80] This is unlike any other rabbinic character that he encounters. Given these factors, it does seem that Stiles was homoerotically enthralled, and that part of the "hidden mystery" that Stiles saw within Karigal may have been tied to this exotic, forbidden allure.[81] In a Platonic manner, he was embracing it and using it as a tool for ecstatic ascendance through beauty.

In fact, in relation to homoerotic mystical allure, Stiles writes to Karigal in relation to "the Messiah and the Greatness & Glory of his Kingdom,"[82] commenting:

> Who is this great King of Glory? He is my Beloved and I am his. I will sing a song unto my Beloved. How beautiful art thou, how pleasant for Delights? But where is He to be found whom my soul loveth? Shall wee seek him among the Lillies, among the souls and pure minds in the Garden of Eden? He is mighty and more exalted than the multitude of the Princes of Hosts, & amidst the ten Saphirots he hath reigned from Eternity, and shall reign over all the Sons of the mighty, the Aralim & the Hassmalim and over all the holy Beings; and unto him all the Superior Powers bow down (with one accord) all as one: Amen. But who is this glorious King? He is the Son of Jehovah.[83]

The homoerotic nature of this passage is undeniable, though here it is being directed toward Jesus rather than toward Karigal. And while it clearly draws on language from the Song of Songs, in the Hebrew version of this letter Stiles attributes the language of the first part of the passage to the *Zohar*.[84] What is more, by drawing in "the ten Saphirots" in the latter part of the passage, he is unequivocally tying his sentiments to Kabbalah. The "Son of Jehovah" is Stiles's "Beloved" and is "pleasant for Delights," not as superadded to his mystical stance above the Superior Powers but in relation to it.

The case could certainly be made that Stiles held Karigal in a correlative, albeit greatly contracted esteem. As an exotic Jew coming from the Holy Land with ancient forms of Wisdom to share, Karigal was perceived in a veritably messianic light. What is more, the love that Karigal advocated to Stiles for all of mankind, and his employment of the biblical "Thou shalt love thy neighbor as thyself" in order to exemplify that advocacy, placed Karigal within the realm of Jesus's second great command.[85] The case could also be made that here Stiles felt comfortable using such love language in his correspondence with Karigal due to his own sentiments toward his friend. Perhaps this was his way of relaying his sentiments toward Jesus, and thus maybe persuading his loving friend not only of Jesus's kabbalistic might but also of his ecstatic mystical love.

On the Mysteries of the Divine Names

Notwithstanding the love language, as a Jewish emissary Karigal's official role was still first and foremost as a scholar, and his encounters with Stiles were certainly under the premise of deep academic exchange.[86] Theoretically at least, the affective takes a back seat to the intellective. Regardless, the rabbi's great erudition on matters of esotericism does not always shine through his reported exchanges with Stiles. One stark case in point is a discussion about *Sefer Yetzirah* five months after Stiles's last meeting with Moses bar David and a little under two months after his first encounter with Karigal. Stiles reports that Karigal had visited him that April evening with the *chazzan* of the synagogue, Isaac Touro, and Karigal had mentioned that the biblical Moses was the first individual to know the Tetragrammaton.[87] Stiles was naturally intrigued and engaged.

In his diary he explains his response to Karigal, which seems to have been based on his studies in *Sefer Yetzirah* with and since Moses bar David:

> I said the Sapher hajitzirah shewed that Abraham had a full manifestation of the mysteries of the Godhead, as amply as Moses had before he went into the Mount—and indeed I question whether any thing respecting the character of God has been revealed in suceeding Ages, which was not opened to Abraham who saw Christs day &c.—& I added, if Abraham knew the Thing he knew the import of the Word Jehovah, tho' he might not know that God had chosen to be called by that Name.[88]

Stiles is entering into Karigal's own territory by referring to the markedly Jewish *Sefer Yetzirah* and by directly engaging Karigal in the rabbinic form of argumentation known as *pilpul*, or casuistic textual analysis. Karigal takes the bait and explains that Abraham knew the character but not the proper name of God. To this Stiles replies:

> God assumed a name variously indicating the character he acted under for the Time being—thus a man is man at all times, but when he speaks as an Ambassador, he calls himself & is known as an Ambassador, when he speaks as a Soverign he is a King, as &c when God describes his Supremacy he calls himself *Elion*, his Dominion *Adonai*, his Power *El*, his Might or Strength *Gibbur*, the imperial Commander, *Lord of Hosts*—by such names God was known to Adam Enoc Noah Abraham—now what was the peculiar Reason for God's taking & changing to be known by the name Jehovah in the Time of Moses, since literally this name denoting nothing of moral Character, but most simply respected Existence or Being in a threefold regard to time *first present & to come*? If he had took a new Appelation from leading forth Israel, or dividing the red sea, or the wonders of Sinai, we might see the reason & meaning of the change of the name. But what was the new Branch of the divine Character taught by Jehovah?[89]

Here Stiles is extrapolating from *Sefer Yetzirah* and turning the notion of the divine name into an entire philosophical discussion hinging on the moral character of God and the different divine personae expressed throughout the Bible. By discussing names as related to the character that God had "acted under for the Time being," Stiles brings to mind Maimonides's notion of *attributes of action*, by which Maimonides means that even for Moses, God's attributes "are His actions, and . . . that His essence cannot be grasped as it really is."[90] In relation to the divine name, Maimonides specifically states:

> All the names of God, may He be exalted, that are to be found in any of the books derive from actions. There is nothing secret in this matter. The only exception is one name: namely, *Yod He, Vav, He*. This is the name of God, may He be exalted, that has been originated without any derivation, and for this reason it is called the *articulated name*. This means that this name gives a clear unequivocal indication of His essence, may He be exalted.[91]

Whether Stiles was aware of this specific Maimonidean source, it certainly parallels his idea quoted above that the biblical names of God signify actions and that the Tetragrammaton, by contrast, signifies "Existence or Being in a threefold regard to time *first present* & *to come*." Yet Stiles turns the idea on its head, showing, through *Sefer Yetzirah*, that Abraham already had a good grasp of such ideas even if he did not have the specific name.[92] In fact, for Stiles the introduction of the new name provides no new insight into a moral attribute relating to any of God's actions.

Karigal's response is rather meager. He does not cite any sources, nor does he offer any of his own theories or opinions. According to Stiles, "The Rabbi replied that the name was a great mystery—& turned to Exodus & talked much on *Ehjeh asher Ehjeh*—but cast no Light."[93] In this specific instance, Stiles seems to be the one casting light by exhibiting more kabbalistic and philosophical acumen than the rabbi whom he esteems as profoundly erudite above all the others. It remains unclear whether Stiles's knowledge stems from his discussions with Moses bar David, who seems to have been a Maimonidean kabbalist, or from his own studies in *Sefer Yetzirah* and other sources. What is clear is that Stiles outperforms Karigal here, and that the rabbi does not seem to have lived up to his stature in this specific instance.

There are many possible reasons for the discrepancy, though all of them are quite speculative. One possibility is that Stiles did not report the full conversation; though given his detailed reports throughout his literary diaries, this seems highly unlikely. Another possibility is that Karigal was caught off guard. However, by this time he had already met with Stiles several times and had even discussed Zoharic matters with him, so this too seems improbable.[94] Yet another possibility is that Karigal was truly acting as one "initiated into the Secrets of Understanding & (sublime) Knowledge and perfected in the hidden mystery of the סוד,"[95] the *sod*, i.e., the kabbalistic secretive realm, and thus deemed it better to leave questions about the essence of God shrouded in mystery rather than discussing them at length with an American Protestant minister whom he had only recently met. As with forbidden erotic attraction on the ground, such initiations into the supernal realms of thought would be strictly prohibited. Whatever the case may be, the gates of amorous dialogue and Jewish mystical exploration had been opened, in this instance if not for Karigal, then at least for Stiles.

Zoharic Messianism and the Conversion of the Jews

If not in relation to *Sefer Yetzirah* and the divine names, then other instances, hinging on the *Zohar*, would bring fuller participation from Karigal. This is despite the statement from George Alexander Kohut in 1902 that for Stiles, the *Zohar* "continued to form a part of his studies for some time, until the arrival of his friend, Rabbi Carigal when, together with him, he pursued nobler investigations."[96] In point of fact, on July 15, 1773, Stiles relates, "The Rabbi has the Zohar in 3 Vol. 4[to] [i.e., "quarto," the size of the page] printed at Constantinople. It is an elegant & sublime accurate Edition. He brought me the 2[d] vol. i.e. on Exodus."[97] The following day he reports having spent a period of time comparing his version of the *Zohar* with that of Karigal. In this instance, Karigal seems to be quite open to textual sharing and elucidation. Kohut's assertion thus does not pass muster.

In fact, Zoharic exegesis, as related to modern eschatology, was an area of immediate dialogue and would come to grip Stiles throughout his relationship with Karigal. In the report of the very first personal meeting at Stiles's home well before the textual exchange in July, on

March 30, 1773, Stiles recounts concerning Karigal, "He spake of Aly Bey, and shewed me a passage in the *Zohar* which he said predicted that the *Russians should conquer the Turks*. I observed that in the Original it was that *Edom* should conquer the *Ismaelites*—he replied that Edom there denoted a Northern Power, and the Ismaelites those of their Religion."[98] Aly Bey, from a family of the Caucasus region, was the Mamluk ruler of Ottoman Egypt, and Karigal seems to be reading recent history into Zoharic eschatology. The Zoharic passage at hand, while not directly cited, seems to be the following:

> In the future the sons of Ishmael will awaken vigorous battles in the world, and the children of Edom will gather against them, and will awaken a battle with them, one on the sea, one on the land, and one close to Jerusalem. And these will rule over these, and the Holy Land will not be given over to the children of Edom.[99]

By reading this as related to the conquests of Aly Bey, Karigal is paralleling the millennialism of those like Increase Mather, and he is opening himself up to further eschatological discussion with Stiles. The end of times as prophesied by the kabbalistic textual tradition is near, and similar to the ideas of Increase Mather, it involves wars between the Ottoman Turks and Christendom; it also includes the fate of Jerusalem.

Stiles, for his part, fully expresses himself on this matter about four months later. On July 19, 1773, in a long letter to Karigal drafted both in Hebrew and in English, which Stiles entitles *The Hope of Israel*,[100] he writes that:

> The Kingdom of the Messiah on Earth will not be Eternal: but one *Olam* only of 1000 years, and this is called the Victory because all Evil will be then overcome, & there shall be Good & Peace on Earth 1000 years, until the Conflagration of the World, and until the Time of the new Heavens & new Earth.[101]

In an otherwise fairly straightforward Puritan brand of millenarianism, here Stiles presents a twist intended specifically for his Jewish interlocutor. Though not explicitly stated in the English version, in the Hebrew letter "the Victory" mentioned here is called *Netzah* by Stiles, and the entire claim concerning the Kingdom of the Messiah is attributed both to Isaiah and to the *Zohar*.[102] Stiles's reference to the prophet is clearly to Isaiah 65:17: "For behold, I create new heavens and a new earth: and the former shall not be remembered, nor come into mind." Stiles's reference to the *Zohar*, though, is not clear. It could be a reference to the notion of the Messiah son of David as related to the *sefirah* of *Netzah*, which is widespread in the later *Tikkunei Zohar* and the *Ra'ya Mehemna* strata of Zoharic literature.[103] This seems to be the most likely reference, though absent a clear citation or indication, it is hard to tell. It could also be related to the idea of *'Olam* as connected to the *sefirot*,[104] variably possibly signifying "World," "Eternity," or even "That which is Hidden."

Whatever the case may be, what Stiles is doing here is replacing the idea of *Netzah* as "Eternity" ("The Kingdom of the Messiah on Earth will not be Eternal") with *Netzah* as "Victory" ("because all Evil will be then overcome, & there shall be Good & Peace on Earth 1000 years"). Part of that eschatological "Victory" will be the appearance of a new Jerusalem, "which God shall cause to descend out of Heaven and it shall rest on Zion in the new Earth, to receive the Saints there."[105] Unlike for Increase Mather and others, the "Zion" here is the earthly Jerusalem, for as Christopher Grasso has shown, Stiles "never argued that Britain or New England was an elect nation in the sense that Israel was, or that either was a type of Israel."[106] Regardless, Stiles's remarks are a clear reference to the book of Revelation 21:2, which states, "I saw the Holy City, the New Jerusalem, coming down out of heaven from God, prepared as a bride beautifully dressed for her husband." Yet Stiles continues on to state that the saints who inhabit the new Jerusalem "shall come in spiritual Bodies," and that they will be neither "male nor female; for all the children of the Resurrection will be like angels of Light."[107] It is worth pointing out that this is highly reminiscent of the luminous garments espoused by Cotton Mather, and the androgynous spiritual bodies of George Keith. Though no evidence of direct influence exists, a common pattern of a kabbalistically tinged soteriology begins to emerge.

Part of the messianic victory for Stiles will also be a restoration of the Holy Tongue, which is an idea that sets Stiles apart and that partially explains his somewhat mystical obsession with Hebrew. This is seen not only in his own Hebrew learning, in his drafting of Hebrew letters to the likes of Karigal, and in his dabbling in Hebrew numerology and his uses of Hebrew as a *cypher*, as discussed above, but also in his defense of the Hebrew vowel points as ancient and divine, as laid out in a sixteen-page letter to Yale tutor John Lewis.

There Stiles makes the case that *Sefer ha-Bahir*, "written a little before Christ," says that "the points move the letters as the soul moves the body."[108] He further quotes the *Zohar* that "the body are the *Letters* and the spirit the *points*. All these proceed in their processions after the vowel sounds and are made to stand in their stature as a living body."[109] This claim is made in light of the expression from the book of Daniel that "those that are Wise shall shine like the firmament," and it goes on to state, in Stiles's translation, "The phrase *those that are wise shall shine* denotes i.e. may be arbitrarily made to denote *letters* and *points*."[110] Stiles goes on to quote the *Tikkunim* on this passage: "What are *those that are wise*, these are the letters of the law. *Shall shine*, they are the points that shine with the letters as the soul in the body."[111] While Stiles's intent here is to show the antiquity of the Hebrew vowel points, his quotes are quite mystical both in content and in terms of their sources. By their very nature, they point to a greater metaphysical structure.

In fact, toward the conclusion of his eschatological *Hope of Israel*, Stiles writes, "Blessed are the Saints for it will be the Lot of their inheritance to behold the Beauty of the Lord and to contemplate all his Works throughout the immense universe forever & ever ages without End. Then they that *are wise shall shine as the Brightness of the Firmament and as the stars forever & ever.*"[112] The idea of the conjoined resurrection of the spiritual bodies of the saints and the revival of the Hebrew language, coupled with this specific verse from the book of Daniel, which incidentally gives name to the *Zohar*, seems to be no coincidence. Stiles seems to be fostering a spiritually living, redemptive role for Hebrew, which like the spiritual bodies of the saints at the end of times, can eternally behold the Beauty of the Lord.

It is worth noting that Abiel Holmes, Stiles's son-in-law, former student, and first biographer, had a much different sense of Stiles's relationship to Hebrew and to Jewish learning. Holmes writes of Stiles:

> His civilities and catholicism, toward the Jews, are worthy of imitation.
> It is to be feared, that Christians do not, what ought to be done, toward
> the conversion of this devoted people . . . they are often persecuted, or

contemned as unworthy of notice or regard. Such treatment tends to prejudice them against our holy religion, and to establish them in their infidelity. Besides this the study of the Hebrew language hath been too much laid aside, and we have, by that means, been less able to convince the Jews. . . . Such *was* the use which the Doctor made of his Hebrew learning.[113]

The textual evidence, as outlined above, overwhelmingly shows that Stiles's Hebrew learning was much more nuanced than what Holmes suggests. Rather than any focus on conversion, it involved both a true desire to uncover pristine Knowledge and a true belief in the present and future soteriological role of the Holy Tongue, as kabbalistically understood.

Jewish Conversion without Compulsion

The conversion of the Jews, both on the national level and the personal level in relation to Stiles's friend Karigal, is in fact curiously absent from Stiles's overall eschatological plan. It is neither mentioned nor discussed in *The Hope of Israel*, and in a letter to Karigal of December 8, 1773, Stiles writes, "So far as respects a suffering Messiah you will differ from me in sentiments—but as to the future glory of the Messianic Kingdom I presume we shall be happy to agree."[114] While there is a recognition of difference regarding the suffering Messiah, there is no pressure for Karigal to believe in the same historical narrative as Stiles. His focus, rather, is more on agreement in regard to the future than on disagreement in regard to the past, or even in regard to the present.

Perhaps more than anything else, this sets Stiles apart from his predecessors such as Increase Mather and even Judah Monis. Nevertheless, Stiles does make his thoughts concerning the Trinity known to Karigal, partially using Zoharic literature. For example, in his *Hope of Israel*, he states that "there are three Degrees in Jehovah or the self existent Being," and that they are all eternal. He goes on to quote Rabbi Eleazar in the *Zohar* concerning this very idea:

> *The mystery of Elohim is this, there are three Degrees, & every one of these degrees subsisteth by itself, and yet all of them are One, and combined to-*

gether in one, nor can one be separated from the other. And again, *these are three Degrees as they are all interwoven (combined) among themselves, and all are united one with another without Division* as it is written if you suffer me to arise & come to the Father—I have heard what is written in the Scripture I am that I am &c.[115]

While the original Zoharic text comes within the context of Divine Judgment, Divine Mercy, and Divine Righteousness as connected to the variant names YHWH, *Elohim*, and *Adonai*, Stiles is clearly reading it in a Christian Trinitarian sense. This is apparent from his inclusion of the notion that one shall "arise & come to the Father," but his omission of the portion of the passage stating that all of these degrees are watered by and flow from the same river, "and that river is called Mother of the Garden, and is above the Garden."[116] The Zoharic paradigm includes the supernal Mother as well as the supernal Father. While later in the same letter Stiles admits, "I am sensible that Jehovah is expounded by *three*, & by *four*, & by the *ten Saphirots* &c . . . and by the name Father, Mother, Son, Daughter, all which is consistent with the secret of the mystery of God,"[117] here that more nuanced sense is somehow lost on him, unwittingly or not.

In any case, Stiles did seem to want to make Christian Trinitarian readings of the *Zohar* known to his Jewish friend, and while conversion was not his top soteriological priority, it did have a place within his overall thought.[118] Given his own Congregational background, which is in line with the Mathers, and given the earlier kabbalistic influence of Judah Monis, we can reasonably surmise that the topic probably came up in Stiles's multiple personal conversations with Karigal. It is also tacitly apparent in a letter addressed to Karigal, dated May 24, 1773. In that letter Stiles writes, "Mayest thou be Blessed of the Most High God, and of the Messiah who is the Lord Jehovah our Righteousness, and the Redeemer of the preferred of Israel, the Light of the Gentiles, and the Salvation of all people to the ends of the Earth." He goes on, wishing for his friend: "May your Eyes behold the King of Zion in his Beauty."[119] Though Jesus is not explicitly mentioned, he is certainly implied.

Perhaps more important than the implicit references, however, is Stiles's use of the phrase "Redeemer of the preferred of Israel." In the Hebrew version ostensibly sent to Karigal, this last phrase, taken in part from Isaiah 49:6, is rendered as "*Go'el l'netzurei Israel*," which means "Redeemer for the safeguarded of Israel"; but it also seems to be playing off the possibility of being read as "*Go'el l'nitzurei Israel*," "Redeemer for the Christianized of Israel."[120] Like the Mathers, Stiles was interested in the conversion of the Jews. However, the textual evidence does not suggest that he saw this as an integral ingredient of the history of redemption.

Rather, Stiles seems to have felt that the conversion of the Jews should follow the pattern of his own perception of Monis as a Christianized Rabbi. It should be organically *as* Jews, into his version of a more simplified apostolic Jewish-Christianity. Like Monis, those such as Karigal should retain their Hebrew and their learning as connected to the past, and should in fact use those tools to help build a new bridge to the future. Stiles wanted to introduce what he perceived to be pristine kabbalistic thought into an old-new form of Christianity, as based on Renaissance notions of *prisca theologia*. This would naturally bring in Jews such as Karigal and others, as it had brought in Monis. But it would also transform Christianity by bringing it back to a primordial sense of Wisdom, on both cosmic and historical layers.

"Universal Kabbalah" as *Prisca Theologia*

Stiles most certainly had a universal vision, not only as based on a future state of redemption but also, and perhaps primarily, as based on a common esoteric past. Toward the very end of *The Hope of Israel* he writes concerning the final eschaton:

> Many of these Things are to be found in the Writings of the Hocamim or Wise men of all the antient nations. And thro' them, as thro' streams from a fountain of water, they have flowed down to us. All which is the Remnant or Relics of the Knowledge which was communicated by the Angel Raziel to Adam & so it was transmitted to Methusselah & Noah, and has been preserved in the Writings of the *Chaldeans, Egyptians, Greeks* and *Ismaelites* or Arabians: in the Books of *Enoch* and *Abraham* and the XII Patriarchs, the *Bahir, Tikkunim, Zohar, Kanah, Binah*, and the *Rabbots* of R. *Bar Nachman*: and in the Writings of *Hesiod, Plato, Zeno, Olian, Ovid, Virgil, Seneca, Fodla*, and the *Druids*: in the Traditions & Literature of *India*, and in the Institution of the *Lama*: and in the Cabala of all people among whom Letters have been found.

This extraordinary list, including not only Jewish but also Chaldean, Egyptian, Greek, Arabic, Druid, and Indian traditions, clearly hearkens back to the *prisca theologia tradition*. Notable here is Stiles's description of this as "the Cabala of all people among whom Letters have been found," and his usage of the Hebrew term "Hocamim" (*hachamim*) to describe the wise men of all the ancient nations.[121] Notable too is his specific mention of the Angel Raziel and the Jewish books "*Bahir, Tikkunim, Zohar, Kanah, Binah*, and the *Rabbots* of R. *Bar Nachman*." The case could certainly be made that this was because Stiles was tailoring his narrative to his specific addressee, the *Hacham* Rabbi Hajim Isaac Karigal. Perhaps if he were writing to a Muslim he would have emphasized Arabic literature, and perhaps if he were writing to an Indian he would have mentioned the Brahmins and written of the Vedas.

Regardless, further evidence does point to Hebrew learning as central to Stiles's Christian Congregational conception of *prisca theologia*. In his *Discourse on Saving Knowledge* discussed above in relation to his use of Monis as a Zoharic source prior to receiving a copy of the *Zohar*, Stiles writes:

> Our fathers, the first ministers of New-England, were well versed in all branches of ecclesiastical literature, and were particularly conversant in the writings of the rabbies, not only the paraphrasts and commentators, but others which cast light upon the doctrine of the holy trinity. They were also well read in Plato and Plotinus, among the ancients, and Aquinas, Marsilius Ficinus, and Gerson, among the later writers on the sublime knowledge of God, and the spiritual life. The ancient libraries of the fathers remaining here to this day, as well as their works, evince this. This kind of reading, which has been too much neglected by their successors, might be resumed with great fruit and utility. I beg leave to recommend to my younger brethren in the ministry, the *platonic writers* and the *rabbinical literature*. If we study the Hebrew only with a view to the bible, it will repay us. It is a glorious language, and throws more light upon the old testament, than all the commentators. The primitive ministers our fathers were generally masters of it.[122]

The mention of Plato, Plotinus, and the ancients, as well as the ancient libraries, rabbinic literature, and Marsilio Ficino, the greatest

Renaissance proponent of the *prisca theologia* tradition, all points to its reference and promotion here. Stiles sees a common wisdom running through many antique traditions. As Christopher Grasso puts it, Stiles understands "the fragmentation of knowledge and language in the world in Neoplatonic terms, as part of a universal plurality emanating from a single unity."[123] Here Hebrew learning is that single unity, and as such it holds a pride of place and outstrips all else in its level of illumination. Moreover, the rabbis hold a place of distinct prominence, since for Stiles they are masters of Kabbalah in the very sense of *prisca theologia*. In fact, in Stiles's 1770 list of important dates and figures in the history of Jewish thought that culminates with Judah Monis, Stiles writes that the Mishnah is "the universal Kabbala and all the Traditions of the ancestors."[124] Here the adjective "universal" is quite operative, indicating inclusivity and perennialism. Such made this type of learning appealing to "the first ministers of New-England," and such, for Stiles, should make it appealing for subsequent generations of American Protestants.

Yet in *The Hope of Israel*, Stiles offers a stark caveat regarding *prisca theologia*, which he casts as a universal Kabbalah. He writes:

> Much of this antient Knowledge is gone to ruin, being swallowed up & polluted in other streams that have issued forth from corrupt fountains. But as Gold mixt with reprobate Silver, or the Iron in the Image of Nebuchadnezzar which mixeth indeed but will not unite & cleave to the clay; so a great deal of this pure Knowledge may be preserved among the Traditions & in the Caballa of the Nations—which all agree with one accord in the Expectation of the King, the *Desire* of all nations, the *Kingdom of Righteousness*, the *Conflagration* and *Renovation*, and *Paradise* of this World in the age to come. And by the help of the fire of Moses & the prophets and of men who have spoken by the prophetic Influence of God we may be able to separate & recover from the Dross the pure Gold of Truth.[125]

Universal does not mean that anything goes. In fact, much of the "Truth" has been lost, and much of what remains has been corrupted. By the same measure, however, much of the remnants can be purified and recovered. In this instance, Stiles points to notions of the final eschaton as veritable indicators. In a circular manner that would be fitting for a

Platonist, by looking to the future redemption, the kabbalistic truths of antiquity can be fully revealed.

Such a notion reappears in Stiles's oration of 1781, though there it is stripped of the eschatological overtones. In that context, he simply writes in a historical manner:

> During the first 400 years of the 2nd Temple, the Hebrew learning was taught with purity both at Babylon and Jerusalem—afterwards the pure science was corrupted and went to ruin, the law being left indeed or preserved, but corrupted by the traditions, or rather the decisions of the Rabbis. However it must be confessed the true *mystical Wisdom* of *the Cabala*, were preserved among a very few of the literati.[126]

It is Stiles's intention, and overall goal, to recover that "true *mystical Wisdom* of *the Cabala*" and to carry it forward into American Protestantism. This is why he meets with rabbis such as Moses bar David and Hajim Isaac Karigal, and this is why he delves into texts such as the *Zohar* and *Sefer Yetzirah*. In doing so, he sees his own learning as a form of enacted hermeneutics. Like Ezra the Scribe, who "became the first president or head of the college of Jerusalem, after the return from Babylon,"[127] Ezra Stiles becomes president of Yale College after learning from Jewish literati from the East. And just as Ezra the Scribe had installed a pure Hebrew learning during the time of the Second Temple, Ezra Stiles seeks to install a pure Kabbalah in America, uncorrupted by superfluous and corrupting laws and traditions. In such a manner, Stiles is directly injecting himself into the center of a plan for an American dissemination of a universal Kabbalah.

Concluding Remarks

In his oration of 1781, after listing several Jewish authors and texts, including some that we have seen him employing and expounding on such as *Sefer ha-Bahir*, *Sefer Yetzirah*, *Sha'arei Tzion*, and the *Zohar*, Stiles writes about several themes that we have reviewed:

> I say in all these I have looked with great attention and unspeakable delight. I have been taught from them the wisdom and knowledge of the

Holy Trinity and invaluable speculations upon the *Divinity and sufferings of Messiah*, upon the glory of his Kingdom, upon the renovation of the universe or restitution of all things, the millennium and the world to come.[128]

He goes on to state, "I have never poured water upon the hands of Elijah, nor sat at the feet of Gamaliel; but I have been taught personally at the mouth of the Masters of Wisdom, at the mouths of *five Rabbies*, Hochams of name and eminence."[129] Of these we have seen some of his most important intellectual exchanges, with Moses bar David and Hajim Isaac Karigal, which were focused on kabbalistic hermeneutics, messianism, and eschatology.

Now, in the oration of 1781, Stiles is summarizing his own Jewish learning, which heavily includes Kabbalah. He is subsequently very publicly claiming, in front of a cohort at Yale College, that "this kind of learning is worthy to be sought after and transplanted into the colleges of America."[130] While one could presumably read this as the very first call for Jewish Studies in American academia,[131] the underlying premise of Stiles's remarks is much more radical. In fact, it is important to emphasize that Stiles's project is not historiographical or academic in our understanding of those terms; rather, his notion is much more doctrinal.[132] He is calling for no less than the transformation of an established American college to mirror the colleges, or yeshivas, of the Jews, and to produce a generation of Congregational ministers heavily steeped in a theology influenced by rabbinic, and by extension kabbalistic thought.

By listing both the books and the living teachers, Stiles is seeking to establish pedigree. This is similar to what he does in his list of 1770, discussed at the outset of this chapter, by mentioning "Rabbi Monis" in an unbroken chain of tradition. Yet here in the oration, it is explicitly Stiles himself who is the recipient of that tradition. And he has certainly come a long way since his initial interest in kabbalistic learning as spurred by Monis. In fact, in many ways he seems to have outdone Monis, as well as his other predecessors discussed in this book. As outlined in the oration, Stiles studied both from Jewish texts and with Jewish adepts. He was perhaps the first known American to own a copy of and to study the *Zohar*. He was the first recorded American to engage in a form of study resembling rabbinic *hevruta*.[133] He was the first to write lengthy letters in Hebrew, and to even draft his rabbinically focused first public address as the president of Yale in that language, which he saw as integral both to understanding divine secrets and to the narrative of the final eschaton.

Whether or not Stiles's ideas resonated with his audience at Yale, or even the greater American public, it is perhaps significant to note that his idea of Yale as a New World, Christian Congregational yeshiva was not entirely lost on the Jewish community. In a letter of April 27, 1790, Isaac Pinto, member of Shearith Israel Synagogue in New York and translator of the first Jewish prayer book to be published in English in America, wrote to Stiles in Hebrew, "To the esteemed man, known at the gates, learned, and a teacher who raises up many students; he is the sagacious, the wise, the intelligent Ezra Stiles, the head of the Yale *Yeshiva* (*Rosh ha-Yeshiva ha-Yalensi*)."[134] Here Pinto is casting Stiles as one on par with the great rabbis of Europe and the East.

Although Pinto's letter was written over eight and a half years after Stiles had given his original oration, Stiles must have been thrilled to have received a letter of this tenor from such a prominent Jew, whom he greatly esteemed.[135] Stiles was being recognized toward the end of his career, just five years before his death, as what he wanted for himself and for American Congregationalism: as a sagacious teacher and *rosh yeshiva* who raises up many students in a universal kabbalistic tradition. In an interesting twist that serves as an apt commentary on his life of Hebrew learning, that recognition did not come from within the ranks of American Protestantism, but from a learned New World Jew.

Conclusion

Jewish Involvement and American Exceptionalism: On Kabbalah and Historiography on Colonial America

Judaism as a Phenomenon Apart?

As has been on display throughout this book, Jewish thought in the form of Kabbalah mixed deeply into the prerevolutionary American Protestant world. It exercised a profound influence on important phenomena such as Christian Quakerism, Puritan-Quaker exchange, New England messianism, perceptions of Jews in relation to Trinitarian ideas, and theological and educational visions for important American institutions such as Yale College. The influence may not have been widespread, but given the stature of the individuals whom we have analyzed, who took up the topic of Kabbalah and specifically related it to Jewish traditions, there is no denying its importance or depth in the shaping of early American religious sensibilities. Yet notwithstanding the evidence displayed throughout this volume, much historiography until now has taken a different view.

In 1970 Jacob Rader Marcus, consummate historian and founder of the American Jewish Archives, wrote a massive three-volume work entitled *The Colonial American Jew: 1492–1776*. It was the first of its kind, and within it Marcus asserted:

> Compared to any or all of the Protestant denominations, American Jews and Judaism represented a phenomenon apart. On the other hand, the Jewish church could hardly have exercised any influence on Protestant America. It has been estimated that there were in the thirteen colonies at least 3000 congregations, of which only seven all told were Jewish, even if Lancaster and Montreal are included.[1]

While Marcus's statement is quite big, his small numbers do not seem to be wrong. According to one more recent historian, Jews made up less than one-twentieth of 1 percent of the entire population of eighteenth-century British North America.[2] Marcus's student, and in many ways successor as the doyen of American Jewish history, Jonathan Sarna, gives a more generous number but concurs: "On the eve of the American Revolution, Judaism remained all but invisible to most colonists."[3] Sarna continues, "No more than one American in a thousand was Jewish, only five cities had significant Jewish populations, and only New York and Newport boasted synagogue buildings."[4] Whatever the actual numbers may have been, it seems clear that between the time that George Keith first set foot on American soil in 1685 and the time that Ezra Stiles gave his first public oration at Yale in 1781, Jews did not comprise a significant block of the overall population.

Notwithstanding, Marcus's notion that Judaism could hardly have exercised any influence on Protestant America is severely brought into question by the evidence discussed throughout this present book. It should be granted that many times, as predominantly seen with George Keith and Cotton Mather, the influence was relegated to texts and ideas. However, as we have seen with Judah Monis's influence on Increase Mather, with Monis's own contested Jewish-Christian identity, and with Monis's influence on Stiles and then Stiles's turn to various rabbis who came through Newport, inspiration and impact did not always remain on the textual level. Our examples thus also bring into question Marcus's claim that American Jews and Judaism represented a phenomenon apart. While Judaism and Jewish institutions as a block may not have wielded much influence over politics or everyday American life, the fact that one (former) Jew could cause messianic stirrings throughout the Harvard Corporation, and the fact that one Congregational minister could be influenced by Jewish sages coming through town as emissaries to the Jewish community, and then officially bring his new visions to bear as president of Yale, seem like highly significant developments.

All of this not only calls into question Marcus's statements, it also seems to run counter to the spin that Conservative rabbi and Jewish historian Arthur Hertzberg put on the Puritan-Jewish colonial narrative in his widely popular *The Jews in America*, originally published in 1989 and reissued in 1997. There Hertzberg writes:

Essays without number have been written to argue that the Puritan theocracy, which was so self-consciously modeled on biblical Judaism, created a pro-Jewish core to the American intellectual and political tradition. This reading is wrong. Because the Puritans knew that they had the truth, they were intolerant of all other believers.[5]

As with Marcus's claims, Hertzberg's remarks are not completely off point. For example, it would be absurd to call the cases of a desire for the conversion of the Jews that we have seen throughout "pro-Jewish," at least in our contemporary sense of the term. Nevertheless, the situation is much more complex than the simple statement that the Puritans knew that they had the truth and were thus intolerant of all other believers.[6] This certainly does not pan out with Stiles, who was an heir to Puritanism, or for that matter with Monis and the Mathers, or with their Quaker contemporary Keith. As we have seen, all of these sought to create their own truths, in part by bringing in and reshaping notions and texts from Jewish Kabbalah. In the case of Keith, the complex plurality of Quaker influence should also be taken into account, both in relation to polemics and the shaping of Puritan thought and in relation to an elevation of kabbalistic thought.

Despite the particularism of Puritanism and Quakerism, both were constantly reformulating themselves, and as has been displayed throughout this book, prominent thinkers in both camps were not closed off to Jewish influence. And despite the extremely small numbers of Jews, seventeenth- and eighteenth-century Judaism in America did not represent a phenomenon apart. Indeed, one point of possible accord with both Marcus and Hertzberg is the fact that in all of the cases covered in this book, the reason for Jewish influence is overwhelmingly theological rather than sociological. That is, it was not that the presence of Jews led to an interest in Judaism, but quite the opposite: in some cases, at least, an interest in Jewish thought led to an eventual interest in encountering and learning from actual Jews.

However, what prompted the theological interest in Jewish Kabbalah was not uniform among the thinkers. Keith's interest was sparked in England, in his encounter at Ragley Hall with Anne Conway and Francis Mercurius van Helmont. Cotton Mather's interest extended from his readings of the likes of Robert Fleming and Jacques Basnage. Increase

Mather's interest was much less text based and rested more on a reading of Jewish history in light of the contemporary false messianism of Shabbetai Tzevi. Monis, as somewhat of a pivotal character in this book, shifted his interest from his Jewish learning upon the European continent to his New World interest in proving the veracity of his Christian faith. Finally, a reading of Monis's treatise and perhaps a direct encounter with him after he had long been Christianized seems to have opened the door for Stiles, as well as wider speculations drawn from readings in Christian thinkers such as John Selden and Ralph Cudworth. Some of these initial interests in Kabbalah were more text based than others, some were more based in historically enacted hermeneutics, and some were more based in Protestant precedent, while others were based within, or at least led to Hebrew and Aramaic sources. And just as there was a divergence in initial interests, the turn from theology to social interaction was not equivalent in all of the instances examined.

In the case of George Keith, the move to communication with Jews only faintly occured toward the end of his kabbalistic Christian Quaker career, when he inquired of Jews in the community of Rhode Island concerning the notion of the *Luz*, the mythological indestructible bone that purportedly survives death and acts as the source for the resurrection body. Prior to that point, it appears that he did not have much occasion to encounter actual Jews, nor did he seem to have much interest. Cotton Mather was also not very interested in discoursing with Jews on an intellectual level concerning mystical and theological matters. This is not surprising given the fact that, as we have seen, his engagement with Kabbalah was always through a distinctly Protestant lens. However, given the role of his father in the conversion of Judah Monis, and given Cotton's now famous sole sentence on Monis, which states, "A Jew rarely comes over to us but he brings treasures with him,"[7] it is surprising that he stuck to this approach and that he did not engage more with Monis; or if he did, then it is surprising that he did not record such engagements. Increase Mather, for his part, seems to have been enthralled by Monis as a learned Jew who could cast Jewish thought in a Christian light, as evidenced from his preface to Monis's published discourses. And Monis seems to have fitted himself into that role as a Christianized Jew. Finally, Ezra Stiles seems to have embodied the fullest expression of a turn from theological interest to social encounter among the figures analyzed here. While he was engaged in textual study throughout his life, as we have seen, he also valued direct encounters with learned Jews. Some of these he carried out in person, while others were done via correspondence; all of them he engaged in to hone his own kabbalistic thinking.

While differences certainly exist among the thinkers examined here, including the impetus for taking an interest in Kabbalah and actual interactions with Jews in pursuit of further kabbalistic learning, one common thread most definitely adheres: Jewish ideas as kabbalistically framed were profoundly taken up by certain diverse sectors of the American Protestant world. Judaism was thus not a phenomenon apart; in relation to its pathways of thought, it was quite integral. And rather than displaying wholehearted intolerance in an arrogant sense that they already had the truth, as claimed by Hertzberg, early Protestants actively discussed and absorbed key elements of Jewish mystical thought, often in the context of their own eschatologies.

Melting Pot or Cultural Pluralism?

While the evidence presented in this book challenges the suppositions of Marcus and Hertzberg, we should be careful not to exaggerate in the other direction. This book has offered the story of five prominent Protestant individuals, and the mark of the importance of their kabbalistic stories is that they all had significant influence on American religious developments. Keith fundamentally shaped early Quaker theology and even created his own Quaker schism. The Mathers were giants in the American Puritan world. Monis taught Hebrew to an entire generation of religious and political leaders coming out of Harvard. As president of Yale and as one of the most important participants in the Republic of Letters of his day, Stiles's influence was immeasurable. But none of these figures were by any means representatives of the Jewish community, and Marcus, as well as Pencak and Sarna in his wake, was right to note the minuscule numbers of Jews. What is more, there were no officially ordained rabbis serving in North America until the arrival of Abraham Rice in 1840, and Hertzberg was right to mention that "the intellectual and religious traditions of American Jewry . . . have shallow roots."[8] This is certainly so in regard to colonial developments.

In the period under examination, there was no permanent authoritative Jewish intellectual voice in British North America, there were no yeshivas, or what Stiles and Karigal would call "colleges" of Jewish learning, and all of the Jewish sages with whom Stiles learned were itinerant emissaries who were only passing through. Even Judah Monis, if we are to take him at his word, was a *Mashkil Venavon* and not a *Hacham*; if we were to translate this into contemporary academic equivalents, he had what might be considered an MA, or even a BA, but not a PhD. He had some Jewish education, but he was not an authoritative expert. Yet none of this much mattered. From George Keith to Ezra Stiles, Jewish kabbalistic thought was more of an idea in the mold of Christian Hebraism than a lived reality in the mold of a sustained ecumenical exchange. Stiles most certainly comes closest to the latter, but lest we become anachronistic, it is important to remember that he issued strong theological judgments in his musings. In so doing, he cast serious doubt on Jewish kabbalistic transmission from the most formative period of rabbinic Judaism: the time of Hillel the Elder onward. Stiles was no religious pluralist in the contemporary sense of the idea but rather a Christian universalist who sought to absorb and subsume variant ideas, including many from Kabbalah, into his own singular system.

From Keith to Stiles, the story of the influence of Jewish Kabbalah in prerevolutionary America is thus a story of American Christian Hebraism. And while Hertzberg's statement about absolute Puritan claims to truth that led to intolerance seems too categorical in that it disregards elements such as a willingness to learn from kabbalistic texts and even from Jewish interlocutors, he is right in alluding to the fact that such learning was far from any expression of philo-Semitism. Regardless, as Hertzberg also correctly alluded to in his above quote, the temptation to paint a more rosy picture of interfaith dialogue and religious pluralism is great. And this is not only the case regarding the Protestant narrative of enlightened acceptance or the general American tale of a pioneering sense of religious pluralism, but also from the vantage point of American Judaism itself.

In fact, in September 1948, longtime member of the American Antiquarian Society and the newly installed president of the American Jewish Historical Society, Lee Max Friedman, published an article entitled

"An Invitation to American Jewish History." Within it he ideologically and sanguinely remarks:

> I have seen it stated that all American history is the study of foreign hu-
> man germs transplanted to American soil, there giving free play to the in-
> terpenetration of influences foreign and native, and the cross-fertilization
> by every heterogeneous element in our spheres of activity. The end re-
> sultant is a novel and surprising new product—the American. Bone of
> the bone, flesh of the flesh, we Jews are an indigenous element in this
> evolution.[9]

This was a reassuring statement in the face of the recent atrocities of the Holocaust. And a few years later, in an address to the same American Jewish Historical Society, Friedman would reiterate, "We have come to accept as a commonplace that life in this new land has from its very beginnings been the resultant of the encounter of American realities with imported ideas, habits, and personalities, and out of this fusion to which every nation, every race, and creed has contributed, our country is built."[10] With the idea that "from its very beginnings" American life was a result of a "fusion" of cultures and creeds, Friedman is clearly sub-scribing to the etiological myth of America as the melting pot. This is a metaphor that arose in the eighteenth century and that gained popu-larity in 1908 with the American staging of Israel Zangwill's play of the same name.[11]

Among his many works, Friedman had written on Cotton Mather and the Jews, on Monis, and on Karigal, and he was thus probably more knowledgeable than anyone of his generation concerning the role of Jews, Judaism, and Jewish thought within that early "melting pot." And as we have seen with the Christian Hebraist adoption and adaptation of Kabbalah by the early American thinkers examined throughout this book, the melting-pot thesis is not entirely wrong. Keith infused Kab-balah so thoroughly into his thought that he rarely distinguished sources and sought to create an organic, universal Christian Quaker theology. Cotton Mather, and to a much greater extent Increase Mather, sought to use Kabbalah to bring Jews into the American Christian fold. Monis readily followed suit, additionally offering his own Christian kabbalis-tic melding of ideas. Finally, Stiles sought to form a universal Kabbalah based on notions similar to the Renaissance *prisca theologia* tradition, with the end result an American apostolic Jewish-Christianity. The crucible was clearly at work.

What is interesting in the case of Friedman's reading is that he holds this up, from the Jewish point of view, as an ideal. Later in the same article, however, he does tack away from the notion of the melting pot and toward the direction of his contemporary, the Jewish philosopher Horace Kallen, and Kallen's novel ideas of cultural pluralism.[12] In fact, using this precise turn of phrase, Friedman writes, "Cultural pluralism is upon what American democracy feeds. Human progress develops from varieties of cultural patterns and conflicting ideas. Uniformity is stagnation."[13] Here Friedman signals a change of tone, which was perhaps deliberate given the title of the article: "E Pluribus Unum: Unity in Diversity." The first half represents the melting pot; the second half represents the ideals of cultural pluralism. In mid-twentieth-century America, the debate was quite relevant. Yet in relation to the prerevolutionary thinkers examined here, with whom Friedman was familiar, there was no endeavor for cultural pluralism; nor was there an interest in democracy. Theirs was a project of unity, not in diversity but out of the old and forged into the new.

As a final caveat, Friedman rather pridefully notes, "Jews are an old people—the oldest to have preserved its history and ideals. American Jews enjoy a precious privilege as Americans and Jews."[14] As we have seen, the idea of the antiquity of Hebraic thought expressed here by Friedman was common to all of the thinkers analyzed in this book. Yet contrary to their concept that something was lost along the way that needed to be recovered and renewed, Friedman seemingly consciously turns this notion of Jewish antiquity in relation to American novelty on its head and adopts it as a mark of pride. In an interesting dialectical spin, just as Jewish kabbalistic ideas had been reinterpreted and adjusted to an old-new theology by the thinkers analyzed here, in the mid-twentieth century that old-new theology was again being reappropriated and masterfully reinterpreted in a historiographical manner. In this case, that reinterpretation was done in order to serve a particular Jewish purpose within the American field of cultural pluralism, by one who was a scholar of Jewish-Protestant colonial relations. But he was also significantly the postwar president of the American Jewish Historical Society, precisely at a time when that institution was seeking to stake its uniquely American post-Holocaust claim within a burgeoning multicultural landscape.

Errand or Exodus in Wilderness?

On the Protestant side of historiography, there is a need to turn with the findings of the present book to the idea made popular by the famed Americanist Perry Miller, and since debated widely, of an errand into the wilderness. Miller was borrowing from the Puritan minister Samuel Danforth, who delivered a sermon on May 11, 1670, entitled "A Brief Recognition of New England's Errand into the Wilderness"; Miller appropriated the phrase and turned it into a full-blown theory of American election. By it, Miller has been understood to mean that the Puritans had a founding mission of soteriological proportions, aimed at ushering in the messianic age by creating a model of Christian reformation to be emulated by England and the rest of Europe.[15] As Miller writes:

> The Bay Company was not a battered remnant of suffering Separatists thrown up on a rocky shore; it was an organized task-force of Christians, executing a flank attack on the corruptions of Christendom. These Puritans did not flee to America; they went in order to work out that complete reformation which was not yet accomplished in England and Europe, but which would quickly be accomplished if only the saints back there had a working model to guide them.[16]

Miller's iconic statement has been extensively critiqued. In an article from 1986, Theodore Dwight Bozeman called it "a minimally developed proposal" and noted concerning Miller, "Neither in the 1952 essay nor elsewhere did he cite explicit evidence from the period 1629–40 other than Winthrop's single reference to a 'City upon a Hill.'"[17] Abram C. Van Engen has recently buttressed this argument by noting that the entire notion of a "City upon a Hill" stood as a common theme of debate between Catholics and Protestants in regard to the "true church" and *not* in regard to the exceptionality of any particular nation.[18] Andrew Delbanco has noted that Miller formulated his ideas of exceptionalism in 1952 shortly after a stint in Europe, where he met with anti-American hostility at the height of the Marshall Plan. Delbanco writes, "His anger was very much at work in his formulation of the Puritans' motives in leaving Europe on the eve of another war. They had, he argued, gone into service, not exile."[19] According to Delbanco, Miller's formulation was thus in some sense more autobiographically apologetic than it was historically plausible.

Miller's notion of complete novelty, expressed in his follow-up statement that in the Puritan perception America was "a bare land, devoid of already established (and corrupt) institutions, empty of bishops and courtiers, where they could start *de novo*,"[20] was critiqued by Sacvan Bercovitch. The latter successfully argued that in fact nothing was de novo, "that the emigrants derived their concept of errand from the Elizabethan premises for national election, and that those premises are most amply set forth in John Foxe's great church history."[21] In fact, the very English rhetorical formula of an *English* Israel, propagated by Foxe for a sense of national election, served as a definitive template for the American Puritan narrative. Bercovitch has shown that Foxe most certainly acted as an important precedent for Cotton Mather, and the model also seems to have been highly important for Increase's notion, examined in this present study, of a New Israel in the New World. Thus, while Miller's concept of the American Puritan errand as a new start was perhaps true and important on the immediate societal level, it is historically problematic on the wider doctrinal level.

Avihu Zakai has taken up the question of service vs. exile in his own reformulation of the errand idea, which focuses on what he calls an "*Exodus* type of religious migration."[22] By this Zakai means a salvation history based on the biblical idea of fleeing the oppressive fleshpots of Egypt for the wilderness of the desert. This is something that offers a definite distinction from the prior formulations of an English Israel, and Zakai urges greater attention to the operative term "wilderness," which "represents an intermediate zone between Egypt and the Land of Promise."[23] The first generation did not see itself as reaching a new Zion as much as a new Sinai.

This accords well with Reiner Smolinski's persuasive argument that the Puritans did not categorically view Boston as an eschatological New Jerusalem, but in fact many maintained, as we have seen with Increase Mather, Judah Monis, and their heir Stiles, that at the end of times a new heavenly Zion would descend onto the old earthly Zion and the Jews as a nationally converted people would reinhabit it.[24] America was not the locus of a New Jerusalem; it was a necessary step in the wilderness before that final salvation. In this sense, Jews actually held a special status of privilege; but that privilege could only fully be realized through their conversion to Christianity. Only then would their return to Zion have any cosmic significance, as only then could they be held up as a paradigm.[25] Such is a case of metaphysical exceptionalism within an exceptionalism. Yet prior to that they are an exception in a completely different, outward sense; this is the sense of being excluded from the paradigm. They are mistaken and in the dark, and only by coming to Christ can they move from the excluded exception to the treasured, core exceptional. The wilderness of America, and its true Godly Christians, would have to prepare the way for them to reach that promised state, eventually in the Promised Land.

Following on the heels of the Bible, and Zakai's notion of an Exodus type of religious migration, it is important to keep in mind that the wilderness is the place where the dramatic national narrative unfolds. Wilderness is a place of hardship and of toil, but it is also a stage for recasting and for nation building. Wilderness represents the unknown, the terra incognita; it holds unforeseen perils but also unexpected opportunities. In this light, the "errand into the wilderness" represents that liminal middle space of exile from the old and an endeavor for the new. In its very liminality, though, I would argue that it does not completely break from the old but draws on it and transforms it. This is a phenomenon that we have seen expressed throughout this book.

As we have witnessed with the case of Increase Mather and Judah Monis, the eschatological impetus for the national conversion of the Jews was, in part, in direct continuity with the worldwide messianic events of Shabbetai Tzevi, which had also affected England. Keith and Stiles, who were not Puritans *sensu stricto*, were drawing on distinctly non-American European and Near Eastern sources in the formulation of their new theologies, with Keith having learned the bulk of his ideas in England from the Conway circle and with Stiles having even learned from various European and Ottoman rabbis. And as we have seen with Cotton Mather, whom Bercovitch showed to have drawn on Foxe for ideas of American chosenness, he was drawing heavily on his European

Protestant predecessors such as Basnage and Fleming in relation to Kabbalah. An examination of our authors thus shows a greater continuity with Europe and the rest of the world, well into the third generation, beyond Puritanism, and even past the shift from Puritan to Yankee culture. The wilderness may have allowed them to synthesize in novel ways, but it was not the locus of a clean break from the past. It was a liminal field that allowed for them to draw on the old and to simultaneously look toward the new.

Conversion, National Reconstitution, and a New Torah

Deeply tied to the notion of liminality in the wilderness, which makes use of the old but opens into the new, is the question of conversion. In fact, many of the narratives portraying the errand from the Old World cast it as a spiritual rebirth for those involved.[26] Just as one who passes through the baptismal font, those who passed over the Atlantic experienced a conversion to a new life of liberty and truth. According to Jerald C. Brauer, "The term 'conversion' designates a profound, self-conscious, existential change from one set of beliefs, habits, and orientation to a new structure of belief and action."[27] In the case of the American national narrative, personal conversion and public reconstitution converge. This is quite significant given the extreme importance of conversion in Calvinist sectors of America as a sign of salvation. But it is also important for the early American narrative beyond Puritanism, as evidenced by the workings of the inner Light in Quakerism, which directs the individual in faith. In the case of Calvinism, we have seen the centrality of the kabbalistically framed conversion of Judah Monis; and in the case of Quakerism, we have seen how George Keith sought to spread his own kabbalistically inflected theologies of Light, thereby affecting the entire community.

Monis offers an interesting paradigm, as his conversion was far from being a merely personal matter. In many ways it was less about his own convictions and more of an injunction for contemporary Congregationalists to undergo an inner conversion. But it was even more than that; it was part of a prerevolutionary national narrative. To his new community, Monis represented Judaism, and as an extension, he represented both the Old World and the Old Testament. Moreover, some of this "old" was represented by Kabbalah, which was now being reconstituted in a "new" Protestant framework. From out of Monis's personal conversion narrative stemmed an overall public reconstitution of the old into the new, in a very liminal manner that set the eschatological stage for redemption from out of the wilderness. Increase Mather's long-held apocalyptic dream was coming true. Yet it was not a mere prophetic fulfillment for Mather. In fact, further into the American future it was picked up on by Stiles, who in his own personal transformation narrative cast himself typologically as Ezra the Scribe. In Stiles's case, personal prophecy led to a very public, national reconstitution of Torah that he hoped to disseminate through national institutions such as Yale College.

In sticking with the liminality of the wilderness and the wilderness's role in both personal and national conversion, it is important to return to Zakai's Exodus trope and to note that the biblical wilderness is the place in which the people of Israel most directly encounter their God. It is the place in which the Torah is revealed, and it is the place in which the Tabernacle is built. This was certainly important for Increase Mather and Judah Monis, for whom America was the liminal "New World" beyond history, as paradoxically read out of the Bible and into history. But it was also quite relevant to Ezra Stiles, who envisioned his new, kabbalistically infused Torah as coming out of America to enlighten the world. Granted, as evidenced by his Yale oration of 1781 and other texts, Stiles saw himself in the mold of the biblical Ezra, whose reconstituted Torah came out of Jerusalem and not out of the wilderness of Sinai. Thus, in this case, the biblically enacted hermeneutics are not perfect. But rarely ever are they. Regardless, there is direct evidence that the theme of American wilderness was indeed important to Stiles and to his idea of disseminating his new kabbalistic Torah.

Stiles's famous sermon entitled "The United States Elevated to Glory and Honour," delivered to the Connecticut General Assembly on May 8, 1783, is quite pertinent. Within that sermon, the wilderness trope has direct resonance; as he writes, "It may have been of the Lord, that Christianity is to be found in such great purity, in this church exiled into the wildernesses of *America*."[28] Within the context of the sermon, he explicitly refers to "God's American *Israel*,"[29] stating that "the *United States* will, by the ordering of heaven, eventually become this people."[30] It is interesting that he does not take it for granted that the United States already *is* this American Israel. Rather, through providence and the acceptance of a new Torah, it shall become so. This is similar to the Levitical theme of national election, in which God does not say that the people *are* holy but that they *shall be* holy, through divine emulation and the upholding of commandments.[31] Given Stiles's knowledge of Hebrew and the Bible, this does not seem coincidental but rather another case of American biblical typology.

Stiles continues with a remarkable passage that is worth quoting in full:

> This great American revolution, this recent political phenomenon of a new sovereignty arising among the sovereign powers of the earth, will be attended to and contemplated by all nations. Navigation will carry the American flag around the globe itself; and display the Thirteen Stripes and New Constellation at *Bengal* and *Canton* on the *Indus* and *Ganges*, on the *Whang-ho* and the *Yang-tse-kiang*; and with commerce will import the wisdom and literature of the east. That prophecy of *Daniel* is now literally fulfilling—ישתאתו ראבים ותראבה האדאעת—there shall be an universal travelling *to and fro, and knowledge shall be increased.*[32] This knowledge will be brought home and treasured up in *America*: and being here digested and carried to the highest perfection, may reblaze back from *America* to *Europe, Asia* and *Africa*, and illumine the world with TRUTH and LIBERTY.[33]

In this extraordinary passage we get a clear sense of American exceptionalism, coupled with eschatological prophecy from the book of Daniel and uniquely peppered with an idea of cultural diversity as based on intellectual elements of Truth and Liberty. Whatever the case may have been for Perry Miller's first generation of Puritans, by Stiles's time an idea had clearly started to solidify that the American errand would extend beyond its initial phase to produce global fruits. For Stiles, those fruits would come out of the new Torah resulting from divine encounters in the wilderness and the newly formed American Israel, and they would spread forth to intellectually nourish the world.

As we have seen in this book, that new Torah coming out of America was kabbalistically conceived. Interestingly, however, in his sermon to the General Assembly, the path to enlightenment for Stiles was not to be a one-way street. In the spirit of his universal Kabbalah, wisdom would also be brought back from the East, would commingle with American ideas and be brought to perfection in America; it would then go back out to reillumine the rest of the world. As Stiles had done with Kabbalah, isolating the "true" pristine strands that had survived from antiquity and forging them into an apostolic Jewish-Christianity that could bring together and enlighten Jews and Christians alike under one rubric, so too could he do that with wisdom traditions from the East. And here this is not an agenda out of Stiles's own fancy, but is from none other than the apocalyptic prophecy of Daniel. Once again, it had biblical sanction. The next phase in the prophetic fulfillment of Stiles's kabbalistic Torah would be akin to later American ideas such as Manifest Destiny.

Concluding Remarks

Stiles's astonishing ideas seem almost eerily contemporary in their proposal that the American flag should be carried around the globe, in their seeming sense of cultural pluralism regarding wisdom literatures of the East, and in their ostensibly American ideals of Truth and Liberty. And indeed, they can help us to understand what are perceived to be some of the foundational ideas of American identity, ideologically construed as connected to a pristine past and a soteriological future. In fact, they were framed at a crucial time of national myth building, and they thus shed great light on early postrevolutionary perceptions of American sacred history, tracing back to what Stiles above calls the "church exiled into the wildernesses of *America.*" Here Stiles was clearly drawing on the tropes of the first-generation Puritans as outlined by Perry Miller, giving some credence to Miller's idea of errand as eschatological world-mission, or at least its perception as such. This is so even if what we have with Stiles is the understanding of a first-generation Yankee and not a first-generation Puritan.

Stiles was perhaps one of the more articulate postrevolutionary voices concerning such matters, but he was not alone in holding such ideas; nor was he the originator. In fact, as we have seen within this book, Stiles's ideas of a soteriological universal Kabbalah, upon which his above-quoted sermon is largely based, were built on some of the prerevolutionary "Judeo-Christian" kabbalistic notions of Monis, as well as on some of the biblio-historical, hermeneutically enacted messianic concepts of the Mathers. In addition, Stiles's concepts held great commonality with the more universalistic, Christian Quaker Kabbalah of George Keith, which was directly connected to the Ragley circle and the Sulzbach kabbalists. It is thus only by understanding these developments that Stiles's above-quoted notion of an American fulfillment of the prophecy from Daniel can make full sense. Knowledge leading to Truth and Liberty shall increase, in Stiles's view, in the same manner in which universal Kabbalah, as direct revelation, shall be uncovered and shall come forth from the colleges of America.

Stiles, as well as Monis, the Mathers, and Keith before him, can certainly be understood both politically and ideologically as laying precedents for notions of American exceptionalism. Here with Stiles, those precedents could be seen as based on the ever so popular idea of intellectual and cultural diversity. They could also be so construed with Monis in his turn to his Jewish "Brethren of the flesh," with Cotton Mather and George Keith in their inclusion of Jewish texts and ideas, and with Increase Mather in his acceptance of Monis and his will to afford a special sacred place for the Jews. On the surface, Stiles indeed seems the most prone of all of these thinkers to modern notions of diversity, not only from his unusual friendships and exchanges with rabbis but also in this final proclamation, with his ideas extending beyond Judaism and into Bengal and Canton.

Yet lest we engage in anachronistic speculation, it is important to keep in mind that for Stiles and all of his predecessors studied in this book, the aim was entirely doctrinal. Despite the sophisticated musings of Lee Friedman, the thinkers studied here did not have an agenda of cultural pluralism. Rather, from Keith to Stiles, all of these thinkers sought to promote the elevated efficacy of their respective takes on Protestantism through variant uses of Jewish Kabbalah. Some, as we have seen, sought to form their own versions of Christian Kabbalah; others used kabbalistic ideas, texts, and events as Protestant-centered polemical springboards.

By understanding their uses of Kabbalah and making that understanding our own springboard, we have gained insight into early developments in American Quakerism, relations between Christian Quakerism and New England Puritanism, the messianic impact of Shabbetai Tzevi on American Protestant eschatology, conversion and kabbalistic polemics, the earliest Jewish-Christian exchanges upon American soil, the earliest American texts and theologies to take Kabbalah into consideration, and an extraordinary movement to bring some of those themes into the colleges of America and from there out into the world. We have also been able to reevaluate and offer correctives to important historiographies, some of which had divorced Judaism from early Protestant developments, others of which had idealized its role, and others of which had proposed an eschatological sense of mission for early Puritans. Through notions of religious dialogue, questions of cultural diversity, ideas of American exceptionalism, and attempts to meld the old with the new, Kabbalah has acted as a lens through which to examine the very complex, often conflicting notions of American historical identity and its various means of *reception* (or Kabbalah) itself.

ACKNOWLEDGMENTS

"I have never poured water upon the hands of Elijah, nor sat at the feet of Gamaliel; but I have been taught personally at the mouth of the Masters of Wisdom." Thus writes Ezra Stiles in his commencement oration of 1781, and it is a sentiment that carries over into the process of composing this present book: due to the obvious constraints of history, my encounters with the subjects in this book were relegated to the texts that they left behind; but I also learned a great deal through personal exchanges with consummate contemporary experts without whom this book could not have been written, and to whom I would like to express my profound gratitude.

Reiner Smolinski read through an earlier version of the entire manuscript and offered detailed, invaluable feedback. His profound knowledge of colonial American thought proved to be indispensable: not only was he readily and amicably available with excellent suggestions based on his extensive work with eighteenth-century English manuscripts, he also saved me from some embarrassing errors. Thank you, Reiner.

Christia Mercer meticulously read through an earlier version of both the introduction and chapter 1, and she gave me some keen insight into the intellectual relationship between George Keith and Anne Conway. From the beautiful gardens of Villa I Tatti in Florence to Le Monde on the Upper West Side of Manhattan and well beyond, Christia has consistently been an incredible dialogue partner and a wonderful friend. Christia, I am grateful for your wealth of knowledge, for your zeal, and for your willingness to share both.

Michael Hoberman has been a congenial interlocutor throughout this project. He provided some important comments on chapter 3 and he willingly and ably acted as a respondent in a dialogue on Judah Monis through the Center for Jewish History. Much appreciated, Michael!

Michael G. Hall also read an earlier version of chapter 3 and offered vital information about the life and thought of Increase Mather. Michael,

I greatly value your willingness to share from your experience and your notes.

My colleagues at Rice University have been extremely supportive and helpful. In particular, Marcia Brennan offered helpful suggestions after reading the introduction and conclusion (the glossary was her wonderful idea), Claire Fanger readily and ably helped me with several Latin passages, and April DeConick helped with Greek. Thank you all for being such supportive colleagues.

Kathleen Canning, dean of the School of Humanities, and Elias Bongmba, chair of the Department of Religion at Rice, allowed me to take an academic leave during the 2019–20 academic year in order to take up residency as a senior NEH scholar at the Center for Jewish History in New York. In addition, Matthias Henze offered unwavering support for this project in his role as director of the Jewish Studies Program at Rice. I am grateful to all three of you.

Several archivists, who are the true gatekeepers of knowledge, gave me key guidance and ready access to essential materials. This includes Nell Carlson of the Andover-Harvard Theological Library, Ashley Cataldo, manuscripts curator at the American Antiquarian Society, and Karen Spicher, archivist of the Ezra Stiles Papers at the Beinecke Rare Book and Manuscript Library, as well as the librarians at the Massachusetts Historical Society and at the Harvard University Archives. Your help has truly been invaluable.

Jennifer Hammer, senior editor at NYU Press, took an early interest in this project and has been a driving force throughout. She has been readily available and incredibly responsive to questions and concerns. Jennifer, I am grateful for your suggestions, for your extensive feedback, and for your tireless work in seeing through the production of this project.

Generous financial support was provided by several organizations, including the Mosle Fund through Rice University, the Sid and Ruth Lapidus Prize through the American Jewish Historical Society, the Jewish Studies Program at Rice, and the National Endowment for the Humanities. As previously mentioned, this last organization allowed me to take up residency as a senior scholar at the Center for Jewish History, during which I was able to write the bulk of this book. I thank Malgorzata Bakalarz Duverger, director of academic programs at the Center for Jewish History, for all of her help and support during a rather strange year in New York.

Sharon and Danielle have accompanied me every step of the way, from our wonderful summer in Cambridge to our difficult year in New York, and from our side trips to archives in the Northeast to our adventures tracing the steps of Ezra Stiles in Newport and in New Haven. As such, this book is as much theirs as it is mine. It has not always been easy, but they have offered life and flare to this project and I would not have wanted to take the journey with anyone else. Shmoldz and Daldul, no words can adequately express the extreme gratitude that I have for what you continually give me.

Finally, Mom and Dad (otherwise known as Carol and Ken Ogren) offered enthusiastic encouragement and support during an otherwise challenging year. They also kindly provided refuge in their Lake Tahoe home at the time that the Covid pandemic hit New York the hardest, thereby saving us from a three-month shelter-in-place in a six-hundred-square-foot Brooklyn apartment with a six-year-old kid and an eighty-three-pound dog. It was during that time of refuge, in that beautiful setting in Lake Tahoe, that I was able to bring this book to completion. The book would probably not have taken the shape that it has without that time. I am forever grateful for your constant support. As I mention in the dedication, you have implanted in me both a curiosity concerning Jewish thought and a deep interest in what it "means" to be an American. It is for this reason that this book on those conjoined topics is dedicated to you.

APPENDIX I

The Cabbala of the Jews

GEORGE KEITH, 1688

Note on the flyleaf by Robert W. G. Vail, head librarian of the American Antiquarian Society:

Jewish Cabala: Seventeenth century manuscript on the Jewish Cabala. Removed from pamphlet volume v 93 which was made up of 17ᵗʰ century Quaker tracts, some of them bearing the autograph of Increase Mather. It is therefore possible that this manuscript also came from the Mather Library.

  R.W.G.Vail
  4/2/35

[THE CABBALA OF THE JEWS]
(from p.c.693)

[1]
So: Friend, having seen what Thou hast lately published in print, as a Compendium of Jacob Behmen's Works, wᶜʰ thou callest yᵉ Temple of Wisdom,[1] it came to my Remembrance, of what I have sometimes formerly thought of J. Behmen's Works, to wit, that he has had some Converse with some Rabbies of yᵉ Jews, wᶜʰ abound in Germany, & has learned from yᵐ some imperfect notions of their Cabbala or mystick Theology, wᶜʰ he not well understanding, has strangely disguised & mingled wᵗʰ some very imperfect & unsound notions of his own, & published to yᵉ World or some for him, who have got his manuscripts as a Divine sort of philosophy, given him by Divine Inspiration, & writt by

209

a Divine impulse. And tho I have a good Esteem of J.B. & have observed diverse good things in him, & doe believe he has felt & justed of yᵉ Word of Life, as every true Christian dos & of yᵉ Powers of yᵉ World to come, & has had Divine Openings of many things, yet I must needs say according to my Sense & judgment of his Books, there is a great mix of fire in yᵐ, & many things that I can in no wise owne to be true Divine Openings, but his own gross mistakes.

I have been informed, yᵗ some Jewish Rabbies, write their mysteries in yᵉ Germane tongue, but in Hebrew Letters, to conceal it from yᵉ vulgar sort: & even yᵉ Jewish Rabbies themselves doe in many things come short of true Divine knowledge of Scripture mysteries pretended unto by them, so yᵗ their present Cabbala is not yᵉ same altogether with that antient Cabbala, yᵗ Moses & yᵉ Prophets had, & therefore we ought not to take any thing upon truth either from yᵉ Jews or from Jacob B. but try all things, by yᵉ Spirit of truth & yᵉ Holy Scriptures.

And that yᵉ choicest & rarest things so accounted in J.B. are in the Sd Cabbala, & that much more distinctly & intelligibly, I may give thee some hints hereafter, tho the

[2]
Cabbala has many more things of these matters & purposes, wᶜʰ I shall not either justify or condemn at present. But (1) I think fit to tell thee some of these things wᶜʰ I dislike greatly in J.B. his Principles.

1. He calls those 7 forms of nature the 7 Spirits of God. [See yᵉ margᵗ. p.s. of Thy Treatise called ye Temple of Wisdom]² whereas yᵉ forms of nature & all created Beings are widely distinct from the 7 Spirits of Gd's infinitely inferiour unto yᵐ if he had Sd, there are 7 forms in nature by way of analogy or Similitude, answering to yᵉ 7 Spirits of God, Rev. 1. but vastly distinct, it had been more safe & consonant to Truth.
2. That he understands 4 of the 7 Forms of nature to be yᵉ anger or Wrath of God, & yᵉ other 3 to be his Love, where he still confoundeth God with nature or Creature, wᶜʰ ought not to be done so, for God yᵉ Creator is infinitely more excellent then all his Creatures.
3. That he calls yᵉ Fire of Wrath, God yᵉ Father, & yᵉ Fire of Love or Light, God yᵉ Son. See p. 6.7.³ as if yᵉ Son were more a God of Love

then ye Father, which is very contrary to Scripture & Divinely enlightened Reason, for as ye Father & Son is one, so their Love is one,
& they are equal in Love, & if we could suppose any inequality, the
Father's Love in that Case is ye greater, as we may well say, it is considering Christ as he is that man called by ye Jews Adam Cadmon.

4. His comparing ye Father, Son & Holy Ghost, to Fire Light & Air,
seems not to me rightly to agree w^t y^t great Mystery, nor indeed
unto ye Cabbala, which places Fire Light, Air, Water, & Earth
Spiritually understood & by way of analogy, not all in ye Deity or
Essence of God wch they call y^e Ænsoph, but in Adam Cadmon
wch they hold to be a middle Being or mediator between God & y^e
Creatures.

5. That he understands 2 Principles to be in God, viz Light & Darkness, Love & Anger, Good & Evil, this is contrary to Scripture, that
sais God is Light, & in him is no Darkness

[3]

at all, & in God there is perfect Unity, his Hieroglyphick being 1,
which being multiplied into itself, ye Square is 1, & that again multiplied into itself, ye Cube is 1, & this ye Root Square & Cube is still
Unity, ye best Hieroglyphick y^t I know, whereby to represent that
glorious mystery of ye Father, Son & Holy Ghost, We cannot find or
conceive these 2 Principles properly but in the Creatures, where y^e
Darkness is posteriour to ye Light, & is ye Effect of ye Fall.

6. That he saith, God moved himself to ye Creation, see p. 83.[4] This
puts me in mind, that I have read in J.B. how God has twice
moved himself, to wit, first in ye Creation, 2dly when Christ came
in ye flesh, & 3dly he is yet to move himself at ye Day of Judgment
& End of ye World. But this is very unsound & unbecoming y^e
nature of God, to allow or conceive any motion in God, whereby
he moveth himself. We find no such expression in Scripture, but
on ye contrary that he is unchangeable, & without any shadow of
Change, but motion in God inferreth a real Change. The antient
Philosophers had better knowledge of God, who called him y^e
Mover of all other things, but reckoned him immoveable within
himself. And if once any new motion be granted in God, they may

also grant y^t there is new knowledge, new Love, new thoughts in God, all which is contrary to Scripture, for whatever is in God, was in him from Eternity & remains to Eternity, no temporal thing belongs to him, as any part or Accident of him, so that it is a good & sound maxim or axiom in ye schools, in deo nulla sunt accidentia. i.e., In God there are no Accidents.

7. That he saith p. 92 The Deity hath exgenerated itself from Eternity out of ye Fiery Wrath, out of ye Fire, by ye sinking thro Death into an other principle of another Source or Quality.[5] All these I greatly dislike as very unsound & offensive to Christian Ears, as containing divers absurdities, (1) as if ye Fierce Wrath were before ye Deity: 2dly as if ye Deity were generated out of ye fierce Wrath: 3dly as

[4]

Sinking thro Death into another Principle wch infers or implies not only a Change in God, but a Death wch is altogether contrary to God's nature y^t is altogether immortal in ye highest sense, & also implying, that God was first a God of anger, & next a God of Love. But if we conceive aright of God, we ought to think, y^t there is no such Composition in God, as J.B. supposeth, his Love & his Anger is one & ye Same in him, but as it respects ye Creatures differently, it receives distinct names, his Love being his most Holy Will to doe good unto his Creatures & reward their Obedience, & his Wrath being his most holy Will to punish Offenders, both which are one in God, but to suppose any fierce burning Wrath like to ye Wrath y^t moveth or riseth in man's heart, upon any new provocation, & stirs his blood & spirits, to be in God, is very gross & unsound so to change ye Glory of ye immortal & incorruptible God, into ye Image of corruptible man.

8. That he saith, ye Souls of men & angels arise out of ye eternal nature, but ye visible things of this World from some temporal being, wch shall have an end, see p. 87.[6] In opposition to this I say, all things, both visible & invisible, have proceeded from God, who is eternal, & ye visible things retain their being or Essence for ever, as well as ye Souls of men & Angels, but are changed after another manner, so as to become Spiritual & invisible, as ye antient philosophy teacheth, Omnia mutantur, nihil interit, i.e. all things are changed, nothing

perisheth. But to say or think, that Souls or Angels, or any other Creatures, are parts of God's own Being or Essence in a proper sense, as J.B. seems to hold, is very unsound and gross.

9. That he understands God made at first 3 kingly Governments of Angels, answering to yᵉ Holy Trinity [see p. 12]⁷ as Michael, Lucifer & Uriel: but wᵗ sais he of Gabriel mentioned in Scripture, & of Raphael mentioned in ye Apocrypha & in yᵉ Cabala? It seems more agreeable to Scripture, to say as

[5]

yᵉ Cabbala, yᵗ there are 4 Kingly Governmᵗˢ of Angels, yᵗ have all stood & remain Holy & pure Angels, to wit, Michael, Gabriel, Raphael & Uriel, answering by way of analogy to yᵉ 4 Elements, Michael answering to Fire, Gabriel to Water, Uriel to Air, & Raphael to ye Earth, & to yᵉ 4 living Creatures In Ezekiel, Michael to yᵉ Lyon, Gabriel to yᵉ Ox, Uriel to yᵉ Eagle, & Raphael to yᵉ Man; & to yᵉ 4 quarters or Corners of yᵉ World, Michael to yᵉ South, Gabriel to yᵉ North, Uriel to yᵉ East, & Raphael to yᵉ West, & also to yᵉ 4 Watches of yᵉ Night, & to yᵉ 4 postures of man's body, to wit, yᵉ right & left side, yᵉ forepart & back, & yᵉ 4 Letters of yᵉ great name הוהי [wᶜʰ we read Jehovah] of wᶜʰ four Angels & Angel-Governmᵗˢ John in Revelations, seems to make mention under the name of winds, & as there are 4 Angels in yᵉ Kingdom of Purity or Holiness [to use yᵉ term of yᵉ Cabala] so there are other 4 contrary unto yᵐ in yᵉ Kingdom of Impurity, that has power to hurt yᵉ Earth & Sea & yᵉ trees. Rev. 7.2. & under these Kings are Captains: there are many other Angel-Hosts & Princes, that I shall not at present medle to enumerate, & yᵗ J.B. hath got yᵉ name of Uriel among the Jews, wᶜʰ is in their Cabala, seems manifest, for I nowhere Find it in Scripture.

10. He seems p. 83. 84. to distinguish between yᵉ Serpent yᵗ deceived Eva, & yᵉ Devil,⁸ as if yᵉ Serpent were some outward Beast, as yᵉ Snake or Serpent commonly so called, wᶜʰ is a gross Conception & contrary to yᵉ Scripture, that expressly calleth yᵗ old Serpent yᵉ Devil. Rev. 20.2.

11. He seemeth to hold, yᵗ yᵉ Soul of man is generated out of yᵉ seed of man, & is not created, wᶜʰ is false, & a most gross Conception:

& from this false Principle he concludes, that Children's Souls, yᵗ come of wicked Parents, when yᵉ Children die in infancy or in yᵉ Womb, reach not God to eternity or yᵉ day of Judgmᵗ. This is merely asserted upon a false Supposition, yᵗ yᵉ Soul is only generated out of yᵉ seed of man, or is only yᵉ seed of male & female mixed together in yᵉ Womb,

[6]

but yᵉ Soul of man is more noble, & is certainly created of God, but when it was created, I shall not at present meddle to determine, only to prove its Creation, see Jesa. 43.7. compared with Gen. 1:27 & 2.7.

12. Again he sais, yᵉ Woman has yᵉ Water Tincture & yᵉ man yᵉ Fire Tincture. This is contrary to yᵉ Cabbala, to wᶜʰ I rather assent, for yᵉ Cabbala understands, yᵗ the woman being yᵉ half of yᵉ man & being made of his side as yᵉ Hebrew word dos signify, Gen. 2.21.22: is the left side of yᵉ man, & yᵉ left side answers to Fire or Anger, and Severity, but yᵉ right side to which man belongs, answereth to Water or Clemency. Hence according to yᵉ Cabbala yᵉ 5 Numerations [in yᵉ Aziluthick System called Adam Cadmon] on yᵉ left hand are called Rigors or Severities, but yᵉ other 5 upon yᵉ right hand are Benignities and Clemencies, & yᵗ yᵉ Fire belongs to yᵉ left hand, appears out of yᵉ New Testament, for yᵉ Goats are set on yᵉ left hand where is yᵉ fire of Anger, answering to Geburah, i.e. Severity or Rigor, & is on yᵉ left hand in ye Aziluthick System; Hence we find, yᵗ women commonly have something in their Nature more fierce & rigid then men & being provoked, are commonly more implacable and less easy to be reconciled then men. But this is to be understood as to yᵉ interiour Nature, whereas to yᵉ exteriour, it may be otherwise, And yᵉ Cabbala sais, that yᵉ Souls of women doe come from yᵉ left side, & yᵉ Souls of men from yᵉ right side in yᵉ Briatick System, otherwise called yᵉ Throne of Glory, that is yᵉ next system unto yᵉ Aziluthick, & is that Throne on which yᵉ heavenly man Adam Cadmon sitteth According to Ezekiel 1,27.

13. And his notion of Election & Predestination p. 60 & 61[9] is altogether false & contrary to Scripture, as a man when he passeth from a State of non-conversion to Conversion, did pass to Election

from Reprobation, as if every man before his Conversion were a Reprobate, after his Conversion became elected; for tho' Election impro

[7]

perly doe at times signify a State of Conversion in Scripture as in Isai. 14,1. 49,7. Zech. 1,7, yet in ye most usual Sense of Scripture in ye N.T. God's Election of men is Sd to be before ye Foundation of ye World, & even unconverted men & unbelievers are Sd to belong to God's Election, & to be elect. Compare Eph. 1.4. wth Ro. 11.7. 28. & 2 Tim. 2.10. Paul Sd, he endured all things for ye Elects sake, y^t they might be Saved, which implyeth they were elect before Converted or Saved. And according to Christ's & Paul's Doctrine, man's Conversion, Faith or Sanctification is not ye Cause of God's Election, but ye Effect of it, for he hath chosen us to be Holy, & not because we are Holy, & he hath first chosen & loved us, before we could love or chuse him, But I have not time at present to open that great Mystery of Election & Predestination, & therefore shall refer it to another Occasion.

14. That he saith, ye Sound of ye 7th Trumpet is already sounding, p. 73.[10] This I am assured, is altogether false, for we are yet but under ye 6th Trumpet. But when ye 7th Trumpet soundeth, not only ye Kingdoms of ye World become the Lord's, but ye time of ye dead to be raised, dos come with it, compared with 1 Cor. 15.52. For ye 7th Trumpet is y^t last Trumpet, for we read but of 7 Trumpets in ye Scripture, & ye 7th is ye last called by Isaiah, ye great Trumpet. Isai. 27.13.

15. That he saith our whole Life is a Continual Sinning & applies Paul's words Rom. 7 to ye best State of ye Saints on Earth, wch is false & unsound Doctrine, & dos but too much gratify Hypocrites & carnal professors, who plead for sin term of life [sic], If he had Sd, y^t there remaineth in ye flesh or mortal body a Seed or principle of Sin, that may tempt to sin, but y^t ye Soul is under no necessity to obey it & when it dos not obey it, it is not defiled by it, that had been more safe.

16. That he saith, at ye end or last Day, ye Earth will be like a Crystal-line Sea,[11] if he mean ye outward Globe of ye

[8]

Earth & Sea, I can see no reason for this, but his own Fancy. I find not that ye Scripture sais any such thing. The Cabbala seemeth to reach to ye mystery of this more truly, & sais, all ye parts of ye Earth shall be changed, after another manner then is here supposed by J.B. wch I shall not at present take time to explain.

17. He seemeth to think, that ye Tree of Life, & ye Tree of Knowledge, were outward things, & y^t ye Fruit of them was eat by ye outward mouth; also y^t Paradise was outward, see p. 26.[12] But in this he is mistaken as in other things: ye Cabbala has a better understanding of these things & more agreeable to Scripture, which I shall not at present open, but refer to another Occasion.

18. He saith, Adam's ~~Fall~~ body before ye Fall, could goe through Earth & Stone uninterrupted by any thing, see p. 30.[13] This also is false & contrary to Scripture, which speaking of ye first man Adam as he was before ye fall, saith ye first man is of ye earth earthly, & that was not first wch is spiritual, but that wch is animal. It is certain, that Adam's body before ye Fall, was very glorious, yet being animal and not Spiritual, it could not penetrate earth & stone as a Spiritual body can doe.

19. He seemeth to hold a Purgatory between heaven & earth, where imperfect Souls, that have ye Work of Sanification begun in y^m, but not perfected, doe remain for sometime; but this also is contrary to Scripture, for all perfect cleansing of ye soul from sin, is upon earth, where Christ shed his blood, & where ye 3 that bear record, to wit, ye Water, Blood & Spirit; & ye Ladder that Jacob saw, reached only between earth & heaven, & ~~earth~~ not between Purgatory or any other middle place & heaven.

20. He saith, Man had no such bestial flesh before ye Fall, but heavenly flesh &c.[14] That man had no such Beastial Flesh, I grant, but y^t his flesh was altogether heavenly, doth not follow, his body was animal, y^t is of a middle degree

[9]

between bestial & heavenly, more excellent then beastial, but yet not heavenly at his first Creation. These are part of ye many & gross mistakes I find in thy Treatise, wch is a Compendium of J.B.

I shall now proceed to give thee some hints wch I promised of some of those things y^t are accounted choice & rare in J.B. his Writings, that I have found more distinctly & intelligibly in ye Cabbala, wch gives me occasion to suppose at least y^t he hath borrowed many of these things from some Rabbies among ye Jews y^t abound in Germany, & ye rather because he useth diverse of those very Words & Terms, y^t are to be found in ye Cabbala. And first as to ye forms of nature wch J.B. sometimes calls 7 & sometimes 10, this doth agree to ye Cabbala, wch saith, there are 10 Divine Lights, y^t have emanated or flowed forth from ye most high & Supream Being, called y^e Ænsoph i.e. Infinite, which no Creaturely Understanding can reach unto, by any Positive Concentration, & y^t ye Sd Ænsoph & Supream Being doth cloth himself wth these 10 Lights, as wth so many Garments, as ye Scripture saith, he is Clothed wth Light as wth a Garm^t, & wth honour & majesty ψ 104.12 by wch he may be apprehended known & enjoyed by his creatures, ye wch Lights are not created Lights, but pure Divine Emanations. Hence is called by James ye Father of Lights: ye wch Term is also used in ye Cabbala. And these 10 Divine Lights or Emanations are understood to be placed in such an order as ye Members of a Man's body, to wch ye Members of ye body of man bear an Analogy, & they make up y^t Aziluthick System called Adam Cadmon, i.e. ye first or great Adam, otherwise called by ye name, ye heavenly Adam, ye great High priest & Bridegroom & Husband of ye Church; And generally they give him all those names given to Christ in ye Scripture, & therefore Christ is y^t Adam Cadmon or heavenly man. Moreover ye Cabbala saith, that every one of these 10 Lights, hath all the other in y^m, so y^t every one is 10, & every one of that 10 is another 10, & so infinitely. Now ye Names of These 10 are in Hebrew & English thus: 1. Kether i.e. ye Crown. 2. Cochma i.e. Wisdom. 3. Binah i.e. Prudence or Understanding. 4. Daath i.e. knowledge And these 4 belong to ye Head of this great man. Kether by

[10]

way of analogy, answering to ye Skul of ye head, y^t contains ye 3 Brains, & Cochmah Binah & Daath to these 3 Brains, Cochmah is ye Brain on ye right side of ye head, Binah that on ye left side, & Daath that behind. 5. Gedulah otherwise called Chesed i.e. Munificence, Bounty or Mercy & Clemency, ye right shoulder arm & hand. 6. Geburah i.e. Fortitude, vigour & Severity, ye left shoulder, arm & hand. 7. Tiphereth i.e. beauty &

body of this great man. 8. Nezah i.e. Victory, yᵉ right thigh, Leg & Foot. 9. Hod i.e. Glory, yᵉ left thigh, leg & foot. 10. Jesod i.e., yᵉ Foundation answering to yᵉ member of generation in yᵉ male. And to this Adam they assign his Wife wᶜʰ is called Malchuth i.e. yᵉ Kingdom having also yᵉ feminine members by way of analogy, & also they call her Mount Zion, & yᵉ heavenly Jerusalem & Sarah, Rebecca & Rachel in high or above, from whence these good women yᵗ lived here below, did borrow their names; even as Eva or Chavah, that signifies Life, borrowed her name from yᵉ Supernatural Chavah i.e. Life who is in yᵉ truest sense yᵉ Mother of all living, much rather then Eva yᵗ was deceived by yᵉ Serpent; & as yᵉ earthly Adam borrowed his name from yᵗ great Adam.

But here it must not be conceived, that any of these members are bodily or corporal, no by no means, they are altogether pure Divine Spiritual Emanations, & they are called Aziluth, which signifies neer or next, as being most near or next to yᵉ Ænsoph or Supream Being, & are yᵉ Son of God come forth or emanated from God as his outspoken word & is yᵉ Image of that in yᵉ mind of God, as yᵉ outspoken word of a man is yᵉ Image of his Word in thy mind or heart; And as God clothed himself with these Divine Garments, sometimes wᵗʰ one sometimes with another, he hath his several names both proper & appellative, as for example, as he is clothed wᵗʰ that Divine light or Garment Geburah, he is called strong, mighty, fearful, terrible, judging Transgressors, a consuming Fire; as he is clothed wᵗʰ Nezah & Hod, he is called Victorious, strong & mighty in battle, overcoming his adversaries: but in Tipheret he is called Bridegroom & Husband of his Church: in Cochmah, Binah &

[11]
Kether he is called Father of mercies & most loving & gracious Father: & in Malcuth he is called King & Lord; in Jesod he is called Just & Holy: but besides his appellative names wᶜʰ are very many, he has in yᵉ Hebrew Bible 10 proper names, each proper name answering to a peculiar Light or Emanation, wᶜʰ 10 proper Hebrew names are these following, 1. Ehejeh i.e. I am or Shall be. 2. Jah, yᵉ first answering to ~~Binah & Daath~~ Kether, yᵉ 2ᵈ to Cochmah. 3. Jehovi answering to Binah & Daath. 4. El answering to Gedula & Chesed, & is alwayes a name of pure Mercy & Bounty. 5. Elohim answering to Geburah, & is always a Name of Justice, Judgment & Severity, unless it have a Name of Mercy adjoined to it. 6.

Jehovah, in Hebrew thus יהוה answering to Tipheret, & is a name ××× partly of Justice & partly of Mercy, but yᵉ Mercy prevailing. 7. Jehova Zebaoth i.e. Lord of Hosts answering to Nezah, & is a name both of great Power & mercy. 8. Elohim Zebaoth i.e. God of hosts, & is a name of great Power & Severity. 9. Elohai i.e. God of Life & El Shaddai i.e. God alsufficient, by which he revealed himself to Abraham, answering to Jesod. 10. Adonai, i.e. Lord, answering to Malchuth. Of these names some are greatest, as, Ehejeh yᵉ greatest of all, next Jah & Jehovah, & yᵉ name Adonai is yᵉ lowest of all his proper names. There are many great Mysteries wrapt up in these names, & he who can read yᵉ Bible in Hebrew with his mind directed to yᵉ Divine Light in his Heart, as he readeth these Hebrew Names, as they occur, may reap much profit in his reading.

And by way of analogy & remote similitude, yᵉ Cabbala saith, every Creature, be it Mineral, Vegetable or Animal, &c. hath 10 forms or Properties in it, answering to these Divine Lights & Emanations, wᶜʰ they sometimes call 7, sometimes 4, sometimes 3, & sometimes 2. When they call yᵐ two, they commonly call ye one dexterum, i.e. belonging to yᵉ left side answering to ye Fire of Fierceness; & when they call yᵐ 3, they say yᵉ 3ᵈ, as yᵉ tongue of yᵉ Ballance qualifieth yᵉ other 2, & is a mean between 2 Extreams or as Glew binding 2 Opposites, as they reckon, yᵉ air is yᵉ Glew of these seeming 2 Elements, Fire & Water; & when they call yᵐ 4, they

[12]
add to these 3, a 4ᵗʰ called Earth, which they call yᵉ house or receptacle of yᵉ other 3, & sometimes they call them 5, calling yᵉ 5ᵗʰ ye Quint-Essence i.e. yᵉ fifth Essence, & sometimes also they call yᵐ 6, answering to yᵉ 6 dayes of yᵉ Creation, & yᵗ degree wherein they are perfected yᵉʸ call yᵉ 7ᵗʰ answering to yᵉ Sabbath or rest, & all this by way of Analogy, to those 10 Divine Lights, & imitating them as yᵉ shadow dos yᵉ body, & deriving a continual influence from yᵐ, without which all is dead, bare & empty. So what J.B. places in yᵉ Root or Center & Circumference or Exit, yᵉ Cabbala, & as I judge more properly, placeth yᵉ one on yᵉ right side, as yᵉ sweet water, yᵉ Light, Love & Meekness, yᵉ other on yᵉ left side, as yᵉ Fire or Fierceness or Severity, which being separated from yᵉ former, is a poison & destroyeth, but when harmoniously joined wᵗʰ yᵉ other, is a

Cause of Life & Fruitfulness. But whereas J.B. placeth yᵉ Fire properly in order of Nature before yᵉ meek property, yᵉ Cabbala dos not so, but placeth yᵗ collaterally, as thus ⅄ or as ye letter Y called Pythagorean letter, wᵗʰ 2 Arms, or as 2 Boughs of one Tree, or as Twins of one Womb, & it is hard to conceive, wᶜʰ of yᵉ 2 is first or last in order of nature, seeing none of yᵐ can be yᵉ one, altogether without yᵉ other but they are in another, only sometimes yᵉ one is more manifest, sometimes the other.

2ᵈˡʸ, J.B. agrees wᵗʰ yᵉ Cab. in affirming yᵗ yᵉ Properties of Nature became divided, & were severed asunder in great part by yᵉ Lapse or Fall of certain created Spirits, as yᵉ faln Angels & hence it is, yᵗ created nature, yᵗ was when first created, so pure & Spiritual, is now become since yᵉ Fall, so impure gross & material, hence also all kind of sickness, death & corruption, by the disharmony & unequal Dividing of yᵉ Properties of Nature; But yᵉ uncreated nature yᵗ did purely & primarily emanate or flow from yᵉ Ænsoph hath suffered no Change within itself, only as to us-ward it has a different way or manner of Acting, insomuch yᵗ when men live Holy & uprightly, this great heavenly Adam or King, who is the true Christ, shineth forth a gracious Aspect upon men, & blesseth them wᵗʰ many both Spiritual & temporal Blessings, sending down upon them, most plentifully yᵉ Rayes & Beams of his Divine Mercy

[13]

& Clemency. But when yᵉʸ transgress his holy Will, these beams of his mercy are withheld & refrained in great part & several judgmᵗˢ & punishmᵗˢ come upon yᵐ, but without any Change upon him. And therefore yᵉ Dividing or contrariety of yᵉ Divine properties called by yᵉ Cabb. Sephiroth i.e. Numerations, or Middoth i.e. Measures, or Aroth i.e. Lights, is only as to us, & not in themselves, which are always in perfect unity one wᵗʰ another; but wⁿ men provoke God by their sins, as when Adam fell, & when these Angels of Lights did fall, yᵉ Cab. Saith, yᵗ these Divine measures or Emanations, as to us-ward, did turn their Faces one from another, to wit, yᵉ Benignities or Clemencies on yᵉ right hand, did turn away their Faces backward from yᵉ Severities on yᵉ left hand & also yᵉ Severities on yᵉ left hand did turn their Faces from yᵉ Benignities, & then nothing but great Misery, Calamity & Affliction could happen to yᵉ Creatures, yᵗ were under these Aspects, for then also yᵉ Properties in created Nature did turn their Faces backward one from another, & y^t caused all ye Strife, jarring & Disorder, that is now in ye Creatures, all which ye Cabbala seemeth to hold forth more intelligibly then J.B.

3dly J.B. agreeth with ye Cab. in saying, this gross, material & visible World, did come from a Spiritual & invisible [*sic*], & y^t all created Nature was at first as a Garden or Paradise; But the Cab. saith, it was but ye inferiour Paradise, for ye superiour Garden or Paradise, was ye Aziluth or Aziluthick Systeme, y^t is above created Nature; & that every thing in this whole visible World to ye lowest grain of Sand or Dust, did preexist in another invisible World, where all were Spiritual, but y^t ye Fall has made things so gross & material by occasion of their Deprivation of Life in great part. And this gives me occasion to hint or glance a little at these 4 Systems or Worlds ye Cab. dos so often mention. The 1st called Aziluth i.e. ye World of Emanation, in wch World or Systeme, nothing could fall or degenerate, for it is for ever in perfect unity wth ye most Supream Being, & is y^t glorious & Divine body, so to speak, wherein God hath made himself spiritually seen & injoyed by Holy Angels & Souls of men, wch is Christ Jesus

[14]

ye Image of ye invisible God, in whom ye Fulness of ye Godhead dwells bodily. This is he who Sd to Moses, when he desired to see his Glory, Thou shalt see my Back-parts or posteriour parts but my faces [so ye Hebrew hath it in ye Plural number Faces] thou shalt not see. And these Back-parts or posteriour parts as ye Cab. saith, are ye 7 posteriour Lights above-mentioned, to wit, Binah, Gedulah, Geburah, Tipheret, Nezah, Hod, Jesod, but ye 3 Superiour, wch were ye Faces, he could not see, nor Kether, Cochmah, & ye last Gate of Binah, which is ye Fiftieth. For ye Cab. saith, Binah hath 50 Gates, & only 49 were opened to Moses, & to none else, & Moses reached higher in ye Aziluthick Systeme then any before or after him, except ye Messiah. And ye lesser Prophets reached commonly no higher then Nezah & Hod, but Joshuah, David & Solomon & others reached to Tipheret, & to some of ye Gates of Binah &a. And whereas all these 10 Lights are called Faces in ye Cab. yet these 3 Superiour are those Fifty called in ye highest sense; Hence those places of Scripture y^t seem to contradict, are reconciled, y^t Moses could not see ye Face of God, & yet God spoke to him Face to Face. And David saw ye Face of God, & so doe all true saints who pray with David, Hide not thy Face from us; but this is ye inferiour Face of God in Binah, Gedulah, Tipheret, &c. & not ye Superiour in Cochmah & Kether, according to wch ye Cab. expounds that profound place in Scripture, Job 28, 20, 21. 22. 23 27. but concerning ye inferiour Wisdom it is to Sd p. 28. The fear of The Lord that is Wisdom &c.

The 2^d World or Systeme mentioned in ye Cab. is Briah or ye Briatick, i.e. ye World of Creation, otherwise called ye Throne of Glory, on which the heavenly Adam sitteth, & ye Father in him according to Ezeckiel 1, 26. And this System is ye Mother of that degree of Souls in men, called Nishmoth, i.e. Minds.

The third World or System Jezirah or ye Jeziratick Systeme, called ye World of Formation, y^t is inferiour to ye former, & of a more diminute & inferiour Light, & is ye Angelical World & Mother of that degree of Souls in men called Ruchoth, i.e. Spirits common to us wth Angels. The great King or Prince or Head of this Systeme, is called

[15]

Imitation, & is by way of Analogy called ye Shoe of ye heavenly Adam, y^t is inferiour both to ye Foot & throne.

The 4th Systeme or World is called Asiah or ye Asiatick System i.e. ye World made or Fabricated, wch is this whole visible World containing Earth, Sea, Air ye Stars, not only ye Planetary system but ye whole Starry Firmament, y^t ye Cab. saith, is full of Spirits good & bad of all sorts, & this is ye lowest, & hath ye most diminute or weakest Light, & is ye Mother of that degree of Souls in men called Nephashoth, i.e. Animal Souls. And ye Cab. saith, all these 4 Worlds are most inwardly connexed & linked together, ye 2^d being ye Vehicle or Garment of ye first, ye 3^d ye vehicle of ye other 2, & ye 4th ye Vehicle of ye other 3, ye wch being more outward hath less Light Glory & Perfection; & ye King or Prince of this last Systeme is called Sandalphon, i.e. ye Slipper to ye Shoe, or that which ye Shoe goeth into, called ye Slipper or Pantaple, to signify ye Lowness & meanness of it. And ye Cab. further saith, that when God made man in ye beginning, he made him an Epitome or Abridgem^t of all these 4 Worlds, & gave him a Degree out of each of them, to wit, ye Nephesh or lowest Degree properly called Soul, out of Asia, ye Ruchoth i.e. Spirits out of Jezirah; & Nishmah i.e. Mind out of Briah, & out of ye Divine

Systeme called Aziluth, he gave him that Nishmah Lenishmah, i.e. Mind of yᵉ mind, otherwise called Chajah, i.e. Life, which hath also its various Degrees too long here to enumerate. The Cab. saith further, yᵗ these 3 latter Systems were framed or composed out of certain Fragments of the Vessels [after some Lapse or Fall] which were first created to receive & enjoy yᵉ Divine Lights & Emanations, & yᵉ Systeme called Briah contained yᵉ first most pure separated parts; the next Systeme called Jezirah contained a 2ᵈ degree of separated parts, but less pure, & yᵉ 3ᵈ & last Systeme called Asia, contained a 3ᵈ degree of separated parts yet less pure, by reason of wᶜʰ in both these latter Systems, to wit, in Jezirah & Asiah, there is a great Mixture of Purity & Impurity or good & evil, wᶜʰ mixt Nature in both these Systems is that called by Moses yᵉ Tree of knowledge of good & evil, wᶜʰ Adam and Eva should not have fed of until yᵉ perfect Separation of yᵉ evil from yᵉ good had been made,

[16]
& then it had been only yᵉ tree of Knowledge of Good & not of evil, for good & evil signifies an unhappy mixture occasioned by the Fragments of yᵉ Vessels, many Ages out of our knowledge or numbring before Adam was made in it; & yᵉ Cabbala sais, that all Devils & unclean Spirits are yᵉ Dross, Dregs or Excrements, after yᵉ Separation is made, or as yᵉ Chaff, when yᵉ Wheat is separated from it, or as yᵉ Shells when yᵉ Kernel is separated, or as yᵉ bark, when it is taken or separated from yᵉ Tree, & as yᵉ Bark, shell & Chaff receive their Life and strength from yᵉ Tree, yᵉ Kernel & Wheat; so all Devils & unclean Spirits receive all their Life from yᵉ more good & pure parts of yᵉ fragmᵗˢ of yᵉ Vessels as men's Souls; & therefore they doe so earnestly desire to dwell ~~upon~~ in men, to have Life & Strength by yᵐ, for otherways they are but as empty dead Shells, after yᵉ Souls of men give them not Life or Strength.

And as concerning yᵗ superiour Garden or Paradise of Eden, yᵉ Cab. dos thus describe it. Eden is Cochmah, Kether is yᵉ East where Eden was, yᵉ Garden or Paradice is yᵉ whole Aziluth, from Binah to Malchuth, yᵉ Tree of Life is Tiphereth, yᵉ other Trees in yᵉ Garden are yᵉ other Divine Measures or Sephirahs infinitely distinguished, as each one into ten, & each of these into other 10, & so infinitely into 100ˢ, 1000ˢ, 10000ˢ, &c. And yᵉ River yᵗ came out of Eden to water yᵉ Garden, is Binah, wᶜʰ cometh out of Cochmah, & reacheth to Malchuth yᵉ lowest, & at Malchuth ends ye Aziluthick System, wch is most immediately united wth y^e Ænsoph or Supream Being, & thence begins ye System of Briah, next follows Jezirah, next Asia, & last of all ye World of ye Shells or Barks, to wit, that of ye Devils, & foul Spirits, that were not perfectly separated from ye pure parts at Adam's first Creation, & by Adam's Fall got more Life & Strength, then formerly they had. And these latter Systems beginning as Briah, are called ye Systems of ye separated & divided Worlds, because it is Sd, ye River having watered ye Garden, it Was thence divided into 4 heads, wch 4 heads signified by 4 streams are 4 Captains or Princes under one General in every System, wch Receive their Food from Malchuth, as her Maidens or Servants, &

[17]

distribute y^m to all ye inferiour hosts in every System, & what remains is to be left to feed ye Cortices i.e. Barks or Shells, as it was Sd to ye Serpent, Dust shalt thou eat. And y^t Adam was placed in ye Garden, Shews, y^t he was advanced to ye Aziluthick System, where he might eat of every tree of ye Garden i.e. he might receive of every one of ye Divine Measures or Sephirahs, a Divine Influence of Light & Life, & converse with God as near as possible. But y^t ye Tree of Knowledge of good & evil was placed in ye midst of ye Garden, shews, y^t both ye Systems of Jezirah & Asiah, y^t have Mixtures of Impurities & evil in y^m [did] stand in ye middle as it were of the Garden: For this Divine Garden dos encompass & enclose all Creatures good & bad, so that all things live & move & have their being in ye same, wch is ye expressed Word y^t is emanated from y^t in the Mind of God himself. And Malchuth ye Wife of this Divine & heavenly Adam is called in ye Cab. ye Ruah Hakkodesh i.e. ye Holy Ghost, & is only called Woman as he is called man by way of Allegory & Analogy, for as ye Woman receiveth Seed from ye Husband, & there of Children are begotten, so Malchuth ye lowest Divine Measure receiveth from Tiphereth & ye other superiour Measures, as Christ Sd concerning ye Holy Ghost, y^t it shall receive of him & deliver unto his Disciples. And she is called Holy, because she receiveth ye Sanctity or Holy Influence y^t comes from the Ænsoph into Kether & descendeth from Kether through all ye Divine Sephirahs into Malchuth, wch is ye last Divine Measure or Vessel. So ye Cabbala.

4^{thly} J.B. agreeth wth ye Cab. y^t saith, Adam before ye Fall, had no Beastial or Brutal body, for he got this Bestial or Brutal body wth ye Fall, by eating ye forbidden Fruit, ye Serpent pouring his venom or poison into him, y^t made him like ye Beasts that perish & subjected him to ye Planets & Starry firmam^t, & so to Sickness & Death. But yet Adam's Body was earthly but of most pure earth, & was very glorious indeed, yet not so subtile & spiritual, as to penetrate Earth & Stone, as J.B. dos Fancy, contrary to Scripture, as I have already observed.

5^{thly} J.B. agreeth wth ye Cabb. y^t saith, Adam & Eva were made both in one body or person, ye woman in ye man, & if the Fall had not hapned, they should have brought forth their children, remaining still in one body without separation both man & woman, & yet

[18]

none of y^m but a Virgin full of Chastity &c. as is Sd, Treatise 26.[15] And thus again it will be at y^e end, when y^e End findeth y^e Beginning, & things come to be as first designed by y^e Divine Wisdom ____ 6^{thly} I find in J.B. an Expression altogether Cabbalistical, p. 34 concerning y^e Soul, y^t it is of y^e Form of a round Globe, & wch divideth itself into 2 parts or Eyes, standing back to back,[16] wch y^e Cab. thus explaineth, viz. Adam & Eva made but one intire man & their Soul was one, & their body one, as an entire Globe, or rather as a Cylinder or round Log of Timber, the wch were joined wth their Backs together & their Faces averse, wch is an Allegory, & is not to be grossly understood. For as is above declared, ye Creatures y^t fell before Adam, provoked God so greatly, y^t these Divine Faces in ye Aziluthick Systeme, to wit, ye Benignity & ye Severity, which formerly looked one towards another, & did qualify & mitigate each other, signified by ye 2 Cherubim in ye Temple y^t looked one toward another, turned their Backs one to another & their Faces averse, & this caused ye like Aversion in ye whole created Nature, for some time, where ye 2 properties, ye Male & Female became divided & averted one from another for some time. But afterwards when God blessed them, & Sd unto them, be Fruitful, these Divine Blessings proceeding from ye Faces of ye Divine Measures turned one towards another, according to word of y^e ψ 85. 10, 11, 12. Mercy & Truth are met together, Righteousness & Peace have kissed each other &c. The Sd Properties in created Nature in Adam & in other things, y^t were joined wth their Backs one to another,

& their faces averse one from an other, were changed, face looking to face, as when 2 half Circles y^t formerly stood thus)(, are so turned in their Figure, or converted one to another, that they stand thus O like an entire Circle, or as 2 halves of a Globe so joined, y^t they make a perfect Globe. For indeed according to ye Cab. Adam & Eva had contained in y^m all ye purest & most refined Spirits or Souls, belonging to ye Asiatick Systeme, yea & his Dimensions or Extent was so great that he reached to all ye Systems, but as a thing is not made perfect at first but by degrees, as in ye great World, even so was it in

[19]
Adam & Eva, y^t were made in one first back to back, & then turned Face to Face, as is before explained.

Thus I have given some hints of J.B.^{s} Philosophy, wherein I find it to agree in divers things wth ye Cab. I could instance more particulars, but these may suffice at present to shew y^t my thought or supposition is not in vain, when I say, it is probable y^t J.B. has borrowed many things among ye Jews out of their Cab. but for want of a right understanding, hath very odly disguised y^m. And if these things I have here delivered very passingly, find good acceptance with thee, & y^t thou find a good & pious Inclination to search further into these things, & be willing to see J.B.^{s} Mistakes [& thy own also in some things] I may possibly as I find freedom & opportunity, say more to these & other things.

Now as I doe not approve of every thing in ye Sd Cab. so I cannot but say, I have found some very excellent things in ye same, wch I greatly approve & savour well, not only agreeing wth ye Holy Scriptures of ye O.T. but especially wth ye N.T. so y^t almost every where y^t I find ~~Sd~~ in ye N.T. any allegory as y^t of Sarah & Hagar, & of ye Servt & Son, or those allegorical & mystical Terms in John's Revelation or any others, in ye Epistles of Peter & y^t of ye Hebrews, & in many of Christ's words, ye Cab. is in a manner ye best outward commentary, to open these so deep places of Scripture in ye NT as well as ye Old; but unless God by his Divine Inspiration & Illumination open ye Understandings of men, it is impossible for y^m to reach into these Mysteries.

But let us not cast Pearls before Swine, nor give Holy things unto Dogs, nor yet feed children wth strong meat, but give milk to Children, & strong food to strong men—As to ye places of Scripture where ye names of these 10 Divine Lights or Emanations in ye Hebrew & English Bible, see 1 Chron. 29, 11. there is some mentioned in due order, & Prov. 24, 3 mentions Wisdom & Knowledge together, as also 3. 19, 20. & ye Crown is mentioned in Pro. called by Crown of Life, Foundation is frequently mentioned.

Postscript

I shall add some more observations & Principles of ye Cab. & ye better to understand what I have already written.

[20]

First, The right Understanding & knowledge of these Divine Lights aforesd, is as it were ye foundation of all true Theology & Philosophy, i.e. of all Divine & natural things, for as these Divine Lights have emanated from ye Ænsoph, i.e. Infinite Being, so all Created Beings have emanated from y^m, & are a Shadowy Resemblance of y^m, but man is ye most excellent Similitude of y^m, beyond all other Creatures, yea beyond ye Angels—

2^ly, The Cab. observeth, y^t in ye work of ye Creation mentiond in Gen. 1 'tis only 10 times expressed (& God Said) wch signifies these 10 Divine Emanations, every word signifying a Divine ~~Measure~~ Emanation, & in Analogy to this, God hath given to men's bodies 10 principal Members, as his two Hands, 10 fingers, & because he is composed of 10, he can goe no further in numbering; & for a Law for him to doe & fulfill, 10 commandm^ts, ye first commandm^t answering to y^e Ænsoph, ye 2^d to Kether, ye 3^d to Cochmah, ye 4th to Binah, ye 5th to Gedulah, otherwise called Chesed, ye 6th to Geburah, ye 7th to Tipheret, ye 8th to Nesah & Hod, ye 9th to Jesod, ye 10th to Malchuth. And thus his fulfilling ye Law of ye 10 Commandments, was his laboring, in ye Garden, & keeping of it all wch hath a Spiritual Signification, & ye 7th day called ye Sabbath according to ye Cab. is Binah, ye 7th Divine Emanation, counting upward from Malchuth or Jesed.

3dly The Cab. saith, ye 3 Metallical Principles, & 7 metals bear a special analogy to these 10 Divine Emanations, as thus ☿ answereth to Kether, ♁ to Cochmah, ♃ to Binah, ☽ to Gedulah ☉ to Geburah, Iron to Tipheret, Tin to Nesah, Copper to Hod, Mercy to Jesod, & ye metallick Female [called ye Moon of ye wise men, & ye Field or Earth, into wch ye Seeds of ye minerals are to be sown, wch ye Cabbalists call Mezaliab, i.e. Water of Salt, see Gen. 36. 29] unto Malchuth.

4^{thly} and as to ye 7 last Emanations, ye Cabbala referreth to ye 7 metals, so also these called ye 7 Planets, & ye 7 dayes of ye weeks as thus:

Geburah	Gedulah	Tipheret	Hod	Nezah	Jesod	Malchuth
Gold	Silver	Iron	Copper	Tin	Mercury	Lead
☉	☽	♂	☿	♃	Venus	♄
1 day	2^d day	3^d day	4th day	5th day	6th day	7th day

[21]

wch seemeth to give a Cabbalistical Reason of these names, given to each day of ye Week, of ye metals & of ye Planets, seeing they so patly agree one to another. And because all things stand in such excellent Harmony & Analogy, ye Cabbalists say, he who hath a right & perfect knowledge of these 10 Lights, knows how to make ☉ & ☽, & y^t called ye Philosophers Stone, wch some Cabbalists seem to have, & they say, ye whole Work of it, is contained in some Hebrew Words & Names of ye Scripture by way of Allegory.

5^{thly} The Cabb. observeth, y^t ye Word Elohim, y^t is one of ye proper Names of God, is used 32 times in ye Work of ye Creation Gen. 1. & neither more nor less, & this signifies ye 32 paths or ways of God in making ye World, all wch are placed in man's heart, for ye Hebrew word y^t signifieth heart, viz. לב Leb, containeth ye number 32. But by reason of sin these Divine Paths or Wayes are dimmed or clouded, until God again reveal y^m, & then a man may understand ye whole Creation. See Ps. 84. 5. ye wch 32 Wayes they understand to be ye 10 Lights, & ye 12 Rotations of y^t great name יהוה answering to ye 12 Celestial signs, & ye 12 Tribes of Israel, together wth ye 7 Planets, & 3 principal Elem^{ts}, Fire, Water & Air, making in all 32.

6^{thly} and ye Cab. further observeth, y^t seeing ye name Elohim is only used in ye Work of Creation, & no other name is joined, until all was finished, & then ye name יהוה i.e. that commonly read Jehovah, is joined to Elohim, as in Gen. 2. 4 we read Jehovah Elohim, translated, Lord God, y^t it signifies, how God made all things in ye whole World by Judgm^t & Justice, as a Judge, as it is written Deut. 32. 4. His works are perfect, all his wayes are Judgment: for ye name Elohim signifies God acting as a

Judge, & holding a Councel, & passing a Sentence of Justice on every thing, that he made in this whole World, wch giveth us an excellent occasion to praise God, & to admire his Councel in all. For every thing is created from a Reason drawn from the Justice of God, according to what is acted in its pre-existing State, as for Example, why one Creature was made a man, another a Cow or Ox, another an Horse, another a Sheep, another a Swine, another thing was made a Tree, another a Stone, & so of the rest,

[22]
wch is a reward of their former Works in a preexistent State in a former World.—And ye Cab. saith further, that God called all ye Creatures together, as they were before, & told every one of y^m, how he was to make y^m, & how he had made all other Creatures subject to man to serve him, & how man was to use y^m, & kill y^m food, many of y^m, & how by these means they were to be elevated & nobilitated in man to become parts of him, & so to partake of his happiness both here & in ye World to come; And that all ye Creatures were glad of these tidings, & most readily assented. But when ye World could not endure by reason of its weakness, to be proceeded with, in ye way of strict Judgment & Justice, therefore God added his other name Jehovah signifying his great Mercy & Clemency to perfect & establish ye works of his hands, according to Ps. 89.2. ye true Translation is thus: By Chesed i.e. Mercy shall ye World be built or established.

7^{thly} the Cab. further saith, that as man is to be saved & restored by ye Lord himself, so all ye Creatures inferiour unto man, are to be saved & restored by him & in him, according to these words in ye Psalm, O Lord thou savest man & beast. For there is no visible Creature but it comes into man by parts & degrees, either immediately or mediately, by that called ye Gilgal, in Hebrew, i.e. ye Wheel or Revolution, for as man eateth and drinketh many things, as Herbs, Corn, flesh or Beasts, birds & fishes, so he also by this means partaketh of ye minerals & metals, & also of ye Sun & Moon & Stars, & all ye elements, & ye earth itself springeth up into Herbs & Fruit & Flesh of beasts, & man eating these things, receiveth part of ye earth daily into him, wch if he be an Holy man, is perfected in him, & through much of what man eateth, turneth to Excrements, yet a part is purified & perfected in him, so that it dos neither turn to

Excrements nor Dust, but is preserved to be his Resurrection-body. And after this manner ye Cab. understands how ye Earth shall be exalted & dignified, not as Ja.B. Fancieth to be made a Globe of Chrystal,[17] for y^t were a very poor degree of Perfection: it is all one to ye earth, whether it be chrystal or sand & Dust. But to conceive, y^t ye Earth shall be glorified

[23]

in man by becoming a part of him, & his body, this is indeed excellent, & thus that cometh to be fulfilled, The Earth shall be filled wth ye glory of God; And is not this ye same wth Paul's Divine Philosophy, who saith, The whole Creation groaneth & travaileth in pain, waiting for ye glorious Liberty of ye Sons of God, because ye Creature itself shall be delivered &c. Ro: 8, 19 20. 21. And because it cannot be supposed, y^t ye whole Earth or any great part of it can be thus restored in one World, therefore ye Cab. saith, there are Worlds to come xx past numbering, as there have been Worlds y^t are past, wch we cannot number but God infinite in knowledge, he knows ye number of y^m; Each World hath Generations of men upon it, in order to elevate ye inferiour Creatures as this hath; This I only relate Historically, without affecting, as I doe other things, ye Truth of wch is left to him y^t is able to try all things, & to hold fast y^t wch is good.

And further ye Cab. saith, The age of this World is but a Week consisting of 7000 years as of 7 days, a 1000 years being as one day, according to Ps. 90 & 2 Pet. And thus 28000 years make up a month or compleat Revolution of the great ☽ & 365000 years make up a year or compleat Revolution of ye great ☉, whereof ye ☽ & ☉ of our World are but Types & Figures: And here it is worth noticeing, whether y^t called by ye late astronomers Procession of ye Equinox or Motion of ye Orb of fixed Stars, formerly called ye Motion of ye 8th sphere, y^t finisheth its Revolution in about 28000 or 27000 years, allowing to each year its motion to be about 48 Seconds, do not point us as wth a Finger to some great mystery yet to be discovered in ye Ages of ye World.

8^thly the Cab. further saith, ye great End of God his making & placing man or mankind in this inferiour World, was by his Holy & good Life to dignify, exalt & nobilitate ye inferiour Creatures to be parts in him & of him, for y^t in all ye Creatures, as in all meats & drinks, there are excellent Spirits, wch are not indeed radical Souls of men, but Scintillae puritatis, i.e. Sparks of Purity, y^t are Spirits or Spiritual Essences, y^t being united unto man, & becoming parts of him partake of his Happiness, & all such Spiritual Essences y^t every good & Holy man dos extract & elevate in eating & drinking or otherwise, he is made Lord & Possessor of y^m for ever as his proper goods & Riches.

[24]

And as every good man dos elevate & nobilitate all meats & drinks in him or whatever comes unto him, by seeing, hearing, smelling & feeling, as well as by tasting [for to ye pure all is pure & every Creature of God is good, being sanctified by ye Word of God's Prayer] so every evil & wicked man by his great sins dos depress & vitiate ye Creatures wch he ought to exalt, & for his so doing, they shall be his Tormentors & Punishers, until he convert & be first changed from evil to good himself, & then he will be able to convert & change y^m.

And as concerning ye high Doctrine of Election, & how it is consistent wth universal Grace, according to ye Cab. ye whole Tree Adam, i.e. he & all souls of his Posterity, y^t did ~~act~~ actually pre-exist in him, & were contained in him, belong to God's Election, & must all be saved before ye end of ye World, & none are lost but Adam Belial, & his Souls called ye Son of Perdition, & altho' these 2 kinds of Souls are mingled here together in this World [ye wch mingling of these 2 kinds of Souls, Seeds, or Natures was occasioned by ye Fall of Adam, for then Adam Belial mentioned, Prov. 6. 12. did impregnate him with his impure souls, so y^t he came to have an equal number of both in him) so as oft both kinds are in one man, yet at last they must be perfectly separated the one from ye other in distinct bodies, ye one making ye number & entire body of ye Elect, ye other ye number & entire body of ye Reprobate; but these things require great deliberation & godly care to inquire into y^m.

I could impart many other things unto Thee of ye mysteries of ye Cab. but am not free or willing at present to commit y^m to writing, & particularly how each Letter of ye Hebrew alphabet dos signify a Divine Influence or Influx, & w^t Letter dos answer to its prop. influence, & how as by ye changing & various setting of these 22 Hebrew Letters, are made all Words & Speeches, so how by these 22 Influences in all ye 4 Systems aforesd, all things in all ye 4 Systems come to exist in these individual Essences & Forms, the God in himself, called y^e Ænsoph, hath no Similitude or Form that created understanding can conceive, & y^t he did expressly forbid to make any Similitude of him, yet Adam Cadmon or yᵉ Son of God as is generated or emanated from yᵉ Father, hath a Similitude, which Scripture sais Moses did See, & so did many of yᵉ prophets, to wᶜʰ yᵉ body of man did

[25]

bear some Analogy, & also the temple of Solomon, & yᵉ Tabernacle, but nothing is here to be understood corporal or material, but all pure Spirit, Light & Life Divine.

See a Description of Adam Cadmon or yᵉ heavenly Man wᶜʰ is Christ Rev. 1 from x. 13 to 18 compared wᵗʰ Ezek. ch 1.

The order of yᵉ Divine Lights

Cab. placeth thus, as on the margin, where in this figure yᵉ 22 Lines reaching from one Light to another, signify the 22 Letters in due Order.

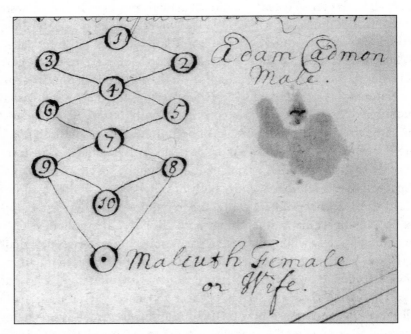

Figure A.1. George Keith, Sefirotic diagram of *Adam Cadmon* in *The Cabbala of the Jews*, mss. Miscellaneous boxes B, commentary on Jacob Behmen and The Temple of Wisdom. Courtesy of the American Antiquarian Society, Worcester, MA.

APPENDIX II

An Oration Upon the Hebrew Literature, Hebrew

EZRA STILES, 1778

[1]

כי עזרא הכין לבבו לדרש את תורת יהוה ולעשות וללמד בישראל חק ומשפט.[1]
האיש חכם וקדוש הזה מצא חן בעיני יהוה ובעיני המלך פרס ובעיני כל ישראל גדול
ליהודים ורצו לרוב אחיו. נלמד בבעלי שכל ובינה בבית מדרש לגלות בבל יהיה הוא מהיר
סופר תורה ובכל חכמת אל נתמלא על כל פנים תם וגדול ואוהב לאלהים ולאדם כי
במפעלות צדק הנכבד הוא. גם ישר וטהור לבבו עם אלהיו. ובאמונת תורה תם תם. עליו
תיזל כטל שפע אורה מלמעלה תזל עליו כטל כמה לא משוגה הוא מין דרך האמת ובכן כל
חיי טוב וחסיד אין זכרון אשר לא נמצא הרע: אך אחד האלה מהוערים בלי רע ואין עוד
שני. לא רע בשמואל ישעיה ודניאל בנוח רע. אברהם משה איוב דוד בכלם הרע אך בעזרא
אין כי אם חמד וצדק.

נותן דת האל על ידי משה וכוון נהפך לרועץ בימי גלות בבל אחריתה יכין ומשעה זאת
על ידי עזרא בימי בית שני. כן תורה במשה ומשנה בעזרא: ובעבור "הזאת" וכל מעשותו
הגדולות שמעו הולך בכל המדינות מהדו ועד כוש שבע עשרים ומאה מדינה וגם שמעו בכל
ארץ צבי ובכל עולמים עד היום הזה.

חמשון מלאכות ~~דברות~~ יעשה לטובת עמו. ראשון התחזק ביד אל הטובה עליו השיב
נדבה אלף[2] ככרים כסף וזהב וכלי קדש לפאר את בית יהוה אשר בירושלם[3] (את כלי
מקדש אשר הוציא נבוכד נזר מין העיר הקודשה):[4] המחזק על ענין נשים זכריות וגבר
הוא כפנחס: גם ישב הוא עם הנביאים אחרונים בכנסת הגדלה והנכבדה של עשרים
ומאה אנשי שם לאשר אחרונם היה שמעון הצדים ועמיהם משנה שני זבחי את בית
שני ואת כלי עבדת המקדש

[2]

אין זכרון בית כנסות קודם עתו אך מצוה הוא לבונה את ביתים באשר להשתחוה ליהוה
כלם כאחד כל מקומות ולשמוע את מקרא בכל הארץ. ולעבדת המקדש והכנסת כהן
וסופר מהיר עזרא כתב הוא את פטסגן ספר תורת משה וגם ספרים כולם אחרים אשר

233

במקרא הכלל ויתן את פטסגנות לכנסות אחד ואחד. ופתגמא של הגביר הסופר הזה נשמרה בישראל ובכל הנצרים עד היום הזה.

משנה בית הנביאים ועזרא ראש הוא ראשון לבית מדרש ירושלמה אחר לשובה מין בבל. בית זה באחרית ימים נתמלא תלמידים וכל חכמה. כמעט עמים העלים ישובו לארץ הקדשה לא יותר לעוד חמשים אלף נפשות עם זרבבל ונחמיה התרשתא ועזרא כהן הסופר. להם בית מדרש נבנה אל ירושלם על מצות משפט אנשי כנסת הגדלה ויתן האיש הזה עזרא לאתה לחכם ולראש. אך בזמן הזה בית מדרש אחרה בקרב האמון העם הנשארים במלכות בבל וזאת בית גדלה לאנשי שם וחכמה. ונשארה עד שנה אלף וחמש מאה שנה לזמן רמב"ם ונצח ישמעלים ושממת נהר-דע לבבל וגלות החכמים מן פומבדיתא ומכל קדם אל מבוא שמש. יהי שממה הזאת אלף שנה לישוע משיחנו מרינו. באחר ימי שפע נבואה ומתים כל אנשי כנסת הגדולה כל עת תרבה דעת לנהר-דיע רבה מאד מאד מאשר לירושלם. כי

[3]

ארבע מאה שנה מבנין בית שני לקח שוב ודעת טהורה אל בבל וגם לירושלם: אחרית יצא לרועץ מוסר טהור ונשמר לבד דעת תורה וזאת הבולה בתנא חכמים: אך נשארות חידות וקבלא למעטים חכמים. בראשית שני מלמדים לראש בית מדרש ירושלמה. באחרית הבית הזאת נפלגה אל שני ביתים של בית הלל הגדול ושל בית שמאי. לא נודע לא נשמע שם רבי קודם הלל וראשון הוא החכם אשר סמך את התלמידיו לשם זה הנכבד. כל משל כמה לו תלמידים ערבעים אשר זכו כי יעמד השמש עליהם כמו על יהושוע בגבעון וגם ערבעים אחרים על אשר הכבוד האל יעמד עליהם. החכם הגדול הזה בן ארבעים שנה יבוא מבבל ארבעים שנה הוא ראש בית מדרש אל ירושלם וארבעים שנה לראש סנהדרין להשבעים ומת הוא בן עשרים ומאה שנה, בזמן כיון ישוע משיחנו נעיר בן שנים ועשר שנה. ואני חשבתי כמו הלל הזקן חי הוא ראש החכמים ומלמדים לזמן ישוע בכך היה הוא אחד למלמדים הרבין על אשר יבוא ישוע בהיכל לנסתו בחידות.

דעת ומוסר לבית שמאי טהור מאד מן לבית הלל אך מנצח זה על מן שמאי במלחמות חכמת ודעת. הבית זאת וזאת. הלל הוא אב תנאים ובימיו

[4]

וממסורתו יוחלו השגיונות אשר משאל ישוע מרינו שיתו את תורת אל לרועץ ומציאות יהוה לתהו. שאל הוא כי זה משל מני-קדם לקדמנים אך לבד מאה שנה שגיונות האלה. היה דעת זה לרבין וחכמים באחרית לזמן בית שני וליום הזה. זאת חכמה על זבחי משפטי וקקת תורה לבדו וגם על כתבי נביאים אשר התנביאו למשיח הנכביד ומלכותו על הארץ. אך אין להם דעת עונות המשיח כיון חלינו הוא נשא ומכאבינו סבלם ואנחנו חשבנהו ונגוע מכה אלהים ומענה והוא מחולל מפשעינו מדכא מעונותינו מוסר שלומנו עליו ובחרתו נרפא-לנו-ויהוה הפגיע בו את עון כלנו Isai. LII.4 את הדברים האלה לא יבינו חכמי והרפי בית שני וגלות ליום הזה: אנחנו מתוך מורישי ללבבנו חנניהם כי נעלו מים מעיניהם. כל

המשוגה הזה יצא מחוקות בית הלל. חוקות עזרא וכנסת הגדלה למדו ישראל דרך אמת וצדק ומעונות של המשיח אך הבית הלל כמה בית אהב החטיא את ישראל.

בכל עת בית ראשון ובית-שני מעטים חכמים יבינו כל אלה בכלל אך מבטחים כול עם אל משיח בעונה ובמברה. אל כתובי מקבלים נשמר אור דעת זה וגם אור חכמת האלהות. ר' שמעון בן יוחי חי הוא עם יחנן הבשיר אל ספר זוהר רב האמת הופיע כמו גם ר' נטרוני וחכמים לזולתם רבים במדרשות ובתלמוד.

[5]

אחרי שמם לטיטוס הרמיי יסב בית מדרש מירושלם וממקום מקום למקום מקם אל ארץ הקדשה ובני הלל נשיאי החכמים שנפצו עד דור[5] וכמה חכמתו של הלל כן לקח וחכמה בקרבם. בימי אדריאנוס מרמם לחרפות ונפץ יד עם קדש ולא עוד יצליח חמכמה בארץ צבי אך יעלה ויציליה אל בבל ימים רבים עד רמב"ס: בימי אדריאן חי הרב וגדול ר' עקיבא שיתן את פתשגן לספר אברהם אבינו ליצירה וחכמת הקבלא: המלאך רזיאל תנא הוא החכמת ליצירה לאדם והוא מכתב אתה עם תלדות אבות בספר: חזון חנוך על רבים הדברים העתידים. ספר אדם וספר חנוך צאו בידי נוח ושם לאברהם והוא יאסף לאלה עמודי כל חכמת הקבלא וכן יסאף השלש ספרים אל ספבר אחד ליצירה ואת זה נחדש או משנה על ידי ר' עקיבא אשר נהרג בימי בר-ככב ואדריאן. זה ספר היצירה אני מבין כי אתו בעיני ראיתי אני.

אחרי הבית שני נעשה עבדה ומעשה מאלך הגדלם של תלמוד. יש תלמוד ירושלם ויש גם תלמוד לבבל ולשניהן לפטסגן אחד הספר משנה ר' יהודה הקדש אוהב הוא לאנטונינוס פילוסופוס: לאקרי אמת יהודה תלמידיו יאסיפו את תנא החכמים לגמרא וכן יצרו את תלמוד ירושלמי שתכלל מאה שנה אחרי שממה. אין נחפץ זאת לחכמי בבל ואלה יאספו אתה מאד יצקו אקרי יהודה עם רבות מחישבות של רבים אחרים החכמי בבל. תלמוד הבבל תכלל חמשה מאה שנה אחר השמם והנכבד ונתמלא מאד מאד מין הראשנה.

[6]

למדנו בתלמוד כי ספר מקרא היום נעשה הוא לפטסגן היום בזמן עזרא. החמשה חמשי תורה בקרב היושבי שמרונים נתנה עליהם בימי שלמנאסר מלך אשור יוצא זה לזמנו: אך חמשה תורה להלל בידינו אין בין זה לזה כמעט. ובכן ידעו אנוחנו כי פטסגן אמה יש זה כמו מין עולומים הקדמנים. וגם בתלמוד ובמעשה יוסף המזכיר נלמדנו המקרא הכלל מתרגום אלה בלשון יונית בימי פטלמי המלך מצרים בזמן בית שני. רבים ספרים אחרים העברים עם ספר מקרא כמו ברית של אבת שנים עשר והגנזים יצאו אל ידי יהודים ונצרים הקדמנים אשר מתרגמים היו אחריתה בלשונים כל הגוים.

בזמן בית שני היהודים לא עוד שמעו את לשון העברי. ובכן משפט עזרא כי הלוים יהיו מבינים את העם מבינים את לתורה—ויקראו בספר בתורת האלהים מפרש ושום שכל ויבינו במקרא. וזה חק ומשפט בכל זמן בית שני על מקרא בית התורה. בזמן החאשמנים יוחלו התרגמים במקרא הנביאים רק לא נכתב התרגם כי מפי מלמדים הקראים נעשה זה. אחריתה הרבים

החכמי תלמידי הלל מכתבים היו את מדרשות על תורה ונביאים וכן נעשה תרגם ירושלמי
ויחנן בן זכי. ואחר שמטה על ידי טיטס נעשה תרגם הנכבדה של ענקלוס גר אשר תכלינה
בלשון אשורית וכשדים מעט שנה אחר שמם בית שני.

[7]

תם התלמוד בבל חמשים ומאה שנה למינין ישוע משיחינו. מין זמן זה לא עוד נכבדה
החכמה העברית כי אם חכמת מסורה וכן נשמרה חכמה הקדמנה עד למנין אלף שנה
לישוע כיון חרבן בית מדרש אליה לבבל. ובזמן זה רב חכמה בבל. ובימים ההם החכמי בבל
נפצו בכל הארצות והפיע אורה חכמה מין האורי גלות לכל עמים וגוים. וזמן זה משנה כל
חכמת בעברית. ובכן נאורו בעלי שם רבים כמו אבן עזרא שלמה יצחקי אך על כלם ר'
משה בן מימון. שנאמר ממשה עד משה לא עוד כמשה. איש חכם וגדול והנכבד הוא.
ובעבור הספר מרה נבוכים יחר אף ליהודים ורגזו מאד עליו ועל הכתביו עד מנוח הכלל איש
חכם ר' דוד קמקי. יצחקי משה גרנדל אבן עזרא בן גרשון ואברבינל ואחרים כתבו מדרשות
על ספרים הקדשים ועל כל מקרא ובמדרשות הזאת נתמלאות רב חכמה.

בכל עת ~~היו בקרב~~ מתי מספר הנצרים אנשים אשר יוכלו רב בחכמה העברית ויבינו את
מקרא בלשון עברי ומתרגומים היו בלשונם של גוים. בזמן משנה תורת ישוע על ידי לותר
מלאנקטון וכאלוין רבים חכמים הנצרים יהיו תלמדי~~ם~~ ר' אליהו ליותא ולרבים היהודים ומהם
נתמלאו בכל חכמה הקדשה בספרי כל מדרשות זהר ר' שמעון בן יוחי תרגמות ושני תלמוד

[8]

שני בוקסטורפים ויטרינגא וגאליוס אנשים הנכבדים בחכמה הזאת וגם בארון האשכנזי
בעל זהר ~~בוכסטורפיו~~ ליגתפוט ועינסוורת ועל כלם שלדן חכם ובעל תלמוד הרברב וגדול
ונכבוד הוא. מין הכלם אנשי שם כל אלה. אך ~~ויטרינגא וסלדן~~ שיוכלו זה אל תלמוד וזה אל
קבלא יש להם כח בינה ושכל ובתפראת האלהים ובחידותם החכמים ויש יתרון הדר להם מן
האחרים כיתרון האור מן-החשך.

היום לא נמצא ספר דת רומיית מכתב קודם ספר של יוסטיניאנוס ופנדקטא שנעשה
בזמן תלמוד בבלי. אלה גנזים לרבים שנה באחרית נמצאו לאלף שנה של ישוע משיחינו: כן
הזהר גנז לאלף שנה אחרי מת שמעון בן יוחי. כמו בפנדיקטא נשאר ונשמר דת רהומיית כן
בתלמוד וגם ספרים אחרים נשמרו משפטי יהודים הקדמונים וגם אורה רבה שנשארה על
העוני משיח על העמודתא טפי~~ם~~ גרים בזמן בית שני על סדרי המלאכים וסדר עלם למלכים
על טהורתו של ספר מקרא הקדש. זכה חכמה הזאות כי מבקשה ושתולה אל ביתי-מדרש
של אמריקא. וחמד חמדתי לראות אתה הפאר תלמדי יאלי וגם החכמי המדינות בזה בא
שמש וקצוה תבל וארץ.

יש לי התרגמים כלם שלמה יצחקי אבן עזרא בן גרשון ספר בהיר ספר יצירה של
אברהם אבינו שערי ציון זהר שמעון בן יוחי מקבל יקיר הנכבד קימקי וגו'. ובהם ובכלם
ובתלמוד וברמב"ם ובארביבל ובכתבי של מקבלים

[9]

Abridgment

ישטטו רבים ותרבה הדעת כי אזרא הכין לבבו לדרש את תורת יהוה ולעשות וללמד בישראל חק ומשפט.

והנון זכאוהי מטול מלתא דם הדותא ומסול דמה דאמרא

במשנת בית הנביאים ועזרא ראש הוא הראשון לבית מדרש ירושלמה אחר לשובה מין בבל. בית זה באחרית ימים נתמלא תלמדים ואורה וכל חכמה. כמעט העם ולא אנשים רבים העלים ישובו אל ארץ הקדשה לא יותר חמשים אלף נפשות עם זורובבל ונחמיה התרשתא ועזרא כהן השופר. על ידיהם בית מדרש נבנה ומקדש אל ירושלם על מצות אנשי כנסת הגדלה ויתנו את איש הזה לאתו לראש ולחכם. אך בזמן הזה יש בית מדרש אחרה בקרב האמון העם נשארים במלכות בבל וגם בזאת בזה נלמדו רבים אנשי שם וגדולים האללה בחכמה ובתבונה. נשארת עד אלף שנה וחמשי מאה שנה לזמן רמב״ם ונצח ישמעלים ושממה נהר-דע לבבל בעת גלות החכמים מן פומבדיטא מקדם למבוא שמש. היה שממה הזאת אלף שנה לישוע משיחנו

[10]

משיחנו בקץ שפע נבואת אל ומתים כל אנשי כנסת הגדלה תרבה דעת לנהר-דע רבה ויותר מאד מאד מאשר בירושלם. מבנין בית שני ארבע מאה שנה היה לקח טוב אל בבל וגם לירושלם. באהרה יצא לרועץ מוסר טהורה ונשמרה לבד דעת תורה וזאת חבולה בתנא חכמים. אך יש נשמרות חידות וקבלא עם כמעטים חכמים עד היום הזה.

בראשית שני מלמדים לראש בית מדרש ירושלמה. באחרית בית הזה נפלגה אל שני בתים של הלל הגדול ושל שמאי.

אין נשמע שם רבי קודם הלל וראשון הוא החכם אשר סמך את התלמידון לשם זה הנכבוד. משל כמה לו היו לתלמידים ארבעים שזכו כי יעמד השמש עליהם כמו על יהושוע אל גבעון וגם ארבעים אחרים אשר האורה כבד-אל יעמד עליהם. חכם הגדול זה כן ארבעים שנה

[11]

יבוא מבבל וארבעים שנה הוא ראש בית מדרש לירושלם וארבעים לראש סנהדרין של השבעים ומות הוא בן ארבעים עשרים ומאה שנה ובזמן כיון ישוע משיחנו נעיר בן שתים ועשר שנה. ואני חשבתי כמו הלל הזקן חי הוא ראש של החכמים ומלמדים לזמן ישוע ובכן היה הוא אחד למלמדים הרבין עם אשר ידבר עמיהם בהיכל ישוע מרינו לנסת אתם בחידות.

וגם הלל הוא אב הפרשים והתנאים. אך דעת ומוסר לבית שמאי טהור מאד מאד מאשר לבית הלל. חקות שמאי אמת וצדק: אך בית הלל כמו בית אחב החטיא את ישראל.

יש תלמוד ירושלמי ויש תלמוד לבבל ולשניהם משנה אחד לרבי יהודה הקדש. אך גמרא של בבלי נתמלא מאד מן האלה לירושלם. אין בתלמוד לקח טוב לקבלא.

[12]

בזמן בית שני היהודים לא עוד שמעו את לשון העברי. ובכן יקראו בספר *בתורת האלהים מפרש ושום שכל ויבינו במקרא*. ובאחרית הימים מכתב יונתן ועקלוס את תרגומים בלשון כשדים. ובזה לשון יש הספר בהיר ובזה ר' שמעון בן יוחאי את ספר זהר מכתב הוא. והמשכילים יזהרו כזהר הרקיע ומצדיקים הרבים ככוכבים לעולם ועד. דניאל ישלח לקץ ימים משיחינו לפדות מחכי קץ ישועתו. רמב"ם וירם ימינו ושמאלו אל השמים וישבע בחי העלם כי למועד מועדים וחצי—תכלינה כל אלה.

[13]⁶

מקבלים וחכמים אחרים רבים בכלם ראה ראיתי בעינין ושעשע רב. למדתי מהם חכמה ודעת קדשים השלשים רב ויקרות מחשבות על אלהותו וענתו וטפראתו של המשיח על כבד מלכותו על החדשה הכלל ואלף שנה ונפלאות עולם הבא. לא צקתי מים על ידי אליהו לא עמדי לרגליו של גמליאל אך אני למדתי מפי בעלי שכל מפי חמשי רבין וחכמי שם ר' משה מלכי לשפט לארץ קדשה והצדים ומשכיל קבלא הוא אחר ר' משה אשכנזי ר' רפאל חיים יצחק קאריגאל לחברון וירושלם כדמות יוסף יפה תאר הוא ויפה מראה ר' טוביה בר יהודה מזרע שלמה יצחקי לדור הששה לדמו איש דברים וגדול מקבל הוא ופילוסופוס ועל כל פנים בדעת לעילה תם תם. זולתם ר' בסקילא וגם ראותי ר' שמואל כהן לירושלים אל דעת שעשועים ותענוגים יקיר הוא ונתמלא. בכלהם אשתעשע כי ידעתי אנשי אורה ובעלי שם אלה. רק כיתרון האור מן החשך כן יתר מאד ר' קאריגאל ויגדל מן כלם בחכמת תלמוד ושכל בעברי ועל כל מקישבות תורה ומשפטי היהודים משכיל רב.

APPENDIX III

An Oration Upon the Hebrew Literature, English

EZRA STILES, 1781

3[1]
Apr. 17, 1781
In Hebrew Oration translated
Ezra VII.10

For Ezra had prepared his heart to teach the law of the Lord and to do it and to teach in Israel Statutes and Judgments.

This wise and holy man found favor in the eyes of the Ld and in the eyes of the King of Persia, & in the eyes of all Israel; he was great among the Jews, and accepted with the multitude of his Brethren. Instructed by the Masters of Wisdom & Understanding at the university of the Captivity in Babylon, he became a ready writer of the Law; and filled with all divine Literature, he was great & perfect on every point. He was beloved of Gd & man, because in works of Righteousness, he was gloriously adorned. His heart was pure & upright with his GOD; and in the Religion of the Law he was completely perfect. The benign Influences of the Light from above distilled upon him like the Dew. So that he erred not from the Way of Truth; and therefore thro' ~~all~~ whole his Life he was good and holy. There is no memorial of his Sin or of an imperfection ~~Crime~~ in him, nor in him was ever found a Crime. He was one of the very few without a Blemish. In Samuel Isaiah & Daniel there was no Blemish. In Noah there was a Blemish; Ab^m Moses Job & David all had their Imperfections; but in Ezra there was nothing but Benevolence & Holiness.

The Law of God was given by the hand of Moses: and when it was injured in the Babylonish Captivity, it was afterward

4

restored & republished by the Hands of Ezra in the days of the second house. Thus the giving of the Law was by Moses, and the new edition of it was by Ezra. And upon the account of this and his other eminent Works, his Fame went forth thro' all the 127 provinces from India to Œthiopia, and thro' the holy Land, & thro' all ages down to this day.

Five eminent services he wrought for the good of his People. First, being strengthened by the good hand of his Gd upon him, ~~he brought back~~ he collected and conveyed the 850 thousand Talents ~~Vessels~~ of silver & gold and vessels, ~~freely given~~ the free Donations of the king, his Counsellors & the Jews for beautifying the House of the Ld at Jerusalem; ~~even all the vessels of the Sanctuary which Nebuchadnezzar carried away from the holy City & the Temple~~. This was the value of a million sterling.[2] He assumed resolution upon the subject of the foreign wives & became courageous therein like a Phineas. This was his second service.[3] He sat with the latter Prophets in the great & illustrious Synagogue of the 120 those men of Renown, the last of whom was Simeon the just. With them he assisted in reestablish^g the Sacrifices of the 2^d house with all the Service of the Sanctuary. There is no mention of Synagogues before his time. Therefore his fourth Labor was the institution of Synagogues for the public worship of Jehovah & Reading of the Law in all places every where throughout the holy Land. And for the service of the Temple & the Synagogues, Ezra as a Priest & a ready scribe, ~~wrote out a copy of~~ transcribed the Law of Moses, & all the other Books of Scriptures, and distributed Copies of the Law to & among each of the Synagogues. The Copy of this eminent

5

Scribe is that which is preserved among the Jews and among the Christians down to this day.

There was a Restoration of the school of the prophets, and Ezra became the first President or Head of the college at Jerusalem, after the Return from Babylon. This was thereupon filled with disciples & with all kinds of Knowledge. A small number of People only returned to the holy Land, not above 50 thousd with Zerubabel, Nehemiah the Tirshata, & Ezra the Scribe. By them the House of instruction was restored at Jerusalem at the command of the Great Synagogue, which appointed

Ezra the Hocham and head thereof. However at this same time there was another House of Instruction amidst the Multitude of Jews still left in the ~~Kingdom~~ Province of Babylon; which was in great ~~for~~ Reputation for men of Wisdom & literary Eminence. This subsisted and remained for 1500 years, even to the time of Maimonides, the Saracenic conquests, and the Dissolution of the College of Nahardia at Babylon, and the Banishments & Dispersion of the Rabbinical literati from Pumbedita and all the East. This Desolation & Ruin was 1000 years after Christ. From the cessation of Prophecy and the Death of the sages of the Great Synagogue, the hebrew Learning was cultivated at Nahardea on the Euphrates, thence called the River of Knowledge, with greater glory than even at Jerusalem.

6

During the first 400 years of the 2^d Temple, the hebrew Learning was taught with Purity both at Babylon & Jerusalem. Afterwards the pure science was corrupted & went to ruin, the Law being left indeed or preserved, but corrupted by the Traditions, or rather the Decisions of the Rabbies. However it must be confessed the true *mystical Wisdom* of *the Cabala*, were preserved among a very few of the literati.

At first there were two Preceptors as colleagues at the Head of the House of Instruction at Jerusalem. Afterwards this House or College was divided into two Houses, that of Hillel, and that of Shammai. The name of *Rabbi* was not known or heard of before the days of Hillel the great, who was the first Hocham who conferred this Degree and Title of Honor upon his Disciples or Scholars. It is said of him that he advanced his Pupils to ~~that~~ such a degree of Eminence in Literature as that fourty of them were worthy to have the sun rest upon them as it did upon Joshua in Gibeon ~~Ajalon~~; and another 40 were worthy to have the Shekinah[4] or divine Glory itself to rest upon them. This great Hocham was educated in Babylon till he was 40 years old; when he was procured from thence & 40 years he was head of the College at Jerusalem; afterwards he was 40 years head of the Sanhedrin, and died aged 120 years, at the time that Jesus Christ was 12 years old. It is my Opinion that Hillel the Old, who was then living & at the Head of the Sages & Doctors when Jesus was 12 æt, was one of the Doctors present in the Temple, when Jesus proved them with hard questions.

7

The Erudition of the House of *Shammai* was far more pure than that of the house of *Hillel*. Yet Hillel prevailed over Shammai in the literary Wars between the two Houses. Hillel was the Father of the Tanaits or Traditionalists: and in his days and from his Institution arose ~~began~~ those Opinions and Documents, which our Lord says, made void the Law, & rendered the Commandments of God of none effect. He expresseth himself indeed "it is said by them of old"—but these Traditions were but an hundred years old. The system of Hillel became ~~was~~ the Erudition of the Learned Hebrews during the latter part of the time of the 2^d Temple, and so ever since down to this day. The subject of this science was the *sacrifices* & outward *ordinances* of the Law only, and the *prophecies of a glorious Messiah* & his Kingdom on Earth. But in this system was *not* taught a *suffering Messiah*, who according to Isai. LIII.4. *hath born our Griefs & carried our sorrows, and we esteemed him stricken smitten [sic] of God and afflicted. And he was wounded for our Transgressions, he was bruised for our Iniquities; the chastisemt of our Peace was upon him & with his stripes we are healed—and the Ld laid upon him the Iniquities of us all.* These Words were not understood by the Rabbies of 2^d Temple & of the subsequent Captivity unto this day. Tho' all the sages understood them well till within 100 years of Christ.[5] We from the bottom of our hearts pity them because these Things are hidden from their Eyes. All this error & mistake

8

has proceeded from the Documents of the House of Hillel. The Documents of Ezra and of the Great Synagogue taught Israel the Truth & Righteousness, and the sufferings of the Messiah: but the House of Hillel like the house of Ahab taught Israel to sin.

During the first & 2^d house, few only of the sages understood all these Things intirely; altho' all the People trusted in a suffering Messiah. In the writings of the Caballists was preserved the Light of this kind of Knowledge and Divinity. R. *Simeon the son of Jochai*, contemporary with St. John the Evangelist, in his book entitled *Zohar* hath shed forth the Light of much Truth: as also Rabbi *Natronai*, and other Rabbies besides them in the *midrashot* and *Talmud*.

After the Desolation by Titus the Roman Emperor the College travelling about from place to place in the holy Land under the Presidency of the sons of Hillel as Princes of the dispersed Rabbins unto the tenth generation.[6] And their Learning was exactly according to the system of Hillel. In the days of Adrian (AD 120) such was the reproachful Treading down and Dispersion of the holy people that Literature no longer flourished in the pleasant Land; but fleeing it was transferred to Babylon, where it prospered and flourished many ages until the time of Rambam or R. Moses Ben Maimon.

9

In the days of *Adrian*, lived the very great Rabbi *Akiba*, who published a copy of the Book of Abraham our Father concerning the Creation, containing the Wisdom and Science of the Cabala. It is said that the Angel Rosiel (the Gd of Secrets) delivered the Instruction concern[g] the Creation to Adam, he wrote it with the account of the Generation of the Patriarchs in a book. Enoch received a vision of many future events. The *Book of Adam* & the *Book of Enoch*, passed thro' the hands of Noah & Shem to Abraham: and he added to them the Pillars of Astronomy[7] and all the *cabalistic Wisdom*; and so conjoyned these three into one Book entitled *of the Creation*. A new Edition of this invaluable Relict of Antiquity was given by R. *Akiba*, who suffered death in the days of Bar-cocab and Adrian. This Book of Abraham I have seen and read.

After the 2ᵈ Temple succeeded the great & laborious Work of the Talmud. There are two Talmuds, the *Jerusalem* and the *Babylonian Talmuds*—the Text of each of which is the *Mishna* of R. Jehudah the Holy, the intimate Friend of *Antoninus* the Philosopher. To the Aphorisms of Jehudah, his Disciples added the tested & decided Opinions of the Rabbies, for the *Gemara*, supplement or Illustration. And thus was formed the Jerusalem Talmud, which was finished 100 years after the Destruction of the Temple. But this Compilation did not satisfy the Rabbies of Babylon And thereupon they augmented the Authorities, and

10
combined with the Aphorisms of Judah, the Opinions and Adjudications of the later Rabins, the Sages of Babylon. It was finished

500 years after the Destruction; and it is a far more complete & glorious work than the former.

We are taught in the Talmud that the copy of the Bible in our day, is formed agreeable to that in the time of Ezra. The Pentateuch now among the Samaritans was given to them in the days of Salmaneser, and hath come down to this time. Now the Pentateuch of Hillel now in our hands differeth but very little from the Samaritan copy.[8] And by this we know that our present Copy is of primæval Antiquity. Moreover we learn from the Talmud & Josephus the Historian, that the whole Scripture was translated into Greek in the days of Ptolemy—K. of Egypt & in the time of the 2ᵈ Temple. ~~Most of~~ Many of the other hebrew Writings, besides the Scriptures, as the Testament of the XII Patriarchs, and the apocryphal or unpublished Books, came or passed into the hands of the Jews & primitive xtians, and were afterwards translated into the Tongues of all the Gentiles. In the time of the 2ᵈ house the Jews no longer understood the Hebrew. And hence it was the ordinance of Ezra that the Levites should *cause the pple to understand the Law. And they read in the book of the Law of Gd, expoundg & givg the sense & caused them to understand*

11

the Reading. And this continued the Statute & ordinance the whole Duration of the 2ᵈ Temple. In the time of the Asmoneans began the readᵍ & Interpretᵃ of the *Prophets* upon Antiochus prohibitᵍ the *Law.*[9] But yet hitherto the Interpretᵃ or Targums were oral only & not written. At length the Rabbies the Pupils of Hillel, wrote Discourse or free Interpretations upon the *Law* & the *Prophets*; and thus was made the brief Targums of Jerusalem and that of Jonᵃ ben Zacchai, a Disciple of the great Hillel.[10] After the Destruction by Titus was made the illustrious & elegant Targum of Onkelos Ger, which he made into the Chaldee a little after the destruction of the 2ᵈ house.

The Babylon Talmud was finished about A.D. 500. From this Period the hebrew learnᵍ did not figure, except in the branch of learnᵍ called the *Masorah*: And thus the antient hebrew literature was preserved (thro' the Fidelity of masoretic criticism) unto the æra of 1000 years after Christ, when the School of Elijah at Babylon was broken up, after it had subsisted there 1600 years. At this time the Learning at Babylon was high. In these days (A.D. 1000) the Sages of Babylon were dispersed thro' all Lands: and there shone forth the Light of Wisdom from the Lights of the Captivity unto all Peoples & Nations. In this æra there was a Mishna or Restoration or Revival of all the Hebrew Literature. There then shone forth

12

many Sages of Eminence and Renown, as *Abn Ezra, Selomoh Itzhaacki,* and above all *R. Moses ben Majemon.* It is said "from Moses to Moses there was not another like unto Moses"—son of Majmon. He was a great Man and a venerable Hocham. But on account of his Book entituled *More Nevochim,* a vehement Controversy arose among the Jews who raged much against him & against his Writgs, until all was appeased by the wisdom of the great Rabbi *David Kimchi.* Itsaaki, Moses, Gerundl, Abn Ezra, Ben Gerson, Abarbinel & others wrote Commentaries upon the all the Scripture [*sic*], and in these commentaries are contained a vast Treasure of Wisdom.

In every age there have been a few Christians who were well acquainted with the hebrew Literature, and understood the Scriptures in the Hebrew Tongue, and translated them from hebrew into the other national Languages. In the time of the Mishna or Renovation of the *Law of Jesus* or the Reformation by the hands of Luther, Melancthon & Calvin, many of the Christian Divines became the disciples of R. Elias Levita & other Jewish Rabbies: and from them were filled with all the sacred Wisdom contained in the *Commentaries,* the *Zohar,* the *Targums,* and both *Talmuds.* The two *Buxtorfs, Vitringa, Galons,* were men of Eminence in this

13

kind of Literature; and also the German Baron who was master of the Zohar & printed it at Sultzbach;[11] & Ainsworth; and beyond & above all the Learned Selden, that great Master of the Talmud, and in all the Branches of the Hebrew Literature he surpassed all the xtian Literati. All these were Men of Renown. But *Vitringa & Selden,* eminent for their knowledge the one for the *Talmud,* & the other for the *Caballa,* were possessed of a strength of Genius understand^g & Discernm^t so that upon the profound & difficult questions among the Literati, their Glory surpassed that of all others as much as Light expelleth Darkness.

In this age is not found the Book nor any code of the Roman Law written before the Institute or Book of Justinian and the *Pandects*, which were compiled in the time of the Babylon Talmud. The Pandect was lost & lay hid many years: but afterwards was found about 1000 years after Christ. Thus also the Zohar lay concealed & unnoticed a thousd years after the Death of its Author R. Simeon ben Jochaj. As in the Pandects have been safely Preserved the great Principles of the Roman Law: so in the *Talmud*, & also in other Books, but in the Talmud especially has been preserved the antient hebrew Jurisprudence: and also therein much Light has been preserved *concerning a suffering Messiah*, concerng *Infant Baptism* under the 2^d Temple, upon the *Chronology of Princes*, upon the *angelic Hierarchy*, & upon the Purity or *Authenticity of the Scriptures*.

14

This kind of Learning is worthy to be sought after and transplanted into the Colleges of America. With Desire I have earnestly desired to see it illuminating the Scholars of Yale College, and also the Literati of different Cities in these Goings down of the sun these Ends of the World.

I have some Rabbinical Authors, which I peruse with great profit & Delight, as all the *Targums*, the Commentaries of *Solomon Ishaaki, Abn Ezra*, & *Ben Gerson*; also the *Bahir* written before X, the *Sapher Jatzira* of Ab^m our father, the *Gate of Zion*, the *Zohar* of Simeon ben Jochaj that most excellent & venerable Caballist, add to these *Maimonides, Kimchi* & others. And in all these, & in *Ramban, Abarbinel*, & in the Writings of the Caballists and many of the later Rabbies, I say in all these I have looked with great attention and unspeakable Delight. I have been taught from them the Wisdom & Knowledge of the Holy Trinity, and invaluable Speculations upon the *Divinity & sufferings of Messiah*, upon the Glory of his K^m, upon the Renovation of the universe or Restitution of all Things, the Millennium and the World to come.

I have never poured Water upon the hands of Elijah, nor sat at the Feet of Gamaliel; but I have been taught personally at the mouth of the Masters of Wisdom, at the mouths of *five Rabbies*, Hochams of name & Eminence; viz, *R. Moses Malachi* of Saphat in the holy Land a

15

Tzadik, and Learned in the Caballa; *R. Moses Askanazi*; R. Raphael Hajim *Isaac Karigal* of Hebron & Jerusalem, like Joseph of a comely aspect & beautiful Countenance. *R. Tobiah Bar Jehudah* of the Blood & sixth Generation from Selomoh Ishaaki—an eloquent man, a great Caballist, a Philosopher, and profoundly versed in the Lights of the celestial Wisdom. Besides these and R. Bosquilla I have been acquainted with *R. Samuel Cohen* of Jerusalem, of a fine Taste & excellently accomplished in elegant & polite Learning. In all of them I took great Delight, for I know them to be Men of Light as well as to be men of name אנשי אורה ובעלי שם. But as Light expelleth Darkness, so far doth R. Karigal surpass & excel all the rest, particularly in the Learning of the Talmud and on all Points & questions of the Law of the Jews, on all which he discourses with singular Ingenuity, a most amiable Candor & profound Erudition.

Apr. 19, 1781

Dec. 1759	R. Moses Malki from Saphat in the holy Land
Nov. 1772	R. Moses Bar David—Ashkenazi
March 1773	R. Karigal from Jerusalem
Nov. 1773	R. Tobiah Bar Jehudah 9th [*sic*; above, "sixth"]
	fr. Selomo Jarchi
June 1774	R. Bosquila from Smyrna
1775	R. Samuel from the holy Land

GLOSSARY OF KABBALISTIC TERMS

A brief note on usage: Only kabbalistic terms that appear in the present work are concisely clarified below. Most of these terms are part of larger systems and often hold multiple roles and meanings. The purpose here is to briefly indicate how the terms are employed by the thinkers analyzed here. In that regard, spellings mirror the transliterations of the thinkers discussed.

ÆNSOPH (EIN SOF): Literally, "that which is without end." This is the infinite, unknown, and unknowable aspect of God, ontically prior to emanation.

ADAM CADMON (ADAM KADMON): Literally, "Primordial Man." The first emanated entity out of Ænsoph, and thus the bridge between Creator and creation. Philosophically associated with Logos as an intermediary, and by extension associated with Christ by Christian kabbalists.

ADAM KADMON: See *Adam Cadmon*.

ATTIKA D'ATTIKIN: Literally, "the Ancient of Ancients," i.e., the Most Ancient One. Often interchanged with *Attik Yomin*, "the Ancient of Days" from the book of Daniel (7:9, 13, 22), and *Attika Kadisha*, "the Holy Ancient One." This also relates to *Adam Kadmon*, to *Arikh Anpin*, and to *Keter*, all of which are taken by many of the thinkers in this book to be related or parallel to the philosophical notion of Logos, as laid out, for example, by Philo of Alexandria.

CABBALA (KABBALAH): Literally, "Reception,'" or "Received Tradition." This variably denotes all of Oral Torah, traditionally believed to have been received by Moses at Mount Sinai, and a specific esoteric tradition developed most fully from the Middle Ages onward, which focuses on a hermeneutics of divine language and the ten *sefirot*.

CHENESETH ISRAEL: Literally, "the Congregation of Israel," which works parallel to "the Church" in Christian theological thought. On the hypostatic plane, this is related to the tenth *sefirah* of *Shekhinah*, or *Malkhut*.

CHAVAH: Literally, "life," and also the Hebrew name of the biblical Eve. On the metaphysical plane, the supernal Chavah is the divine Mother, who according to some thinkers is the female cohort of *Adam Kadmon*.

EDOM: Literally, "Red," the Edomites were an ancient biblical people who lived in a southern region of what is now modern-day Israel and Jordan. The Hebrew Bible etiologically relates the Edomite kingdom to Esau, who was born red and hairy. In medieval Jewish polemical literature, Edom came to be associated with Rome and the Church.

EIN SOF: See *Ænsoph*.

GALGAL (GILGAL): Literally, "Wheel," or something that rotates. In the kabbalistic thought of those who employ it in this book, it refers to variant notions of reincarnation.

GAON: Literally, "Genius." This term came to refer to the institutional heads of the major Babylonian Talmudic academies of Sura, Pumbedita, and Baghdad, roughly from 580 to 1040 CE.

GEMATRIA: Hebrew numerology, by which the letters of the Hebrew alphabet correspond with numeric values. The first ten increase consecutively from one to ten, the next nine increase by tens from twenty to one hundred, and the next three increase by one hundred from two hundred to four hundred. Gematria is used as a hermeneutical device.

GILGAL: See *Galgal*.

HACHAM (HOCHAM): Literally, "Wise Man." A title used for an accomplished rabbinic sage.

KABBALAH: See *Cabbala*.

LURIANIC KABBALAH: A school of Kabbalah developed by Isaac Luria (1534–1572), taught to his students during the last few years of his life in the city of Tzfat, and propagated after his death throughout Europe and the Near East. Much of it is a systematization of and development on ideas found in the *Zohar*, such as emanatory processes and the four worlds. It became a popular base for Christian Kabbalah through the *Kabbalah Denudata*, published in 1684.

LUZ: Literally, a "nut" or an "almond." In rabbinic literature and in subsequent kabbalistic texts, it became associated with a small bone within the spinal column that cannot be destroyed and that will act as the point of physical regeneration at the time of resurrection.

MASHKIL VENAVON (MASKIL V'NAVON): Literally, "Educated and Sagacious." A title in seventeenth- and eighteenth-century Italy for an individual with basic rabbinic training and education.

MERKAVAH: Literally, "Chariot." In rabbinic literature, *ma'aseh merkavah*, i.e., "the act of the chariot" is considered one of the explicitly mentioned esoteric realms of contemplation. It usually relates to Ezekiel's vision of the chariot in the first chapter of the book of Ezekiel, and to the chariot that took Elijah up to heaven in 2 Kings 2:11. The *merkavah* as a vehicle has been variously seen as a bridge between the heavenly and earthly realms.

'OLAM (PL. 'OLAMOT): Literally, "World." There are four "worlds" in Zoharic and Lurianic thought, which represent four different planes of existence related to four descending orders of creation. These are:

AZILUTH: Literally, "Emanation," this is the highest world and the ontological point from which Æensoph extends from itself.

BRIAH: Literally, "Creation," this is below *Aziluth*, is the first mentioned creation in the first verse of the Bible, and is a material creation of something from nothing out of the emanated divine essence.

JEZIRAH [*Yetzirah*]: Literally, "Formation," this is the third level and the formation of the created matter of *Briah*, like the formation of a vessel from formless clay.

ASIAH: Literally, "Fabrication," this is the combining of formed vessels into actionable existence. It relates to our own lived earthly realm.

PARTS OF THE SOUL: In Jewish thought there are variant parts of the soul often related to five different levels, though the thinkers in this book focus heavily on four, related to breath. These are:

NEFESH: This is the lowest level and is sometimes related to the Greek notion of a vegetative faculty. Related to the world of *Asiah*.

RUACH: This is the second level and is sometimes related to the Greek notion of an animal faculty, or the seat of the emotions. Often this is translated as "spirit." Related to the world of *Jezirah*.

NESHAMAH: This is a much higher level, often considered divine in essence, and is sometimes related to the Greek notion of an intellective faculty, or the seat of reason. Related to the world of *Briah*.

NESHAMAH L'NESHAMAH: This is the *Neshamah* of the *Neshamah*, i.e., that which gives the *Neshamah* life and existence. Related to the world of *Aziluth*.

PARTSUFIM: Literally, "Faces" or "Countenances." These are different configurations related to emanation within the divine realm. Notions such as *Adam Kadmon* and *Attika d'Attikin* are closely related to this and are often counted among the *partsufim*, but the thinkers in this book, drawing mainly on the *Idra* sections of the *Zohar*, focus on two specific anthropomorphic configurations. These are:

ARIKH ANPIN: Literally, the "Long Countenance." This is related to the *sefirah* Keter and is the first point of emanation from out of *Ænsoph*. It is called *Macroprosopus* in the *Kabbalah Denudata*. It looks toward the infinite and it is the concealed aspect of God.

ZE'IR ANPIN: Literally, the "Lesser Countenance." This is related to the six *sefirot* from *Hesed* to *Yesod* and it draws on the overflow from *Arikh Anpin*. It is called *Microprosopus* in the *Kabbalah Denudata*. It looks toward creation and it is the revealed aspect of God.

RUACH HA-KODESH (RUACH KUDSHA): Literally, "the Holy Spirit." In Judaism, this refers to divine influence, or influx into the tangible universe. In rabbinic literature and beyond it relates to prophetic inspiration and divine revelation, and is related to the *Shekhinah* as the earthly indwelling of God.

RUACH KUDSHA: See *Ruach ha-Kodesh*.

SEFIRAH (PL. SEFIROT): Taken together, these are ten hypostases that intervene, in gradient order, between the infinite, unknowable, and ungraspable *Ænsoph* and the physical universe of human existence. They are variably seen as tools and essences of the divine, and they act as both a means of effectively filtering the divine flow into the universe and a ladder for mystical ascent. They are to be taken as a unified whole, and separation is paramount to idolatry; nevertheless, they are gradients on a continuum and they have differing names and functions. They are, in descending order:

KETHER (KETER): Literally, "Crown." This is the highest level, sometimes indistinguishable from *Ænsoph* itself. Sometimes it is seen as the blurred and ultimately unknown first point from out of *Ænsoph* into emanated existence.

COCHMAH (HOKHMAH): Literally, "Wisdom." This *sefirah* is associated with the supernal Father and is often seen as the active beginning of creation.

BINAH: Literally, "Understanding." This is associated with the supernal Mother and is often seen as the womb that receives divine influx from *Hokhmah* and gives birth to the seven lower *sefirot*.

DAATH: Literally, "Knowledge." This is an intermediary between the upper three and the lower seven, which is not always counted. When counted, then either *Keter* is seen separately as *Ænsoph* or *Malkuth* is seen as a separate divine feminine entity.

GEDULAH/HESED: Literally, "Greatness" (*Gedulah*) or "Benevolence" (*Hesed*). Paradigmatic of the divine masculine and the forces of mercy.

GEBURAH/DIN: Literally, "Fortitude" (*Geburah*) or "Judgment" (*Din*). Paradigmatic of the divine feminine and the forces of discernment.

TIPHERET (TIFERET): Literally, "Beauty." This is a central, and centered, *sefirah* that mediates between the forces of mercy and discernment. Often seen as the subsuming body of the divine masculine and the male cohort of *Malkuth*.

NESAH: Literally, "Eternity" or "Victory." Associated with the masculine side of mercy and paired with *Hod*.

HOD: Literally, "Splendor." Associated with the feminine side of discernment and paired with *Nesah*.

JESOD (YESOD): Literally, "Foundation." This is the conduit through which all of the divine forces converge before flowing forth in a unified manner into the *Shekhinah*.

MALCUTH/SHEKHINAH: Literally, "Kindgom" (*Malcuth*) or "Indwelling" (*Shekhinah*). Associated with *Cheneseth Israel*, and the final point between the divine and the earthly realms. Ultimate receptacle of the divine flow, this is often seen as the cohort of *Tiferet* and the paradigm of the centered divine feminine.

SHA'ASHU'A: Literally, "Enjoyment," this denotes divine delight, sometimes in an autoerotic manner that gives birth to creation. It is the ontically first feeling and act that constitutes the paradoxical intermingling of indistinct masculine and feminine forces within the *Ænsoph*, and thus the very beginning.

SHEMA': Literally, "Listen," this is a central prayer to Judaism affirming the oneness or uniqueness of God, and taken directly from Deuteronomy 6:4–9.

SOD: Literally, "Secret." This often designates the esoteric realm of Jewish thought and frequently specifically relates to Kabbalah.

TA'AMEI HA-MITZVOT: Literally, "reasons for the commandments," this is a speculative practice of explaining the purposes of divine commandments that may otherwise seem to have no logical explanation. In kabbalistic thought, this usually involves explanations related to the supernal realms, sometimes in a theurgic manner.

URIM AND THUMMIM: Literally, "Lights and Purities." These were two elements within the breastplate worn by the high priest, as commanded in Exodus 28:30. They were used for communication between the high priest and the supernal realm, specifically in instances of divination.

YEHID HA-KADMON: Literally, "the Primordial Singular." This is an aspect of God as Unity in *Ænsoph*, but also as metaphysical Unity in an ontological state of postemanation, of the Emanator and the Emanated.

YESHIVA (PL. YESHIVOT): Literally, "a state of sitting." A yeshiva is a Jewish institution of learning that focuses on traditional religious texts and ideas. It is a place of intellectual exchange and community by which innovation emerges from tradition.

NOTES

INTRODUCTION: KABBALISTIC "DIAMONDS IN A DUNGHILL"

1 The literature on American exceptionalism abounds. As representative examples from the viewpoint of the history of politics and foreign policy, see Godfrey Hodgson, *The Myth of American Exceptionalism* (New Haven, CT: Yale University Press, 2009) and Hilde Eliassen Restad, *American Exceptionalism: An Idea That Made a Nation and Remade the World* (London: Routledge, 2015). For a more recent, successful exposition from the history and historiography of colonial America, see Abram C. Van Engen, *City on a Hill: A History of American Exceptionalism* (New Haven, CT: Yale University Press, 2020).

2 William Pencak, *Jews and Gentiles in Early America, 1654–1800* (Ann Arbor: University of Michigan Press, 2005), 1.

3 *The Papers of Thomas Jefferson: Retirement Series*, vol. 6, ed. J. Looney (Princeton, NJ: Princeton University Press, 2010), 548, quoting William Enfield, *The History of Philosophy: From the Earliest Times to the Beginning of the Present Century* (London: J. Johnson, 1791), 208.

4 *Papers of Thomas Jefferson*, vol. 6, 548. The Mishnah is the first major work of rabbinic literature, which is composed of the views and sayings of the sages known as the *Tannaim*, or "reviewers," who were active roughly from the first decade of the Common Era to 200 CE. It was compiled and codified by Judah ha-Nasi around 200 CE. The Gemara is composed of commentary and analysis on the Mishnah by a group of rabbis known as the *Amoraim*, or "those who speak," who were active roughly from 200 CE to 500 CE. The Mishnah and Gemara together make up the Talmud. The *Cosri* (more commonly transliterated as the *Kuzari*) is a famous twelfth-century book of Jewish philosophy by the Spanish Jewish poet and thinker Judah Halevi. Kabbalah, the *Yetzirah*, and the *Zohar* will be discussed at length below, and throughout this book. It is important to note that all of these elements brought by Jefferson represent what is known as Oral Torah, which will also be discussed below in greater detail.

5 *Papers of Thomas Jefferson*, vol. 6, 549.

6 Ibid.

7 For a full exposition of Jefferson's attitude toward Judaism and Jews more generally, see Robert M. Healey, "Jefferson on Judaism and the Jews: 'Divided We Stand, United We Fall!'" *American Jewish History* 73, no. 4 (June 1984): 359–74.

8 *Papers of Thomas Jefferson*, vol. 6, 549.

9 Ibid., 618.

10 "From John Adams to François Adriaan Van der Kemp, 16 February 1809," *Founders Online*, National Archives, https://founders.archives.gov, n.d.

11 Ibid.

12 Cf. Matthew 3:12.

13 It is worth mentioning that in addition to the occasional correspondence with both Jefferson and Adams, there is evidence of a working relationship between Adams and Stiles. On the concluding page of the Hebrew version of Stiles's *Oration upon the Hebrew Literature*, which will be discussed in detail in chapter 5 and is reproduced in full in appendices II and III, there is a note that Stiles was seeking Adams's advice concerning the planning of lectures for the professorship of law. Whether this is a reference to *the* John Adams is impossible to tell, but the fact that it involves a legal professorship indicates that it may very well be.

14 It bears mention that in kabbalistic thought, "Truth" is a central concept. The word for "Truth," אמת, is made up of the first, the middle, and the last letter of the Hebrew alphabet, representing the entire spectrum of beginning, middle, and end. Truth is also an animating principle, as the mythical Golem comes alive by the very word "Truth" itself. Meaning as such, and even life itself, hinges on the ability to master the "Truth."

15 For a fuller exposition, which will form the basis of much of what will be discussed here, see Brian Ogren, "Kabbalah," in *The Cambridge Handbook of Western Mysticism and Esotericism*, ed. Glenn Alexander Magee (New York: Cambridge University Press, 2016), 95–106.

16 משה קבל תורה מסיני ומסרה ליהושע, ויהושע לזקנים, חקנים לנביאים, ונביאים מסרוה לאנשי כנסת הגדולה. All translations from Hebrew or Aramaic are mine unless otherwise noted.

17 Exodus 19:8.

18 Exodus 20:14.

19 See, for example, BT *Eruvin* 54b.

20 George Keith, *The Cabbala of the Jews*, 1. The manuscript is currently cataloged as "Commentary on Jacob Behmen and the Temple of Wisdom, mss. Miscellaneous boxes B, American Antiquarian Society, Worcester, MA." Former librarian of the American Antiquarian Society, Robert W. G. Vail calls it *The Cabbala of the Jews*, which is how I will reference it throughout this book. There is no pagination in the manuscript, and my own page distinctions are according to the order of pages.

21 Ibid., 19.

22 Beinecke Library, Ezra Stiles Papers, note on Rabbinical Authors, Literature, etc., December 10, 1770, 6. See also Stiles's letter to John Lewis dated February 15, 1775, 14.

23 Ibid., letter to John Lewis, 14.

24 See, for example, Cotton Mather, *Biblia Americana: America's First Bible Commentary*, vol. 1 (Genesis), ed. with introduction and annotations by Reiner Smolinski (Tübingen: Mohr Siebeck, 2010), 317–19.

25 Ibid., 319.

26 Judah Monis, *The Whole Truth* (Boston: Daniel Henchman, 1722), 20.

27 Works on Pico and the Kabbalah abound. For what is still the seminal study, see Chaim Wirszubski, *Pico della Mirandola's Encounter with Jewish Mysticism* (Cambridge, MA: Harvard University Press, 1989). For more recent full treatments, see *Giovanni Pico e la Cabbalà*, ed. Fabrizio Lelli (Firenze: Olschki, 2014), and Giulio Busi and Raphael Ebgi, *Giovanni Pico della Mirandola: Mito, magia, Qabbalah* (Milano: Einaudi, 2014). For more on Francesco Giorgi and the Kabbalah, see Frances Yates, *The Occult Philosophy in the Elizaethan Age* (London: Routledge, 1979), 33–42 and 148–56, and more recently the works of Saverio Campanini, including his careful edition of Francesco Zorzi, *L'armonia del mondo*, ed. Saverio Campanini (Milano: Bompiani, 2010). For representative works on Reuchlin and the Kabbalah, see the English translation of his *De arte cabalistica*, entitled *On the Art of the Kabbalah*, trans. Martin and Sarah Goodman with introductions by G. Llyod Jones and Moshe Idel (Lincoln: University of Nebraska Press, 1993); Elliot R. Wolfson, "Language, Secrecy, and the Mysteries of the Law: Theurgy and the Christian Kabbalah of Johannes Reuchlin," *Kabbalah: Journal for the Study of Jewish Mystical Texts* 13 (2005): 7–41; Joseph Dan, "The Kabbalah of Johannes Reuchlin and Its Historical Significance," in *The Christian Kabbalah: Jewish Mystical Books and Their Christian Interpreters*, ed. Joseph Dan (Cambridge, MA: Harvard College Library, 1997), 55–95.

28 See Cotton Mather, *Magnalia Christi Americana: or, the Ecclesiastical History of New-England From its First Planting in the year 1620 unto the Year of our Lord, 1698* (London: Printed for Thomas Parkhurst, MDCCII [1702]), 119.

29 Sacvan Bercovitch, *The Puritan Origins of the American Self* (New Haven, CT: Yale University Press, 2011), xviii.

30 Ibid., xxxi. For Erich Auerbach's lengthy essay on the subject, see his *Scenes from the Drama of European Literature* (Minneapolis: University of Minnesota Press, 1984), 11–78.

31 Ibid., xxii.

1. AMERICAN CHRISTIAN QUAKERISM AND JEWISH MYSTICISM

1 On a cover page, Vail had penciled in "Removed from pamphlet volume v93 which was made up of 17th century Quaker tracts, some of them bearing the autograph of Increase Mather. It is therefore possible that this manuscript also came from the Mather Library." Vail then signs off and dates his note "4/2/35."

2 The manuscript does get brief mention in Brian Regal and Frank J. Esposito, *The Secret History of the Jersey Devil: How Quakers, Hucksters, and Benjamin Franklin Created a Monster* (Baltimore: Johns Hopkins University Press, 2018), 34, though there its author, as I will show, is misidentified as an unknown "Quaker in Massachusetts." The author, in fact, seems to have been George Keith.

3 *Cabbala of the Jews*, 1. There are no page numbers written on the epistle, but for the sake of clarity I will indicate the page according to its order within the manuscript.

4 Regal and Esposito, *Secret History*, 2.

5 Ariel Hessayon, "Jacob Boehme and the Early Quakers," *Journal of the Friends Historical Society* 60, no. 3 (2005): 212–13.

6 Daniel Leeds, *The Temple of Wisdom for the Little World* (Philadelphia: William Bradford, 1688), title page.

7 Leeds, *Temple of Wisdom*, preface.

8 Hessayon, "Jacob Boehme," 192.

9 Ibid.

10 Henry J. Cadbury, "Early Quakerism and Uncanonical Lore," *Harvard Theological Review* 40, no. 3 (July 1947): 204.

11 It is significant to note that among other developments, this theology gave rise to one of the first antislavery tracts written in North America, *An Exhortation & Caution to Friends Concerning Buying or Keeping of Negroes*, published by William Bradford and attributed to George Keith. That tract states, "All such who are sincere *Christians* and true Believers in Christ Jesus, and Followers of him, bear his Image, and are made conformable unto him in Love, Mercy, Goodness and Compassion, who came not to destroy men's Lives, but to save them, nor to bring any part of Mankind into outward Bondage, Slavery or Misery, nor yet to detain them, or hold them therein, but to ease and deliver the Oppressed and Distressed, and bring into Liberty both inward and outward." The argument is that only through *both* an outward Christ as a model *and* an inward Light as an image can true salvation be achieved, both on the individual and universal levels. Katharine Gerbner argues that the *Exhortation* should not be ascribed to Keith alone but should be seen as a communal effort of the Christian Quakers. See her article "Antislavery in Print: The Germantown Protest, the 'Exhortation,' and the Seventeenth-Century Quaker Debate on Slavery," *Early American Studies* 9, no. 3 (2011): 552–75.

12 For a detailed study of the Christian Quakerism of George Keith, see Madeleine Ward, *The Christian Quaker: George Keith and the Keithian Controversy* (Leiden: Brill, 2019).

13 George Keith, *Fifth Narrative of His Proceedings at Turner's Hall; Detecting the Quaker's Errors* (London: B. Aylmer, 1701), 14.

14 Keith, *The Way Cast Up, and the Stumbling Blocks Removed before the Feet of Those Who Are Seeking the Way to Zion* (1677), 157–58. The biblical reference is to John 17:23.

15 For Keith's full biography, see Ethyn Willliams Kirby, *George Keith (1638–1716)* (New York: D. Appleton-Century, 1942).

16 *The Conway Letters: The Correspondence of Anne, Viscountess Conway, Henry More, and Their Friends 1642–1684*, ed. Marjorie Hope Nicolson, rev. with an introduction and new material by Sarah Hutton (Oxford: Clarendon Press, 1992), 402.

17 For more on this entire relationship, see Sarah Hutton, *Anne Conway: A Woman Philosopher* (New York: Cambridge University Press, 2004), 148; Alison Coudert,

The Impact of the Kabbalah in the Seventeenth Century: The Life and Thought of Francis Mercury van Helmont (1614–1698) (Leiden: Brill, 1999), xv–xvi and 179–82.

18   This text was originally written in English and then translated into Latin; only the Latin version is still extant. A team led by Christia Mercer is carrying out a new translation with critical notes that will appear in *Oxford New Histories of Philosophy*, with Andrew Arlig, Laurynas Adomaitis, and Jasper Reid (from here on, *Principles*, Oxford). For a current translation, see Anne Conway, *The Principles of the Most Ancient and Modern Philosophy*, trans. and ed. Allison P. Coudert and Taylor Corse (New York: Cammbridge University Press, 1996).

19   *Conway Letters*, 408.

20   The use of the word "men" instead of "humans" here is deliberate, in that it reflects Conway's own usage. Whether women were understood to be privy to the same processes is an interesting question. We might assume that for Conway the answer would be yes, though it is interesting that she writes of "many soules of man," either out of convention or possibly as reflecting Keith's ideas.

21   וייצר יהוה אלהים את-האדם עפר מן-האדמה ויפח באפיו נשמת חיים ויהי האדם לנפש חיה.

22   *Zohar* 1:205b-206a: ונשמתא איהי כלילא בתלת דרגין, ועל דא תלת שמהן אינון לנשמתא, כגוונא דרזא עלאה.
נפש, רוח, נשמה. נפש הא אוקמוה דאיהי תתאה מכלא. רוח איהו קיומא דשלטא על נפש, ואיהו דרגא עלאה עלה, לקיימא עלה בכלא כדקא חזי. נשמה איהי קיומא עלאה על כלא ושלטא על כלא, דרגא קדישא עלאה על כלהו. In the translation here, I have purposefully left the terms *Nefesh*, *Ruach*, and *Neshamah* in the Hebrew due to the unique way in which they are used here and elsewhere. For a fuller explication, see the glossary of this current volume.

23   Ibid.: בגין לאתערטא בדרגא עלאה קדישא. Actualization and purification in this context are fundamentally related to a fulfillment of the commandments.

24   George Keith, *The True Christ Owned, as He Is* (London, 1679), 65–66. For another example of the distinction of the parts of the soul, from Keith's *The Way Cast Up* of 1677, and possible Zoharic influence through Knorr, see Michael Birkel, "Immediate Revelation, Kabbalah, and Magic: The Primacy of Experience in the Theology of George Keith," in *The Early Quakers and their Theological Thought, 1647-1723*, ed. Stephen W. Angell and Pink Dandelion (New York: Cambridge University Press, 2015), 262.

25   It is worth noting that this median position is an accounting that would first put Keith at odds with Presbyterianism and Anglicanism but would later get him into trouble with orthodox Quakerism.

26   For a deft analysis of this distinction within Conway, see Christia Mercer, "Anne Conway's Metaphysics of Sympathy," in *Feminist History of Philosophy: The Recovery and Evaluation of Women's Philosophical Thought*, ed. E. O'Neill and M. P. Lascano (Cham, Switzerland: Springer, 2019), 49–73. The explicit citation from Conway (from the *Principles* IV 2 [21]) is on page 62, where Mercer comments in a footnote, "Conway is quite explicit about her reliance on 'the ancient hypothesis of the Hebrews' for her account of 'the first-born son of God.'"

27   *Conway Letters*, 408.

28 Cf. Moshe Cordovero, *Pardes Rimonim* 3:7: והנה אצילות הכתר נקרא אריך אנפין והוא העלם
ראשון אל המאציל. העלם ב' הוא זעיר אנפין והוא כולל כל ח' ספירות שהם מחכמה עד יסוד וזהו סוד
העלם שני אל המאציל.

29 *Zohar* 2:62b: בההיא שעתא נטיף טלא קדיש מאתיקא סתימאה ומליא לרישיה דזעיר אנפין, אתר
דאקרי שמים. ומההוא טלא דנהורא עלאה קדישא הוה נגיד ונחית מנא לתתא. וכד הוה נחית הוה
מתפרש גלידין גלידין, ואקריש לתתא. הדא הוא דכתיב דק ככפור על הארץ.

30 *Principles*, Oxford, ch. 6, S.11.

31 *Principles*, Oxford, ch. 8, S.4.

32 *Zohar* 2:62b.: תאנא, בההוא שעתא אשתלימו ישראל לתתא כגוונא דלעילא.

33 Herzog August Bibliothek, Cod. Guelph Extrav. 30.4, fols. 20–21. Sarah Hutton has dated the letter to November 17, 1675 (*Anne Conway*, 191). It should be
noted that in the letter, Keith mentions his and Knorr's mutual friends Henry
More and Francis Mercury van Helmont, but he curiously leaves out any mention
of Anne Conway, who was the entire impetus behind his introduction to Kabbalah.

34 Ibid.: "Hic est ille primus homo, de quo Judaei Cabbalistae tam multa loquuntur,
tum Macroprosopos quem Arich Anpin nominant, tum Microprosopos, quem
Dseir Anpin vocant. Christus enim et Magnus homo est et parvus, Magnus enim
est, per quem omnia facta sunt visibilia et invisibilia, et Parvus, qui in Utero
Mariae virginis per novem menses jacere potuit, cum carnem assumpsit."
I thank my colleague Claire Fanger for willingly and quite ably checking my
translation.

35 Birkel, "Immediate Revelation," 261; Birkel, "Robert Barclay and Kabbalah,"
Quaker Studies 21, no. 1 (2016): 6.

36 Hutton, *Anne Conway*, 193.

37 Herzog August Bibliothek, Cod. Guelph Extrav. 30.4, fol. 20: "Anima verò huius
magni hominis, cuius centrum residet in parvo homine, qui de Maria secundum
carnem natus est, extenditur per universos sanctos, et quodam sensu per uni-
versum genus humanum immo per universam creationem." I thank both Claire
Fanger and Christia Mercer for their added nuances in regard to the translation
from Latin.

38 Ibid., fol. 16.

39 J. William Frost, "Unlikely Controversialists: Caleb Pusey and George Keith,"
Quaker History 64, no. 1 (Spring 1975): 33; Regal and Esposito, *Secret History*, 39;
Ward, *Christian Quaker*, 69.

40 Cf. Coll. 283 of the Monmouth County Historical Association Archives (George
Keith's account ledger of 1686); British Library add. mss. 23, 217, fol. 21 (letter from
George Keith to Anne Conway).

41 *Cabbala of the Jews*, 6.

42 Harold S. Jantz, "Christian Lodowick of Newport and Leipzig," *Rhode Island History* 111, no. 4 (October 1944): 107.

43 Christian Lodowick, *A Letter from the most Ingenious Mr. Lodowick Rhode-Island,
Febr. 1. 1691, 2* (Boston: Bartholomew Green, 1692), 1.

44 R.W.G. Vail's shelflist of 1935 includes no less than three works by George Keith, among other texts, that were bound together with the kabbalistic manuscript. See American Antiquarian Society Octavo Vol. # 19.15, vol. 693.

45 Lodowick, *A Letter*, 2.

46 Ibid., 6.

47 *Cabbala of the Jews*, 24.

48 Lodowick, *A Letter*, 6.

49 This is a reference to Isaac Luria (1534–1572), whose teachings on reincarnation made their way into the *Kabbala Denudata* via the *Sefer ha-Gilgulim* of his student Hayyim Vital, translated into Latin with the title *Tractatus de Revolutionibus Animarum*.

50 Ibid.

51 Francis Mercurius van Helmont, *Two Hundred Queries Moderately Propounded Concerning the Doctrine of the Revolution of Humane Souls, and Its Conformity to the Truths of Christianity* (London: Rob. Kettlewell, 1684), 7.

52 For detailed discussions, see Coudert, *Impact of the Kabbalah*, 244–51; Hutton, *Anne Conway*, 206–212.

53 *Cabbala of the Jews*, 22.

54 What is written in the manuscript is reminiscent of the theory of revolution, or metensomatosis, known as *din b'nei halof*, i.e., "the law of differentiation and change," which was propounded by the fourteenth-century Jewish kabbalist Joseph ben Shalom Ashkenazi. Ashkenazi writes, "It is known that every eaten thing transmigrates according to its eating, such as the food that is suitable for the sustenance of an animal and is eaten by it; it will become an animal, and from it will be manure that is suitable for insects, and from the manure insects. And that which is suitable as human food for the human will return to be human, and that which is suitable for waste will be excrement. Thus it is with wild animals and with birds and with domestic animals and with fish and with unclean creatures and with all creeping things that creep upon the land. And from this you have learned that every inanimate object, plant, animal and speaking creature, all undergo *din b'nei halof* in ascent and in descent" (Ashkenazi, *Commentary on Sefer Yetzirah*, 8:2–3). For a full discussion of this concept in Ashkenazi's thought, see Brian Ogren, *Renaissance and Rebirth: Reincarnation in Early Modern Italian Kabbalah* (Leiden: Brill, 2009), 195–98; Jonnie Schnytzer, "Metempsychosis, Metensomatosis and Metamorphosis: On Rabbi Joseph ben Shalom Ashkenazi's Systematic Theory of Reincarnation" (in Hebrew), *Kabbalah: Journal for the Study of Jewish Mystical Texts* 45 (2019): 221–44.

55 Rhode Island Historical Society mss. 9003, vol. 14, p. 223.

56 Lodowick, *A Letter*, 6.

57 For the detailed evidence of this, beyond Lodowick's explicit mention of the "Learned Noble Man," see Henry J. Cadbury, "Christian Lodowick," *Journal of the Friends Historical Society* 33 (1936): 24. See also Jantz, "Christian Lodowick," 108–09.

58 Lodowick, *A Letter*, 6–7.
59 Jantz, "Christian Lodowick," 112; Cadbury, "Christian Lodowick," 22–23.
60 *Cabbala of the Jews*, 9.
61 Conway, *Principles*, Oxford, ch. 5, S.1. Christia Mercer serendipitously brought this passage to my attention at the precise time that I was reviewing the Antiquarian Society manuscript, inadvertently, though very significantly, solidifying the notion of a connection to Keith.
62 *Cabbala of the Jews*, 11.
63 Ibid., 12.
64 Keith, *True Christ Owned*, 50.
65 What is being discussed here are the highest four kabbalistic worlds of existence from out of nothing, or from the One God, which are *Aziluth*, or Emanation, *Briah*, or Creation, *Yetzirah*, or Formation, and *Asiah*, or Fabrication (Keith uses the term "Faction"). All of these are discussed at length, both in the Antiquarian manuscript and in Keith's *True Christ Owned*. *Azilulth* is manifested here by *Adam Kadmon* as the first man, the first entity emanated from the depths of God.
66 Hutton, *Anne Conway*, 199. While this may initially be true, I would add an important caveat that later in life Keith may have had greater exposure to kabbalistic texts and ideas than Conway had, as he possibly had access to texts such as the *Kabbala Denudata*, which was published after Conway's death.
67 Lodowick, *A Letter*, 1.
68 Ibid., 5.
69 Ibid.
70 Ibid.
71 Keith, *Fifth Narrative*, 13.
72 This all seems to relate back to Conway's notion of Logos as at once both divine and the first emanated being.
73 Ibid.
74 Keith, *True Christ Owned*, 15.
75 Conway, *Principles*, Oxford, ch. 7, S.3.
76 Ibid.
77 Birkel, "Immediate Revelation," 263–64; Birkel, "Robert Barclay," 10–12. For the Jewish esoteric standard, see BT *Hagigah* 2:1: "One may not expound upon the subject of forbidden relations in the presence of three, nor the work of creation in the presence of two, nor the work of the chariot (*merkavah*) in the presence of one, unless he is wise and understands of his own knowledge" (אין דורשין בעריות בשלשה, ולא במעשה בראשית בשנים, ולא במרכבה ביחיד, אלא אם כן היה חכם ומבין מדעתו).
78 Lodowick, *A Letter*, 4.
79 *Cabbala of the Jews*, 9.
80 Ibid., 15: "These 4 Worlds are most inwardly connexed & linked together, the second being the Vehicle or Garment of the first, the third the vehicle of the other 2," etc.

81 Keith, *Fifth Narrative*, 13.

82 *Cabbala of the Jews*, 9.

83 Ibid., 13.

84 Ibid., 13–14.

85 Lodowick, *A Letter*, 5.

86 Proverbs 20:27.

87 James 1:21.

88 John 1:14. Here the idea that "the Word was made flesh, and dwelt among us" is slightly altered to fit the Quaker notion of the internal Light.

89 Keith, *The Way Cast Up*, 143.

90 For Plato's theory of a tripartite soul, which was adopted and built upon by medieval and early modern philosophers and kabbalists alike, see his *Republic*, IV.

91 Keith, *True Christ Owned*, 72–73.

92 Ibid., 48–49.

93 *Cabbala of the Jews*, 15.

94 Abraham Cohen de Herrera, *Gate of Heaven*, trans. from Spanish with introduction and notes by Kenneth Krabbenhoft (Leiden: Brill, 2002), 67–68.

95 Ibid., 68.

96 Ibid., 346.

97 Francis Mercurius van Helmont, *Seder Olam: or, the Order, Series, or Succession of all the Ages, Periods, and Times of the World*, trans. from Latin by J. Clark, M.D. (London: Sarah Hawkins, 1694), 16–17.

98 Ibid., 17.

99 Ibid., 18

100 *Cabbala of the Jews*, 10.

101 Lodowick, *A Letter*, 6.

102 Cyril O'Regan, *Gnostic Apocalypse: Jacob Boehme's Haunted Narrative* (Albany: SUNY Press, 2002), 194.

103 Cecilia Muratori, *The First German Philosopher: The Mysticism of Jakob Böhme as Interpreted by Hegel*, trans. from Italian by Richard Dixon and Raphaëlle Burns (Dordrecht: Springer, 2016), 50, 158, 279–80.

104 Gershom Scholem, *Major Trends in Jewish Mysticism* (New York: Schocken Books, 1995), e-book ed., 548–51; Elliot R. Wolfson, "The Holy Cabala of Changes: Jacob Böhme and Jewish Esotericism," *Aries: Journal for the Study of Western Esotericism* 18 (2018): 21–53. It is significant to note that O'Regan himself also participates in such speculation.

105 O'Regan, *Gnostic Apocalypse*, 196.

106 *Cabbala of the Jews*, 12.

107 Ibid., 2.

108 Ibid., 2–3.

109 Leeds, *Temple of Wisdom*, 70.

110 It is significant to note that the Latin *principium*, which Boehme seems to have had in mind here, denotes both "principle" and "beginning."

111 Wolfson, "Holy Cabala," 39.
112 Ibid., 42.
113 Leeds, *Temple of Wisdom*, 3.
114 Scholem, *Major Trends*, 550.
115 *Cabbala of the Jews*, 9.
116 Wolfson, "Holy Cabala," 32.
117 Leeds, *Temple of Wisdom*, 5.
118 Hans Lassen Martensen, *Jacob Boehme: His Life and Teaching or Studies in Theosophy*, 74, quoted in Wolfson, "Holy Cabala," 32, n. 41. This connection is also reflected in O'Regan, *Gnostic Apocalypse*, 199.
119 *Cabbala of the Jews*, 17.
120 O'Regan, *Gnostic Apocalypse*, 196.
121 Elliot R. Wolfson, *Language, Eros, Being: Kabbalistic Hermeneutics and Poetic Imagination* (New York: Fordham University Press, 2005), 471, n. 435. For a detailed account of the androgynous Adam in Boehme, see Andrew Weeks, *Boehme: An Intellectual Biography of the Seventeenth-Century Philosopher and Mystic* (Albany: SUNY Press, 1991), 113–21. Writings on the androgynous nature of God in Kabbalah abound. For some of the most representative treatments, see Wolfson, *Language, Eros, Being*, 142–89; Moshe Idel, *Kabbalah and Eros* (New Haven, CT: Yale University Press, 2005), 53–103; Charles Mopsik, *Sex of the Soul: The Vicissitudes of Sexual Difference in Kabbalah* (Los Angeles: Cherub Press, 2005), 1–4 and 28–38.
122 *Cabbala of the Jews*, 17.
123 Ibid., 18.
124 I intend to write a more in-depth article on this topic.
125 V5, 36, quoted in Muratori, *First German Philosopher*, 279.
126 Ibid.
127 *Cabbala of the Jews*, 2.
128 Keith, *Fifth Narrative*, 13.
129 John Smolenski, *Friends and Strangers: The Making of a Creole Culture in Colonial Pennsylvania* (Philadelphia: University of Pennsylvania Press, 2010), 151.
130 George Keith and Peter Boss, *The Tryals of Peter Boss, George Keith, Thomas Budd, and William Bradford, Quakers for several great misdemeanors* (London: reprinted for Richard Baldwin, 1693).
131 Smolensky, *Friends and Strangers*, 151.
132 Keith and Boss, *Tryals*, 1.
133 Ibid., 8.
134 Lest one claim, as many scholars have, that Keith's idea of revolutions involved the twelve human revolutions meant for the eventual acceptance of the Gospels by pagans and pre-Christians, it is important to keep in mind Keith's own claim that "there are many Revolutions, and of many sorts" (*Truth and Innocency Defended against Calumny and Defamation, in a late Report Spread abroad Concerning the Revolution of Humane Souls* [Philadelphia: William Bradford, 1692], 2).

135 Rufus Jones, *The Quakers in the American Colonies* (London: Macmillan, 1911), 458.

2. FROM CHRISTIAN QUAKERISM TO AMERICAN PURITANISM

1 This is a play on Luke 12:32, where Jesus states, "Fear not, little flock: for it is your Father's pleasure to give you the kingdom." For more on how this plays into general seventeenth-century Protestant notions of chosenness, see Van Engen, *City on a Hill*, 52.

2 Cotton Mather, *Little Flocks Guarded against Greivous Wolves* (London: Benjamin Harris & John Allen, 1691), 14.

3 Ibid.

4 Ibid., 6.

5 Mather, *Little Flocks*, 15.

6 Lodowick, *A Letter*, 6.

7 Ibid., 7.

8 Ibid. For Keith's reference, in which he uses the Hebrew term *Gilgal*, see his *Cabbala of the Jews*, 22.

9 This is an idea put forth by van Helmont in his *Two Hundred Queries*, and if it is true that Keith collaborated, or even imbibed from this work, then the claims may be true. For more on the controversy with Pusey, see Ward, *Christian Quaker*, 17; Frost, "Unlikely Controversialists," 25–26; Birkel, "Immediate Revelation," 265. For Keith's denial of the claim, though willingness to entertain the idea on a rational level, see his *Truth and Innocency Defended*, 4.

10 Mather, *Little Flocks*, 19.

11 Ibid., 23.

12 Ibid., 28.

13 Interestingly, this is a narrative that, a few years later when Keith would convert to Anglicanism and become an active member of the Society for the Propagation of the Gospel in Foreign Parts, would work better from within Quakerism. Perhaps Mather was referring to Keith's Presbyterian upbringing, or to his seemingly orthodox stance regarding the historical Christ.

14 Mather, *Little Flocks*, 28. This all comes in the context of Keith's critique of Mather's *Memorable Providences, relating to Witchcrafts and Possessions* (Boston: Richard Pierce, 1689). See Keith, *A Refutation of Three Opposers of Truth, By plain Evidence of the holy Scripture* (Philadelphia: William Bradford, 1690), 46–72.

15 Mather, *Little Flocks*, 46–47.

16 Ibid., 47.

17 George Keith, *A Serious Appeal to all the more Sober, Impartial & Judicious People in New England* (Philadelphia: William Bradford, 1692), 43.

18 Ibid.

19 As we will see, Christian Hebraic authority is of great importance to Mather. For Buxtorf's lengthy discussion, referenced here by Keith, see Johannis Buxtorf, *Lexicon Hebraicum et Chaldaicum* (Basileae: Ludovici König, 1607), 154–64.

20 Keith, *Serious Appeal*, 43. For Buxtorf's attribution of the pronunciation *Jehova* or *Jehovi* to Galatinus, see his *Lexicon Hebraicum*, 157. Galatinus's discussion of this issue appears in his *Opus de Arcanis Catholicae Veritatis* (Basileae, 1550), 77–78. For an academic history of the pronunciation of the name, calling into question the idea that Galatinus was the originator, see George Foot Moore, "Notes on the Name יהוה," *American Journal of Theology* 12, no. 1 (January 1908): 34–52; Moore, "Notes on the name יהוה," *American Journal of Semitic Languages and Literatures* 28, no. 1 (October 1911): 56–62.

21 For more on Galatinus and the Tetragrammaton, see Robert J. Wilkinson, *Tetragrammaton: Western Christians and the Hebrew Name of God: From the Beginnings to the Seventeenth Century* (Leiden: Brill, 2015), 329–31.

22 Galatinus, *Arcanis*, 75: אין לאל שם אשר אנו נוכל להשיג הכרח לפי שעצמותו הוא שמו ושמו עצמותו וכמו שמעצמותו לא נוכל להשיג ידיעה עם כל זה כל שמותיו יש להם הוראה לפי ששם ארבע אותיות הוא יותר עצמיי לפעולותיו ומראה ידיעה יותר שלמה ויותר עצמיית כפי מה שאנו יכולין לקבל ומזה מצטרפים כל שמותיו ולפי זה השם נקרא שם המפורש לא שהוא יהיה שמו העצמיי אבל אנו אומרים אותו לפי שזה הוא כל מה שכחינו יוכל להשיג ויותר גבות לא נוכל לעלות. This is followed by a Latin translation.

23 Galatinus, *Arcanis*, 80: מזה השם המפורש הוא נגזר שם שנים עשר אותיות כי הוא אב בן ורוח הקדש אשר בלשונינו העברית שם שנים עשר אותיות נכתב כך.

24 BT *Kiddushin* 71a: אמר הקב"ה לא כשאני נכתב אני נקרא נכתב אני ביו"ד ה"י ונקרא באל"ף דל"ת. ת"ר בראשונה שם בן שתים עשרה אותיות היו מוסרין אותו לכל אדם משרבו הפריצים היו מוסרים אותו לצנועים שבכהונה.

25 Incidentally, it is the specific combination of the vowels for *Adonai* with the Tetragrammaton that gave rise to the mistaken pronunciation *Jehovah*, which Buxtorf attributes to Galatinus himself.

26 Keith, *Serious Appeal*, 44.

27 Ibid.

28 Cotton Mather, *Biblia Americana: America's First Bible Commentary*, vol. 5 (Proverbs–Jeremiah), ed. with introduction and annotations by Jan Stievermann (Tübingen: Mohr Siebeck, 2015), 593. This passage shows up in Galatinus, *Arcanis*, 42.

29 Ibid.

30 *Zohar* 3:134: וקרא זה אל זה ואמר קדש קדש קדש (ישעיהו ו' ג'). הא תלת אינון. וספר תורה. לקבליהון, נרתקו קדש, וההיכל קדש, והוא קדש, והתורה נתנה בג' קדושות. For other Zoharic references, see Yehuda Leibes, *Studies in the Zohar*, trans. Arnold Schwartz, Stephanie Nakache, and Penina Peli (Albany: SUNY Press, 1993), 229, n. 8.

31 Cotton Mather, *Biblia Americana: America's First Bible Commentary*, vol. 2 (Exodus–Deuteronomy), ed. with introduction and annotations by Reiner Smolinski (Tübingen: Mohr Siebeck, 2019), 390–91. This is almost an exact translation of Riboudealdus, who writes: "Alij tandem volunt Vrim & Thumim fuisse nomen Tetragrammaton intra Pectoralis duplicationem positum, quo mediante Sacerdoti futura revelabantur" (Philippo Riboudealdo Cabilonesi, *Sacrum Dei Oraculum Urim & Thummim* [Genevae, 1685], 240).

32 Mather, *Biblia Americana*, vol. 2, 392.

33 Riboudealdo, *Sacrum Dei*, 241.

34 BT *Yevamot* 49b.

35 *Zohar* 2:234b: כתיב ונתת אל חשן המשפט את האורים ואת התומים, והא אוקמוה. את האורים,
    דנהרין, רזא דאספקלריא דנהרא, ודא איהו גליפו דאתוון דשמא קדישא, ברזא דארבעין ותרין דבהו
    אתברון עלמין, והוו משקעין ביה. ואת התומים, רזא דאינון אתוון, דכלילן באתר דאספקלריא דלא נהרא.
    ואיהי אתנהגא בע"ב אתוון גליפין, דאינון רזא דשמא קדישא, וכלהו אקרון אורים ותומים.

36 For what is still one of the best expositions of vision and interpretive hermeneu-
    tics within the *Zohar*, see Elliot R. Wolfson, *Through a Speculum That Shines:
    Vision and Imagination in Medieval Jewish Mysticism* (Princeton, NJ: Princeton
    University Press, 1994), 326–92.

37 Rashi on Exodus 28:30: הוא כתב שם המפרש, שהיה נותנו בתוך כפלי החשן, שעל ידו הוא מאיר
    דבריו ומתמם את דבריו. Cf. BT *Yoma* 73b.

38 Johannis Buxtorfi Fil., *Exercitationes Ad Historiam* (Basileae: Deckeri, 1659),
    280.

39 The reason for this may be the notion of prophetic evidence, which Jan Stiever-
    mann explains, especially in the case of Mather, as "geared toward demonstrating
    the absolute and exclusive truth of the Christian religion over against other reli-
    gions, especially Judaism" ("The Debate over Prophetic Evidence for the Author-
    ity of the Bible in Cotton Mather's *Biblia Americana*," in *The Bible in American
    Life*, ed. Philip Goff, Arthur E. Farnsley II, and Peter J. Thuesen [New York: Ox-
    ford University Press, 2017], 52). According to this principle, it is the accuracy of
    text of the Bible that ultimately matters, and not postbiblical texts written by Jews.
    See also Stievermann, *Prophecy, Piety, and the Problem of Historicity: Interpreting
    the Hebrew Scriptures in Cotton Mather's "Biblia Americana"* (Tübingen: Mohr
    Siebeck, 2016), 61, where Stievermann reiterates this point and explicitly mentions
    Mather's use of Galatinus.

40 Mather, *Biblia Americana*, vol. 1, 316.

41 See, for example, the introduction to the commentary on *Sefer Yetzirah* of Joseph
    ben Shalom Ashkenazi 1:1; and Cordovero, *Pardes Rimonim*, 12:1.

42 Keith, *Serious Appeal*, 43.

43 Mather, *Biblia Americana*, vol. 1, 318.

44 Richard H. Popkin, "Can One Be a True Christian and a Faithful Follower of
    the Law of Moses? The Answer of John Dury," in *Secret Conversion to Judaism in
    Early Modern Europe*, ed. Martin Mulsow and Richard H. Popkin (Leiden: Brill,
    2004), 34.

45 Mather, *Biblia Americana*, vol. 5, 193.

46 Ibid., 192, citing Robert Fleming, *Christology: A Discourse Concerning Christ*, vol.
    1 (London: Andrew Bell, 1705), 235, who is loosely quoting Stephan Rittangel,
    Veritas religionis Christianae (Wibium Bleck, 1699), 45.

47 Rittangel, 45: "*Sapientiam summam*, sive secundam Numerationem Intellec-
    tualem in mundo archetypo, h.e. Verbum Dei viventis, à *Corona Summa*, Deo
    Patre, prima, inquam, *Numeratione intellectuali* in mundo archetypo ab omni

aeternitate è Non-termino Infinitudinis Divinae Essentiae ineffabili generatione productum."

48 Mather, *Biblia Americana*, vol. 5, 192, from Fleming, *Christology*, 235, which in turn is from Rittangel, 54; Rittangel, for his part, is translating and quoting from *Tikkunei ha-Zohar* 120a: אית אדם דלית ספירה דלא אתקריאת אדם, אבל אדם קדמאה עלאה דכלהו, כתר עליון, סתים וטמיר, סתים דכל סתימין, עלת העלות, קדמון לכל קדומים, בגין האי אדם קדמון אתמר בעלת העלות ואהיה אצלו אמון, ולההוא קדמון אמר נעשה אדם בצלמנו כדמותנו . . . דא חכמה עלאה דאיהי בדיוקנא דכתר.

49 George Keith, *The Presbyterian and Independent Visible Churches in New-England and else-where, Brought to the Test, and examined according to the Doctrine of the Holy Scriptures* (Philadelphia: William Bradford, 1689), 31.

50 A similar passage to the one quoted here appears in Keith's *Cabbala of the Jews*, and it will be discussed in further detail below.

51 Mather, *Biblia Americana*, vol. 5, 194.

52 Ibid., 194–95; cf. Fleming, *Christology*, 239.

53 Ibid., 196; cf. Fleming, 244.

54 Ibid., 193; cf. Fleming, 237.

55 Fleming, 237.

56 Mather, *Biblia Americana*, vol. 5, 198.

57 *Cabbala of the Jews*, 9.

58 Ibid.

59 *Zohar* 3:296a. This is the translation of Daniel Matt, *Zohar: Pritzker Edition*, vol. 9 (Stanford, CA: Stanford University Press, 2016), 843: אמה דדכורא, סיומא דכל גופא, ואקרי יסוד.

60 Ibid.: וכל תיאובתא דדכורא לגבי נוקבא, בהאי יסוד עייל לנוקבא, לאתר דאקרי ציון, דהתם הוא אתר. כסותא דנוקבא, כבית רחם לאתתא.

61 Ralph Cudworth, *The Union of Christ and the Church in a Shadow* (London: Richard Bishop, 1642), 7–12.

62 Mather, *Biblia Americana*, vol. 5, 463, quoting Patrick, *Song*, preface, section 3, who is summarizing Cudworth.

63 Ibid., 464.

64 Ibid., 197.

65 Ibid.

66 Mather, *Little Flocks*, 47.

67 Ibid., 64–65.

68 Proverbs 20:27: נר יהוה נשמת אדם, חפש כל-חדרי-בטן.

69 Cotton Mather, *Coheleth: A Soul upon Recollection* (Boston: S. Kneeland, 1720), 6.

70 Keith, *Presbyterian and Independent Visible Churches*, 29.

71 Ibid., 29–30.

72 Mather, *Biblia Americana*, vol. 2, 1046–47, quoting Simon Patrick, *A Commentary upon the Fifth Book of Moses, Called Deuteronomy* (London: Chiswell, 1704), 100–101.

73 It is worth noting that *Sefer Yetzirah* does not promote a trinity and explicitly emphasizes a unity of the structure of ten *sefirot*. This is also a mistake made by Mather's contemporary, the convert from Judaism Judah Monis, as we will see in chapter 4. There Monis is drawing on an anonymous thirteenth-century Provençal text of pseudo-Hai, but his mistake may very well have originated with the text of Patrick, perhaps even through Mather. As we know, Mather was certainly in contact with Monis, and as we will see in the next chapter, Mather's father and teacher Increase played a key role in Monis's conversion.

74 For more on this, see Elke Morlok, *Rabbi Joseph Gikatilla's Hermeneutics* (Tübingen: Mohr Siebeck, 2011), 310.

75 Joseph Gikatilla, *Sha'arei Orah* (Offenbach, 1715), 45a: אברהם כנגד החסד יצחק כנגד הדין יעקב מכריע ביניהם איש תם יושב אהלים. This last phrase is from Genesis 25:27.

76 Ibid., 39a: והסוד הוא שאמר במראות הצובאות אשר צבאו פתח אהל מועד. ואהל מועד הוא סוד אדני. ומשה רבינו ע"ה נכנס באהל מועד ומדבר עם יהוה שהיא אספקלריאה מצוחצחת פנים בפנים. ושער הנביאים מדברים עם יהוה ע"י אדני שהיא אספקלריאה שאינה מצוחצחת. וזהו סוד וארא אל אברהם אל יצחק ואל יעקב באל שדי ושמי יהוה לא נודעתי להם.

77 Lodowick, *A Letter*, 6–7.

78 Mather, *Biblia Americana*, vol. 5, 704, copied from John Gregory, *A Sermon upon the Resurrection* (London: J. Grismond, 1663), 70. This last verse is from Song of Songs 5:2.

79 See, for example, *Zohar* 1:137b, where the term *betu'el rama'ah*, i.e., "deceitful house of God" is used, and *Zohar* 2:28b and 3:222a, where a more nondescript bone of the spinal column is referenced.

80 Cf. *Ecclesiastes Rabbah* 12:5 and *Leviticus Rabbah* 18:1, where the *Luz* of the spine is written of as indestructible. For more on the history of the idea of the bone, and its usage in Christian as well as Jewish sources, see Edward Reichman and Fred Rosner, "The Bone Called Luz," *Journal of the History of Medicine and Allied Sciences* 51, no.1 (January 1996): 52–65.

81 Cf. *Zohar* 3:128b, 3:135b. Daniel Matt notes that the motif of dew reviving the dead appears in the eighth- or ninth-century midrashic *Pirkei de-Rabbi Eliezer* 34: "In the time to come, the blessed Holy One will bring down a dew of revival, reviving the dead, as it is said: *Your dead will live, my corpses will arise . . . . Awake and shout for joy, O dwellers of the dust! . . . For your dew is a dew of lights . . . and the earth will cast forth spirits of the dead*" (Isaiah 26:19). See *Zohar: Pritzker Edition*, vol. 8, 328, n. 25; 384, n. 227.

82 Cf. Christian Knorr von Rosenroth, *Kabbala Denudata*, vol. 2 (Frankfurt, 1684), 393–94.

83 Mather, *Biblia Americana: America's First Bible Commentary*, vol. 3 (Joshua–2 Chronicles), ed. with introduction and annotations by Kenneth P. Minkema (Tübingen: Mohr Siebeck, 2013), 320.

84 Examples abound. For a representative sample, see *The Threefold Paradise of Cotton Mather: An Edition of Triparadisus*, ed. Reiner Smolinski (Athens: University

of Georgia Press, 1995), 123, and Smolinski's comment, 397, n. 32; see also Kenneth P. Minkema's comment in Mather's *Biblia Americana*, vol. 3, 320, n. 282; Mather, *Biblia Americana*, vol. 1, 414, and Smolinski's comment, n. 333; Robert E. Brown, "Introduction" to Mather, *Biblia Americana: America's First Bible Commentary*, vol. 9 (Romans–Philemon), ed. with introduction and annotations by Robert E. Brown (Tübingen: Mohr Siebeck, 2018), 49–50; Stievermann, *Prophecy, Piety*, 183–84, 187–88.

85 For a lengthy treatment of this subject, beyond the sources cited in the previous note, see John S. Erwin, *The Millennialism of Cotton Mather: An Historical and Theological Analysis* (Lewiston, NY: Edwin Mellen Press, 1990), 116–52. See also Margaret Humphreys Warner, "Vindicating the Minister's Medical Role: Cotton Mather's Concept of the 'Nishmath-Chajim' and the Spiritualization of Medicine," *Journal of the History of Medicine and Allied Sciences* 36, no. 3 (July 1981): 278–95. There has been speculation that a kabbalistic idea stands at the heart of this notion, though the evidence to support this claim is scant. It should also be noted for our purposes that while it bears resemblance to Keith's notion of the "Neschama Christi," it is quite different, and there is no evidence of any connection between the two concepts.

86 William B. Hunter Jr., "The Seventeenth Century Doctrine of Plastic Nature," *Harvard Theological Review* 43, no. 3 (July 1950): 197–213.

87 Mather, *Biblia Americana*, vol. 9, 324.

88 Ibid., 324–25; cf. Whitby, *Paraphrase and Commentary on the New Testament*, vol. 2 (London: Awnsham and John Churchill, 1703), 194.

89 Ibid., 325.

90 Raymundi Martini, *Pugio Fidei Adversus Mauros et Judaeos, cum observationibus Josephi de Voisin* (Leipzig, 1687), part III, 618, fol. 491. *Zohar* 3:113b.

91 *Zohar* 3:113b: אמר רבי פנחס עתיד הקדוש ברוך הוא ליפות לגוף הצדיקים לעתיד לבא כיופי של אדם הראשון כשנכנס לגן עדן.

92 Mather, *Threefold Paradise*, 136. Cf. Mather, *Biblia Americana*, vol. 1, 474–75.

93 *Zohar* 2:229b: נשמתא לא סלקא לאתחזאה קמי מלכא קדישא עד דזכאת לאתלבשא בלבושא דלעילא לאתחזאה תמן.

94 Ibid.: אדם הראשון כד הוה הגנתא דעדן הוה מתלבש בלבושא כגוונא דלעילא, ואיהו לבושא דנהורא עלאה. כיון דאתתרך מגנתא דעדן, ואצטריך לגוונין דהאי עלמא, מה כתיב ויעש יהוה אלהים לאדם ולאשתו כתנות עור וילבישם. בקדמיתא הוו כתנות אור, אור דההוא נהורא עלאה, דשמש ביה בגן עדן . . . ואי לא אתלבש בקדמיתא בההוא נהורא, לא ייעול לתמן . . . והכא כגוונא דא, עשו בגדי שרד לשרת בקדש, לאעלא בקודשא.

95 Mather, *Little Flocks*, 43, quoting Isaac Pennington, *A Question to the Professors of Christianity whether they have the True, Living, Powerful, Saving Knowledge of Christ, or No* (London, 1667), 49.

96 Ibid.

97 Mather, *Little Flocks*, 44.

98 Ibid., 43.

99 Keith, *Serious Appeal*, 26.

100 As Reiner Smolinski has brought to my attention, in Christian theology Proverbs 8:22, "The Lord brought me forth as the first of his works, before his deeds of old," is often referenced as Christ's preincarnate existence and as the second element of the Trinity. While here Keith is not referencing Proverbs directly, the idea, as related to *Adam Kadmon,* carries over.

101 Keith, *Serious Appeal,* 26.

102 *Cabbala of the Jews,* 1.

103 Mather, *Biblia Americana,* vol. 5, 704.

104 Michael Hoberman, "'They have with faithfulnesse and care transmitted the Oracles of God unto us Gentiles': Jewish Kabbalah and Text Study in the Puritan Imagination," in *Kabbalah in America: Ancient Lore in the New World,* ed. Brian Ogren (Leiden: Brill, 2020), 11–30.

105 For more on Mather's complex relationship to the *prisca theologia* tradition more generally, but especially in regard to pagan wisdom, see Harry Clark Maddux, "Euhemerism and Ancient Theology in Cotton Mather's 'Biblia Americana,'" in *Cotton Mather and Biblia Americana—America's First Bible Commentary: Essays in Reappraisal,* ed. Reiner Smolinski and Jan Stievermann (Tübingen: Mohr Siebeck, 2011), 337–59.

106 Massachusetts Historical Society, Cotton Mather Papers, *Biblia Americana,* vol. 5, "Appendix to Acts," 70; quoted from Jacques Basnage, *The History of the Jews, from Jesus Christ to the Present Time,* trans. Thomas Taylor, A.M. (London, 1708), 664.

107 For more on this, see Scholem, *Major Trends,* 156–204.

108 Mather, *Biblia Americana,* vol. 2, 1032–41. For the published version, with both Latin and Hebrew, see *Epistola Ludovici Carreti ad Iudaeos: quae inscribitur Liber visorum divinorum* (Paris: Wecheli, 1554). It should be noted that Carretus's tract was included in three editions of Buxtorf's *Synagoga Judaica* (1604, 1614, and 1622), and given Mather's relationship with Catholic text as filtered through Protestant authorship, it is probable that one of these editions was his source. For more on Carretus, see Smolinski, "Introduction," *Biblia Americana,* vol. 1, 161–63 and Robert Bonfil, "Chi era Ludovico Carretto, apostata?" in *E andammo dove il vento ci spinse: la cacciata degli ebrei dalla Spagna,* ed. Guido Nathan Zazzu (Genova: Marietti, 1992), 51–58.

109 Cotton certainly did hold a certain "missionary zeal," as Lee M. Friedman calls it, but it was not driven by the same mystical eschatology prodded by actual historical events as was that of his father Increase. For more on this, see Lee M. Friedman, "Cotton Mather and the Jews," *Publications of the American Jewish Historical Society* 26 (1918): 201–10.

3. SABBATEANISM AND MYSTICAL CONVERSION IN THE NEW WORLD

1 Massachusetts Historical Society, Cotton Mather Papers, *Biblia Americana,* vol. 5, "Appendix to Acts," 82, quoting from Basnage, *History of the Jews,* 701. Tzevi's name is variably spelled in English. I will use the less archaic

"Shabbetai Tzevi" throughout, unless there is a differing spelling within a direct quote.

2 Ibid., 80, Basnage, 697.

3 Ibid.

4 Sabbateanism and Shabbetai Tzevi have been widely written about, though Gershom Scholem's *Sabbatai Sevi: The Mystical Messiah, 1626–1676* (Princeton, NJ: Princeton University Press, 1973) still stands as the most comprehensive treatment of Shabbetai Tzevi's kabbalistic background, his prophet, and the movement as a whole.

5 See, for example, Scholem, *Sabbatai Sevi*, 131.

6 See Yaacob Dweck, "Introduction to the Princeton Classics Edition," in Scholem, *Sabbatai Sevi*, lxi; Ze'ev Gries, *Sifrut ha-Hanhagot: Toldoteiha U'mekomah b'Hayei Hasidav shel ha-Besht* (Jerusalem: Mosad Bialik, 1989); Moshe Idel, "'One from a Town, Two from a Clan': The Diffusion of Lurianic Kabbala and Sabbateanism: A Re-examination," *Jewish History* 7 (1993): 79–104.

7 Michael McKeon, "Sabbatai Sevi in England," *AJS Review* 2 (1977): 139.

8 Paul Rycaut, *The History of the Turkish Empire from the Year 1623, to the Year 1677* (London, 1687), 174; cf. Hannah Adams, *The History of the Jews from the Destruction of Jerusalem to the Nineteenth Century*, vol. 2 (Boston: John Eliot, 1812), 19.

9 Richard H. Popkin, "Three English Tellings of the Sabbatai Zevi Story," *Jewish History* 8, nos. 1–2 (1994): 43–54. For an expanded version, see Richard Popkin, "Christian Interests and Concerns about Sabbatai Zevi," in *Millenarianism and Messianism in Early Modern European Culture*, vol. 1, ed. Matt D. Goldish and Richard H. Popkin (Dordrecht: Springer, 2001), 91–106. It is worth noting that the main focus of Popkin's exposition, Paul Rycaut's *The History of the Turkish Empire*, was the main source for the first full American publication on Shabbetai Tzevi, namely, the twelfth chapter of Hannah Adams's *History of the Jews*. Within that context, Adams rather uncharitably writes, "We have seen the Jews during sixteen centuries obstinately persisting in rejecting the true Messiah, and frequently duped by impostors who assumed this character. This infatuation continued unabated, notwithstanding the repeated disappointments which often involved this miserable people in terrible calamities" (vol. 2, 19). This may give a partial answer to Popkin's query in his article regarding Rycaut: "It would be interesting to find out what people in New England at the end of the eighteenth century made of the package" ("Three English Tellings," 51). For Adams, as for Increase Mather and other New England divines, as we will see, the fascination ties into a notion of "false" messianism that plagues the Jews, and that can be remedied by the "true" messianism of Jesus of Nazareth.

10 Whether the elder Mather was influenced by Basnage is hard to tell. Unlike his son he does not copy full passages, and he does not seem to cite Basnage anywhere in his musings related to Shabbetai Tzevi.

11 Increase Mather, *A Dissertation Concerning the Future Conversion of the Jewish Nation* (London: R. Tookey, 1709), 21.

12 Here Mather explicitly quotes Luke 2:1, Acts 11:28, and Colossians 1:23. As Reiner Smolinski has brought to my attention, Mather here seems to be responding to Joseph Mede's conjecture that the New World of America was to be excluded from the millennial kingdom established by Christ in the Old World and cast as an outer darkness ripe for Gog and Magog. For more on this, see Smolinski, "Israel Redivivus: The Eschatological Limits of Puritan Typology in New England," *New England Quarterly* 63, no. 3 (September 1990): 370–73.

13 Mather, *Dissertation*, 32.

14 This, again, is a reversal of Joseph Mede's negative exclusion of the American hemisphere.

15 Here I am indebted to Sacvan Bercovitch's deft understanding of the Puritans' reading of their own history: "The Biblical Basis of the American Myth," in *The Bible and American Arts and Letters*, ed. Guiles Gunn (Philadelphia/Chico, CA: Fortress/Scholars' Press, 1983), 224.

16 Mather Family Papers, 1613–1819, American Antiquarian Society. For Hall's analysis, see his *The Last American Puritan: The Life of Increase Mather* (Middletown, CT: Wesleyan University Press, 1988), 76.

17 Cotton Mather, *Parentator: Memoirs of Remarkables in the Life and the Death of the Ever-Memorable Dr. Increase Mather. Who Expired, August 23, 1723* (Boston: B. Green, 1724), 61. In private correspondence, Smolinski has noted that Cotton Mather's language that "some" were waiting for the "Consolation of Israel" was probably deliberate in that it excludes himself from the expectation. By this point Cotton had become an allegorist in regard to Romans 11, which states that "All Israel" shall be saved.

18 Mather, *The Mystery of Israel's Salvation, Explained and Applyed* (London: John Allen, 1669), "An Epistle to the Reader," A3.2. This specific passage was already noted in relation to Sabbateanism by Scholem, *Sabbatai Zevi*, 549.

19 Moshe Idel, *Messianic Mystics* (New Haven, CT: Yale University Press), 184. Works on Sabbateanism as a mass movement abound. For representative treatments, see *Jerusalem Studies in Jewish Thought*, vols. 16-17 (2001): *The Sabbatian Movement and Its Aftermath: Messianism, Sabbatianism and Frankism*. For our purposes, perhaps most representative of the mass movement's impact on Christianity are the works of Richard Popkin. See especially Popkin, "The Sabbatian Movement in Turkey (1703–1708) and Reverberations in Northern Europe," *Jewish Quarterly Review* 94, 2 (2004): 300–317. More recently, see Matt Goldish, "Sabbatai Zevi and the Sabbatean Movement," in *The Cambridge History of Judaism*, vol. 7, *The Early Modern World, 1500–1815*, ed. Jonathan Karp and Adam Sutcliffe (New York: Cambridge University Press, 2018), 491–521.

20 Mather, *Parentator*, 62.

21 Mather, *Mystery of Israel's Salvation*, "An Epistle to the Reader," b.5.2.

22 Revelation 16:10, 16:12.

23 For more on this, see Richard W. Cogley, "The Fall of the Ottoman Empire and the Restoration of Israel in the 'Judeo-Centric' Strand of Puritan Millenarian-

ism," *Church History* 72, no. 2 (June 2003): 304–32; Nan Goodman, "Sabbatai Sevi and the Ottoman Jews in Increase Mather's *The Mystery of Israel's Salvation*," in *American Literature and the New Puritan Studies*, ed. Bryce Traister (New York: Cambridge University Press, 2017), 38-53.

24 For a concise history of the Sabbatean debacle, see Gershom Scholem, "Shabbetai Zevi and the Shabbatean Movement," *Kabbalah* (New York: New American Library, 1978), 244–86.

25 For what is still the best, most detailed account of this idea, see Gershom Scholem, "Redemption through Sin," *The Messianic Idea in Judaism* (New York: Schocken Books, 1971), 78–141. For more specific textual examples brought by Scholem, see pages 97 and 119.

26 Unfortunately, *The Mystery of Israel's Salvation* in published form seems to be the sole known record of the lectures at this point. This is corroborated by Michael G. Hall in e-mail correspondence of September 14, 2019.

27 Hall, *Last American Puritan*, 77.

28 Mather, *Mystery of Israel's Salvation*, 85.

29 Ibid., 87; this idea shows up in *Seder 'Olam Rabbah*, ch. 30.

30 Ibid., 89.

31 Ibid., 87.

32 Mather, *Dissertation*, 10. The last line is a quote from 1 John 2:18.

33 Ibid., 12.

34 Mather, "The Preface" to *The Truth: Being a Discourse Which the Author Delivered at his Baptism, Containing Nine Principal Arguments the Modern Jewish Rabbins do make to prove, the Messiah is yet to Come* (Boston: Daniel Henchman, 1722), ii.

35 Ibid.

36 This is the title of Monis's three-part discourse published in 1722. The first part, i.e., *The Truth*, seems to be the only portion he read publicly. The third part, i.e., *Nothing but the Truth*, is the most kabbalistically oriented and will further be discussed at length.

37 The fairly idiosyncratic transliteration of Hebrew, here and throughout, is within Monis's original texts. In her recent article "'A Pure Language (or Lip)': Representing Hebrew in Colonial New England" (*Studies in American Jewish Literature* 37, no. 2 [2018]: 117–44), Rachel Wamsley claims that this is an invention of Monis. George Foot Moore, by contrast, claims that "the monstrous system of transliteration for English-speaking students which makes Hebrew look like the speech of the lost Ten Tribes whom so many New England theologians recognized in the American Indians, is unmistakably that of the Italian Jews of his time" (Moore, "Judah Monis," *Proceedings of the Massachusetts Historical Society* [May 1919]: 5–6).

38 For more on this narrative, see Eran Shalev, *American Zion: The Old Testament as a Political Text from the Revolution to the Civil War* (New Haven, CT: Yale University Press, 2013), 19; see also Robert H. Pfeiffer, "The Teaching of Hebrew in Colonial America," *Jewish Quarterly Review* 45, no. 4 (April 1955): 365.

39 John Winthrop, "A Modell of Christian Charity (1630)," *Collections of the Massachusetts Historical Society* 7 (1838): 46.

40 The discourse of exceptionalism surrounding the Great Migration was brought to the fore in 1953 by one of the key founders of American Studies, Perry Miller, in his "Errand into the Wilderness," *William and Mary Quarterly* 10, no. 1 (January 1953): 3–32. Miller's thesis has raised serious debate, as the conclusion to this present study will address. For the most recent full treatment, see Van Engen, *City on a Hill*.

41 Mather, *Magnalia Christi Americana*, 119.

42 Bercovitch, *Puritan Origins*, x.

43 Mather, *Mystery of Israel's Salvation*, 58.

44 Ibid.

45 Niel Caplan and Benjamin Colman, "Some Unpublished Letters of Benjamin Colman, 1717–1725," *Proceedings of the Massachusetts Historical Society* 77 (1965): 127.

46 Benjamin Colman, *Moses a Witness unto our Lord and Savior Jesus Christ* (Boston, 1722), 26.

47 Ibid., 126. Colman remarks, "He wrote out the Books of Moses for a Synagogue in Holland some years agoe," which we can take to mean that he scribed a Torah scroll. See also Milton M. Klein, "A Jew at Harvard in the 18th Century," *Proceedings of the Massachusetts Historical Society* 97 (1985): 136.

48 Caplan and Colman, 126.

49 Mather, "Preface," iv.

50 See his dedicatory preface to the entire three-part publication, entitled "The Dedication," i ("To my Brethren *According to the Flesh*. Dear and Beloved Brethren"); *Nothing but the Truth*, 4, 19.

51 Mather, *Dissertation*, 12.

52 Monis, *Nothing but the Truth*, 17.

53 Yaacob Dweck, *Dissident Rabbi: The Life of Jacob Sasportas* (Princeton, NJ: Princeton University Press, 2019), 17.

54 Dweck, *Dissident Rabbi*, 220. For Dweck's full exposition concerning Sasportas on Christianity, see chapter 5.

55 Sasportas, *Ohel Yaacov*, #3, 2a, cited with a slightly different translation in Dweck, 218. The Hebrew is: המאמין באיש ההוא של אדום נקרא מין.

56 Mather, *Dissertation*, 2.

57 This was pointed out by Michael Hoberman in his *New Israel/New England: Jews and Puritans in Early America* (Amherst: University of Massachusetts Press, 2011), 110.

58 Pawel Maciejko, "The Peril of Heresy, the Birth of a New Faith: The Quest for a Common Jewish-Christian Front against Frankism," in *Holy Dissent: Jewish and Christian Mystics in Eastern Europe*, ed. Glenn Dynner (Detroit: Wayne State University Press, 2011), 225. Maciejko references Jacob Sasportas, *Tzitzat Novel Tzevi*, ed. Isaiah Tishby (Jerusalem: Mosad Bialik, 1954), 39; Rivka Shatz-Uffenheimer, "Tzitzat Novel Tzevi u-Madurato ha-Shlemah," *Ra'ayon ha-Meshihi me-az Girush*

Sefarad (Jerusalem: Magnes Press, 2005), 139–61; Matt Goldish, *The Sabbatean Prophets* (Cambridge, MA: Harvard University Press, 2005) 143; Dweck, *Dissident Rabbi*, 85–122.

59 In fact, if this had been the case, then one would expect that he would have at least mentioned Sasportas's stance on Sabbateanism. Because there is absolutely no mention of this or of Sabbateanism within his treatise, I take the anti-Sabbatean connection as a mere, albeit unusual and intriguing, coincidence of history.

60 Cited in Arthur A. Chiel, "Judah Monis, the Harvard Convert," *Judaism; a Journal of Jewish Life and Thought* 23 (1974): 229.

61 Ibid., n. 2; Moore, "Judah Monis," 5. Incidentally, this designation of Monis as a *Maskil* would have worked nicely into Increase Mather's narrative. In his *Mystery of Israel's Salvation*, he bases himself on Daniel 12:3 and writes concerning the final conversion of the Jews, "There shall be a wonderful spiritual glory upon the Ministers of God in those days, *those that be Teachers (*המשכילים*) shall shine as the brightness of the Firmament, and they that turn many to righteousness as the Stars for ever and ever*" (114). Whether Mather was aware of the Jewish mystical implications of this verse is unclear, but as a *Maskil* and as a "teacher," Monis perfectly fit Mather's paradigm here.

62 For more on this, see Moore, "Judah Monis," 5.

63 George Alexander Kohut, "Judah Monis," *American Journal of Semitic Languages and Literatures* 15, no. 1 (October 1898): 52.

64 Ibid., 52–54.

65 Ein Harod Mus. 107.

66 Even though Monis was born seven years after Tzevi's death and thus long after Tzevi's apostasy, Sabbateanism was still rampant, in various forms, throughout the world. In fact, as Pawel Maciejko has recently pointed out, "Most of the controversies that took place in the Jewish world between the mid-seventeenth and the mid-nineteenth century were associated in one way or another with Sabbatianism. Sabbatai's followers developed a set of theological doctrines in which Jewish tradition was reinterpreted in novel and highly unorthodox ways and was merged with Muslim and later Christian elements" (*Sabbatian Heresy: Writings on Mysticism, Messianism, and the Origins of Jewish Modernity* [Waltham, MA: Brandeis University Press, 2017], xi). It is worth pointing out that some followers had held that Tzevi's apostasy, and even death, were deliberate parts of the cosmic story of salvation.

67 Louis Ginzberg already identified several of the pieces of this manuscript for George Foot Moore in 1919. See Moore, "Judah Monis," 26. For more on this manuscript, see also George F. Moore, "A Cabalistic MS. From the Library of Judah Monis," *Publications of the American Jewish Historical Society* 28 (1922): 242–45; Mordecai Glatzer, *Hebrew Manuscripts in the Houghton Library of the Harvard College Library*, catalog, ed. Charles Berlin and Rodney Gove Morris

(Cambridge, MA: Harvard University Library, 1975). Apparently the surmise that the first half of this manuscript is in Monis's handwriting comes from the signature at the end of the copied *Emet l'Ya'akov*, "ע"כ אני יהודה מוניש מצאתי" (Until here, I, Judah Monis have found), ms. HUG 1580.74, fol. 44a.

68 Ms. HUG 1580.74, fols. 187a–187b.

69 Heinrich Cornelius Agrippa, *De occulta philosophia* (Colonia, 1533), cclxxiii–cclxxiv. For more on these ciphered alphabets from out of the tradition of Agrippa, see Saverio Campanini, "The Quest for the Holiest Alphabet in the Renaissance," in *A Universal Art: Hebrew Grammar across Disciplines and Faiths*, ed. Nadia Vidro, Irene E. Zwiep, and Judith Olszowy-Schlanger (Leiden: Brill, 2014), 196–245. Campanini notes that "the alphabets published by Agrippa enjoyed enormous popularity in contemporary esotericism, but were also reproduced in innumerable *grimoires* and in many collections of amulets" (220–21). He also points out that Agrippa was strongly influenced in these matters by the Venetian Christian kabbalist Francesco Giorgio.

70 Ms. HUG 1580.74, fol. 186b. ו"צי, which I interpret here as ישראל צדיק וישר, could also be ישמרהו צורו ויחיהו, among others.

71 "פירוש" "ענין הגלגולים עם ענין העגל," "ענין הקשר של מורי הקשר של מורי זלה"ה עם החברים והחברים בעצמם זה עם זה," "מאמר פסיעותיו של אברהם אבינו." "This last one was printed at the end of Abraham ben Mordecai Azulai, *Hesed l'Avraham: Sapir G'zerato* (Amsterdam, 1685).

72 Fürth, 1695. See Harvard Andover Theological Library, S.C.R. (206.435). I thank Nell Carlson of Harvard Andover for granting me access to this rare book. While there are unfortunately no marginal notes by Monis (or Martyn), it does bear Martyn's name and the date 1764, indicating that it was most probably a part of Monis's kabbalistic library.

73 Monis, *The Whole Truth*, 7.

74 See his dedicatory preface to the entire three-part publication (n. 52 above).

75 Monis, *The Truth*, 19.

76 Mather, *Mystery of Israel's Salvation*, 73.

77 Monis, *Nothing but the Truth*, 4.

78 Klein, "A Jew at Harvard," 137.

79 Hoberman, *New Israel/New England*, 92.

80 Bercovitch, *Puritan Origins*, 19–20.

81 In fact, Cambridge's Christian community continued to refer to Monis as "the converted Jew" or "the Christianized Jew," and some derisively, or with a sense of authority that he was perceived to hold concerning Judaism, referred to him as "Rabbi Monis." For more on this, see Klein, "A Jew at Harvard," 142.

82 Hoberman, *New Israel/New England*, 88.

83 Klein, "A Jew at Harvard," 140.

84 Shalom Goldman, *God's Sacred Tongue: Hebrew and the American Imagination* (Chapel Hill: University of North Carolina Press, 2004), 39.

4. NOTHING BUT THE TRUTH

1 Moore, "Judah Monis," 20–21; Klein, "A Jew at Harvard," 141. Klein notes, "By his own admission, Monis was not 'A Master of the English tongue,' and modern analysts find too much detailed Protestant theology and too much virulent anti-Catholicism to suggest anything but the intrusion of other hands into the composition of these discourses." Moore quite wittily quips, playing off Genesis 27:22, "The voice is the voice of Jacob, but the hands are the hands of Esau."

2 For a full analysis of this question, see Goldman, *God's Sacred Tongue*, 41–45. See also George Alexander Kohut, "Judah Monis, M.A., the First Instructor in Hebrew at Harvard University (1683–1764)," *American Journal of Semitic Languages and Literatures* 14, no. 4 (July 1898): 218–19; and George Alexander Kohut and John Parry, "Early Jewish Literature in America," *Publications of the American Jewish Historical Society* 3 (1895): 113–14.

3 Monis, *Nothing but the Truth*, 2. George Foot Moore claims that this strange transliteration of Hebrew was typical of Italian Jews of Monis's time. See Moore, "Judah Monis," 5–6.

4 Judah Monis, *Nothing but the Truth* (Boston: Printed for *Daniel Henchman*, and sold at his Shop, 1722).

5 Moshe Idel, *Kabbalah: New Perspectives* (New Haven, CT: Yale University Press), 263.

6 In private correspondence, Reiner Smolinski has pointed out that Newport and New York would not have been out of Monis's reach. Notwithstanding, there is no evidence that he had any contact with those communities or that his treatises had any circulation within them. Were his conversionary impulses active and focused, we would expect to see evidence from within those communities; none so far has been laid bare.

7 Monis, *Nothing but the Truth*, 1.

8 Ibid., 8.

9 Ibid.

10 Moses Maimonides, *Mavo l'Perek Helek* (Berlin: Papplauer Buchhandlung, 1901),
והיסוד השני: יחודו הש"י כלומר (שנאמין) שזה שהוא סבת הכל אחד ואינו כאחד הזוג ולא כאחד 21:
המין ולא כאיש האחד [המורכב] שהוא נחלק לאחדים רבים ולא אחד כמו הגוף הפשוט האחד במנין
שמקבל החלוק [והפרידה] לאין סוף אבל הוא יתעלה אחד באחדות שאין כמותה אחדות [בשום פנים]
וזה היסוד השני מורה עליו מה שנאמר שמע ישראל ד' אלהינו ד' אחד.

11 Monis, *Nothing but the Truth*, 15.

12 Ibid.

13 Ibid.

14 Ibid.

15 Monis, *Dickdook Leshon Gnebreet: A Grammar of the Hebrew Tongue* (Cambridge: Jonas Green, 1735), 94.

16 For Wamsley's analysis of the Creed as transformed by Monis, see her "'A Pure Language (or Lip),'" 131–34.

17 BT *Berakhot* 61b: .יצתה בת קול ואמרה אשריך רבי עקיבא שאתה מזומן לחיי העולם הבא

18 Deuteronomy 6:5: .ואהבת את יהוה אלהיך בכל-לבבך ובכל-נפשך ובכל-מאדך

19 BT *Berakhot* 2:1: .היה קורא בתורה, והגיע זמן המקרא, אם כון לבן, יצא. ואם לאו, לא יצא

20 *Encyclopaedia Judaica*, 2nd ed., vol. 18 (2007), 455.

21 Ms. HUG 1580.74, fol. 79a: לקיים מ"ע לומ' ק"ש ולאהוב השי"ת דכתיב ואהבת את ה' אלהיך: This may be בכל לבבך לסתום עיניו בפ' ראשון ביד ימינו: בסוד עולימתא שפירתא דלית לה עיינין. an abbreviated version of *Shulchan 'Aruch shel Rabbenu Yitzhak Luria*. See the version printed in Vilna (1880), 17a: כשיאמר שמע יסגור עיניו בידו הימנית בסוד עולימתא שפירתא דלית לה עיינא כנזכר בסבא דמשפטים.

22 *Zohar* 2:95a: מהו עולימתא שפירתא ולית לה עיינין ,וגופא טמירתא ואתגלי, איהי נפקת בצפרא ואתכסיא ביממא, אתכשטת בקשוטין דלא הוו.

23 Tzahi Weiss, "Who Is a Beautiful Maiden Without Eyes? The Metamorphosis of a Zohar Midrashic Image from a Christian Allegory to a Kabbalistic Metaphor," *Journal of Religion* 93, no. 1 (January 2013): 70. For a list of the extensive scholarly literature on the topic, see Weiss, 61, n. 2.

24 Elliot R. Wolfson, "Beautiful Maiden without Eyes: *Peshat* and *Sod* in Zoharic Hermeneutics," in *The Midrashic Imagination: Jewish Exegesis, Thought, and History*, ed. Michael Fishbane (Albany: SUNY Press, 1993), 186.

25 Monis, *Nothing but the Truth*, 12.

26 Ibid., 16.

27 Ibid. The "we" here refers to Christians, thereby placing Monis firmly within their ranks.

28 Ibid., 12.

29 The modern dating of *Sefer Yetzirah* is still far from definitive, but it places it anywhere between the Second Temple period and the Islamic Hellenistic renaissance of the ninth century. For the early dating, see most recently Yehuda Liebes, *Torat ha-Yezirah shel Sefer Yezirah* (Jerusalem: Schocken Books, 2000), 73. For the presumed later dating, see Steven M. Wasserstrom, "Further Thoughts on the Origins of *Sefer yesirah*," *Aleph: Historical Studies in Science and Judaism* 2 (2002): 201–21.

30 תֶּרַח עוֹבֵד צְלָמִים הֲוָה, חַד זְמַן נְפִיק לַאֲתַר, הוֹשִׁיב לְאַבְרָהָם מוֹכֵר תַּחְתָּיו. הֲוָה אָתֵי בַּר אֵינַשׁ בָּעֵי דְּיִזְבַּן, וַהֲוָה אָמַר לֵהּ בַּר כַּמָּה שְׁנִין אַתְּ, וַהֲוָה אָמַר לֵהּ בַּר חַמְשִׁין אוֹ שִׁתִּין, וַהֲוָה אָמַר לֵהּ וַי לֵהּ לְהַהוּא גַּבְרָא דַּהֲוָה בַּר שִׁתִּין וּבָעֵי לְמִסְגַּד לְבַר יוֹמֵי, וַהֲוָה מִתְבַּיֵּשׁ וְהוֹלֵךְ לוֹ. חַד זְמַן אֲתָא חַד אִתְּתָא חַד אִתְּתָא טְעִינָא בִּידָהּ חָדָא פִּינַךְ דְּסֹלֶת, אָמְרָה לֵיהּ הֵא לָךְ קְרֵב קֳדָמֵיהוֹן, קָם נְסִיב בּוּקְלְסָא בִּידֵיהּ, וְתַבְרִינּוּן לְכָלְהוֹן פְּסִילַיָּא, וִיהַב בּוּקְלְסָא בִּידָא דְּרַבָּה דַּהֲוָה בֵּינֵיהוֹן. כֵּיוָן דְּאָתָא אָבוּהּ אָמַר לֵיהּ מַאן עָבֵיד לְהוֹן כְּדֵין, אָמַר לֵיהּ מַה נִּכְפּוֹר מִינָךְ אֲתַת חָדָא אִתְּתָא טְעִינָא לָהּ חָדָא פִּינַךְ דְּסֹלֶת, וַאֲמַרַת לִי הֵא לָךְ קְרֵיב קֳדָמֵיהוֹן, קְרֵיבִית לְקָדָמֵיהוֹן הֲוָה דֵּין אָמַר אֲנָא אֵיכוֹל קַדְמָאי, וְדֵין אָמַר אֲנָא אֵיכוֹל קַדְמָאי, קָם הָדֵין רַבָּה דַּהֲוָה בֵּינֵיהוֹן נְסַב בּוּקְלְסָא וְתַבְרִינוֹן. אָמַר לֵיהּ מָה אַתְּה מַפְלָה בִּי, וְיָדְעִין אִינּוּ. אָמַר לֵיהּ וְלֹא יִשְׁמְעוּ אָזְנֶיךָ מַה שֶּׁפִּיךָ אוֹמֵר

31 Monis, *Nothing but the Truth*, 3.

32 For more on this text, see Gershom Scholem, *Origins of the Kabbalah* (Princeton, NJ: Princeton University Press, 2018), 347–54.

33 Monis, *Nothing but the Truth*, 9.

34 Bahya ben Asher, *Midrash Rabbenu Bahya ʿal Hamisha Humshei Torah* (Jerusalem, 1972), 143: קבלת הגאון בשמותיהם שהם אור קדמון אור מצוחצח אור צח ושלשת שמות אלו: אלו כלם ענין אחד ועצם אחד דבקים דבוק אמיץ בשורש כל השרשים.

35 Ibid.: ואע"פ שמצינו שלש עשרה מדות ולא מצינו שלש עשרה ספירות סוד העניו מפני שהשלש המאורות העליונות שהם על עשר ספירות אין להם התחלה כי הם שם ועצם לשורש השרשים.

36 Scholem, *Origins of the Kabbalah*, 354.

37 Iosephi Ciantes Romani, *De sanctissima trinitate ex antiquoroum Hebraeorum testimonijs euidenter comprobata* (Rome, 1667), 5: "Nunc vobis, inquit, declarabo tres sublimes Luces, quae Supra decem Sephirot, seu Spiritus, sunt—- quorum nomina a nostris veteribus Sanctis accepimus; Lucens intrinsecam, antiquam; Lucem clarificatam; Lucem claram—- Hae tres luces sunt in Infinito in Deo."

38 "convincere gli Ebrei coi loro stessi principij," quoted in Yossef Schwartz, "Kabbalah and Conversion: Caramuel and Ciantes on Kabbalah as a Means for the Conversion of the Jews," in *Unʾaltra modernità Juan Caramuel Lobkowitz (1606–1682): enciclopedia e probabilismo*, ed. Daniele Sabaino and Paolo C. Pissavino (Pisa: Edizione ETS, 2012), 177.

39 Schwartz explains, "Ciantes' work is probably mainly directed to Jewish intellectuals, which again might explain his decision to concentrate solely on Jewish sources, which he quotes very accurately" (ibid., 184).

40 Ibid., 176.

41 Profiat Duran, *Kelimat ha-Goyim* in *Ha-Sofe le-Hokhmat Yisrael* 3:143, cited in Scholem, *Origins of the Kabbalah*, 354.

42 Monis, *Nothing but the Truth*, 10.

43 Ibid.

44 Isaiah Tishby, *Wisdom of the Zohar*, vol. 3 (New York: Oxford University Press, 1989), 973.

45 For Liebes's continuation of Tishby's discussion, see his "Hashpaʿot Nozriot al Sefer ha-Zohar," in *Jerusalem Studies in Jewish Thought* 2, no. 1(1982–83): 44–45. For the English version, see Leibes, "Christian Influences on the *Zohar*," *Studies in the Zohar*, trans. from Hebrew by Arnold Schwartz, Stephanie Nakache, and Penina Peli (Albany: SUNY Press, 1993), 140.

46 Liebes, "Christian Influences," 139.

47 Ibid., 142–43.

48 *Zohar* 2:43b. The pericope *Bo* is Exodus 10:1–13:16.

49 Ibid., 140; and Liebes, "Hashpaʿot Nozriot," 44–45.

50 Monis, *Nothing but the Truth*, 10. Caps and italics are in the original. The Aramaic passage, at least in the printed versions of the *Zohar* is as follows: שמע ישראל י' אלהינו י' הא כלהו חד, ועל דא אקרי אחד. הא תלת שמהן אינון, היך אינון חז, אוף על גב דקרינן אחד, היך אינון חז. אלא בחזיונא דרוח קדשא אתיידע, ואינון בחיזו דעינא סתימא, למנדע דתלתא אלין אחד. ודא איהו רזא דקול דאשתמע, קול איהו חד, ואיהו תלתא גווניו, אשא ורוחא ומיא, וכלהו חז, ברזא דקול. (ולאו אינון אלא חד). אוף הכא י' אלהינו י' אינון חז. תלתא גווניו, ואינון חז. ודא איהו קול דעביד בר נש ביחודא ולשוואה רעותיה ביחודא דכלא מאין סוף עד סופא דכלא, בהאי קול דקא עביד בהני תלתא דאינון חז. ודא איהו יחודא דכל יומא דאתגלי ברזא דרוח דרוח קדשא.

51 This is a term from the book of Daniel, which takes on theosophical significance in Kabbalah. See Daniel 7:9, 7:13, 7:22.

52 *Zohar* 2:43b: ‏ודא איהו קול דעביד בר נש ביחודא, ולשוואה רעותיה ביחודא דכלא, מאין סוף עד סופא‏ ‏דכלא, בהאי קול דקא עביד בהני תלתא דאינון חד.‏

53 It is reasonable to surmise that Increase Mather and his ilk were unaware of such textual gymnastics. One could make the claim that Monis was thus involved in a form of subterfuge, but such recontextualizations of prooftexts were actually part and parcel of rabbinic thought, and it is thus just as reasonable to assume that Monis was rereading with faithful intent.

54 For examples of biblical references, see Psalm 51:13, Isaiah 63:11. For rabbinic references and for a full discussion of the idea within Judaism generally, see Alan Unterman et al., "Ru'aḥ Ha-Kodesh," *Encyclopaedia Judaica*, 2nd ed., vol. 17 (2007), 506–9.

55 Adam Afterman, "The Rise of the 'Holy Spirit' in Kabbalah," *Harvard Divinity Bulletin* 46, nos. 3-4 (Autumn/Winter 2018), https://bulletin.hds.harvard.edu/the-rise-of-the-holy-spirit-in-kabbalah/

56 Ibid.

57 Nigel Voak, "Richard Hooker and the Principle of 'Sola Scriptura,'" *Journal of Theological Studies*, New Series, 59, no. 1 (April 2008): 96.

58 Numbers 23:9.

59 Isaiah 11:1.

60 Monis, *Nothing but the Truth*, 11. This is Monis's translation of *Zohar* 3:203b: ‏כל יחודא שלים הכא איהו. יי' אלקינו יי'. דהא רזא דיליה מראש צורים איהו ואתייחד ברישא בגזעא‏ ‏ושבילא. יי' דא רישא עלאה אוירא דסלקא. אלקינו דא גזעא דאתמר גזע ישי. יי' דא שבילא דלתתא ועל‏ ‏רזא דא אתייחד ביה כדקא יאות.‏ The pericope *Balak* is Numbers 22:2–25:9.

61 This same passage was taken up in the same manner in the late nineteenth or early twentieth century by another convert from Judaism to Christianity, Leopold Cohn. In his pamphlet *Do Christians Worship Three Gods?*, Cohn writes, "It will interest the reader to know that the most sacred Jewish book, the Zohar, comments on Deuteronomy 6:4—'Hear O Israel, Jehovah our God, Jehovah is one,' saying 'Why is there need of mentioning the name of God three times in this verse?' Then follows the answer 'The first Jehovah is the Father above. The second is the stem of Jesse, the Messiah who is to come from the family of Jesse through David. And the third one is the way which is below (meaning the Holy Spirit who shows us the way) and these three are one'" (*Do Christians Worship 3 Gods?* [New York: American Board of Missions to the Jews, n.d.], 4–5). Cohn is clearly taking greater liberties with this passage than Monis.

62 Tishby, *Wisdom of the Zohar*, 973.

63 Monis, *Nothing but the Truth*, 11. This is Monis's translation of *Zohar* 2:133b: ‏יהו"ה: דא רשימו דאת י', רישא עלאה דבשמא קדישא. אלהינו: דא איהו רזא דרשימו דאת ה' עלאה,‏ ‏את תנינא דבשמא קדישא. יהו"ה: דא משיכו דאתמשך לתתא ברזא דרשימו דאת ו', דאינון תרין אתוון‏ ‏אתמשכו למהוי באתר דא, ואיהו אחד. כל הני תלתא אינון חד, ביחודא חד.‏

64 Ibid.

65 *Zohar* 2:133b: בההיא שעתא דאתחברו בעלה ומטרוניתא כחדא, כדין כרוזא נפיק מסטרא דדרום, אתערו חילין ומשיריין דגלי רחימותא לגבי מאריכון. כדין אתער חד ממנא עלאה, בוא"ל שמיה, רב משריין, ובידיה ארבע מפתחן, דנטיל מארבע סטרי עלמא, וחד מפתחא אתרשים באת י', וחפתחא אחרא אתרשים באת ה'. וחד מפתחא אתרשים באת ו'. ואנח להו תחות אילנא דחיי. אינון תלת מפתחן, דאתרשימו בתלת אתוון אלין, אתעבידו חד. כיון דאתעבידו חד, ההוא מפתחא אחרא, סליק וקאים ואתחבר בההוא אחרא כללא דתלת, וכל אינון משריין וחיילין עיילין לאינון תרין מפתחן גו גנתא וכלהו מיחדי כגוונא דלתתא.

66 Monis does mention "Rabbi Menasseh Ben Israel" on pages 33 and 35 of *The Whole Truth*, and while he mentions the *Consiliador* on page 35, he does not quote from this or any of Menasseh ben Israel's works.

67 Monis, *Nothing but the Truth*, 17.

68 Ibid.

69 Moshe Hallamish, "On the Question of Connections between R. Moshe Elbaz and the Ari" [Hebrew], *Daʿat: A Journal of Jewish Philosophy and Kabbalah* 50–52 (2003): 515–16; Dan Manor, "R. Moses bar Maimon (Elbaz): Kabbalistic Exegesis and its Sources" [Hebrew], *Kabbalah: Journal for the Study of Jewish Mystical Texts* 7 (2002): 200. Incidentally, the passage being quoted by Monis is not only from Elbaz and not from Sasportas; it is on page 14b of Elbaz's *Heikhal ha-Kodesh* and not, as Monis writes, on page 15.

70 Moshe bar Maimon Elbaz, *Sefer Heikhal ha-Kodesh* (Amsterdam, 1653), 14b: שמע יתכוין לשם עין שם היא המלכות והיא מלה בפני עצמה ולכן העין רבתי להראות כי שם הוא מלה בפני עצמה והיא מדת המלכו' הנקראת שם וכשמוציא עין רבתי מפיו בהברת העין יתכוין לשבע ספירות כולם שהם סוד החתן מן יסוד עד חסד וכשאומר שמע יתכוין ליחד שם עם עין ויעשם חיבור אחד כמו שעשה מהם הכתוב מלה אחת שמע וכשאמר ישראל יתכוין לאם הבנים שהיא למעלה מן השבע ונקראת ישראל כי שם הם נשמותיהן של ישראל י' אבא עלאה אלהינו ראש הלבן יתברך עתיקא דכל עתיקין היחיד הקדמון נשמת הנשמות וכאשר תעלה מחשבת האדם למקום הזה ימשוך הנשמה אל הכתר כשיאמר אלף של אחד שהוא כנגד ראש הלבן.

71 This is markedly different from the common Christological idea, stemming from exegesis on the Song of Songs, of the Bride as the Church and the Groom as Christ, as it places the Bride within the theosophical realm.

72 Elbaz, 14b: באלף של אחד אין להאריך כי הוא כנגד המופלא והיא מדה אחת ברגע ישוטט בה מחשבתו.

73 Ibid.: ומשם ימשוך הנשמה אל חית שהיא סוד חכמה עליונה עם השמנה ספירות כלם שהם עלמא דדכורא בחשבון חית עד היסוד ויאריך בחית כשיעור שתשוטט מחשבתו בכל המדות מן החכמה עד היסוד להמשיך להם הנשמה . . . ולאחר שמייחד עלמא דדכורא ויעשם אחד בנשמה אחת ובאהבה באחו' במלת אחד יתכוין להמשיך אל הנשמה עוד הנשמה דלת שהיא השכינ' שהיא דלת ויחבר אותה עם אח' ויהיה אחד כי נשמתם אחד והם גוף אחד כמו שגוף האדם הוא מחולק לאיברים ונשמו אחת כן למעלה וזהו הייחוד האמתי שהוא מקובל ומרוצה והנה דלת רבתי ג"כ לחלק המלה לעשות ממנה אחד כי אלמא דדכורא הרומז בא"ח כמו שביארנו הוא את לדלת שהיא השכינה כי הם אחים מן האב והאם.

74 Manor, "R. Moses bar Maimon (Elbaz)," 203.

75 For more on the concept and its historical development in Judaism, see Gershom Scholem, "Adam Kadmon," *Encyclopedia Judaica*, 2nd ed., vol. 1 (2007): 378–79. For a discussion of the Lurianic casting of this concept, see Scholem, *Major Trends*, 616, 638–39.

76 Ms. HUG 1580.74, fol. 3a: הוא אדם קדמון הנק' עתיקא דעתיקין מפני שהוא למעלה מעתיק יומין
דאצי' ומפני זה נק' עתיק דעתיקין ונק' ג"כ טמירא דטמירין מפני שהוא טמור.

77 Van Helmont, *Adumbratio*, 5, quoted in Coudert, *Impact of the Kabbalah*, 127.

78 Conway, *Principles*, 23.

79 Monis, *Nothing but the Truth*, 20.

80 Ibid.

81 See, for example, Hayyim Vital, *Sefer Otzrot Hayyim* (Livorno, 1783), 3. The catalog of the Institute for Microfilmed Manuscripts at the National Library of Israel
counts over 210 manuscripts of *Otzrot Hayyim* that were scribed before 1785.

82 Herrera, *Gate of Heaven*, 326.

83 Genesis 36:31.

84 *Zohar* 3:135b, translated here by Matt, *Zohar: Pritzker Edition*, vol. 8, 382: וכיון
דאתתקן אדם אתקרון בשמהן אחרנין ואתבסמו בקיומא ביה וקיימין בדוכתייהו.

85 Ms. HUG 1580.74, fols. 37a-b: וכיון שניתקן בחי' אדם ויצא לעולם בחי' שם מ"ה החדש הנק' אדם
שיצא מתוקן זכר ונקיבה אז אלו המלכים שנשברו שקודם היו נק' נקודות דשם ס"ג אז כשיוצא שם מ"ה
אז נק' אלו הנקודות דס"ג נק' ב"ן כדי שיוכלו להתבסם ולהתקן עם שם מ"ה שאם היו עדין נק' שם ס"ג
לא היו יכולים להתקן בשם מ"ה . . . נקראו אלו הנקודות בשמות אחרים שקודם היו נק' ס"ג ואה"כ
נקראו ב"ן ואה"כ נתבסמו בשם מ"ה הנק' אדם.

86 Monis, *Nothing but the Truth*, 22.

87 See *Zohar* 3:235b and Yosef Shlomo Delmedigo of Candia, *Sefer Novlot Hokhmah*
(Basel, 1629), 172b.

88 Translated and quoted in Giuseppe Veltri, *Renaissance Philosophy in Jewish Garb:
Foundations and Challenges in Judaism on the Eve of Modernity* (Leiden: Brill, 2008),
27, from Knorr von Rosenroth, *Kabbala Denudata. Tomus primus, pars prima: loci
communes*, 343: Est autem חכמה quasi כח מה is est vis מה qui est numerus אדם.

89 Monis, *Nothing but the Truth*, 22.

90 Ibid.

91 Ibid., 23.

92 Ibid., 21–22.

93 This is according to a system of gematria known as *mispar katan*, for which all
"0"s are disregarded, plus a system of assigning numerical value to vowel and
punctuation points. Thus, 9–1=ק-ץ, 9–1=צ-י, 9–1=ט-א. According to this reckoning,
29=רוח הקדש. Added to this is a vowel and punctuation system for which each dot
is worth 10, *patach* is worth 6, and *kamatz* is worth 16. Accordingly, the vowel and
dot value of *Ruach ha-Kodesh* would be 72; the entire word together, vowels and
all, would be worth 101.

94 Monis, *Nothing but the Truth*, 23.

95 Ibid., 25.

96 The idea of the performative nature of Monis's work was highlighted by Michael
Hoberman, who writes, "Monis's conversion pamphlet was more performative
than functional, as was evidenced by his having directed its first words to the
Jews, or, as he put it, 'My Brethren, According to the Flesh.' While it may very well
have been the case that the author imagined a Jewish audience (his pamphlet was

circulated in London, as well as in Boston, so from a purely practical standpoint, it could possibly have reached members of at least one organized Jewish community), his prefatory remarks, although ostensibly directed to other Jews, were calculated to achieve an effect among Christians" (Hoberman, *New Israel/New England*, 107).

97 Monis, *The Whole Truth*, 1.

98 Humphrey Moore, *A Treatise on the Divine Nature, Exhibiting the Distinction of the Father, Son and Holy Spirit* (Boston: Samuel T. Armstrong, 1824), 29.

99 Ibid.

100 *The Jewish Expositor and Friend of Israel* (February 1821): 41–56; (March 1821): 81–96; (April 1821): 125–34; (May 1821): 165–74; (July 1821): 245–57; (August 1821): 285–91; (September 1821): 325–32. Significantly, there Monis is explicitly referred to as "Rabbi Judah Monis."

101 Monis, *Nothing but the Truth*, 5.

102 The lack of a Jewish response should come as no surprise given the fact that Jews made up less than one-tenth of a percent of the population in British North America, none of those were great kabbalists or Talmudic scholars, and none of them were living in the Boston area. It is worth noting in this context that Monis's treatise was published in English in Boston, indicating that it was actually intended for an American Protestant audience from the outset, with its purported conversionary purpose (described above) as a smokescreen; while it may not have been aimed toward changing Protestant views of Jewish thought, it may very well have aspired to convince the Boston Protestant community of Monis's sincerity (including his intent to convert other Jews). Had it truly been intended globally for his "Brethren of the flesh," it would have been written in Hebrew.

5. UNIVERSAL KABBALAH IN THE COLLEGES OF AMERICA

1 Stiles is indeed off by two years, since, as we have seen, Monis converted in 1722. It should also be noted that Stiles's catalog follows a chronological order throughout, but then at the end it lists the conversion to Christianity of "Rabbi Jehiel" in 1746, and then backtracks to 1720 to culminate with Monis. The Rabbi Jehiel written about was was Jehiel Hirschlein of Buchau am Federnsee, who indeed converted in 1746 and took on the name Christian Gottlieb. See Elisheva Carlebach, *Divided Souls: Converts from Judaism in Germany, 1500–1750* (New Haven, CT: Yale University Press, 2001), 117; and George Alexander Kohut, *Ezra Stiles and the Jews: Selected Passages from his Literary Diary Concerning Jews and Judaism* (New York: Philip Cowen, 1902), 45; see also *The Literary Diary of Ezra Stiles, D.D., LL.D.*, vol. 1: January 1, 1769–March 13, 1776, ed. Franklin Bowditch Dexter (New York: Charles Scribner's Sons, 1901), 77, entry of November 18, 1770.

2 Beinecke Library, Ezra Stiles Papers, letter of December 10, 1770.

3 Ibid.

4 See, for example, his letter to Rabbi Raphael Haim Isaac Karigal (spelled variably throughout his notebooks as Carigal, Carregal, et al.), dated May 24, 1773, which

in its entirety discusses Ezra the Scribe and his changing of the Hebrew letters of the Pentateuch; letter to John Lewis dated February 15, 1775, especially pages 6–10; and his oration given at Yale in 1781. All of these are found in the Beinecke Library, Ezra Stiles Papers.

5 Beinecke Library, Ezra Stiles Papers, oration given at Yale in 1781, 3.

6 Ibid.

7 Ibid. For purposes of clarity, abbreviations have been spelled out. The "all" in brackets here is penned in the manuscript and crossed out.

8 Stiles, oration of 1781, 14.

9 Ibid. The original statement from *Pirkei Avot* 1:1 is: משה קבל תורה מסיני ומסרה ליהושע, ויהושע לזקנים, וזקנים לנביאים, ונביאים מסרוה לאנשי כנסת הגדולה.

10 Ezra Stiles, diary entry of April 29, 1769, in *Literary Diary*, vol. 1, 10. Stiles's reading of Monis is curiously absent from Arthur A. Chiel's otherwise meticulous account of Stiles's Hebraic learning in his article "Ezra Stiles: The Education of an 'Hebrician,'" *American Jewish Historical Quarterly* 60, no. 3 (1971): 235–41.

11 Ezra Stiles, *A Discourse on Saving Knowledge* (Newport: Solomon Southwick, 1770), 14.

12 Ibid.

13 Monis, *Nothing but the Truth*, 10.

14 Stiles, *Discourse on Saving Knowledge*, 14–15.

15 Monis, *Nothing but the Truth*, 11.

16 Ibid., 12.

17 Stiles, *Discourse on Saving Knowledge*, 15.

18 Beinecke Library, Ezra Stiles Papers, "Memoir concerning my learning Hebrew," May 12, 1768, 6–7.

19 Beinecke Library, Ezra Stiles Papers, letter of December 27, 1769.

20 Beinecke Library, Ezra Stiles Papers, letter of September 27, 1770. For purposes of clarity, I have spelled out some of Stiles's abbreviations. I thank Reiner Smolinski for helping me decipher some of the obscure handwriting and archaic terminology, such as "Œconomy."

21 Ibid.

22 Beinecke Library, Ezra Stiles Papers, letter of September 28, 1770.

23 Stiles, *Literary Diary*, vol. 1, 298.

24 Boaz Huss, "The Text and Context of the 1684 Sulzbach Edition of the *Zohar*," in *Tradition, Heterodoxy and Religious Culture: Judaism and Christianity in the Early Modern Period*, ed. Chanita R. Goodblat and Howard Kreisel (Beer-Sheva: Ben-Gurion University Press, 2006), 117.

25 Ibid., 122.

26 *Kabbala Denudata* 1:2:3–4, quoted in Coudert, *Impact of the Kabbalah*, 114.

27 Ibid.

28 Coudert, *Impact of the Kabbalah*, 114.

29 Beinecke Library, Ezra Stiles Papers, letter of September 27, 1770.

30 Ibid.

31 Beinecke Library, Ezra Stiles Papers, diary entry of October 29, 1772.

32 Ibid.

33 Ibid.

34 George Foot Moore, "Ezra Stiles' Studies in the Cabbala," *Proceedings of the Massachusetts Historical Society*, Third Series, vol. 51 (October 1917–June 1918): 290–306.

35 Moore, "Ezra Stiles' Studies," 299.

36 Beinecke Library. I thank Karen Spicher, archivist at the Beinecke Rare Book and Manuscript Library, for bringing this letter to my attention and for sending me a copy.

37 Ibid.

38 Stiles, *Literary Diary*, vol. 1, 7.

39 Moore, "Ezra Stiles's Studies," 299–300.

40 Beinecke Library, Ezra Stiles Papers, diary entry of November 9, 1772. For the printed version, see *Literary Diary*, vol. 1, 299.

41 Ibid. This, and other important information, is curiously missing from Dexter's printed version of the diary. Jarchi is a regular epithet for the eleventh-century French exegete more commonly known as Rashi.

42 Ibid.

43 Stiles references his meeting with Malki at the end of his oration of 1781 and in various other places, including his literary diary of December 30, 1771. For more on this figure, see Arthur A. Chiel, "The Rabbis and Ezra Stiles," *American Jewish Historical Quarterly* 61, no. 4 (June 1972): 295–97. The Stiles Papers at the Beinecke Library also include a list of questions that Stiles posed to Malki, and their answers, dated December 6, 1759; within that list there is no mention of the *Zohar* or other classical kabbalistic texts.

44 Beinecke Library, Ezra Stiles Papers, diary entry of November 9, 1772.

45 What Stiles references joins several other sketches of concentric circles that he had made throughout his life, though it is clearly the intended diagram. This can be determined from the above quote, in a portion omitted here for the sake of narrative continuity, in which Stiles references page 233, which is the manuscript page of this diagram. The erroneous date must have been added later. I thank April DeConick for helping me verify the translations from the Greek. For Dionysius's hierarchy and a detailed explanation, see Paul Rorem, *Pseudo-Dionysius: A Commentary on the Texts and an Introduction to Their Influence* (New York: Oxford University Press, 1993), 47–90.

46 Yossi Chajes, "Kabbalistic Diagram as Epistemic Image" [Hebrew], *Pe'amim: Studies in Oriental Jewry* 150–152 (2017): 235–88; Chajes, "Imaginative Thinking with a Lurianic Diagram," *Jewish Quarterly Review* 110, no. 1 (Winter 2020): 35 (for references to Lüthy's work discussing this idea, see n. 16 on page 35).

47 For the best treatment of this to date, see Wolfson, *Through a Speculum*, especially 13–16.

48 Stiles, *Literary Diary*, vol. 1, 225. At a later point he would say of Dionysius that he was "a most lofty & sublime Writer!" See his *Literary Diary*, vol. 3, 399.

49 Beinecke Library, Ezra Stiles Papers, letter to Thomas Wright, April 10, 1775, 485.

50 *Luthers Werke, Kritische Gesamtausgabe* (Weimar: Bohlau, 1883), 5:503; and John Calvin, *Commentarii in Acta Apostolorum* (Amsterdam: Jacob Schipper, 1671), 167, both quoted in Eric M. Parker, "'Saint Dionysius': Martin Bucer's Transformation of the Pseudo-Areopagite," in *From Rome to Zurich: Between Ignatius and Vermigli: Essays in Honor of John Patrick Donnelly, SJ* (Leiden: Brill, 2017), 121.

51 Moses Maimonides, *Mishneh Torah* [*Sefer ha-Mada', Hilchot Yesodei ha-Torah*, 3:1] (Tel Aviv: Rishonim, 1946), 14: הגלגלים הם נקראים: שמים, ורקיע, וזבול, וערבות, והם .תשעה גלגלים Here Maimonides mentions four of the seven firmaments laid out by Reish Lakish in BT *Hagigah* 12b: .וילון, רקיע, שחקים, זבול, מעון, מכון, וערבות

52 Moses Maimonides, *The Guide of the Perplexed*, vol. 2, trans. with an introduction and notes by Shlomo Pines (Chicago: University of Chicago Press, 1963), 257. See also pages 268 and 301.

53 For more on this trend, see Gershom Scholem's now classical article, "From Philosopher to Cabbalist (a Legend of the Cabbalists on Maimonides)" [Hebrew], *Tarbiz* 6, no. 3 (1935): 334–42. Literature on the complex relationship between Maimonidean thought and Kabbalah abounds. For a representative sample, see Moshe Idel, "Maimonides' *Guide of the Perplexed* and the Kabbalah," *Jewish History* 18, nos. 2–3 (2004): 197–226; Idel, "Maimonides and Kabbalah," in *Studies in Maimonides*, ed. Isadore Twersky (Cambridge, MA: Harvard University Press, 1990), 31–81; Idel, "Some Images of Maimonides in Jewish Mysticism," *Studia Judaica* 17 (2009): 36–63; Elliot R. Wolfson, "Beneath the Wings of the Great Eagle: Maimonides and Thirteenth-Century Kabbalah," in *Moses Maimonides (1138–1204): His Religious, Scientific, and Philosophical "Wirkungsgeschichte" in Different Cultural Contexts*, ed. Görge K. Hasselhoff and Otfried Fraisse (Würzburg: Ergon Verlag, 2004), 209–37.

54 Beinecke Library, Ezra Stiles Papers, diary entry of November 16, 1772. It is worth noting that this is very similar to a conversation that Stiles would have about a year later with another Polish rabbi, Tobiah bar Jehudah. In his diary entry of November 19, 1773, Stiles writes of Rabbi Tobiah, "We had much conversation on the Zohar and particularly the X Saphirots. He said that the Sapher Haujtzirah was now in the same state as in Abrahams Time; that Rabbi Akiba made no change in it—only he selected it as a part of a larger Book called the Sapher Razael, which was communicated by the Angel Razael to Adam, from Adam to Seth, who delivered it to Enoch, he to Methuselah, he to Noah, he to Shem, & Shem delivered it to Abraham." For more on this fascinating figure, see Chiel, "The Rabbis and Ezra Stiles," 304–07; Chiel, "Ezra Stiles' Rabbi Tobiah," *American Jewish Historical Quarterly* 59 (1969): 228–29; and Chiel, "Ezra Stiles and the Polish Rabbi," in *Studies in Jewish Bibliography History and Literature: In Honor of I. Edward Kiev*, ed. Charles Berlin (New York: Ktav, 1971), 83–89. Since there is no need to repeat

Chiel's findings, and since I have not uncovered any new documentation related to Rabbi Tobiah, I do not discuss him in this chapter.

55 Stiles, *Literary Diary*, vol. 1, 322.

56 Beinecke Library, Ezra Stiles Papers, diary entry of January 11, 1773.

57 This is cataloged in the Stiles Papers as correspondence of Stephen Sewell to Ezra Stiles, February 29, 1772, and on the other side of the page is a series of gematriot, or Hebrew numerological calculations, as well as a quotation from the *Zohar*, Midrash Ruth. Given that the letter from Sewell to Stiles there has nothing to do with Kabbalah, and that Sewell exhibits no known affinity to Kabbalah in his writings or papers housed at Harvard, it seems highly unlikely that Sewell was the one who wrote those notes. It seems more likely that Stiles jotted them on the envelope at a later date that is impossible to determine, and that they then got cataloged along with the correspondence from Sewell to Stiles.

58 *Sefer Yetzirah*, with commentaries (Jerusalem: Levin-Epstein, 1965), 17b: והרב זקני ז"ל ביאר ספר ספור ספרי שכ"ל משכי"ל מושכ"ל. For more on Botarel, see Tzipora Brody, "Rabbi Moses Botarel: His Commentary on *Sefer Yetzirah* and the Image of Abu Aharon," *Jerusalem Studies in Jewish Thought: Gershom Scholem (1897–1982): In Memoriam* (2007): 159–206.

59 Moses Maimonides, *The Guide of the Perplexed*, vol. 1, transl. Shlomo Pines (Chicago: University of Chicago Press, 1963), 163.

60 It is somewhat surprising that Stiles does not capitalize on the triad here to further a Christian Trinitarian reading, especially given his obsession with Trinitarian readings in the *Zohar*. The absence of such an attempt here may signal that the ideas expressed have not been reformulated by Stiles but are wholly those of an interlocutor such as Moses bar David.

61 Beinecke Library, Ezra Stiles Papers, diary entry of January 11, 1773.

62 Juan Vernet, "al-Ṣafr," *Encyclopedia of Islam*, 2nd ed. (2012). Consulted online on March 25, 2020, http://dx.doi.org.ezproxy.rice.edu.

63 The provenance of the term "abracadabra" is not known, though it first occurs in the writings of a second-century-CE Gnostic physician named Severus Sammonicus. For more on this term, especially in relation to Jewish magical thought, see Dov Noy, "Abracadabra," *Encyclopaedia Judaica*, 2nd ed., vol. 1 (2007), 280. See also Joshua Trachtenberg, *Jewish Magic and Superstition: A Study in Folk Religion* (Philadelphia: University of Pennsylvania Press, 2004), 80–83.

64 Vernet, "al-Ṣafr."

65 Ibid.

66 Beinecke Library, Ezra Stiles Papers, diary entry of January 11, 1773.

67 See the discussion in the previous chapter surrounding Monis, *Nothing but the Truth*, 20, and Monis's ms. HUG 1580.74, fols. 37a-b.

68 Beinecke Library, Ezra Stiles Papers, correspondence of Stephen Sewell to Ezra Stiles, February 29, 1772. At the top of the note is written "Genesis—Zohar p. 27 Midrash Ruth." There is a passage from Midrash Ruth in the Genesis section on page 27 of the Sulzbach edition of the *Zohar*, but it does not match up with the

translated passage here. This is clearly parallel to the notions of *Adam Kadmon* as discussed by Monis, and also George Keith.

69 What is outlined there is a system known as מילוי האותיות, or "the filling of letters," by which each letter is spelled out and the total numeric value is calculated. יוד הא ואו הא as 45, or מה, is a perfect example of this ciphering and deciphering system.

70 Karigal was a *shadar*, or "emissary," dispatched, according to Matthias Lehmann, as part of a modern Jewish movement to propagate "the enduring centrality of the Holy Land as well as the obligation of Jews everywhere to provide financial support for their coreligionists in Palestine" (*Emissaries from the Holy Land: The Sephardic Diaspora and the Practice of Pan-Judaism in the Eighteenth Century* [Stanford, CA: Stanford University Press, 2014], 2).

71 Stiles, oration of 1781, 15. Stiles numbers only five rabbis but actually mentions six whom he has encountered.

72 Beinecke Library, Ezra Stiles Papers, letter to Karigal, July 19, 1773, 3.

73 Arthur A. Chiel claims that this was "a case of *amor intellectualis* at first sight" ("The Rabbis and Ezra Stiles," 300). While the intellect was unquestionably operative within this relationship, there also seems to be a superadded layer of mystical sensuality.

74 Beinecke Library, Ezra Stiles Papers, letter of Karigal to Stiles, May 29, 1773, quoted in Edmund S. Morgan, *The Gentle Puritan: A Life of Ezra Stiles 1727–1795* (New York: W. W. Norton, 1962), 143. Cf. *Literary Diary*, vol. 1, 387, entry of June 14, 1773, which reports the quote as: "Your Love has made such an indelible impression upon the inmost Tho'ts & Affections of my Heart that Volumes of Book are not sufficient to write the thousandth part of the eternal Love wherewith I love thee."

75 *Literary Diary*, vol. 1, 387.

76 Beinecke Library, Ezra Stiles Papers, letter of July 19, 1773. The italicized portion, which is emphasized in the manuscript, is a quote from 2 Samuel 1:26.

77 Beinecke Library, Ezra Stiles Papers, letter of March 1774. Cf. Psalm 119:103.

78 Laura Leibman, *Messianism, Secrecy and Mysticism: A New Interpretation of Early American Jewish Life* (Portland, OR: Vallentine Mitchell, 2012), 58, 76 n. 1.

79 Stiles, oration of 1781, 15.

80 See, for example, the entries of March 8, 1773, April 8, 1773, and May 28, 1773.

81 Lest I be accused of presentism, I am not making the case that Stiles was a homosexual, a term that would not have even had resonance at the time. Rather, I am making the case that regardless of Stiles's sexuality, the language here has clear erotic overtones, common to the masculine high culture of the times; it is indeed part of the rhetoric of the period associated with elite homosocial communities, as outlined by Eve Kasosfky Sedgwick in *Between Men: English Literature and Male Homosocial Desire* (New York: Columbia University Press, 1985); I thank Marcia Brennan for pointing me toward this reference. It should be noted that regardless of the embeddedness of such language in elite homosocial culture, given

the context, Stiles seems to have been utilizing it in a mystical, ecstatic manner similar to the Platonic sublimation of physical beauty, as will be further substantiated below.

82 Beinecke Library, Ezra Stiles Papers, letter of July 19, 1773, 3.

83 Ibid., 3–4.

84 In the Hebrew version of the letter Stiles writes, in English, "Zohar 3.38" after גן עדן, or "Garden of Eden" in the above passage, though nothing in *Zohar* 3.38 directly matches. See, however, *Song of Songs*, especially chapter 6.

85 Matthew 22:39.

86 Hoberman states that while their "mutual admiration may have had its origin in their respective scholarly achievements and shared interests, its strongest foundation lay in their fondness for each other" (*New Israel/New England*, 177). The attraction indeed seems to have been the foundation, with scholarly interests stemming from that.

87 Clearly this does not mesh with the biblical narrative, where Abraham refers to God directly by way of the Tetragrammaton. See, for example, Genesis 14:22 and 15:7. This, rather, is a Maimonidean idea, as taken from the *Guide*, I:63 (see vol. 1, 153–56).

88 Beinecke Library, Ezra Stiles Papers, diary entry of April 26, 1773.

89 Ibid.

90 Maimonides, *Guide*, I:54, vol. 1, 123.

91 Ibid., I:61, 147.

92 Again, this does not quite fit with the biblical narrative. Cf. Genesis 14:22 and 15:7.

93 Beinecke Library, Ezra Stiles Papers, diary entry of April 26, 1773.

94 See, for example, the diary entry of March 30, 1773, where Stiles states, "He spake of Aly Bey, and shewed me a passage in the *Zohar* which he said predicted that the *Russians should conquer the Turks*. I observed that in the Original it was that *Edom* should conquer the *Ismaelites*—he replied that Edom there denoted a Northern Power, and the Ismaelites those of their Religion" (*Literary Diary*, vol. 1, 357–58). Stiles does not give the precise Zoharic passage consulted.

95 Beinecke Library, Ezra Stiles Papers, Letter to Karigal, July 19, 1773, 3.

96 Kohut, *Ezra Stiles and the Jews*, 53. It is important to note that Kohut was a Reform rabbi and that his language here of "nobler investigations" than the *Zohar* fits with early twentieth-century hyperrationalist Reform sensibilities.

97 Beinecke Library, Ezra Stiles Papers, diary entry of July 15, 1773.

98 Stiles, *Literary Diary*, vol. 1, 357–58.

99 *Zohar* 2:32b: וזמינין בני ישמעאל לאתערא קרבין תקיפין בעלמא ולאתכנשא בני אדום עלייהו ויתערון קרבא בהו, חד על ימא, וחד על יבשתא וחד סמוך לירושלים. וישלטון אלין באלין, וארעא קדישא לא יתמסר לבני אדום.

100 There is no clear connection here to Menasseh ben Israel's popular treatise of the same name.

101 Letter of July 19, 1773, 25. These are topics that Stiles also covered on November 23, 1772, with Rabbi Tobiah bar Jehudah. Tobiah did not seem to want to engage

and simply responded that "these Inquiries bewildered & lost us in the Incomprehensiblity of Futurity, & it was best to leave them to God." The English version of this letter was published by Edwin Wolf 2nd, "Ezra Stiles Writes a Hebrew Letter," in *Studies and Essays in Honor of Abraham A. Neuman*, ed. Meir Ben-Horin, Bernard D. Weinryb, and Solomon Zeitlin (Leiden: E. J. Brill, 1962), 516–46.

102 Hebrew letter of July 19, 1773, 20: מלכותו של משיח לארץ לא היתה עולם בלי קץ עלמים כי עולם אחד לאלף שנה לבדו זה נקרא נצח בעבור כל עון נצח חולת טוב ושלום על הארץ אלף שנה עד משרפה התבל ועד השמים החדשים וארץ החדשה. ישעיה חזר.

103 For reference to this, see Idel, *Messianic Mystics*, 365, n. 36. An example from the *Zohar*, called forth by Idel, is *Zohar* 3:243b.

104 Cf. *Zohar* 1:24a.

105 Letter of July 19, 1773, 31.

106 Christopher Grasso, *A Speaking Aristocracy: Transforming Public Discourse in Eighteenth-Century Connecticut* (Chapel Hill: University of North Carolina Press, 1999), 255. For similar ideas in other colonial thinkers, see Smolinski, "Israel Redivivus."

107 Ibid., 26.

108 Beinecke Library, Ezra Stiles Papers, letter to John Lewis, February 15, 1775, 4.

109 Ibid., 5. Here he is quoting *Zohar* 1:15b.

110 Ibid.

111 Ibid.

112 Letter of July 19, 1773, 32.

113 Abiel Holmes, *The Life of Ezra Stiles* (Boston: Thomas & Andrews, 1798), 171–72. This also seems to be the reading of George Foot Moore in his "Ezra Stiles' Studies," 298.

114 Beinecke Library, Ezra Stiles Papers, letter of December 8, 1773, 1.

115 Letter of July 19, 1773, 5, translating and citing *Zohar* 3:65a. Stiles first raises this passage in his literary diary of November 5, 1772, where he also mentions: "The *Three* in God are sometimes called *Middot*, &c. The *Sapher Jetzira* (said to be by Abraham) calls these three middot ההויות the beings, the Jehovahs, the self existences."

116 *Zohar* 3:65a: והאי נהרא אתקרי אם לגנתא, ועילא מגנתא.

117 Letter of July 19, 1773, 9.

118 Hoberman correctly states that "while Stiles certainly would have delighted in the prospect of perhaps converting, or at least *witnessing* the conversion of Jews, the largest motivating factor behind his inquiries about Judaism was his belief that his *own* religion might be enriched or enhanced by a fuller understanding of its Jewish roots" (*New Israel/New England*, 170). Chiel, for his part, emphasizes Stiles's desire for the conversion of those who are his friends, for the sake of unity in Christian brotherhood, in his "Ezra Stiles and the Jews: A Study in Ambivalence," in *A Bicentennial Festschrift for Jacob Rader Marcus*, ed. Bertram Wallace Korn (New York: Ktav, 1976), 72.

119 Beinecke Library, Ezra Stiles Papers, letter of May 24, 1773.

120 Ibid.: ברוך אתה לאל עליון ולמשיח שהוא יהוה צדקנו וגאל לנצירי ישראל אור גוים הוא וישועת כל
עמים לקצה הארץ. Evidence that this somewhat sophisticated, subtle Christian
reading of the Isaiah passage was understood by Stiles and was being used by him
in his discourse with Karigal can be found in the lines of the letter that shortly
follow: ראשונים נוצרים שהיו יהודים והם כהנים וחכמים יודעי בינה וספרי רבותיכם יתנו את הדעת זה
לאנשים קדשים אחריהם. In Stiles's own English translation: "The first Nazarenes or
Christians, who were Jews and themselves Priests and wise men knowing in the
Literature and Book of your Rabbins, delivered this learning to holy men after
them." He clearly knew the notion of *Notzrim* as "Nazarenes or Christians" (and
asserted that they were Jews), and by extension, he knew that *Nitzurim* were those
who had been Christianized.

121 For more on early modern notions of kabbalistic universalism and the *prisca theo-
logia* tradition, see Moshe Idel, "Kabbalah, Platonism, and Prisca Theologia: The
Case of R. Menasseh ben Israel," in *Menasseh ben Israel and His World*, ed. Yosef
Kaplan, Henry Méchoulan, and Richard H. Popkin (Leiden: Brill, 1989), 207–19;
Idel, *Kabbalah in Italy, 1280–1510: A Survey* (New Haven, CT: Yale University
Press, 2011), 165–76; Idel, "Prisca Theologia in Marsilio Ficino and in Some Jew-
ish Treatments," in *Marsilio Ficino: His Theology, His Philosophy, His Legacy*, ed.
Michael Allen and Valerie Rees (Leiden: Brill, 2002), 137–58; Ogren, *Renaissance
and Rebirth*, 163–84.

122 Stiles, *Saving Knowledge*, 18.

123 Grasso, *Speaking Aristocracy*, 265.

124 Beinecke Library, Ezra Stiles Papers, letter of December 10, 1770. To be sure, Stiles
is using the term "Kabbala" here more broadly to include all received wisdom.
This broader definition follows him throughout his ruminations and shapes his
thinking about Jewish and universal esoteric thought.

125 Letter of July 19, 1773, 33.

126 Stiles, oration of 1781, 6.

127 Ibid., 5.

128 Ibid., 14.

129 Ibid.

130 Ibid.

131 This statement is not made merely in jest. According to Shalom Goldman,
when Stiles "assumed the presidency of Yale he not only made Hebrew language
instruction mandatory, but also took on the teaching of Hebrew" (*God's Sacred
Tongue*, 52). He jokingly explained that he wanted his students to know Hebrew,
if for nothing else then so that they could understand the angels singing psalms
once they reached heaven (Morgan, *Gentle Puritan*, 378; *Literary Diary*, 3, 306).
Given the tenor of his oration, one could naturally surmise that he would have
liked to have made rabbinic learning mandatory too.

132 For more on the way this distinction plays out with the *prisca theologia* tradition, with which Stiles is clearly engaged as we have seen, see Wouter Hanegraaff,
Esotericism in the Academy: Rejected Knowledge in Western Culture (New York:

Cambridge University Press, 2012), 6–7. Kohut makes the claim that in regard to the rabbis, Stiles "prizes their learning only for the 'scattered Remains of the ancient Doctrines of the Trinity & a suffering Messiah'" ("Ezra Stiles and His Friends," *Menorah Journal* 3, no. 1 [February 1917]: 42). As we have seen, however, his relationship to the tradition is much more complex than that.

133 In another context, Alexander Guttman raises the specter that in 1780, Stiles (accurately) took upon himself the role of *posek*, or halakhic decisor. This is simply another example of Stiles crossing religious boundaries and taking on learned Jewish religious praxis. See Alexander Guttman, "Ezra Stiles, Newport Jewry, and a Question of Jewish Law," *American Jewish Archives* 34, no. 1 (1982): 98–102.

134 Beinceck Library, Ezra Stiles Papers, letter from Isaac Pinto of April 14, 1790:
לאיש מכובה. בשערים נודע. מלומה. מלמד ומעמיד תלמידים הרבה. ה"ה החכם הנבון המשכיל עזרא סטיליז ראש הישיבה הילנסי. שלום

135 In his *Literary Diary*, Stiles refers to Pinto as "A Learned Jew at N. York" (*Literary Diary*, vol. 3, 392).

CONCLUSION: JEWISH INVOLVEMENT AND AMERICAN EXCEPTIONALISM

1 Jacob R. Marcus, *The Colonial American Jew 1492–1776*, vol. 1 (Detroit: Wayne State University Press, 1970), 860.

2 William Pencak, *Jews and Gentiles*, 1.

3 Jonathan D. Sarna, *American Judaism: A History* (New Haven, CT: Yale University Press, 2004), 28.

4 Ibid.

5 Arthur Hertzberg, *The Jews in America: Four Centuries of an Uneasy Encounter: A History* (New York: Columbia University Press, 1997), 19.

6 Hertzberg seems to have had a bit of an ax to grind. For example, he goes on to remark, "Stiles, who prided himself on writing letters to Rabbi Carigal in Hebrew (it was very bad Hebrew), wrote continually in his diary that the rabbi was a rabbi and thus the representative of a bad doctrine. Jews, no matter how intriguing they might be as individuals, remained outsiders. They could become part of America only if they ceased being Jewish" (32–33). Snubs at Stiles's "bad Hebrew" aside, this is blatantly false. Stiles did not write that Karigal, or any other Jewish intellectual whom he encountered, was the representative of a "bad doctrine." He also frequented the synagogue in Newport, thus fully understanding that there was a permanent community there. As we have shown, his relationship was naturally much more complex than simply seeing Judaism as a "bad doctrine" or Jews as naturally un-American.

7 Cotton Mather, *The Diary of Cotton Mather: 1709–1724* (Boston: Massachusetts Historical Society, 1892), 741, entry of July 17, 1724.

8 Hertzberg, *Jews in America*, 1.

9 Lee M. Friedman, "An Invitation to American Jewish History," *Publications of the American Jewish Historical Society* 38, no. 1 (September 1948): 13–14.

10 Lee M. Friedman, "E Pluribus Unum: Unity in Diversity," *Publications of the American Jewish Historical Society* 40, no. 3 (March 1951): 210.

11 As J. Hector St. John de Crevecoèur now famously wrote about America in 1782 and then republished many times, "Here individuals of all nations are melted into a new race of men, whose labors and posterity will one day cause great changes in the world." *Letters from an American Farmer* (Belfast: James Magee, 1783), 34. For Zangwill's work, see his *The Melting-Pot: Drama in Four Acts*, rev. ed. (New York: Macmillan, 1917).

12 Kallen had written an article entitled "Democracy versus the Melting Pot" in 1915, and he published a book entitled *Culture and Democracy in the United States* in 1924. While Friedman does not explicitly cite Kallen, the latter's views had gained quite a bit of ground and the former's references to cultural pluralism seem unmistakably connected to them.

13 Friedman, "E Pluribus Unum," 208.

14 Ibid., 213.

15 Theodore Dwight Bozeman has noted that scholars frequently overlook the idea posited by Miller that "errand" had a dual intent. One was practical in the sense of actual business, i.e., the Puritans were on an errand *for themselves*, to set up a working society. The other is a greater aim, by which they were seen as "despatched for a further purpose" (Bozeman, "The Puritans' 'Errand into the Wilderness' Reconsidered," *New England Quarterly* 59, no. 2 [June 1986]: 232).

16 Perry Miller, "Errand into the Wilderness," *William and Mary Quarterly* 10, no. 1 (January 1953): 14.

17 Bozeman, "Puritans' Errand," 233.

18 Van Engen, *City on a Hill*, 49. Van Engen further writes, "So indispensable did this sermon become to Perry Miller that he actually began inventing facts to support its significance. By 1954, he was claiming that the sermon had been 'printed,' though it never was. One year later he explained that it 'was sent back to London for printing, and was reimported to Massachusetts Bay, so that all might heed.' It never was" (242).

19 Andrew Delbanco, "The Puritan Errand Re-Viewed," *Journal of American Studies* 18, no. 3 (December 1984): 346.

20 Miller, "Errand into the Wilderness," 15.

21 Bercovitch, *Puritan Oigins*, 72.

22 Avihu Zakai, *Exile and Kingdom: History and Apocalypse in the Puritan Migration to America* (New York: Cambridge University Press, 1992), 65, 123.

23 Ibid., 66.

24 Smolinski, "Israel Redivivus." Needless to say, the picture is actually quite messy and complex since, as Smolinski also notes, several of the Puritans do refer to New England as a New Jerusalem. Cotton Mather himself even refers to the Holy City in America.

25 This rhetorical paradigm holds sway for much of Evangelical Christian Zionist discourse until this very day. For an interesting analysis, see Stephen Spector,

Evangelicals and Israel: The Story of American Christian Zionism (New York: Oxford University Press, 2009).

26 Bercovitch notes that this is certainly the case with Cotton Mather in his *Magnalia*, where he writes of an evangelical call and a paradise regained. See *Puritan Origins*, 115.

27 Jerald C. Brauer, "Conversion: From Puritanism to Revivalism," *Journal of Religion* 58, no. 3 (July 1978): 227.

28 Ezra Stiles, *The United States Elevated to Glory and Honour*, 2nd ed., corrected (Worcester, MA: Isaiah Thomas, 1785), 98.

29 Ibid., 9.

30 Ibid., 10.

31 Leviticus 19:2, 20:26, 21:6.

32 Daniel 12:4. Here the Hebrew is fully mistaken. It should be: ישטטו רבים ותרבה הדעת.

33 Stiles, *United States*, 89.

APPENDIX I

1 Reference here is to Daniel Leeds, *The Temple of Wisdom for the Little World* (Philadelphia: William Bradford, 1688). All notes in this section will be limited to direct citations from this work, to which Keith is responding in his epistle.

2 Leeds, 1: "The understanding of the thing here called Quality, is the Foundation of the whole Revelation of Jacob Behme's, and all Mysteries of which his Writings are only a description; for all along the seven Qualities are called sometimes 7 Sources, 7 Species, Powers, Operations or Faculties of a thing; also the qualifying or fountain Spirits, which give Model, Image or Frame, the Power, Virtue, Figure, Constitution, Substance, Essence and distinct Beeing of all things that ever were or can be, in, from, and to all Eternity in God, and all Creatures in Heaven, Hell, or in this World. Also the Forms or Properties of Nature, which is the solliter or power of God. And so they are the seven Spirits of God, as in the Revelations of John c. 1."

3 Leeds, 7: "The first Principle: the dark World, or Fire of Wrath, hence God the Father is called an angry zealous jealous God, and consuming Fire. The second Principle: The Light World, or Fire of Love, hence God the Son, the Word; the Heart of God is called a loving and merciful God."

4 Leeds, 82–83: "Of the Serpent that deceived *Adam*, and of all created Things: When God said, *Let all sorts of Beasts come forth each according to his property* [or kind] then came forth Beasts out of every property of Nature, as it was manifest in the severation [of the two Kingdoms, viz. Time and Eternity] when God moved himself to the Creation; for the Devil would domineer over the Love and Meekness of God, and put his desire also into the Anger, tht is, into the austeer Might, where the poyson-Life ariseth, viz. into the Fiat of the wrathful Property out of which Form are proceeded Vipers, Serpents, Toads, and other venomous Worms."

5 This is a direct quote. There, however, it is related primarily to man, who is the similitude of God: "Man is the greatest *Arcanum*, or secret Mistery that God ever

wrought, he hath the figure and is the similitude, shewing how the Deity hath exgenerated it self from Eternity out of the fierce Wrath out of the Fire, by the sinking through Death into another Principle, of another Source or Quality."

6 Leeds, 87: "Whatsoever is arisen from the eternal Fixity, as Angels, and the Souls of men, doth remain undestroyable in its fixt Beeing; but whatsoever is arisen in the unfixt Beeing, viz. with the motion of Time, that doth again enter into the first motion, whence it hath taken its original, and is a Map of its form, which it had here like a Picture, or as in an Image in a Glass without life; for so it was from Eternity before the times of this world, which the Most-high hath introduced into an Image into the comprehensible natural Life in time, to behold the great Wonders of his Wisdom in a creatural being, as we plainly see."

7 Leeds, 12: "When God Almighty had decreed in his Counsel that he would make Angels and Creatures out of himself, then he made at first three Kingly Govern-ments or Dominions answerable to the number of the holy Trinity, and each Kingdom had the order or ordinance Power and Quality of the divine Beeing."

8 Leeds, 83–84: "The Devil was a fair Angel, and the Serpent the subtile Beast, and Man the likeness of the Deity: Now all three were corrupted by Imagination and Pride, and got the Curse of God for their false Lust [or cunning.] All whatso-ever is eternal proceedeth originally from one ground, as Angels and Souls; but the Serpent is not out of the eternal ground, but out of the beginning of Time; all things were good in the beginning, also the Devil was good while he was an Angel; so also the Serpent [was good in its Creation before the Curse.]"

9 Leeds, 60–61: "Of the Eternal Predistination, and Election of God: When the Scripture speaks of God's eternal purpose, or Predistination, it speaketh not of a purpose or predestination that hath been long before, for in God there is no beginning, but there is an eternal beginning, where the beginning and the end is all one, the first is continually the last, and the last first: whatsoever God hath be-gun from Eternity to foresee that he beginneth now also at this day always every *moment* to foresee I can say with good ground thus, that if I were in my Mother's Body or Womb comprehended in his Anger then God hath from Eternity seen me & apprehended me in his Anger, & I were from Eternity elected in his *anger*. But if I convert in Repentance so that God's love apprehendeth me then I am from Eternity forseen out of the Anger into the Love; for in God all is eternal whatsoever at this day beginneth to alter in the eternal, that is from Eternity to Eternity, equally in the Eternity, the matter consists only in the Conversation of the Will . . . . And though it standeth written, *that it standeth not in man's willing*, that is only concerning those that desire God, and yet will not go forth out of their sinful Will, they keep their Sin, and yet will be saved; therefore it lieth not in his willing, but in this, that man go out from Sin into God's Grace, and then it lieth in the mercy, and that God doth readily, for he hath promised it."

10 Leeds, 72–73: "Let none wait for the outward Prophet, he appeareth or shineth inwardly in the Spirit, the outward man will not know him; the right way into the eternal Life is in man: Whosoever will enter in with *Sion*, and praise God in

Jerusalem, hath now the acceptable time, the sound of the seventh Trumpet is already sounding, the Fountain of *Israel* is open; let none think that the sound of the Trumpet will come from this or the other place: for as the lightning breaketh up in the East, and shineth to the West; so from the beginning to the end is the coming of the Son of Man."

11 Leeds, 56–57: "When this outward dominion shall pass away, in the very place where the world now stands, there will be meer *Paradise*, for the Earth will be of an heavenly Essentiality, so that we shall be able to dwell any where, and be able to pass through and through it . . . . There will be no Cold or Heat any more, also no Night; there is no Death any more, also no Fear, no Sorrow, no Sickness. The Earth will be like a Christaline Sea, and the Wonders of the World will be seen wholly perspicuously, and the Brightness of God shall be the Light thereof, and the holy *Jerusalem*, the great City of God, shall be therein."

12 Leeds, 26: "But that Moses saith, *The Tree of Life stood in the midst of the Garden*; and presently next after setteth down, and the *Tree of Knowledge of Good and Evil*: Here lieth the Vail before Moses his eyes, and the earthly sinful man cannot behold him. The precious Pearl lieth in the [knowledge of] the difference of these two Trees, and yet it is but only one, but manifest in two Kingdoms—He saith *the Tree of Life*, thereby he understandeth the Property of the eternal Life in the Tree, viz. the second Principle; and by the Words, *of the Tree of Knowledge of Good and Evil*, he understandeth the wrath of the Anger of God, which was manifest by the Essence of the outward World, in earthliness, in the Tree of which Adam should not eat; for he should have eaten with the inward Mouth, and not with the earthly Desire, but with the heavenly, for he had such Fruit growing for him, which the inward Mouth could enjoy; indeed the outward Mouth did also eat thereof; but not into the Worms Carkess, for as the Light swalloweth up the Darkness, so the Coelestial swallowed up the Terrestrial, and changeth it again into that whence it proceeded."

13 Leeds, 30: "Man had no such bestial Flesh before the Fall, but heavenly Flesh; no *heat*, nor *frost*, no *sickness*, no *misshape*, or *mischief*, also no *fear* could touch or terrifie him, his Body could go through Earth and Stone uninterrupted by any thing; for that could be no eternal man which earthliness could limit."

14 Ibid.

15 Leeds, 26: "Adam *was a man, and also a Woman, and yet none of them [distinct] but a Virgin full of Chastity, Modesty and Purity*, viz. *the Image of God he had, both the Tinctures of the Fire and Light in him, in the Conjunction of which the one Love*, viz. *the Virginal center stood, being the fair Paradisical Rose-Garden of delight, wherein he loved himself.*"

16 Leeds, 34: "So we must understand that the Soul is in the form of a round Globe according to the Eye of God, through which the Cross goeth, and which divideth it self in two parts, *viz.* into two Eyes, standing Bck to Back, *viz.* a holy divine Eye, and a wrathful hellish Eye in the Fire; this it should shut and secretly reign there-with through the Anguish [*viz.* through Death] in the second Principle of Love."

17 Leeds, 56: "There will be no Cold or Heat any more, also no Night; there is no Death any more, also no Fear, no Sorrow, no Sickness. The Earth will be like a Christaline Sea, and all the Wonders of the World will be seen wholly perspicacously, and the Brightness of God shall be the Light thereof, and the holy Jerusalem, the great City of God, shall be therein."

APPENDIX II

1 עזרא ז י

2 In the English version, Stiles writes 850 thousand talents of silver and gold.

3 This is expanded in the English version to say that the king, his counselors, and the Jews donated such vessels, etc.

4 This is crossed out in the English version.

5 Here is missing the "tenth" generation: העשירי

6 The manuscript jumps pages because of the abridgment, brought below, which is inserted into the middle.

APPENDIX III

1 The manuscript includes two pages of unrelated notes, but the oration itself begins on page 3.

2 This sentence does not appear in Stiles's Hebrew version.

3 This sentence does not appear in the Hebrew version.

4 In the Hebrew version Stiles interestingly does not reference the *Shekhinah*.

5 This sentence is not in the Hebrew.

6 The meaning of this sentence is not clear.

7 Astronomy is not mentioned in the Hebrew version.

8 In the Hebrew version he seems to be saying the opposite, i.e., that they have very little in common.

9 There is no mention of Antiochus prohibiting the Law in the Hebrew version.

10 The Hebrew version does not mention that he was a disciple of Hillel.

11 In the Hebrew version he does not mention the printing at Sultzbach, but he does mention Lightfoot, whom he does not mention here.

INDEX

Page numbers in *italics* indicate figures and tables

ABOUT THE AUTHOR

BRIAN OGREN is the Anna Smith Fine Associate Professor of Judaic Studies in the Department of Religion at Rice University. He is the author of *Renaissance and Rebirth: Reincarnation in Early Modern Italian Kabbalah* (2009) and of *The Beginning of the World in Renaissance Jewish Thought* (2016), and the editor of *Time and Eternity in Jewish Mysticism* (2015) and of *Kabbalah in America* (2020).